THE ANNOTATED FRANCHISE AGREEMENT

Nina Greene
Dawn Newton
Kerry Olson
EDITORS

Forum on Franchising
AMERICAN BAR ASSOCIATION

Cover design by Jill Tedhams/ABA Design

Printed in the United States of America.

22 21 20 19 18 5 4 3 2 1

Library of Congress Cataloging-in-Publication Data

Names: Greene, Nina, editor. | Newton, Dawn, editor. | Olson, Kerry, editor.
Title: The annotated franchise agreement / edited by Nina Greene, Dawn Newton, Kerry Olson.
Description: First edition. | Chicago : American Bar Association, 2018. | Includes bibliographical references and index.
Identifiers: LCCN 2018037987 (print) | LCCN 2018038050 (ebook) | ISBN 9781641052726 (ebook) | ISBN 9781641052719 (print : alk. paper)
Subjects: LCSH: Franchises (Retail trade)—Law and legislation—United States.
Classification: LCC KF2023 (ebook) | LCC KF2023 .A948 2018 (print) | DDC 346.7304/8—dc23
LC record available at https://lccn.loc.gov/2018037987

CONTENTS

CHAPTER 2

CHAPTER 3

CHAPTER 4

Operation of the Business 83

CHAPTER 9

CHAPTER 10

ABOUT THE EDITORS

Nina Greene is a partner in the Miami office of Genovese, Joblove & Battista, P.A., where she practices in the areas of franchise, trademark, and complex commercial litigation. She has represented franchisors throughout the United States in matters involving protection of trademarks, franchise terminations, discrimination claims, covenants not to compete, unfair competition, business torts, and many other issues. She has lectured on numerous franchise issues for the ABA Forum on Franchising and the International Franchise Association (IFA). Additionally, Greene is the chairperson for the South Florida Chapter of the Women's Franchise Network of the IFA and is a member of the IFA Supplier Forum Advisory Board. Greene has been selected to appear in Best Lawyers of America, the International Who's Who of Business Lawyers and the International Who's Who of Franchise Lawyers. She is also a committed volunteer and is the chairperson who oversees all advisory boards throughout the United States for Best Buddies, a nonprofit organization dedicated to ending the social, physical, and economic isolation of individuals with intellectual and developmental disabilities. Greene earned her LLM in taxation from Temple University School of Law, her juris doctor from the University of Miami School of Law, and her bachelor of arts from the University of Pennsylvania.

Dawn Newton is a partner in the Bay Area law firm of Donahue Fitzgerald LLP and co-chairs the firm's intellectual property group. She primarily represents franchisors in start-up and emerging franchise brands and operates as their outside general counsel. In addition, she represents technology companies and manufacturers in protecting their trademarks worldwide. Dawn is a member of the Governing Committee of the ABA Forum on Franchising and co-chaired the 40th Annual Meeting of the Forum in Palm Desert, California. She currently serves as the forum's program officer, and in 2010 she was honored to be a recipient of the forum's future leader award. Dawn is recognized as a certified specialist in franchise and distribution law by the state bar of California's Board of Legal Specialization and is a past chair and commissioner of the Franchise and Distribution Law Advisory Commission of that board. She has been named a best lawyer in franchising in the San Francisco region since 2013 by Best Lawyers.

Kerry Olson is chief legal officer, general counsel, and secretary of CKE Restaurants Holdings (Carl's Jr. and Hardee's). Previously she was a partner in the Minneapolis office of Faegre Baker Daniels LLP and spent more than 12 years in-house at major brands, including serving as EVP and global general counsel at Carlson Hotels, Inc.; VP and assistant general counsel at International Dairy Queen, Inc.; and associate general counsel at Buffalo Wild Wings, Inc. Kerry is a frequent speaker locally and nationally on topics related to franchising, and is an active participant in the franchise community and industry, having held several leadership roles. She is a past chair of the International Franchise Association's Women's Franchise Committee and Legal Legislative Committee, as well as a past division director of the ABA's International Franchise and Distribution Steering Committee. In 2011, Kerry was honored as part of the "40 under Forty" list published by the *Minneapolis St. Paul Business Journal*. Franchise Times has included her in its list of "Legal Eagles" in 2006, 2007, 2008, 2009, and 2018 and named Kerry as one of "20 to Watch" in 2010. Kerry graduated summa cum laude, Phi Beta Kappa, from St. Olaf College in 1997. She earned her law degree, magna cum laude, from the University of Minnesota Law School in 2000, where she was awarded membership in Order of the Coif.

ABOUT THE AUTHORS

Corby Anderson is a partner in the Charlotte office of Bradley, Arant, Boult Cummings LLP, where she co-chairs the firm's Franchise Industry Team. Her practice focuses on commercial litigation, with an emphasis on franchising and intellectual property. She has represented clients in trials and appeals involving franchise, trademark, copyright, trade secret, unfair competition, and false advertising claims, among other disputes. She regularly counsels clients on privacy, IP, advertising, social media, and franchise matters. For the ABA Forum on Franchising, Corby co-authored *Annual Franchise and Distribution Law Developments 2017* and co-presented the plenary session on annual developments at the 40th annual forum. She has spoken and written for past forum meetings on strategic IP protection (2014), social media (2010), and trademark dilution (2007). Corby served as editor in chief of *The Franchise Lawyer* (2013–2016) and on the editorial board of the *Franchise Law Journal* (2006–2011). For the International Franchise Association, Corby was co-presenter of the legal symposium's Judicial Update (2016). She founded the Charlotte chapter of the IFA's Franchise Business Network. For the North Carolina Bar Association, Corby is a regular presenter of a program on "The Anatomy of a Franchise Lawsuit." Corby has been recognized in Chambers USA, Best Lawyers in America, Business North Carolina's Legal Elite, and Who's Who Legal: Franchise. She earned a BA degree, magna cum laude, from the College of William and Mary and a JD degree from the University of Virginia School of Law.

Bethany L. Appleby is chief legal officer for Franchise World Headquarters (Subway). She is a member of the Governing Committee of the ABA Forum on Franchising and past editor in chief of the ABA's *Franchise Law Journal*. Before going in-house, Bethany was co-chair of the Franchise and Distribution Practice Group at Wiggin and Dana LLP. She received her bachelor's degree from Yale University, magna cum laude, and graduated with highest honors from the University of Connecticut School of Law.

Amy Cheng is the co-founder of Cheng Cohen LLC in Chicago, Illinois. Amy concentrates her practice in domestic and international commercial transactions, general corporate, and franchise, licensing, and distribution law. She represents franchisors on the structuring and operation of their franchise programs through all phases of development. She also represents non-U.S.-based franchisors expanding into the U.S. market. Amy has extensive experience in structuring and drafting agreements for complex franchise, licensing, and distribution relationships and in regulatory compliance. Her experience includes advising clients in connection with complex issues arising from the ownership of multiple brands, non-traditional opportunities, system restructuring, and brand acquisition. Amy also has extensive experience in representing private equity firms in connection with their acquisitions of franchise companies. Amy is a current member of the International Franchise Association Supplier Forum Advisory Board and a member of the Franchise Advisory Board for the Illinois attorney general. For her work in the field of franchise law, Amy was named a Legal Eagle by the Franchise Times; recognized by Who's Who Legal, Leading Lawyers, Chambers and Partners; and selected by her peers for inclusion in The Best Lawyers of America and was The Best Lawyers' 2014 Chicago Franchise Law "Lawyer of the Year." In 2016, Amy was bestowed with the Crystal Compass Award for outstanding leadership by the International Franchise Association's Women's Franchise Committee and was also inducted in to the 2016 class of Women of Influence by the *Chicago Business Journal*.

Harris J. Chernow is the chair of Reger Rizzo & Darnall's Franchise and Distribution Practice Group. He has developed a national reputation through his franchise, transactional, and dispute resolution practices where he represents franchisors, franchisees, and distributors in conjunction with his corporate and business, M&A, retail development, and leasing practices. His franchise clients include franchisors, multi-unit franchise owners, area developers, master franchisees, distributors, and businesses desiring to expand through franchising, as well as distribution systems in all franchise industry groups, including a significant hotel and lodging specific practice, representing brands, owners, and management. In addition, Harris represents businesses of all sizes, including financial service companies, manufacturers and service-oriented companies, along with professionals and individuals in a wide range of matters, with general business and corporate matters, mergers and acquisitions, structuring transactions, real estate, employment, day-to-day counseling, and dispute resolutions. By virtue of a broad base of legal experience, he serves as "general counsel" to a number of his clients. Harris is frequently called upon to serve as a neutral mediator and arbitrator. Harris is a frequent speaker and author on numerous franchise and business topics. He is a member of the American Bar Association's Forum on Franchising, currently serving on its Marketing Committee, and was a long-term member of the Governing Committee, served as its Finance Officer for five years, served on the forum's Publications Committee, was chair of its Litigation and Alternative Dispute Resolution (LADR) Division, served on the forum's Nominating Committee for the Board of Governors, served as liaison to its solo and small firm practitioners group, and served as liaison to its paralegal group. Harris is also a member of the International Franchise Association (IFA) and has served on the IFA's Legal Symposium Task Force. He is co-chair of the Montgomery County Franchise Law Committee, chair of the Philadelphia Franchise Law Committee, and member of the New Jersey Bar Association's Franchise Law Committee. Harris is also active with a variety of other professional and community-related organizations.

Marisa Faunce is a partner with the law firm of Plave Koch PLC in Reston, Virginia. Marisa counsels franchisors, licensors, and manufacturers on transactional, regulatory, and intellectual property issues. She has extensive experience in structuring and revamping franchise programs, drafting franchise, license and area development agreements, and counseling franchisors with regard to regulatory (FDD) compliance issues. Marisa is also a trademark attorney and manages domestic and international trademark portfolios for franchisors. She is the chair of the International Franchise Association's Women's Franchise Committee and a member of the Supplier Forum Advisory Board. She has been recognized by Chambers USA, Best Lawyers in America, Franchise Times Legal Eagles, and the International Who's Who of Franchise Attorneys. Marisa is an Order of the Coif graduate of the Marshall-Wythe School of Law at the College of William and Mary and she received her undergraduate degree from the University of Virginia.

Michael D. Joblove is a founding shareholder of Miami-based Genovese Joblove & Battista and leads the 35-lawyer firm's franchise practice whose clients include Miami-based Burger King Corporation and Benihana, and a host of other franchise clients. Joblove is "AV" rated by Martindale-Hubbell and is a Fellow in the Trial Lawyer Honorary Society of the Litigation Counsel of America. He is also listed in Best Lawyers in America and has been named the Best Lawyers' 2011 and 2017 Miami Franchise Lawyer of the Year. He is also ranked in Chambers & Partners USA, Florida Trend, South Florida Legal Guide, Franchise Times, and Florida Super Lawyers. In addition, he has been selected by Who's Who Legal, to appear in the International Who's Who of Franchise Lawyers and the International Who's Who of Business Lawyers.

Kathryn Kotel is a retired executive and franchise counsel. Ms. Kotel was senior vice president, general counsel, and head of business affairs for TGI Friday's Inc. from 2009 to 2017. She worked for McDonald's Corporation from 1995 to 2009, most recently as vice president, U.S. general counsel. Prior to joining McDonald's, she was a partner in Keck, Mahin & Cate in its Franchise and Distribution Practice Group. She also served as in-house counsel for Convenient Food Mart. Ms. Kotel was a member of the ABA's Forum on Franchising Governing Committee and its Membership Officer from 2008 to 2014. Ms. Kotel received her BS from the University of Illinois and her JD, with distinction, from The John Marshall Law School.

Beata Krakus is a partner of Greensfelder, Hemker & Gale, P.C., and part of the firm's Franchising & Distribution Practice Group. She works with franchisor clients in domestic and international franchise transactional matters, as well as related areas such as distribution and sales representative arrangements, and other commercial contracts. She has advised, structured, and prepared franchise programs for many different franchise concepts including real estate brokerages, hotels, restaurants, and fitness and personal health systems. Prior to joining Greensfelder, Ms. Krakus was an associate with Sonnenschein Nath & Rosenthal LLP. She also practiced in Warsaw, Poland, with the Swedish law firm of Magnusson Wahlin. Ms. Krakus is a member of the Governing Committee of the ABA Forum on Franchising and also serves as the information officer for the organization. She has served as an associate editor for *The Franchise Lawyer*, has herself written articles for the *Franchise Law Journal* and other franchise law publications, and has spoken repeatedly at the ABA Forum on Franchising and International Franchise Association Legal Symposium. She is recognized by International Who's Who of Franchise Lawyers and by Chambers USA and Chambers Global.

Robert A. Lauer is a partner in the Austin office of Haynes and Boone, LLP, and a member of the firm's Franchise and Distribution Practice Group. Mr. Lauer's practice focuses on all aspects of domestic and international franchise transactions. Mr. Lauer was named to Chambers, Global Franchising, Band 3, 2011, Band 4, 2012, and Band 3, 2013 to 2018; Chambers USA, Franchising (Nationwide), Up and Coming, 2012, and Band 4, 2013 to 2018; the International Who's Who of Franchise Lawyers, Law Business Research, 2010 through 2017; The Best Lawyers in America for Franchise Law in 2008 through 2017; and a "Texas Rising Star" by *Law & Politics* magazine and *Texas Monthly* for 2005 and 2007 through 2012. Mr. Lauer is also the speaker for the Texas Bar Association's Ten Minute Mentor video tutorial on "What Every Texas Attorney Should Know About Franchise Law." He is a member of the ABA Forum on Franchising (and former member of the International Division's Steering Committee from 2008 to 2011) and current officer of the International Bar Association's International Franchising Committee (treasurer to serve from January 2017 to December 2018). Mr. Lauer is a 1997 cum laude graduate of St. Mary's University School of Law where he served as an associate editor of the St. Mary's *Law Journal*, and a 1994 graduate of Trinity University in San Antonio, Texas.

Ann MacDonald is a partner in Schiff Hardin LLP's Chicago office, where she handles litigation and pre-litigation matters for a range of clients. She spends much of her time representing hospitality companies and franchisors in litigation across the country and helping clients assess litigation risk for changes to their business terms and resolve disputes relating to business partnerships gone sour. Ann has been recognized by the Chicago Law Bulletin in its annual Leading Lawyers publication.

She graduated from Washington University School of Law in St. Louis, where she was an editor for the *Global Studies Law Review*, and has served as president of the Chicago Council of Lawyers.

Himanshu Patel is a partner at the law firm of Zarco Einhorn Salkowski & Brito, P.A., where he concentrates his practice in the areas of complex commercial litigation, franchise arbitration, litigation and mediation, general business and corporate law, and appellate practice. Himanshu graduated from Vanderbilt University in December 1994 with a BA degree in economics. He then earned his JD in 1998 from the Brandeis School of Law at the University of Louisville. Himanshu holds the maximum "AV" (pre-eminent) rating by the Martindale-Hubbell Directory. Himanshu has been named a Florida Rising Star by Florida Super Lawyers, and has been listed in the Cambridge Who's Who Registry Among Executives and Professionals as a representative for Miami, Florida, as well as the Cambridge Worldwide Who's Registry. Himanshu has also been recognized in the *Wall Street Journal* and *Miami Magazine* as a Top Young Attorney in Florida and as one of Florida's outstanding young lawyers in franchise and dealership law. Since joining Zarco Einhorn Salkowski & Brito, P.A., Himanshu has authored several articles discussing various issues in the franchise industry, including "Is Your Franchise Agreement Complete: Be Aware of the Merger and Integration Clause," "A Comparison of Franchise Disclosure Requirements under United States Law and International Law," and "Is the Franchisee Responsible When the Guest is Injured on Hotel Property?" Himanshu also co-authored the following articles: (1) "Common Issues in Hospitality Franchising," which was presented at the 2004 Hospitality Law Conference in Houston, Texas; (2) "Common Discovery Issues in Franchising," which was presented in 2009 at the 32nd Annual Forum on Franchising in Toronto, Canada; and (3) "Changes in System Standards: What Is the Extent of the Franchisor's Latitude?" which was presented at the 35th Annual Forum on Franchising in Los Angeles, California.

Rebekah Prince is a partner at Barnes & Thornburg where she focuses her practice on franchising and corporate matters. She has handled the purchases and sales of both public and private franchise companies and she regularly advises clients on the structuring of domestic and international franchise ventures including registration, disclosure, and the development of franchise systems. She also has significant experience representing buyers, sellers, and investment advisors in connection with financings, mergers, and acquisitions of companies. Since 2012, Ms. Prince has been annually recognized by Franchise Times as a Legal Eagle. She is also recognized as a leading franchise lawyers by Who's Who Legal: Franchise 2017. Ms. Prince is a frequent speaker and author on franchise-specific topics. She earned her BS from Washington & Lee and received her JD from the University of Texas School of Law.

Iris Figueroa Rosario is a principal in Gray Plant Mooty's Washington, D.C. office in the Franchise and Distribution Practice Group. She advises clients on their contracts and represents clients in federal and state courts and before international arbitration panels on a variety of commercial civil litigation matters. She has litigated numerous franchise cases, including cases touching upon issues of underreporting, unapproved products, tax fraud, immigration/employment violations, trademark violations, and covenants not to compete.

Brian B. Schnell has more than 30 years of experience in franchising and product distribution, and serves as the chair of the franchise practice at Faegre Baker Daniels in the firm's Minneapolis office. Brian represents franchisors with headquarters based across the United States and abroad. Brian's experience uniquely includes serving as the COO and Chief Legal Officer during 2012 for one of the country's leading healthcare franchisors. In the role, he led the company's field operations team and the franchise administration and legal groups. With this unique legal and business experience, Brian counsels both emerging and mature franchisors in a variety of industries, ranging from companies with thousands of locations worldwide to companies in the initial stages of building franchise systems. His clients operate in dozens of industries where franchising plays a key role in the U.S. and global economies. Brian is a frequent (and well-respected) speaker and author on franchising. He is a past chair of the International Franchise Association (IFA) Supplier Forum and a member of its Legal/Legislative, Awards, and Membership Committees. He also serves on the board of trustees for the IFA Educational Foundation. As the first male to receive the IFA Women's Franchise Committee Crystal Compass, Brian earned distinction for the 2009 honor based on his leadership in franchising.

Joseph Sheyka is senior counsel in the Chicago office of DLA Piper LLP (US). He is a member of the American Bar Association Forum Committee on Franchising, the Franchising Committee of the Antitrust Section of the ABA, and the International Franchising Committee of the Business Law Section of the International Bar Association. Mr. Sheyka is a frequent lecturer on franchising and distribution topics and is author of *Franchising in the United States*, published in the Canadian Franchise Guide.

Andra Terrell received her BS from Johns Hopkins University in 1992 and her JD from Howard University School of Law in 1995. She is a member of the Maryland Bar. Mrs. Terrell currently serves as senior director and assistant general counsel for Cajun Operating Company, d/b/a Church's Chicken, at its corporate headquarters in Atlanta, Georgia. She also is a board member of, and counsel to, the Church's Foundation. Prior to her tenure at Church's, Mrs. Terrell was the assistant general counsel for Luxottica Retail (an Italian eyewear manufacturer and retailer, and the franchisor of more than 400 and operator of 200 Pearle Visions in the United States and Canada, and franchisor of approximately 100 Oakley locations outside the United States), at its corporate office in Mason, Ohio. Mrs. Terrell also worked as the general counsel of Decorating Den Systems, Inc., an Easton, Maryland-based franchisor of home decorating services in the United States and Canada. Mrs. Terrell is a member of the American Bar Association (Forum on Franchising), and has been active in the Corporate Counsel Steering Committee and Diversity Caucus, as well as serving as the liaison to the ABA Commission on Disability Rights. She is also a member of the International Franchise Association (IFA), and served two terms on its task force.

Trish Treadwell is a partner in the Litigation and Employment practice group at Parker Hudson. She uses a fresh, flexible, and experienced approach to counsel clients in preventing, solving, and litigating franchise, employment, and general complex business issues. Ms. Treadwell regularly writes and speaks on franchise and employment topics. She has contributed as both an author and an editor to the *Franchise Law Journal*. Ms. Treadwell received a Bachelor of Arts with honors from Oglethorpe University and her JD from Georgia State University College of Law.

Larry Weinberg is a partner at the Toronto law firm of Cassels Brock & Blackwell LLP. Since 1989, he has had a practice that specializes in franchise law and providing all necessary legal services to franchisors. He is a member of the International Franchise Association, where he served as a member of the IFA board of directors and as chair of its Supplier Forum Advisory Board, and the Canadian Franchise Association, where he serves as chair of the CFA's Legal and Legislative Committee and on the CFA board of directors. He is also currently co-chair of the International Bar Association's International Franchising Committee and is a past chair of the Ontario Bar Association's Franchise Law Section. Larry was the founder of, and to date has organized and chaired four Ontario Bar Association annual franchise law conferences. He is a member of the American Bar Association's Forum on Franchising, and in 2006, he was the first Canadian lawyer to be appointed director of the ABA Forum's International Division and to a leadership role on its Governing Committee. In 2009, he had the honour of being co-chair of the ABA's 32nd Annual Forum on Franchising conference. In 2004, he acted as co-editor of the ABA Forum on Franchising's book entitled *Fundamentals of Franchising—Canada*. In 2017, he again acted as co-editor of the second edition of this publication. As well he was co-editor and co-author of the Canadian Franchise Association's first and still only official book publication entitled *How to Franchise Your Business*. He is a co-author of the chapter on Canada for the ABA Forum's book entitled *International Franchise Sales Laws*. In 2004, 2005, and each year from 2009 to 2018 Larry was named by Franchise Times to their "Legal Eagles" list of the top franchise lawyers in the United States and Canada. He and Cassels Brock are each listed in the *Lexpert* Canadian legal directory as being among the leaders in Canada in franchise law. In 2014, 2015, and 2016 Larry received Who's Who Legal's one and only worldwide Lawyer of the Year award for franchise law, and in 2014, the *Lexpert* Zenith Award. Larry was called to the Bar of the Province of Ontario in 1989.

Elizabeth M. Weldon is a partner at Snell & Wilmer L.L.P. in Costa Mesa, California. Elizabeth concentrates her practice on business litigation, franchise litigation, and intellectual property litigation. She represents franchisors in disputes including breach of contract, trademark and trade name infringement, business competition torts, and franchise law claims, and also represents both large and small businesses in business litigation and intellectual property disputes. She frequently writes and speaks about various franchise litigation topics. Elizabeth graduated with a JD from the William & Mary School of Law in 2001. She was the director of the Forum's Litigation and Dispute Resolution Division during 2015–2017 and will be a member of the Governing Committee beginning in August 2018. She is currently on the board of directors of Girls Inc. of Orange County.

Will K. Woods is a partner in the Dallas office of Baker & McKenzie. He leads the firm's Franchise and Distribution Group and concentrates his practice in franchise and distribution law. He counsels clients on structuring cross-border and domestic franchise transactions, distribution of products and services, and franchise registration and disclosure matters. Mr. Woods represents franchisors across many industries throughout their business life cycle: in the start-up stage; as middle-market franchisors; and as mature, global franchisors. He represents many of the leading hotel, lodging, and hospitality franchise companies and has vast experience in negotiating complex franchise transactions both in the United States and in many other countries around the world and in counseling clients across industries with respect to system restructuring and related relationship issues. Mr. Woods is a frequent author and speaker on franchise and distribution related topics. Mr. Woods is an active member of various trade and bar associations, including the International Franchise Association and the ABA Forum on Franchising. He is consistently listed in Chambers USA (Franchising) and Chambers Global (Franchising) as a leading franchise lawyer in the United States and globally, has been named in Franchise Times' "Legal Eagles" as one of the top 101 franchise lawyers in the United States and Canada, has been listed in the International Who's Who of Franchise Lawyers, and has been named one of the Best Lawyers in Dallas by *D Magazine*. He is currently on the Governing Committee of the American Bar Association Forum on Franchising. Mr. Woods received his BBA from Baylor University in 1994 and his JD, cum laude, from Baylor University School of Law in 1998. He is a member of the Texas Bar.

FOREWORD

The American Bar Association Forum on Franchising takes great pride and pleasure in introducing *The Annotated Franchise Agreement*, which we hope and expect will be an extremely valuable resource for all of our members, whether they represent franchisors or franchisees and whether they practice in-house with a franchisor, in a government or academic setting, or in a private practice.

The franchise agreement is the core and the foundation of the franchise relationship, yet, as the editors rightly point out, one size does not fit all. This necessitates an in-depth examination of the agreement as yet another element of our continuing efforts to fulfill our mission to be the preeminent forum to study and discuss the legal aspects of franchising.

Business executives sometimes refer to material portions of any contract as "boilerplate," meaning that certain language is perceived to be standard in all agreements and perhaps does not deserve the attention that is merited by other portions of the agreement. *The Annotated Franchise Agreement* demonstrates that every provision of the franchise agreement has a meaning and a purpose that must be carefully considered in light of many factors, including the size and maturity of the franchise system, the nature of the goods and services to be provided to customers or clients of the franchisees, the culture of the system, and the regulatory environment in which the system operates. And because the goal of the typical integration clause is to make the franchise agreement stand alone, it must be drafted in a clear, concise, straightforward, and readable fashion, free from ambiguity.

Carrying out an enterprise of this depth and breadth takes a small army of dedicated, experienced, and knowledgeable practitioners willing to give unstintingly and generously of their time and effort for the benefit of their fellow members of the forum.

Our expression of gratitude must begin with the editors: Nina Greene, Dawn Newton, and Kerry Olson. It is indeed an honor and privilege to thank them for their consistent and persistent commitment to completing this ambitious and much-needed book. They have been expertly and creatively overseen first by Jim Goniea and then by David Oppenheim in their successive roles as chair of the Forum's Publication Committee. We are also deeply grateful to Teresa Koller, the Publication Committee member who served as liaison for *The Annotated Franchise Agreement*.

The core of the work done on this book was provided by our impressive team of chapter authors. Each of them is a longtime forum contributor with a wealth of experience and wisdom. I commend Corby Anderson, Bethany L. Appleby, Amy Cheng, Harris J. Chernow, Marisa Faunce, Michael D. Joblove, Kathryn Kotel, Beata Krakus, Robert A. Lauer, Ann MacDonald, Himanshu Patel, Rebekah Prince, Iris Figueroa Rosario, Brian B. Schnell, Joseph Sheyka, Andra Terrell, Trish Treadwell, Larry Weinberg, Elizabeth M. Weldon, and Will K. Woods.

I know that you will find *The Annotated Franchise Agreement* to be filled with practical and useful information to assist and guide you in your practice of franchise law for years to come.

Eric H. Karp
Chair, Forum on Franchising
2017–2019

INTRODUCTION

We sincerely hope that *The Annotated Franchise Agreement* will be a useful resource guide. It is designed especially for business attorneys who may be relatively new to drafting franchise agreements, whether that person is a seasoned transactional attorney who is less familiar with franchising or a newer associate or corporate counsel who wants to understand the caselaw and reasoning behind some of the typical structures of a franchise agreement.

From many readers, the editors can anticipate an initial question: Where can we download the franchise agreement template? The answer is that this reference book does not come with a cut-and-paste-ready template, for two specific and important reasons.

First, a careful review will show that, despite the comprehensive coverage, the sections discussed in this book do not fit together like perfect puzzle pieces. Some provisions overlap with one another slightly, covering some of the same information in more than one place. Some sections include multiple samples, each appropriate for a different situation. In other sections, the sample language is drafted in a way that lends itself very well to a specific type of franchising, such as food service or the hotel industry, and is not as well suited to the many other types of business franchising that exist in the United States. The authors selected these sections to illustrate some of the points their comments make about how and why to draft certain terms in various situations.

Second, and even more importantly, one of the goals of this book is to persuade the reader that there is no one-size-fits-all franchise agreement template. A well-drafted franchise agreement is the product of careful analysis of many considerations, including the type of business at issue, its business goals and objectives, the specific obligations of the franchisor and franchisee in a particular system, the level of sophistication of both franchisor and prospective franchisees in that system and the power dynamic between them, regulatory issues, judicial direction, and the culture of that franchise system. While each franchise system's agreement will invariably deal with many if not most of the same issues, they may be addressed in an entirely different manner from one franchise agreement to the next.

A good franchise agreement is also, by necessity, a reflection of where the brand is in its life cycle. Quite often, a "mom and pop" franchise start-up will have a franchise agreement that is more generous to franchisees in various ways, including lower fees. It may exert slightly fewer controls over a franchisee's latitude to be creative or regional in its product or service offerings than a well-established system under a famous brand. At the same time, the start-up will typically promise less in the way of support and franchisor obligations, while the famous brand can be expected to offer a robust and extremely consistent level of support including, for example, high production value advertising and sophisticated research and development programs focused on developing new products and services and responding to trends. As the start-up matures, establishing more units and accumulating more brand recognition, these elements change, and the franchise agreement changes along with it. Thus, the sample agreement language in this guide is a jumping off point for the drafter to modify to fit the specific franchise system at issue.

Understanding the meaning and purpose of a clause in a franchise agreement is key to being able to provide quality advice to clients, whether they are franchisors or franchisees. There is a real risk to taking one form of franchise agreement and believing it can be used in another, or any other, franchise system, which, unfortunately, some franchisors and lawyers may do at times. Although often intended as a cost-saving measure, this can result in a system using forms of agreement inappropriate to the type of franchise being offered. Those systems can then spend more on marketing the franchise, as they try to explain to prospects the content of a form that is not appropriately tailored to the situation. But the real long-term cost may be much more significant: more and costlier legal disputes result when interpretation of the contract wording becomes the focus. It should go without saying that inappropriate or incorrect provisions result in substantial problems.

The Annotated Franchise Agreement owes its origins to a paper written by editor Kerry Olson, Robin M. Spencer, and chapter author Larry Weinberg in 2010 and presented as a 75-minute workshop at the 33rd Annual Forum on Franchising in San Diego, California. Although that paper was a hefty 100 pages in length, to the authors it was clear that many important matters had been left out. This book, which incorporates some of the original language in the 2010 paper, attempts to fill in some of those omitted topics, in addition to updating the agreement language in ways that have become important in franchise systems in the intervening years.

The scope of this book is the core franchise agreement. This book does not cover the exhibits and attachments to the franchise agreement, but practitioners should be aware that virtually every franchise agreement includes these additional documents. A typical franchise agreement has at least some of the following agreements attached to it:

- *Territory Definition:* A description or map of the territory granted to the franchisee
- *Personal Guaranty:* A form of personal guaranty which the individual owners are required to sign if the franchisee is not a natural person
- *Nondisclosure Agreement:* A form of nondisclosure and noncompetition agreement that the franchisee is required to use to bind its employees to duties not to disclose the brand's confidential information or unfairly compete with the brand
- *Acknowledgment:* An acknowledgment to be executed by the franchisee, confirming that the franchisee has not relied on outside information or representations not made within the franchise agreement and any disclosure document which may have been provided
- *Collateral Lease Assignment:* A form of lease addendum that must be made part of the lease for the physical premises where the franchisee will operate its business, ensuring that the franchisor may assume the lease in the event the franchisee defaults or its franchise agreement is terminated
- *Telephone Number Assignment:* An agreement that telephone numbers either belong to the franchisor or will be assigned to the franchisor, in the event of termination of the franchise
- *Software License Agreement:* A software license agreement permitting the franchisee to use and sometimes sublicense brand-specific software or mobile apps
- *ACH Agreement:* An agreement allowing the franchisor to draw fees directly from the franchisee's designated bank account

This is a non-exhaustive list, and many systems have additional agreements appropriate to their business formats. The same care which a drafter takes in creating the franchise agreement should also be taken in drafting these ancillary agreements.[1]

The franchise agreement is the key document that establishes the franchise relationship. This relationship is characterized legally, in broad strokes, by a franchisor granting a franchisee a temporary or time limited right to use the franchisor's system and trademarks to conduct business.[2] In many systems, the term of a franchise agreement is ten years, and the franchise agreement's individual provisions set out the rights and obligations of each party over that decade-long relationship in detail. For this reason, it is critical that prospective franchisors and franchisees understand the purpose and drafting issues behind each provision in the agreement, as well as the historic rationale for such a provision, in order to ensure they are willing to enter into it.

---

1. Alan R. Greenfield & Kathryn M. Kotel, *Ancillary Agreements; The Other Contracts Needed in the Franchise Relationship*, ABA 35th Annual Forum on Franchising W-20 (2012).

2. W. Andrew Scott, Business Labels: Identifying the Signs of a Franchisee Relationship, 79 A.B.A.J. 86 (1993).

Despite the variation from one franchise agreement to the next, virtually all such agreements contain the same key concepts, regardless of the industry or business. This book explores the common and often complex terms and conditions found in franchise agreements by providing, for each section:

- One primary sample provision (which appears in italics), and where appropriate, reference to alternatives or variations on how a particular issue may be addressed;
- A discussion on the provision's meaning and typical purpose; and,
- Where appropriate, practical perspectives on the clause, franchisee negotiation points, and statutory and judicial considerations.[3]

Of course, every industry, business, and relationship has unique considerations, and each consideration may affect and alter the sample provisions. So while the text provides some variations of clauses, the full myriad of possible provisions is beyond the scope of this book.

A franchise agreement should be drafted with precision and care. It should be clear (with concise and simple language), user friendly, and comprehensive. The sections should build logically on one another, should be placed under appropriate headings, and should be easily found by any person reading it. To make the agreement as comprehensible as possible, drafters might consider approaching the project as if they are writing a "story," so that users can see the big picture of the franchise relationship.[4]

Drafters must keep in mind that the typical franchise agreement is a long and complicated document. If a franchise agreement is not logically built, and/or if provisions are not easy to find, then the agreement could, at best, become a source of confusion and frustration in the franchise sales process as well as during the ongoing business relationship and, at worst, add to the time, cost, and complication of disputes between a franchisor and franchisee.

Given the importance of a well-structured franchise agreement, commentators have noted that several general approaches have emerged to structuring the basic framework of the agreement. Some drafters prefer to take a "life cycle" approach and set out a sequential outline of what will happen in the franchisee/franchisor relationship.[5] Another approach is the "highlight-the-deal" approach where the key aspects of the relationship are covered first, followed by a sequential life-cycle approach for the remainder of the agreement.[6] Lastly, some may use a "franchise disclosure agreement" approach, where the agreement follows the order of the information required by the Franchise Disclosure Document (FDD). This last approach often misses key provisions and is rarely used. Even though it is uncom-

3. The clauses in this agreement are simply sample clauses drawn from typical franchise agreements. They are not intended to be comprehensive, the "gold standard," or clauses recommended by the authors.

4. Richard M. Asbill, Rupert M. Barkoff, & Andrew C. Selden, *Franchise Agreements: New Approaches to Old Problems*, ABA 25th Annual Forum on Franchising 1, 4 (2002).

5. *Id.* at 7–9.

6. *Id.*

mon for drafters to follow the general structure of the FDD, they nevertheless should consider drafting in anticipation of franchise disclosure.

This book follows the life-cycle approach for the most part, which the editors believe is used most frequently. However, it is important to note that even within the life-cycle approach there is no single right way to order the provisions, and drafters should not feel constrained by the order in which this book considers the typical sections of the agreement. As noted in Chapter 2, sometimes a blended approach can be beneficial. The goal is an effective franchise agreement that embodies and clearly articulates the parties' respective rights and obligations and provides an opportunity to assist in the resolution of disputes.

The sample franchise agreement language used in this book is modeled primarily on restaurant franchising, arguably the most common type of franchised business. This "standard" franchise structure presents an excellent starting point for understanding the key provisions in a franchise agreement. Drafters working on behalf of other types of systems, such as hotels, consulting service providers, janitorial systems, or mobile businesses, however, must consider the elements present in their systems, which may not be covered by the sample provisions presented here.

A few other editorial choices are also worth mentioning. As is briefly alluded to in Chapter 3, there is some dispute among franchise practitioners about the appropriateness of the term "sole discretion" in a franchise agreement, and as to the proper interpretation of what standard is meant by this phrase. While many agreements grant "sole discretion" to the franchisor as often as possible, some practitioners have made conscious efforts to use other terminology, and still others have included language defining whether "discretion" should be measured under the business judgment rule or the implied covenant of good faith and fair dealing.[7] The sample provisions in this book include the word "discretion" in many instances, and the authors' perspectives on this issue are reflected in these chapters.

In addition, we refer throughout the book to the agreement as a "franchise agreement" and to the parties as "franchisor" and "franchisee." This is simply a decision to make the language in this book uniform. Some franchise systems call their agreements "license agreements" or may use other names to define the parties and these are generally all appropriate. And we avoided repeating dollar figures in both words and numbers (e.g., "three hundred dollars ($300)") because this is a notoriously easy way to have one number changed and the other number unchanged, leading to disputes. We also removed virtually all the numbers from the sample provisions, even where a period of time such as 30 days or 12 months might be fairly standard, to avoid biasing the reader toward a particular period of time or dollar amount. As is repeatedly emphasized in this book, the best franchise agreements are customized to the particular system to which they belong, with the franchisor making specific choices rather than adopting "boilerplate" language to set its practices.

7. Brian B. Schnell & Ronald K. Gardner, Jr., *Battle Over the Business Judgment Rule and the Path to Peace*, 35 Franchise L.J. 167 (Fall 2015).

This book could not have come together without extraordinary contributions from a number of people. The editors are deeply grateful to all of the prominent practitioners who authored chapters, contributing an enormous amount of time and attention to making this book a reality and tolerating occasionally unexpected deadlines and difficult requests. Their experiences and suggestions make this guide a rich and detailed exploration of the language of franchise agreements and the statutory and judicial considerations which should inform drafters. This book also could not have come together without the attention and efforts of two different ABA Forum on Franchising Publications Officers, James Goniea and David Oppenheim, and Publication Committee member Theresa Koller whose patient and sometimes impatient prodding helped keep this project on track. The editors also thank Lee Plave for his contributions.

Nina Greene
Dawn Newton
Kerry Olson

1

Introductory Terms, Grant, Territory, and Reservation of Rights

Robert A. Lauer and Larry Weinberg

I. Parties to the Agreement

This Franchise Agreement (the "Agreement") is made as of _________, 20___ (the "Effective Date"), between ________________, a ________________ with its principal business located at ________________ ("Franchisor"), and ________________, a ________________ with its principal business located at ________________ ("Franchisee"). Franchisor and Franchisee may be collectively referred to as the "Parties". If Franchisee is a corporation, partnership, limited liability company or other legal entity, certain provisions to this Agreement also apply to its owners, jointly and severally.

Discussion:

Most lawyers will agree that identifying the parties to the franchise agreement should be one of the easiest drafting formalities in preparing and signing a franchise agreement, but that is not always the case, especially where an outside attorney prepares the form of franchise agreement and the franchisor and its personnel (many times non-lawyers) are left to fill in the blank spaces before execution of the documents. Problems may arise due to a number of issues, normally related to the identity and description of the "franchisee." From confusion as to which entity is the proper franchisee (many times an issue if a sophisticated franchisee signs a development agreement with one entity and then each franchise agreement with a sole purpose entity), to using an incomplete name, or misidentifying the entity type, or jurisdiction of formation, to simply forgetting to add in the name at all, the rather simple process of documenting who is executing the agreement may become complicated. As a result, one alternative to the standard language would be to use a format that does not leave anything to chance, and therefore does not leave blank spaces requiring that names, etc., be inserted as in the preceding sample. Such an example is as follows:

> This Franchise Agreement ("Agreement") is entered into by and between Franchisor and Franchisee and is effective as of the Effective Date. The Summary Page to this Agreement is an integral part of this Agreement.

This sample provision, and the use of a summary page, is representative of an attempt to avoid multiple blank spaces in the franchise agreement to be completed electronically or by hand when preparing a deal-specific franchise agreement. Presumably, the franchisor entity information should never be an issue if the franchise agreement form is prepared properly and the only blank spaces are for a signature and perhaps a signatory name and title if there are multiple potential signatories, but the existence of any blank spaces creates the potential for an error or omission.

With respect to the franchisee, ideally the person or entity that is the franchisee is identified one time in a summary page, exhibit/schedule or even just once in the signature block to avoid having to complete multiple times, or missing blank spaces where the information is meant to be inserted. Some franchisors routinely have an individual or both spouses listed on the franchise agreement as the franchisee, and in that case it is important to list the full names of all of the individuals and be very clear that they are collectively the franchisee on a joint and several basis. With respect to an entity, the information that should be clearly indicated in the franchise agreement includes the full proper name of the franchisee entity, the type of entity and the jurisdiction of formation. In addition, while not the norm in the United States, in certain more formalistic international jurisdictions, franchise agreements might also contain a reference in the parties section stating who is authorized to sign the franchise agreement on behalf of the franchisee and their title, or even the company number of the franchisee entity (for instance, this is routinely seen in Australian franchise agreements).

Because there are so many different types of entities that can be created in different jurisdictions, it is key to have a working knowledge of the general differences among corporations, limited liability companies (LLC), limited partnerships, sole proprietorships, trusts, and even anachronisms such as unincorporated associations. From a practical standpoint, the franchisors are often provided a name and might even receive an entity type and jurisdiction, but the entity has not actually been formed by the time the franchise agreement is ready to be signed. It is crucial to require the franchisees to provide evidence that the entity is actually formed and valid, or to do the due diligence directly. Often times, the prospective franchisee has an existing company that the franchisor vets as part of the process, but at the last minute the franchisee decides to use a different entity or create a new entity for tax purposes, separation of assets and/or to further minimize personal liability. Unfortunately, many franchise lawyers, including the authors, can readily recall files where a franchisor has sought to enforce a franchise agreement after many years of the business being operated, only to discover that the franchisee entity was not correctly named, or validly formed at the time it supposedly entered into the franchise agreement, or individual names were left off,[8] or some entity or individual did not sign the franchise agreement notwithstanding it may have been originally contemplated that they do sign.[9]

Although generally outside the scope of the parties provision in the franchise agreement, it is important to confirm and document the direct and indirect owners of the franchisee entity. Another practical consideration flowing from the franchise entity choice involves the implications on federal court jurisdiction in the event of future disputes. For example, if the franchisee is an LLC, the franchisor should ensure that it knows who the members of the LLC are as well as their state of citizenship, just as they should know names of all of the shareholders (within reason), directors, and officers of a corporation. With respect to LLCs, this is important for federal diversity jurisdiction, among other reasons, if a claim does later arise.[10]

II. Recitals

Franchisor owns a unique system for the development, opening and operation of distinctive quick service restaurants currently featuring chicken, ribs, pizza and other food and related products focusing on take out, drive thru and delivery services for individuals, families or large party gatherings with limited dine-in services;

Franchisor owns certain trade names, trademarks, service marks, logos, emblems and indicia of origin which are used in association with the restaurant system, including but not limited to (as of the date hereof) the trade name and trademark "_____®" (the "**Proprietary Marks**");

8. Generally, a franchise agreement will only be enforced against parties that signed the agreement. However, courts have been willing to enforce covenants not to compete against non-signatories when the non-signatory aided or assisted the franchisee in violating the covenant not to compete. *See* Emma Cano, Darci Cohen, & Diane Green-Kelly, *Unsigned Obligations: When Are Non-Signatories Bound?*, ABA 37th Annual Forum on Franchising W2, at 19 (2014).

9. For example, the sale of goods in a franchise relationship may implicate the Uniform Commercial Code and the statute of frauds. At least one court has held that an unsigned franchise agreement is unenforceable under the statute of frauds because it could not be performed within one year. Midwest Energy, Inc. v. Orion Food Sys., Inc., 14 S.W.3d 154 (Mo. App. 2000).

10. In federal court, the citizenship of an LLC is based on the citizenship of all of the LLC's members. Rolling Greens MHP, L.P. v. Comcast SCH Holdings, L.L.C., 374 F.3d 1020, 1022 (11th Cir. 2004) ("a limited liability company is a citizen of any state of which a member of the company is a citizen").

> The distinguishing features of the _______ restaurant system (the "**System**") include, but are not limited to, food selection and presentation, unique recipes, unique methods and procedures, specially designed premises with distinctive decor, equipment, equipment layouts, interior and exterior accessories, color schemes, products, services, methods of operation, management programs, standards, specifications, proprietary marks, information, and the Manual (as more particularly defined in this agreement);
>
> Franchisor has the right to license others to use the System and the Proprietary Marks in the operation of ________ restaurants;
>
> Franchisee wishes to acquire from Franchisor the right and license to operate a ______ restaurant utilizing the System, and the Proprietary Marks, upon the terms and conditions hereinafter set forth.
>
> Now therefore this Agreement witnesses that in consideration of the mutual covenants and agreements herein contained the parties hereto do hereby covenant and agree with each other as follows:

Discussion:

The recitals to the contract have traditionally been the place where the person drafting is provided the opportunity to present background information to assist the reader in understanding the context in which the parties are entering into the contract. As noted in the preceding example, the recitals establish that the franchisor owns or has rights to the key elements of the franchised business model being licensed for use by the franchisee pursuant to the franchise agreement, namely the trademarks and the System as well as that body of knowledge used in the operation of the franchised business (see Chapter 1, Section III for further discussion of the definition of the term "System").

In more limited instances the recitals will be used to extol the advantages of the System, such as recitals will use terminology that refers to such characteristics as the "valuable goodwill" that already exists in the System because of the franchisor's "high standards of quality and service." An example is a recital that will say the following:

> By reason of a uniform business format or system and high standards of quality and service, Franchisor has established demand for its products and services and built up valuable goodwill;

However, this is not a recommended approach. In some contracts the recitals are explicitly stated to form part of the contract. But even if they are not so incorporated, there should be legitimate concern that a court would view the words on the page not as mere puffery, but instead as intended to have some meaning and provide some guidance on the interpretation of the contract.[11]

11. For example, in one much discussed Canadian case, 21 franchisees were awarded significant damages where the franchisor "represented" in the contract's recitals, among other things, that it had and maintained "high and uniform standards," and then was found, as part of the breaches of contract, to have failed to protect and

There is also the question of what value is served if the recitals are used to recite the advantages of the System. In a practical setting, by the time the franchisee is delivered the contract for signing, a decision has been made on whether to sign based on other information, such as the information in the Franchise Disclosure Document (FDD). And what if the recited advantages are not accurate at the time the contract is entered into, or cease to be accurate at some future date? In that case the franchisor is inviting complaint or, worse, a claim for damages or rescission. So it is language that serves no real purpose, and could potentially be used later against the franchisor.

III. Definition of Key Terms

The key terms or "Definitions" section in a franchise agreement is used to define and explain the words, phrases, or terms that will be used throughout the agreement. The person drafting the franchise agreement should never assume that a word, phrase, or term will mean what they want it to mean, or be understood by the reader, unless they define it. The absence of or a mistake in one or two words in a definition could mean a substantially different agreement between the franchisor and the franchisee. As such, great care should be taken when defining these terms. There are a few different ways a drafter may approach defining terms in a franchise agreement: (1) including a separate section in the document to call out all defined terms used in the document; (2) including the definition in the body of the agreement when first used; or (3) a combination of the two. The authors of this book have followed the third type of approach, defining certain terms at the onset (as done in this chapter) as well as including the definition in the text of the agreement when appropriate. As an example, you will note that "Annual Convention" is not included in the listing of terms in the following text, but rather is defined in Chapter 3.

A. The System

> **System** means the operational guidelines, opening guidelines, initial and ongoing training programs, business methods, designs, knowhow, arrangements and brand standards for developing and operating the Franchised Business, including those pertaining to conversion, site selection, construction, building design, signage and layouts, trade dress, equipment, ingredients, recipes, methods of preparation and specifications for products and services, delivery, training, methods of inventory control and requirements and policies regarding personnel, accounting and financial performance, advertising and marketing programs and information technology, all of which Franchisor may improve, further develop or otherwise modify from time to time.

---

enhance the brand and maintain those standards. Bertico Inc. c. Dunkin' Brands Canada Ltd., 2012 QCCS 2809 (CanLII) (Quebec Superior Court), appeal dismissed 2015 QCCA 624 (Quebec Court of Appeal), application for leave to appeal denied (S.C.C. Docket no. 36475) (Supreme Court of Canada).

Discussion:
System is the industry standard term used to define the bundle of intellectual property and other rights, such as knowhow, that are being licensed for use by the franchisee pursuant to the franchise agreement. It is important for the franchise agreement to define what is included in the system so that the franchisor can adequately protect its intellectual property rights in the elements that make up the system. The sample clause includes some of the typical elements included in the definition of a restaurant franchised business system. An alternative version of a definition can be found earlier in this chapter, in Section II (sample recitals). There may very well be a longer list of features to any one franchisor's system, or if the business is one that is a retail store, or solely service oriented, references to ingredients, recipes, premises, and building design may not be necessary.

Either in the body of the agreement, or in this definition, the franchise agreement should contemplate that the then current system will evolve and change over time, as that is a fundamental feature of most businesses, and that the franchisee must abide by and adhere to such changes. Such an acknowledgment is in the example provided. If something is missing from the definition, then the franchisor risks losing the right to adequately control the system, the franchisee's use of it, and perhaps even any intellectual property rights it may assert, thereby preventing the full capture of its value. The franchisor's explicit right to dictate changes to the system should however still be set out in the terms and conditions of the franchise agreement, and not just appear in the definition. See, for example, Chapter 4, which contains provisions and discussion related to modernization and other modifications to the system.

B. Gross Sales

Gross Sales means the aggregate of all revenues, sales and other income of Franchisee from whatever source derived, regardless of whether collected by Franchisee or collected in the form of check, cash, credit or otherwise, arising out of, in connection with or relating to the Franchised Business including, without limitation, (a) income from the sale of any products or other items; (b) income from any services provided; and (c) all proceeds from any business interruption insurance, but excluding (i) all refunds and discounts made in good faith to a customer; (ii) any sales, use, retail sales and equivalent taxes which are collected by Franchisee for or on behalf of any governmental or other public body and actually remitted to such body; and (iii) the value of any coupon, voucher or other allowance authorized by Franchisor and issued or granted to customers of Franchised Business which is received or credited by Franchisee in full or partial satisfaction of the price of any product or service offered in connection with the Franchised Business. Franchisor reserves the right to institute policies in the Manual or otherwise in writing and from time to time, regarding the inclusion in Gross Sales of any pre-paid goods or services (including, without limitation, gift cards and gift certificates) and the delivery and redemption thereof.

Discussion:
It is important to explain gross sales or gross revenues in the franchise agreement because the ongoing amounts to be paid to the franchisor by the franchisee under the agreement will often be based on a percentage of gross sales, however defined.[12] Most commonly, the franchisee pays a continuing royalty based on a percentage of gross sales. Additionally, advertising fees are often paid as a percentage of gross sales.[13] For additional discussion on fees, please refer to Chapter 2.

Given its importance, the franchisor will want to give a broad definition for gross sales so that it can ensure that the franchisee is not able to categorize income under a different label and thereby argue that payment is not due to the franchisor. The definition may include specific language to ensure that revenue from new or nontraditional sources are included in the definition, such as Internet sales, phone sales, home delivery, catering, or other forms of sales, which helps to avoid confusion or misunderstanding. Some agreements also add a reference to "other consideration" in addition to the phrase "other income" included in the sample clause. This language allows the franchisor to assess fees on the value of goods or services the franchisee may provide as part of a barter transaction.

It is common for the definition of gross sales to specifically exclude sales taxes from the calculation, as this is truly a pass-through tax and not brought into income by the franchisee. In more unusual cases, there will be other exclusions from gross sales, but these need to be considered on a case by case basis. For instance, a franchisor may choose not to collect continuing royalties on certain sales (such as on sales made at cost to employees), or reduce gross sales by the equivalent value of any refunds given to customers (assuming the initial sale was included in gross sales to begin with), or a franchisor may be restricted from collecting continuing royalties on certain goods sold (for instance, liquor sales in certain jurisdictions).

C. Trademarks

> **Trademarks** means collectively, those trademarks, service marks, trade names and other commercial symbols and related logos as set forth in Exhibit A, together with such other trade names, trademarks, service marks, symbols, logos, distinctive names, and elements, trade dress, logos, designs, insignia or other items which may be designated for use with the System by Franchisor from time to time.

Discussion:
Along with the system, the trademarks associated with the system are the franchisor's most valued asset.[14] As noted, the essence of what is being licensed under a franchise agreement is use of the system and trademarks. It is crucial that the

12. Asbill, Barkoff, & Selden, *supra* note 4, at 26.

13. *Id.* at 26–27.

14. Francis J. Duffin & Bryan S. Watson, *Best Practices in Protecting and Enforcing Trademarks, Copyrights, and Other Intellectual Property Rights*, 28 Franchise L.J. 132 (Winter 2009).

franchisor carefully define the trademarks. The version included here deals with that in a particular way, by contemplating that a specific list of the trademarks being licensed will appear in an exhibit to the contract. Sometimes contracts are more general and do not include an itemized list of the trademarks. In some instances, not all of the system trademarks are licensed to every franchisee, because of different business formats or multi-branded units for instance, which may be a reason to not include a standard list in every agreement. A variety of approaches can work, but the key aspect of any approach should be to include a catch-all for future trademarks that the franchisor may develop or use and add to the system.

In some instances, as in the example provided, the definition will be so comprehensive that it includes other related and unrelated intellectual property rights as part of the definition of trademarks, such as trade dress, the copyrights in the manuals, and materials produced by or for the franchisor. Trade dress refers to the physical attributes related to the appearance of a retail outlet, or other physical or tangible item. Historically, this was not capable of registration as a trademark, and instead, infringers would be pursued in tort for passing off. That being said, the physical appearance of retail store premises, such as the now iconic and novel look of an Apple® store, has recently been approved for registration as a trademark in both the United States and Canada.[15] Therefore if the franchisor's premises, product, or packaging has a distinctive physical appearance, then trade dress should be included in the definition, or set off as a separate defined term, as in the following example.[16] Otherwise, the franchisor cannot capture the full value associated with this physical appearance. Therefore, franchisors should carefully review which aspects of their trademarks bring value to the system, and explicitly describe them in the definitions. Following is a separate definition of trade dress:

> **Trade Dress** means decorative, nonfunctional components of a Franchised Business that provide the establishment of a distinctive, memorable appearance.

D. Copyrighted Materials

> **Copyrighted Materials** refers to and includes all versions, variations and adaptations of the following materials in tangible form, either produced by Franchisor, produced on its behalf as works for hire, or derived from works produced by or on behalf of Franchisor: (i) all manuals and training modules used in a Store's development, operation and marketing activities, including but not limited to the Manual, (ii) training materials (including printed, audio, video or electronic materials), (iii) Store plans and specifications, (iv) menu board designs and graphics, (v) product identification posters, photographs and graphics, (vi) advertising and marketing materials, (vii) labels, forms and reports provided by Franchisor, (viii) any computer software developed for use in the operation of Stores, (ix) all Trade Dress and Trade Dress elements, and

15. Buffalo Wild Wings, Inc. v. Buffalo Wings & Rings, LLC, No. 09-CV-1426 (D. Minn. June 8, 2011) (order granting summary judgment on trade dress infringement claim).

16. Duffin & Watson, *supra* note 14.

(x) any other materials protected by copyright law or marked or identified by Franchisor as protected by copyright.

Discussion:
Another much less discussed intellectual property right associated with franchising is the copyright that subsists in the written or tangible expressions of the ideas that the franchisor produces for use in the system. Copyright is a form of intellectual property right that "provides the author of an original work of authorship with certain exclusive rights with respect to that work."[17] Again, if the franchisor fails to identify its copyrights adequately, then it will not be able to capture the full value of those rights. So, at the very least, legal counsel should advise their clients to assert copyright on such materials by including a claim of copyright on the work, namely the © symbol along with the year of first publication and the name of the copyright owner. Copyrights may be registered, but because registration is not required to assert rights and recover provable damages, it is less commonly done. That being said, there are certain statutory benefits in asserting rights if the copyright is registered, including the right to seek statutory damages and attorneys' fees in federal court. In the United States, registered copyrighted materials must be deposited in the Library of Congress. Because most franchisors consider (and should consider, if appropriate) their manuals to constitute trade secrets, they typically do not want to deposit a copy for copyright purposes lest they lose trade secret protection. In some instances, a franchise agreement will be so comprehensive that it includes other unrelated intellectual property rights as part of the trademarks, such as the copyrights in the manuals and materials produced by or for the franchisor. We include in the preceding text a franchise agreement definition of copyrighted materials, although it is not that commonly included as a separately defined term.

E. Manual

Manual means, collectively, all manuals, policy statements, directives, books, pamphlets, bulletins, memoranda, letters, notices, computer media (i.e. computer software, CDRom) or other publications, documents or electronic media prepared by or on behalf of Franchisor for use by Franchisees generally or for Franchisee in particular, that contain prescribed or recommended standards, procedures, policies and advice relating to the operation of the Franchised Business' operation and management, to marketing the products and services offered, and setting forth information, advice, standards, requirements, operating procedures, recipes, instructions or policies relating to the operation of Outlets, as Franchisor may amend from time to time.

Discussion:
The manual is of critical importance in any franchise relationship. The manual sets out the system standards that the franchisee must abide by in operating the franchised business, and can include such items as the store operating procedures,

17. *Id.*

recipes, and other policies.[18] Historically it would be delivered to the franchisee in binder "hard copy" form. Today, it is usually a mixture of hard copy and electronically delivered information (which itself may be in text, audio or video form), with more and more being delivered and made available to the franchisee in electronic form (via e-mail, access to extranet, or the like). The definition of the manual needs to take into account the methods by which the information is delivered.

The franchise agreement should provide the franchisor with the right to revise the manual on an ongoing basis, and there must be provision made for the franchisee to accept and abide by all parts of the manual and any changes, typically at the franchisee's cost. For a more in depth discussion on manuals, see Chapter 5, Section XIX, which includes more detailed clauses regarding the manual.

F. Franchised Business

Franchised Business means the business operated by Franchisee under this Agreement.

Discussion:
It is important to identify the specific business that the franchisee is going to operate. Once this identification is made, the rest of the franchise agreement can refer to the specific location merely through a defined term, such as "franchised business." Throughout the course of this book the term "franchised business" is used, although drafters may choose to include more specific references depending on the concept and industry, such as "store" or "restaurant" as appropriate.

G. Control Person and/or Principal Owner, Etc.

Owner means each person or entity that has a direct or indirect legal or beneficial ownership interest in Franchisee, if Franchisee is a business corporation, partnership or other legal entity.

Principal Owner means each Owner with an ownership interest greater than XX%, if Franchisee is a business corporation, partnership, or other legal entity.

Managing Owner means one of Franchisee's Owners who meets Franchisor's requirements and is approved by Franchisor, and who is appointed by Franchisee to supervise and manage all aspects of Franchisee's business and to deal exclusively with Franchisor and its staff for purposes of administering and coordinating the relationship created by this Agreement. Franchisee's first Managing Owner is identified on the Summary Pages.

Discussion:
Administratively, it is important to label and be able to identify one or more franchisee control persons, managing stockholders, or other key persons operating the

18. Heather Carson Perkins, Sarah J. Yatchak & Gordon M. Hadfield, *Franchisor Liability for Acts of the Franchisee*, 29 Franchise L.J. 174, 180 (Winter 2010).

franchised business in the definition section of the franchise agreement. The names or labels provided in the preceding samples are common examples, but these terms vary greatly from one form of franchise agreement to another.

The franchisor and its legal counsel need to consider how much detail they want, and who they need to specify under the contract by way of ownership and/or management. These issues also become important later in the context of who will also be required to provide a personal guaranty. Most frequently, the people are identified in the franchise agreement using simpler concepts and rather arbitrary percentage ownership thresholds, such as is found in the preceding sample version.

The control person may very well be the same person as the principal owner or guarantor. Although a franchisee is most usually a corporation or other legal entity (i.e., a limited liability company), the franchisor is usually keenly interested to make sure that it is aware of the person(s) in charge and managing the business on a day-to-day basis.

The control person also may be the key manager, but that is not necessarily the case. A franchisor will therefore need to consider early on whether it will permit a franchisee to use employee managers to run the franchised business, or insist that a control person fulfill this role. In some businesses it is critical to the franchisor that the owner also be an operator. In other situations, it is not important at all. Where a franchisor permits multiple unit ownership by the same franchisee, it may of course be impossible to insist that the franchised businesses be run day to day by an owner-operator.

H. Confidential Information

Confidential Information means Franchisor's proprietary and confidential information relating to the development and operation of Stores, including:

1. Information Systems and software programs prescribed for use in Stores;
2. Identity of suppliers and knowledge of Brand Standards for and suppliers of certain fixtures, furnishings, equipment, products, materials and supplies;
3. Methods of training and management relating to Stores;
4. The Brand Standards, the Manual, any other proprietary materials and knowledge, know-how or experience used or obtained in developing and operating Stores;
5. Sales, marketing and advertising programs and techniques for Stores;
6. Knowledge of operating results and financial performance of Stores, other than Franchisee's Store;
7. Operator and employee recruiting, interviewing, orientation, training and evaluation policies and procedures;
8. Franchisor's initial and refresher training programs;
9. Site selection criteria, general contractor and architect criteria and Trade Dress for Stores, and plans and specification for the development of Stores;
10. Guest Information and other information (including earnings information) regarding Franchisor's personnel and Customers and those of other franchisees and licensees of Franchisor;

11. Franchisee recruiting methods and procedures, and selection criteria;
12. Business performance measurement systems; and
13. All other information that Franchisor provides Franchisee and designates proprietary or confidential, including information provided to Franchisee through the Intranet or the Manual.

Discussion:

Invariably a franchisor will ascribe to the notion that at least some parts of the know-how relating to the system are comprised of confidential information. So most if not all franchise agreements will have provisions that deal with or deem many types of information as confidential in nature. Misuse or disclosure of confidential information is a default under the contract and often is noncurable, leading to termination without opportunity to cure.

Included here is a relatively comprehensive definition of confidential information. It is included because it goes to some length to identify the types of information in the specific system that the franchisor wishes to be treated as confidential. Of course, the types of information that are truly proprietary and worthy of being treated as confidential vary from system to system, and by the type of business. Often it is difficult to identify it with any certainty in advance, such as early on when the franchise agreement is being drafted. So, perhaps more often the definition in the franchise agreement is more general in nature, and includes a definition such as the following:

> "Confidential Information" means any trade secrets or confidential information concerning the System, proprietary and marketing information including the Manual, technical knowledge, research data, processes, programs, designs, product or marketing plans, financial or personnel data, sales, supplier, customer, employee or investor information, or the like, relating to the business affairs or operations of Franchisor or its franchisees, whether in oral, written, electronic, graphical or other form provided that Confidential Information does not include any information that:
>
> 1. was publicly known and made generally available in the public domain prior to the time of disclosure by Franchisor;
> 2. becomes publicly known and made generally available after disclosure by Franchisor through no action or inaction of Franchisee; or
> 3. is required to be released or disclosed by law or judicial order.

In some instances, as with this second example, the franchise agreement will seek to deem all information shared with the franchisees as confidential, and therefore subject to duties of nondisclosure and proper use. However, it is likely more realistic to limit enforcement to situations where the information is in fact confidential, proprietary, and not public.[19] Enforcement of the confidentiality provisions

---

19. *See, e.g.*, Millet v. Crump, 687 So. 2d 132, 135 (La. App. 5th Cir. 1997) ("[A]n agreement not to use confidential information is enforceable if . . . the information used is in fact confidential.") (internal quotations and citations omitted); Am. Potato Dryers, Inc. v. Peters, 184 F.2d 165, 172 (4th Cir. 1950) ("[I]t would be absurd to

of the franchise agreement against a franchisee where the information was already made public by someone else, or was never truly confidential, is likely not simple, nor worth the effort.

IV. Grant and Reservation of Rights

A. Grant of Rights

1. Franchisor grants to Franchisee a Franchise, and Franchisee accepts the Franchise and obligation to develop and operate, the Franchised Business and to offer and sell approved products and services from the Premises, using the System and Marks in accordance with Franchisor's Brand Standards.
2. The Franchise includes the following rights and licenses:
   (a) Authorization to operate Franchised Business under the Marks and in accordance with the System;
   (b) Authorization to provide Catering Service in the Designated Area; and
   (c) Authorization to advertise and promote the Franchised Business using the Marks in accordance with the Brand Standards and Franchisor's instructions.
3. Franchisee will acquire no rights or authority under this Agreement or as an element of the Franchise:
   (a) To sell any product or service to any wholesale customer;
   (b) To operate a Kiosk or Special Outlet, except as expressly authorized by Franchisor in writing; or
   (c) To sell any product or service from catalogues or an Internet Website.
4. Franchisee's use of any of the Marks or any element of the System in the operation of a business at any other address or in any other channel of distribution without Franchisor's express prior written authorization will constitute willful infringement of Franchisor's rights in the Marks and the System.
5. Franchisee's right to operate the Franchised Business and to use the Marks or any element of the System for the operation of the Franchised Business is contingent upon Franchisee's full compliance with all federal, state and local laws, rules and regulations, and Franchisee's timely procurement and maintenance of any and all permits, certificates or licenses necessary for the full and proper conduct of the Franchised Business including, without limitation, licenses to do business, trade name registrations and sales tax permits.

Discussion:

The grant clause is one of the most important provisions in a franchise agreement, yet the core of it may only be one sentence long in many franchise agreements, such as the following:

designate as a confidential disclosure that which is publicly known."); Sarkes Tarzian, Inc. v. Audio Devices, Inc., 166 F. Supp. 250, 265 (S.D. Cal. 1958) ("[M]atters which are generally known in the trade or readily ascertainable by those in the trade cannot be made secret by being so labelled [sic] in an agreement.").

> Subject to the provisions of this Agreement and for the term hereinafter specified, Franchisor hereby grants to Franchisee a nonexclusive right to operate a Franchised Business at and only at the Premises and a nonexclusive license to use the System and Trademarks solely and exclusively in the operation thereof.

Still, especially in this day and age of multiple avenues of distribution of products and services, the grant needs to be very clear as to the scope of rights franchised to the franchisee. As a foundational matter, the grant in a typical franchise agreement is not the sale of assets; it is the granting of temporary (and many times conditional) rights to use the trademarks and system during the term of the franchise agreement. Key points to cover include the type of business covered, the geographic location for the business, exclusivity, the duration of the grant, and any key conditions or limitations.

(i) Appropriate Parties

A franchisor must consider if there are other affiliates that might need to be included in this granting provision, whether due to different trademark ownership, mandatory product or supply purchases from an affiliate, etc. Ultimately, the question of who is granting the rights is more important with respect to reserved rights afforded the franchisor (exclusivity and other similar protections afforded the franchisee, as further detailed next related to exclusivity and reserved rights), but many franchise companies will attempt to limit overarching liability exposure by using a single-purpose franchisor entity in lieu of a parent or other affiliates that may be a public company, an operator of multiple company-owned locations, a manufacturer, distributor or seller of products, a service provider or owner of other unrelated assets that the "company" desires to insulate from the franchise system. Inadvertent inclusion of parents or affiliates in the grant can open these entities to potential exposure.[20]

The language of the franchise agreement clarifies that it is the franchisee receiving the rights, and not the franchisee's owners, officers, directors, employees, and so on. There are a number of reasons that the franchisors want to make sure the grant is solely to the franchisee and not its affiliated parties, not the least of which relates to potential litigation and rights afforded the franchisee. Accordingly, while in certain instances in the franchise agreement the franchisor will want to bind certain guarantors or owners to all or certain terms of the franchise agreement, the franchisor wants to take care to not expressly grant franchise rights to the guarantors or owners or else they may be able to claim standing in a dispute that could

20. Franchise agreements often define "franchisor" to specifically exclude "parents or affiliates." The issue of who is granting the rights often arises when a franchisee seeks to compel a franchisor and the franchisor's affiliated parties to arbitrate. When the franchise agreement defines the "franchisor" to specifically exclude "parents or affiliates," the affiliate or parent will most likely not be bound by the arbitration clause in the franchise agreement. *See* World Rentals & Sales, LLC v. Volvo Constr. Equip. Rentals, Inc., 517 F.3d 1240 (11th Cir. 2008) (lender/affiliate not bound by arbitration clause since "franchisor" defined to exclude "parents or affiliates").

range from matters relating to who received disclosure to whose harm should be compensated in a suit.[21]

(ii) Rights Granted

The sample provision includes several defined terms such as the franchise, the franchised business, the marks, the system, and other similar defined terms to enable the franchisor to clearly define the parameters for the rights being granted. Although defined terms are discussed elsewhere, for purposes of discussion the franchise here is "the right to develop and operate the franchised business and to offer and sell approved products and services." Alternatively, a provision may refer more specifically to the franchised business as a unit or store, in which case the "store" would be further defined as "an establishment (often a restaurant) that operates on a year-round basis at a fixed (permanent) location or at an approved kiosk location under the marks and system." Thus, it is clear that the rights relate to a permanent store at a specific physical (i.e., bricks and mortar) location that uses both the system and the marks. All elements are required, so the rights do not apply if one or more of the elements are missing. Some franchisors may go further to distinguish sizes or product offerings of the franchised business, or differentiate the specific marks that are part of this system versus another "system" or offering. This is especially important when it comes to multi-brand operators who in some cases may use all of or certain aspects of the marks and/or the system across multiple concepts. Further down in the provision the language covers certain additional rights (here, operating the store, providing catering service, and advertising and promoting the store).

(iii) Rights Excluded

The business scope of rights has grown exponentially in importance over the past 15 years with the growth of the Internet and alternative methods of distribution, and setting forth what is excluded from the grant of rights can sometimes be as important as describing what is included. In the sample provision, for instance, the right to sell to any wholesale customer, to operate a kiosk or special outlet, or to sell from catalogues or an Internet website are all specifically excluded.

Although greater depth on the various types of reserved rights that the franchisors withhold from the franchisees and/or reserve for themselves and their affiliates is presented later in this section, the goal for most franchisors is to provide as narrow a business scope as possible while still being able to sell franchises. Thus, in an ideal scenario, the rights being granted are clearly set forth and limited by

---

21. *See* Jon S. Swierzewski, *Standing in Franchise Disputes: Check the Invitations, Not Every Party Gets Inside*, 26 FRANCHISE L.J. 107 (Winter 2007); *see also* Long John Silver's Inc. v. Nickelson, 923 F. Supp. 2d 1004 (W.D. Ky. 2013) (only signatory to franchise agreement, and not her husband and his other franchisees, had standing to bring fraud claim against franchisor); Gold's Gym Franchising LLC v. Brewer, 400 S.W.3d 156 (Tex. App.—Dallas 2013, no pet.) (shareholders of corporate franchisee were not parties to franchise agreement and therefore shareholders could not have breached the franchise agreement because guaranty agreements signed by shareholders were separate contracts between and among separate parties).

definition, description, and/or exclusion. The bottom line is, even if the franchisor and its personnel cannot currently envision moving into a specific line of distribution, it cannot hurt to provide for it as technology is continuously improving. Just consider that 25 years ago the concept of doing taxes "online," or ordering your food through an "app" on your mobile phone or watch was probably inconceivable to persons who now do both with regularity. Even five years ago, most of us would not have envisioned home and office communication devices such as Amazon's Alexa, Google Home, or Apple Homepod as the future for ordering pizza, products, and other items. There is even a TV ad for a major pizza brand that touts ordering pizza through a button on your shoe.

(iv) Geographic Rights and Restrictions—Brick and Mortar

The provision clearly states that the rights are specific to the premises, which is most commonly set forth on the cover page or an exhibit to the franchise agreement, similar to the "summary page" described earlier in this chapter. Note that this provision includes expanded rights, in that the franchisee may provide catering service in a designated area and advertising and promoting the store. As with the business scope of rights, the geographic scope of rights has perhaps grown exponentially in importance over the past 15 years with the growth of the Internet and alternative methods of distribution discussed previously. While exclusivity and various retained rights are discussed in greater depth later in this section, it is crucial that the franchisor be very clear where the franchisee can exercise these rights.

Many franchise systems are storefront-based product businesses (hence the store address concept in the previous discussion), but even those types of businesses must address off-site concepts such as delivery, catering, take-away, online ordering, and other similar concepts where a customer does not come to and stay at the location for the duration of the customer experience. This is all the more important where there are franchisees placed close together, and many franchise systems have experienced relationship and even legal complications where an original franchisee who had no brand-based competition and was permitted to expand their coverage is unceremoniously told to reign in their activities after a new franchisee comes into the area. When a system allows delivery, catering, and other services offsite, it is of course crucial to provide parameters as to distances, maintenance of product specifications (for instance, food temperature and/or presentation), and maintenance of quality specifications (uniforms, delivery vehicles, tableware, etc.).

(v) Geographic Rights and Restrictions—Service Industry and Mobile Units

The geographic component is even more important in service- and/or mobile-based franchise systems where there may not be any store front for customers to gather, and instead the nature of the business entails the franchisee marketing to, and then traveling to, the customers. The size and description of the geographic area in which the franchisee can market and serve customers is crucial. While generally speaking the size is a business decision, the insertion of the description into the franchise agreement is crucial, and mistakes such as inserting a larger development area into the smaller franchise territory blank can be both embarrassing and damaging. Along those lines, there are myriad ways to describe the franchise territory, from the use of counties or city limits to zip codes to roadways to metes and bounds to electronic or hand-marked demarcations on a map, and of course there are myriad ways to create confusion with respect to the franchise territory, from misspelled city or county names to unconnected roads to unclear maps to even referencing a map that is never prepared or attached. Ultimately, from a drafting standpoint, the goal would be clarity and simplicity so that the person in charge of completing the franchise agreement for execution has clear and concise direction to fill in these key terms.

Particularly in mobile-based franchise systems, the franchisor must analyze different scenarios and ideally reserve the right to create and modify policies regarding territories, encroachment, and other similar territorial rights and restrictions. For instance, the growth of food truck franchises creates a new host of issues because the traditionally brick and mortar/single location restaurant franchise can be both a fixed and mobile location.[22] Consider a scenario where two food truck franchisees have territories that are adjacent to each other, and each decides to park at the edge of their respective territories to take advantage of a particular "hot" area or even a special event. The food trucks could literally find themselves on the other side of the street from each other in what they each consider their own protected areas. Depending on the business model, the franchisors may need to consider issues such as having an area of protection and a separate area of operation so that while no other franchisee will go in the larger area of protection, the franchisee can only go within the smaller area of operation to provide a buffer between the franchisees.[23]

(vi) Other Conditions

Other nonbusiness and nongeographic conditions may also be placed on the rights being granted. The sample provision states that the rights to use the system and marks must be exercised "in accordance with Franchisor's Brand Standards." In other words, the franchisee must follow the system and operate in accordance with the system as a continuing condition to the overarching grant of rights. This is the foundation of a franchise; the franchisee has to operate under the brand's operating system, and if the franchisee fails to do so there are ramifications that can range from a penalty to a revoked right to a denied privilege to a formal default to an outright termination. In addition, depending on the nature of the franchise, especially franchises in the medical field or other highly regulated areas, the grant may go further and confirm that the franchise rights must be exercised "in accordance with all applicable laws." While outside the concept of this particular section, the overarching thought that goes through any franchise agreement drafter's mind must

22. *See* Chris Egan & Suzie Trigg, *Food Trucks, Kiosks and Other Alternative Venues: Structuring and Drafting Issues*, ABA 37th Annual Forum on Franchising W-17, at 23 (2014).

23. Although outside the scope of this section, the advent of mobile businesses tethered with the growth of technology has led to interesting control, privacy, and related topics such as tracking devices on mobile food trucks or other mobile businesses.

be whether a particular concept, right, or obligation is something that must be contained in the franchise agreement itself, or may be ripe for general coverage in the franchise agreement with ability to modify from time to time in the brand standards.

B. Exclusive or Nonexclusive Territory

> 1. So long as Franchisee, its Affiliates and the Principals are in full compliance with this Agreement and all other agreements between Franchisee, its Affiliates and the Principals and Franchisor and its Affiliates, then Franchisor will not operate or authorize anyone except Franchisee to commence operation of a Store using the Marks and System from a physical location in the Designated Area.

Discussion:

Although the grant of rights section of the agreement clearly outlines who receives the rights, the extent and limitation of the business and geographic scope, and any other conditions, the franchisee will invariably want and need to know how the franchisor, its affiliates, other franchisees, and other related parties might impact their business (i.e., encroachment by the franchisor, other franchisees or third parties with rights in alternative methods of distribution). This is perhaps the most important practical franchise relationship concept in the grant provision. Ultimately, a franchise agreement's section relating to exclusivity (or nonexclusivity) of the franchisee's rights is a classic example of competing franchisor and franchisee objectives. It exemplifies the difficult balance that a franchisor must strike when considering the attractiveness of the franchise offering versus the need to reserve control and flexibility over the expansion of the brand (whether that is through additional outlets or other channels of distribution). The language of the franchise agreement must consider all of these objectives. A clearly drafted section regarding territory helps set expectations of the parties and may assist in dispute resolution.

(i) No Exclusivity/Location Only

Franchisors generally try to avoid locking themselves into express contractual obligations to franchisees, and more importantly franchisors also try to avoid setting express limitations on their current and future rights with respect to the brand. The franchisors will many times couch this in negotiations with franchisees as an inability to compromise the franchisor's freedom or flexibility to expand and enhance the brand. In this sense, a franchisor's ideal provision would read something like the following site-specific grant/reservation of rights:

> The rights granted to Franchisee are site specific, for use only at the location identified in this Agreement, and provide no rights of exclusivity to Franchisee. Accordingly, Franchisee's rights do not include (i) an exclusive area or protected territory within which Franchisor or its affiliates agree not to issue competing franchises or operate competing businesses, (ii) any right to sell products and items identified by the Marks at any location other than the Authorized Location or through any other channels or methods of distribution, including the Internet (or any other existing or future form of electronic commerce) and pre-packaged retail sales, (iii) any right to sell products and

items identified by the Marks to any person or entity for resale or further distribution, or (iv) any right to exclude, control or impose conditions on the location or development of future stores at any time.

This is a clean and easy provision to manage for a franchisor, and as discussed next some franchisors operate in a specific segment or have sufficient market power to take this position in their agreements and relationships. In the language of the example provision, the franchisor will give no exclusivity rights, and the franchisee will be given no guaranty that the franchisor, its affiliates, or other franchisees will not directly compete. In other words, the franchisee gets no exclusivity on any territory and the franchise rights are truly "site only." In these situations, anyone, including the franchisor, can open a competing outlet nearby. More advanced and mature franchisors are the most likely to have this kind of language in their franchise agreements.[24] Sophisticated franchisors can do this in theory because there is enough value attached to their trademarks that the consumer demand for the franchises themselves, and the franchise's products or services, is high. Because the demand is high, locations in close proximity will likely still succeed. These franchisors generally want to add a number of franchise outlets in densely populated areas and keep exclusive areas small so that they can dominate the market and outpace their competitors.[25] In effect, the argument is that what is good for the brand (global domination/closing out competitors) is good for the franchisees. Similarly, the brand popularity, track record, or history is enough to incentivize demand by prospective franchisees, regardless of territorial exclusivity.

Understandably so, the notion that the franchisor, its other franchisees, or the "brand" as a whole could compete with the franchisees in their area causes a great deal of consternation for franchisees.

(ii) Exclusive Territory

Commercial reality dictates that many franchisors need to incorporate some types of exclusivity in favor of the franchisee in their standard franchise agreements to effectively sell franchises. Newer or smaller franchisors, in particular, might have to provide for some exclusivity of territory to attract franchisees.[26] This is especially important where there is no track record of the franchisor and its personnel in terms of being aggressive or cautious when it comes to locating franchisees, or developing and implementing new concepts or alternative methods of distribution.

If the franchisor is going to provide some amount of exclusivity, the issue becomes how much.[27] Thus, the greatest tension in the grant/reserved rights section of the franchise agreement is the determination of what is fair or reasonable

24. Joseph J. Fittante, Jr. & Dennis E. Wieczorek, *Advanced Drafting*, ABA 27th Annual Forum on Franchising, at 3–5 (2004).

25. Joe Mathews, Don DeBolt & Deb Percival, Street Smart Franchising 189 (Entrepreneur Press 2006).

26. Scott A. Shane, From Ice Cream to the Internet: Using Franchising to Drive the Growth and Profits of Your Company 133 (Pearson Education Inc. 2005).

27. *See generally* Julie Lusthaus, *Just How Exclusive Is an Exclusive Territory?*, http://ed-lawfirm.com/wp-content/uploads/2015/05/Just-How-Exclusive-is-an-Exclusive-Territory-August-2013-Issue.pdf (last visited Sept. 19, 2018).

in terms of exclusivity, and what it does and does not entail. There is no one size fits all option, and the Federal Trade Commission (FTC) appears to mainly be concerned with clarity of description based on its answer to Frequently Asked Question (FAQ) 37, which relates to describing a territory as exclusive where there are carve-outs for alternative venues that reduce the franchisee's rights.[28]

If an exclusive territory is warranted or necessary, the franchisor has to consider the needs that it and the franchisee wish to see protected. This is a function of the type of business being operated. For instance, when provided in a retail restaurant franchise, territorial protection is most often afforded to a franchisee by providing a relatively straightforward geographic area, defined in the agreement with sufficient certainty, such that the franchisor agrees that it will not open physical units in the territory, nor franchise others to open units in the territory.

However, in other situations, the territory needs to be considered and articulated in a different manner, such as exclusivity with respect to market segment, or by specifying that the franchisee will in fact only seek customers from within the territory. This last right (restriction) is most often seen in service franchises where the franchisee is expected to seek out customers at their addresses, but as we all know today, with Internet and other marketing techniques it is very difficult to limit marketing to specific territories, and franchisees are loath to reject a potential customer because the potential customer's physical address, or even the location at which they need a particular product or service, falls outside of what the franchisee would likely deem an artificial barrier to them effectively operating their business.

If some form of exclusivity is granted, the franchisor must then take care to ask, answer, and address the same types of questions as when the grant provision was drafted. While seemingly duplicative, case law in the area of grants, reserved rights and encroachment, good faith and fair dealing, and similar claims necessitate it.[29]

---

28. *See* FTC Amended Franchise Rule FAQs, FAQ 37, http://www.business.ftc.gov/documents/amended-franchise-rule-faqs#37:

> May a franchisor state in Item 12 that it grants an "exclusive territory" if it reserves the right to open franchised or company outlets in so-called "non-traditional venues" like airports, arenas, hospitals, hotels, malls, military installations, national parks, schools, stadiums and theme parks? Answer: No. Pursuant to FAQ 25, a franchisor may state in Item 12 that it grants an "exclusive territory" only if the franchisor contractually "promises not to establish either a company-owned or franchised outlet selling the same or similar goods or services under the same or similar trademarks or service marks" within the geographic area or territory granted to a franchisee. A reservation of rights to open outlets selling the same goods or services under the same trademarks or service marks within a franchisee's territory negates any such commitment and triggers the Item 12 requirement to include a disclaimer stating that franchisees will not receive an exclusive territory. FAQ 25 notes that it is consistent with the disclosure scheme in Item 12 for a franchisor to grant an exclusive territory yet reserve the right to make sales in the territory through other channels of distribution or competitive brands because Item 12 elsewhere specifically requires detailed disclosures about such potential competition. The required disclosures about "other channels of distribution such as Internet, catalog sales, telemarketing or other direct marketing" are limited by the examples provided, however, to sales not requiring a franchised or company outlet physically located in a franchisee's exclusive territory.

29. The implied duty of good faith and fair dealing is generally invoked when the franchise provision is ambiguous. For example, when the contract language is unclear, franchisees have brought encroachment claims under a theory of breach of the implied duty of good faith and fair dealing. Scheck v. Burger King Corp., 798 F. Supp. 692

(iii) Appropriate Parties

The provision states that the franchisor "will not operate or authorize anyone except franchisee to commence operation of a store from a physical location in the Designated Area." The grant relates to the franchisor opening a unit itself or granting a franchise to a third party to open a unit, but by design the provision does not expressly mention or limit the franchisor's parents, owners, officers, directors, affiliates, successors or assigns, and so on (although in most circumstances it would be difficult to carve out legitimate successors or assigns to the franchisor's rights under the franchise agreement). Further, while in theory (if not always in reality) the franchisor would have the sole overarching rights to make any such third party grant, there can be more complicated trademark and system ownership rights that create potential loopholes for the franchisor or related third parties to use to their advantage to circumvent a narrowly defined grant of reserved rights. To that end, in practice some more sophisticated franchisees may demand greater coverage as to all of the franchisor's related entities and even owners, officers, or employees of the franchisor and its related entities. This is of course a product of negotiation since not many franchisors will unilaterally provide broad coverage in their standard forms, but it can be a slippery slope to entertain since a sophisticated franchisee may legitimately question how a franchisor can make its parent entity comply if it is not a party to the franchise agreement, but no franchisor wants to make its parents, affiliates, or subsidiaries direct parties to the franchise agreement for even the narrowest of terms. Ultimately, a compromise may be an express default if a related party to the franchisor violates the provision.

As discussed in the grant section, Section IV, the exclusivity is limited to the franchisee, and does not include its parents, owners, officers, directors, affiliates, and so on. Limiting the number of entities or persons who are afforded the rights is the best way of limiting the potential exposure and claims both in connection with a claim that the reserved rights were breached, but also (as noted previously) in connection with a claim that these ancillary persons were the franchisee or third party beneficiaries of the franchise grant and therefore harmed by the alleged breach.

(iv) Rights Granted

The language outlines an agreement of the franchisor to not operate or authorize anyone except the franchisee to commence operation of a store from a physical location in the designated area. This limits the exclusivity to the defined store, and

(S.D. Fla. 1992) (even though franchise agreement denied territory exclusivity to franchisee, the court determined that franchisee "is entitled to expect that Burger King will not act to destroy the right of the franchisee to enjoy the fruits of the contract"); *but see* Burger King Corp. v. Weaver, 169 F.3d 1310 (11th Cir. 1999) (overturning *Scheck* and holding that if franchisee's franchise agreement did not grant him a right to an exclusive territory, Burger King Corporation incurred no duty to refrain from licensing new franchises in the area). However, when the franchise agreement unambiguously states than a franchisee can expect no exclusive territory, the implied duty of good faith and fair dealing will not override or replace the express terms of the contract. *See* Camp Creek Hospitality Inns, Inc. v. Sheraton Franchise Corp, ITT, 139 F.3d 1396, 1403 (11th Cir. 1998) (noting prevailing view that implied covenant cannot be used to contradict express contract terms).

not other types of locations, which is generally in the reserved rights section of the franchise agreement discussed later in this chapter.

(v) Geographic Rights and Restrictions

Here, the limitation relates to a physical location in the designated area. Thus, there is no express prohibition on the franchisor's right to offer and sell on the Internet, through other retail outlets such as supermarkets or convenience stores, or outside the designated area.

(vi) Other Conditions

Drafters should consider what other nonbusiness and nongeographic conditions may be placed on the rights being granted. Here, the franchisee, its affiliates, and the principals must be in full compliance with the franchise agreement and all other agreements between franchisee, its affiliates, and the principals and franchisor and its affiliates. Thus, while the grant of exclusivity is limited to the franchisor and the franchisee, the conditions to the grant are broader and include all of the related parties of the franchisor and the franchisee. This is especially important where the franchisors are part of a larger multi-concept group and/or the franchisee is part of a larger, multi-unit or even multi-concept franchisee with multiple affiliated entities. All that said, in the authors' experience, it is fairly rare for a franchisor to actually invoke a franchisee's (or related parties') pending breach of the specific franchise agreement (much less a different franchise agreement) to actually place another company-owned or franchised unit in the otherwise protected area, in part because many defaults are susceptible to cure and could likely be cured before the franchisor could take action to open a unit and in part because in most instances a termination of the franchise is a more attractive option to the franchisor than trying to place another unit in the same geographic area. That said, confirming to a breaching franchisee that the pending default permits the franchisor to re-open the territory to another company-owned or franchised unit can be a useful shot across the bow tactic to hasten a defaulting franchisee to pursue cure.

While generally outside the scope of a franchise agreement grant of exclusivity, many development agreements will have interim measures related to breach that can include elimination, reduction, or restructuring of an existing larger protected development area as part of the rights afforded the franchisor, and in theory similar interim measures could be instituted in a franchise agreement, but in the authors' experience it is much more limited and generally industry specific (for instance, turning off promotion/access to a reservation system in the hotel industry).

C. Reservation of Rights and Alternate Channels of Distribution

1. Reservation of Rights
   (a) Franchisor and its Affiliates (and their respective successors and assigns, by purchase, merger, consolidation or otherwise) reserve all rights that this

Agreement does not expressly grant to or confer upon Franchisee, including, without limitation and notwithstanding Section __ above:

(i) The right to establish and operate and license others to establish and operate Special Outlets in the Designated Area, regardless of proximity to or competitive impact upon the Franchised Business;

(ii) The right to establish, operate and license others to establish and operate Stores, Special Outlets or other establishments located anywhere outside the Designated Area's physical boundaries, regardless of proximity to or competitive impact upon the Franchised Business and regardless of whether these establishments market their products and services in, or draw customers from, the Designated Area;

(iii) The right to distribute private label products, pre-packaged food products, memorabilia, and other products and merchandise, whether or not identified by or associated with the Marks, to or through any commercial establishments that are not affiliated with Franchisor or associated with the Franchise Network, including (for example) department stores, supermarkets and convenience stores, both inside and outside the Designated Area, regardless of proximity to or competitive impact upon Franchisee's Store;

(iv) The right to distribute private label products, pre-packaged food products, memorabilia, and other products and merchandise whether or not identified by or associated with the Marks, to all Persons whether inside or outside the Designated Area through catalogues, telemarketing campaigns, an Internet website and other direct-order techniques;

(v) The right to distribute catalogues and similar sales solicitation materials in the Designated Area, broadcast television and radio commercials for direct-order merchandise into the Designated Area, initiate telephone contact with and accept telephone orders from residents of the Designated Area, and fill orders for direct-order merchandise in the Designated Area, regardless of proximity to or competitive impact upon the Franchised Business;

(vi) The right to operate, and grant to others the right to operate, retail food establishments (including Stores) identified by tradenames, trademarks, service marks or trade dress, other than the Marks, pursuant to such terms and conditions as Franchisor deems appropriate, both inside and outside the Designated Area and regardless of proximity to or competitive impact upon the Franchised Business;

(vii) The right to advertise and promote sales of any products and/or services (including those offered by Stores) both inside and outside the Designated Area and advertise and promote franchises, regardless of proximity to or competitive impact upon the Franchised Business; and

(viii) The right to acquire or be acquired by (regardless of the form of the transaction) a business which operates or licenses others to operate premises within the Designated Area, and Franchisor or its successors or assigns will have the right to operate and license other to operate such businesses under the trademarks or service marks of such other business at, from and/or physically contiguous to the Franchised Business's premises within the Designated Area regardless of proximity to or competitive impact upon the Franchised Business.

(b) Franchisee acknowledges and agrees that Franchisor has no express obligation or implied duty to insulate or protect Franchisee's revenues from erosion as the result of the Franchised Business competing with other foodservice businesses or with Special Outlets in the ways and to the extent this Section provides or contemplates. Franchisee expressly waives and relinquishes any right to assert any claim against Franchisor based on the existence, actual or arguable, of any such obligation or duty.

Discussion:

The core of the grant clause was one sentence, and the core of the exclusivity clause was one sentence, but the reserved rights provision set forth here is almost a page long. The example provision illustrates how results in certain cases can significantly impact the language commonly included in franchise agreements. In a nutshell, the approach has trended toward being short and direct in the exclusivity clause, and then whittling away at the exclusivity in the reserved rights section. Although it may seem logical that a franchise agreement would contain a similarly brief catch-all reservation that "reserves all rights that this Agreement does not expressly grant to or confer upon Franchisee," as witnessed in certain historical encroachment cases, this catch-all might not be enough and therefore a laundry list of reserved rights are detailed both for legal reasons and practical relationship reasons since it is always easier to get the franchisor's position across when it can point to a specific statement in the FDD and provision in the franchise agreement to back up a specific action (e.g., "we expressly told you we might build a location in a special outlet in your Territory," or "we expressly told you we might create a frozen item under this brand and sell it in Costco"). Although it may cause concern for the prospective franchisee and result in difficult discussions for those on the franchise development side of the business, case law has made it critical to clearly "call out" the respective rights (or the limitation on such rights, as the case may be) related to territory.[30]

(i) Encroachment Considerations

Where the franchise agreement is unclear or ambiguous regarding the level of territorial protection, the franchisees have attempted to bring encroachment claims under a breach of implied duty of good faith and fair dealing theory. For example in *Scheck v. Burger King Corp.*, the franchise agreement contained the following provision relating to territory:

30. *See* Scheck v. Burger King Corp., 798 F. Supp. at 692 (the court concluded from the agreement's grant of a franchise at a particular location coupled with silence on the subject of territorial protection that the franchisor's implied duty of good faith included a duty not to encroach); *but see* Burger King Corp. v. Weaver, 169 F.3d at 1317 (overruling *Scheck* and commenting on a franchise agreement that expressly negated any implied territory or protection). By the time of this 1999 case, Burger King had modified its franchise agreement to expressly negate any claim of protection from encroachment. *See generally* Carmen D. Caruso, *Franchising's Enlightened Compromise: The Implied Covenant of Good Faith and Fair Dealing*, 26 FRANCHISE L.J. 4 (2007).

> This license is for the described location only and does not in any way grant or imply any area market or territorial rights proprietary to FRANCHISEE.[31]

The *Scheck* court held that even though the franchise agreement expressly denied a right to an exclusive territory, it didn't necessarily imply that Burger King had the different right to open additional units without considering the effect of the new units on the franchisee's operations.[32] As such franchisee "is entitled to expect that Burger King will not act to destroy the right of the franchisee to enjoy the fruits of the contract."[33]

However, following *Scheck*, the franchisors were largely able to prevent any encroachment claims by inserting express language in their franchise agreements that negated any claim to implied territorial protection. For example, in *Weaver*, the Eleventh Circuit concluded that a claim of encroachment based on the implied covenant of good faith and fair dealing could not be maintained where the express language of the franchise agreement provided that the franchisee did not have a right to an exclusive market area.[34] The prevailing view is that the implied covenant should only "supplement or interpret the provisions of a contract" and cannot be used "to achieve a result contrary to the express contract terms."[35] As such, the franchisors have been able to defeat encroachment lawsuits by inserting express language in their franchise agreements that negate any implied territorial protection.

As is evident in the sample provision, if the franchisor grants some designated or exclusive territory to the franchisee, it must carefully consider and include in the franchise agreement the rights it reserves (or carves out) for itself, namely the parameters under which the franchisor *can* operate or franchise competing businesses or offer and sell competing products and services inside or outside the so called exclusive territory.

As detailed previously, all franchise attorneys know that vague language can lead to claims of encroachment. Claims of encroachment may occur when a franchisor opens a new location (whether as a corporate or franchise location) within certain proximity to the franchised business, and the new location lures customers from the original franchised business, or claims may occur when the franchisor conducts the sale of the franchise system's products and services through alternate channels of distribution.[36] Alternate channels are any methods used to offer products or services to the franchise system's consumer that are different than the method used by the franchises of the system. The issues surrounding alternate channels

---

31. Scheck v. Burger King Corp., 756 F. Supp. 543 (S.D. Fla. 1991), *reconsid. denied*, 798 F. Supp. 692 (S.D. Fla. 1992).

32. *Id.* at 549.

33. *Id.*

34. Burger King Corp. v. Weaver, 169 F.3d 1310, 1317 (11th Cir. 1999).

35. Burkhardt v. City Nat'l Bank of Detroit, 226 N.W.2d 678, 680 (Mich. Ct. App. 1975).

36. For a compilation and history of encroachment case law by legal theory, see Erika L. Amarante, Andraya C. Frith & Karen B. Satterlee, *Territory, Exclusivity and Encroachment: Thinking Ahead of the Curve and Dealing with the Fallout*, ABA 32d Annual Forum on Franchising W23, at 17–36 (2009). *See also* Ann Hurwitz & Brian B. Schnell, *Tough Issues: Drafting Challenges for Franchisors Operating in the New Economy*, ABA 23d Annual Forum on Franchising, at 6 (2000).

have become especially pronounced with the advent of the Internet, as online sales became a new channel of distribution that was not previously contemplated.[37] But there are many others, and the previous example contemplates several.

To avoid claims to the extent possible, the agreement should speak to acceptable/unacceptable proximity. If this section is left ambiguous, it could lead to problems between the franchisor and the franchisee about whether the franchisor breached the terms of this agreement by opening an outlet on the perimeter of the territory. It is not sufficient to reserve a "general right" above and beyond this agreement.[38] Parties also should be aware that particular state franchise statutes restrict the franchisors' freedom with respect to locating new locations, in an effort to protect the franchisees from encroachment, and those restrictions override contractual terms and reservations of rights.[39]

Some franchisors (particularly those with no grant of exclusivity in the franchise agreement) may supplement their system expansion standards with site clearance procedures, rights of first refusal, minimum performance quotas, impact policies, and so forth. Such additional considerations may be included in the franchise agreement, but they also may be beyond the scope of the franchise agreement and be included instead in policy statements, system memos, and the like.

(ii) Appropriate Parties

As detailed in the preceding text, the first (and most crucial) step is to make clear who is reserving the right. It is not just the franchisor itself; it is the "Franchisor and its Affiliates (and their respective successors and assigns, by purchase, merger, consolidation or otherwise)." One of the most crucial errors a drafter can make is to inadvertently bind an existing affiliate or "yet to be created" or even "yet to be affiliated" entity to an agreement or overarching restriction that it was not meant to be a party to. This is particularly important in industries where brands are bought and

37. *See, e.g.*, Emporium Drug Mart, Inc. v. Drug Emporium, Inc., summarized in (CCH) Bus. Franchise Guide ¶ 11,966 (AAA Sept. 2, 2000) (arbitrators held franchisor's Internet sales encroached franchisee's contractual exclusivity); *see also* Armstrong Bus. Services, Inc. v. H&R Block, Inc., No. WD 60348 (Cir. Ct. Jackson Cnty., Mo., Oct. 2003) (jury found franchisor's Internet program encroached franchisee's rights), discussed in Gary R. Duvall, *Using the Web More Effectively*, 24 Franchise L.J. 173 (Winter 2005).

38. Asbill, Barkoff, & Selden, *supra* note 4, at 20–25.

39. *See, e.g.*, Ind. Code § 23-2-2.7-1(2) ("It is unlawful for any franchise agreement entered into between any franchisor and a franchisee who is either a resident of Indiana or a nonresident who will be operating a franchise in Indiana to contain any of the following provisions: (2) Allowing the franchisor to establish a franchisor-owned outlet engaged in a substantially identical business to that of the franchisee within the exclusive territory granted the franchisee by the franchise agreement; or, if no exclusive territory is designated, permitting the franchisor to compete unfairly with the franchisee within a reasonable area."); *id.*, § 23-2-2.7-2(4) (Unlawful for franchisor to "[e]stablish[] a franchisor-owned outlet engaged in a substantially identical business to that of the franchisee within the exclusive territory granted the franchisee by the franchise agreement or, if no exclusive territory is designated, competing unfairly with the franchisee within a reasonable area . . ." (exemptions omitted)); Iowa Code § 523H.6 (imposing extensive encroachment restrictions); Wash. Rev. Code § 19.100.180(2)(f) (encroachment restrictions); Wis. Code §§ 135.03, 135.04 (governing "changes in competitive circumstances").

sold, and private equity companies accumulate brands both across different industries and segments but also across similar industries and segments.[40]

(iii) Reservation of Rights inside the Territory

The first reservation is the right to establish and operate and license others to establish and operate special outlets inside the designated area. There are multiple variations of the special outlet concept, but generally speaking in most cases the franchisor wants to reserve to itself the right to develop "brand" stores at special locations such as airports, military bases, stadiums, and other captive audience locations. The underlying idea is that those types of locations require a different type of store, and in most cases a different type of operator.[41] In addition, these locations often do not compete with traditional units in the same manner—that is, the captive audience is not choosing between the special outlet and the traditional outlet, and traditional outlet customers are not getting access to the captive locations just to shop at the special outlet. Many times these special outlets require contracting with a government or quasi-government entity,[42] or an entity with special rights and privileges to contract with the government. Other times, the contracts are subject to requests for proposal (RFPs) that may only be open to certain groups. Finally, in many cases, RFPs have already been conducted and won, and the only way the franchisor can locate a brand store in the particular special outlet is to contract with the party that won the RFP, which is more than likely a large concessionaire such as Delaware North, Compass, Aramark, and others. Of course, many prospective franchisees are loath to accept the concept of a special outlet in their territory[43] and may attempt to negotiate either a right of first offer to see if they can develop and operate a special outlet themselves if the opportunity arises or a nonexclusive grant so that the franchisor and the prospective franchisee are essentially in a race as to the development of a special outlet.

(iv) Reservation of Rights outside the Territory

The second reservation relates to the right to establish, operate, and license others to establish and operate stores, special outlets, or other establishments located anywhere outside the designated area's physical boundaries. It seems axiomatic, but again case law has dictated that the franchisor specifically state what the franchisor

---

40. *See* Charles Modell & Sherin Sakr, *Competing Brands under Common Ownership*, ABA 37th Annual Forum on Franchising W-19 (2014).

41. *See, e.g.*, Jeffrey A. Brimer, *Franchising in Unique Venues*, *in* Collateral Issues in Franchising (ABA Forum on Franchising 2013).

42. Generally speaking, airports and other quasi-government venues require competitive bidding for direct concessionaire status, and the competitive bidding will contain references to anticipated brands. *See generally* Suzanne Trigg & Joyce Mazero, *Non-Traditional Generation: Franchise Systems Coming of Age within Non-Traditional Venues*, 30 Franchise L.J. 227 (Spring 2011).

43. Reasons could range from a desire to reap the financial rewards of a prime special outlet location, to concern that the special outlet operator may be subpar and hurt the goodwill and brand reputation in the market.

did not give the franchisee, what the franchisor retains for itself, and what the franchisor may do in that reserved area. As with special outlets as noted previously, although definitely not the norm, some franchises will negotiate standstills, rights of first offer, and/or rights of first refusal to allow the franchisee to have the first opportunity to develop stores outside the reserved area. These rights can be free or paid for separately, and can be for a short or longer period of time, but in most instances the franchisee must be in compliance to exercise any such right. For instance, where a younger franchise concept is selling the franchise in a new geographic area where no other franchises exist within 1,000 miles, the prospective franchisee may try to negotiate a short standstill period to allow their location to get open and the franchisee to determine whether it desires to expand without an immediately triggerable right of first offer or right of first refusal looming overhead, and then request a right of first offer or right of right refusal for a longer period after the standstill expires.

(v) Alternative Distribution

The third reservation relates to non-brand store operations and sales, such as producing and selling private label products, pre-packaged food products, memorabilia, and other products and merchandise and selling them at physical locations in the designated area. This particular reservation includes items that may or may not be identified by or associated with the marks and includes (for example) department stores, supermarkets, and convenience stores. Many franchise attorneys have had clients come to them to discuss private labeling agreements, and the ability to negotiate supermarket or department store contracts with companies such as Walmart, Costco, and so forth. These contracts can be extremely lucrative, but can also be relationship killers if the franchisees believe that their customers are buying products at Walmart instead of visiting their retail location. *Carvel Corp. v. Noonan* is a case involving the franchisor–franchisee sales competition.[44] In this case, Carvel had sold its ice-cream products only through the franchisees for decades, but after experiencing declining revenues, Carvel decided to introduce a supermarket program that added sales by Carvel through supermarkets. The franchisees then sued, arguing that Carvel tortiously interfered with their prospective business relations by implementing the supermarket program.[45] The *Carvel* court determined that in order to sustain a valid claim for tortious interference, in the absence of an illegal act or malicious motive, a franchisee must demonstrate that the franchisor engaged in egregious conduct. Since the franchisor's acts that induced customers to buy its products from supermarkets rather than from franchised locations was not sufficiently egregious, the franchisees did not have a viable tortious interference claim.[46] Some franchisors will alleviate or mitigate these relationship issues with

44. *See* Carvel Corp. v. Noonnam, 818 N.E.2d 1100 (N.Y. 2004) (confirming that contract law should govern in a dispute as to whether Carvel's sale of products in grocery stores created a valid claim for tortious interference with prospective economic relations).

45. *Id.*

46. *Id.*

sharing or reverse royalty provisions as part of their form offering or negotiated in specific transactions that allow for the franchisees to receive some type of payment from these types of sales that occur in their designated areas, especially where there is no practical way for the franchisee to actually produce or sell the product to these other types of retailers. Others will take the position that the retail sales will enhance the brand name and provide "free" marketing to the franchisees in their territories. While each situation is likely to be different, the view points of the franchisor and the franchisee with respect to these types of retail sales are definitely going to be different.

The fourth reservation relates to the same type of non-brand store operations and sales of items such as private label products, pre-packaged food products, memorabilia, and other products and merchandise in the designated area, but instead of a physical location the sales occur through catalogues, telemarketing campaigns, an Internet website, and other direct-order techniques. Internet sales of certain types of products and services have created a sea change in some industries and segments. For instance, some of the earliest controversies and case law in this area related to Internet sales. H&R Block found itself at the forefront of these issues in 2002 when it sought to perform tax returns via the Internet without compensation to the franchisee's whose markets included the residences of those new online customers.[47] Additionally, Drug Emporium lost its argument that its unfortunately named "Online Drug Store" was not a store for purposes of its reserved rights provisions and therefore could not offer and sell drugs through such "Online Drug Store" into the territories of its franchisees without their consent or compensation.[48] Internet encroachment claims by the franchisees have been largely unsuccessful.[49] In any event, many franchise agreements now reserve the right of the franchisor to sell via the Internet. These issues are also prevalent when the franchisor is also a manufacturer of a product that can be sold not only through retail franchised outlets, but also through the Internet directly to third party distributors or end user customers. No manufacturer wants to intentionally restrict its current and future methods of distribution, and the authors are aware of a number of industries in which the franchisors maintain both retail franchise locations and distribution networks for their manufactured products, and these systems take great care to manage legal and relationship issues arising from concurrent, dual distribution of their products at different levels of the supply chain.

The fifth reservation relates to alternative or special advertising techniques such as catalogues and similar sales solicitation materials, broadcast television and radio

47. *See, e.g.*, Armstrong Business Services, Inc. v. H&R Block, 96 S.W.3d 867, 874–79 (Mo. Ct. App. 2002) (refusing to address the issue in connection with an expiring agreement).

48. *See* Emporium Drug Mart Inc. of Shreveport v. Drug Emporium, Inc., No, 71-114-0012600, AAA (Sept. 2, 2000); *see generally Inside the Drug Emporium Decision*, 20 FRANCHISE L.J. 101, 149 (Winter 2001).

49. Newpaper, LLC v. Party City Corp., CCH Fran. Guide ¶ 15,148 (D. Minn. 2013) (dismissing breach of contract claim based on franchisor's Internet sales made in franchisee's territory); Pro Golf of Florida, Inc. v. Pro Golf of America, Inc., No. 05-71380, 2006 WL 508631 (E.D. Mich. Mar. 1, 2006) (determining that unless franchise agreement specifically addressed Internet sales, Internet encroachment claims should be precluded under territorial exclusivity clause).

commercials for direct-order merchandise, telephone contact with residents, and filling of orders for direct-order merchandise, all in the designated area.

(vi) Operating under a Different Trademark or Price

The sixth reservation relates to operating other retail food businesses (including similar businesses) in the designated area, under different tradenames, trademarks, service marks, or trade dress. This relates back to the concept that the franchise is for a "store," and nothing else. There are a number of franchisors that have multiple different, separate offerings arising from a single core trademark (for instance, a full service offering, a delivery or express offering, a kiosk offering, etc.) or multiple similar product or service offerings under different trademarks (for instance, at one point in its history, Blockbuster was aggressively purchasing competitors and depending on the grant and exclusivity provisions in the Blockbuster and competitor franchise agreements converting the unit to Blockbuster or maintaining operations of the competitive video stores under their original brands). As with other reserved rights, and although definitely not the norm, some franchises will negotiate rights of first offer or rights of first refusal to allow them to have the first opportunity to develop any other type of retail food business that the franchisor (or its affiliates) may pursue inside the designated area. Again, these rights can be free or paid for separately, and can be for a short or longer period of time, but in most instances the franchisee must be in compliance to exercise any such right.

(vii) Advertising and Promotion

The seventh reservation relates to traditional advertising and promotion of sales of any products and/or services. The franchisors that maintain advertising funds and/or budgets will invariably advertise into the franchisee territories, and where there are specific advertisements for a particular product or service (such as a limited time only item) or a particular price for a product or service, the franchisor's message and advertising may not match exactly what the local franchisee is doing for its own advertising or units. The reservation can dovetail with pricing considerations in the franchise agreement (addressed elsewhere in this book) since it is fairly common for a large franchisor to pursue pricing-based advertising initiatives in national advertising that can have an effect on the franchisee either because they decide to follow the advertised price or refuse to follow the advertised price. Most franchise attorneys are well aware of the antitrust and pricing reasons for "at participating locations only" qualifiers in advertising, but a pricing-based advertising campaign that airs ads in the designated area could also potentially be couched as a form of encroachment claim if the franchise agreement does not expressly state that the franchisor can advertise as it deems fit into the designated area.[50]

---

50. The franchise agreement may provide that the franchisor will direct national advertising programs in its discretion or in collaboration with franchisees. Where a franchise agreement provides that the franchisor has sole discretion to administer the advertising fund, a franchisee will not be able to state a claim for breach of contract or breach of implied duty of good faith and fair dealing arising from the franchisor's marketing strategy. *See* America's

(viii) Mergers and Acquisitions

The eighth reservation relates to mergers and acquisitions that result in other brands, other owners, and other parties coming together and potentially having directly or indirectly competitive operations in the designated area. This is an area of the franchise agreement that is ripe for both abuse by the franchisor and compromise between the parties.[51] In an ideal world for the franchisor, franchise systems can be bought/sold without contractual limitations, but no franchisee would consider it fair that its long-time franchisor could potentially purchase or be purchased by a rival competitor and then have the existing rival brand compete with the franchisee in the designated area. Very few, if any of the franchisees, would consider it a positive result even if those rival brand stores were now under the same franchisor or parent umbrella as their franchised store. Thus, this is an area where franchise drafting for ultimate flexibility must be weighed against fairness and salability.

(ix) Other Considerations

To complete the reservation, many franchisors will expressly state and require the franchisee to acknowledge that the franchisor has no express obligation or implied duty to insulate or protect the franchisee's revenues from erosion as the result of franchisor-initiated or related competition, and to expressly waive and relinquish any right to assert any claim against the franchisor based on the existence, actual or arguable, of any such obligation or duty. While some may argue this last provision is belts and suspenders on an already overly long reservation of rights provision, franchise litigators defending an encroachment case will generally applaud the inclusion of a provision that would enable them to walk through express "no duty" language in the franchise agreement as part of a deposition or trial.

Favorite Chicken Co. v. Cajun Enters., Inc., 130 F.3d 180 (5th Cir. 1997) (franchisee could not assert breach of contract claim based on franchisor's failure to allocate sufficient advertising funds to the franchisee's local market because franchisor was granted "sole discretion" with respect to advertising placement).

51. *See* Modell & Sakr, *supra* note 40.

2

Fees, Initial Terms, and Renewal

Joseph Sheyka and Elizabeth M. Weldon

V. Initial Fees and Other Fees

This section of the franchise agreement is devoted to stating and explaining the fees the franchisee is required to pay to the franchisor, including the method of payment, penalties for late payment, and related terms.

The Editors' Introduction describes some of the different approaches to structuring a franchise agreement. This section is one of the places where the drafter's choice of structure will make a significant difference in how this section is written. In a very traditional "life-cycle" franchise structure, the initial franchise fee(s) and the royalties are included in this section, and sometimes the advertising fee is also included here. Other fees that the franchisee will incur are not included in this section, and are instead included in the sections of the franchise agreement where that subject is first raised. Under that structure, for example, the transfer fee would be stated in a section discussing transfer, the relocation fee under a section outlining the procedure for relocation, and so on.

An alternate approach to the structure of this fee section blends in an element of the "highlight the deal" structure by listing all of the fees that the franchisor will or may charge the franchisee. Some franchisors and franchisees prefer this approach because it creates a clear section in the franchise agreement where all fees are summarized and no fees appear to be hidden or are hard to locate in the event of a dispute over what can be charged.

In Section V.C. of this chapter, the authors include example language of how drafters might incorporate additional fees into this section, even though some of the later provisions in other chapters of this book have references to the amounts of these fees. A well-drafted agreement will state the fee only once, not in both places.

A. Initial Franchise Fee

> In consideration of the Franchisee receiving the opportunity to establish the Franchised Business, and conduct it at the Premises, the Franchisee shall pay to the Franchisor, upon the execution of this agreement, an initial, non-recurring, non-refundable franchise fee in the amount of $XX. The Initial Franchise Fee shall be deemed to be fully earned by the Franchisor upon the execution of this Agreement by the Franchisor and in consideration of the grant by it to the Franchisee of the opportunity to establish the Franchised Business as herein provided. The Franchisee shall not be entitled to a refund of any part thereof, regardless of the date of expiration or termination of this Agreement, except as specifically provided herein.

Discussion:

(i) Form and Basis of Fee

Almost every franchise relationship requires the franchisee to pay an upfront initial franchise fee to the franchisor. As seen in this sample language, the initial franchise fee is essentially the price of entry that the franchisee pays for the right to be a franchisee in the system, to learn the system's methods and procedures, to receive training, to use the name and marks of the system, and to open a franchised business. It does not include the costs of opening and running the franchised business, however.

Some drafters instead choose to use language that splits the total initial franchise fee into multiple different fees for the services the franchisor provides. These fees can differ by system, and examples include items such as a training fee, a real estate or site inspection fee, an opening support fee, an opening advertising fee, a technology fee, or a recruitment fee. An example of this type of language might look like this alternate sample provision:

> The Franchisee agrees to pay the Franchisor upon execution of this agreement an initial franchise fee in the amount of $XX for the rights granted to the Franchisee under this Agreement. Additionally, the Franchisee agrees to pay the Franchisor upon execution of this Agreement the following amounts in exchange for the pre-opening services provided to the Franchisee under the terms of this Agreement and in connection with the opening of the Franchised Business: (i) $XX for assistance in the selection of the site for the Franchised Business and in the negotiation of the lease for the premises of the Franchised Business; (ii) $XX for the initial training program to be conducted by the Franchisor as herein provided; (iii) $XX for assistance in the set-up of the Franchisee's point of sale system at the Franchised Business and for other technology related matters; and (iv) $XX for the on-site support and supervision in connection with the opening of the Franchised Business. The payments for initial assistance and support shall be deemed fully earned by the Franchisor upon completion of these services. The

> Franchisee shall not be entitled to a refund of the initial franchise fee or other initial payments or any part thereof, except as specifically provided herein.

In selecting the type of provision to use, drafters should consider the discussion of changes in accounting rules for franchise fees later in this chapter. These rules may increase the use of paragraphs like this more detailed provision.

The initial franchise fee is not meant to be calculated dollar for dollar against items and services the franchisee receives from the franchisor, but rather is more focused on covering, at least in part, the franchisor's expenses incurred in working with franchisees to open the franchises.[52] The amount of the initial fee, whether stated in a lump sum or split into different kinds of fees, may include differing considerations such as the cost of training, certain rights granted to the franchisee (such as territory exclusivity), cost of development aid, and cost of initial opening aid, among other considerations.[53] While this fee likely relates to the franchise rights and services provided by the franchisor, it is not meant to represent the full present value of the franchisee's potential future profits from the franchised business.[54] The franchisor and franchisee may agree to a lower initial fee than could otherwise be charged, with the franchisor to be further and continuously compensated in the future via additional fees and continuing royalties from the franchisee.

(ii) Determining Amount of Fee

Attorneys drafting franchise agreements should remind their client that their role is lawyer, not accountant, and the application and effect of financial rules should be determined with an accountant with knowledge of franchising or an experienced franchise consultant. Many clients seek the franchise lawyer's experience on proper royalty levels and structure. While the lawyer can share what he or she has seen in other systems, where appropriate, financial input should come from other advisors.

That said, it is important for drafters to have a core understanding of the factors that influence the initial fees. The amount of the initial franchise fee will vary depending on the industry-specific market rates and for reasons aside from industry standards. As one treatise on franchising notes,

> [c]onsiderations influencing its amount include the nature and extent of the up-front services offered by the franchisor and the cost of providing those services; the franchisee's ability to pay; the amount charged by competitive franchise systems; the trademark's value; the 'attractiveness' of the

52. Kenneth F. Darrow, Mark Siebert, & Phyllis Alden Truby, *The Structural Elements of a Franchise System and Their Economic and Legal Implications for Start-Up and Existing Systems*, ABA 30th Annual Forum on Franchising 38–39 (2007) (calling for a "cost-plus" approach to determining the initial fee).

53. Harris J. Chernow, Kerry J. Olson, & Rebekah K. Prince, *Is That a Fair Deal? Best Practices for Negotiation of the Franchise Agreement*, ABA 35th Annual Forum on Franchising W-6, at 13 (2012); Darrow, Siebert, & Truby, *supra* note 52, at 35–36.

54. Roger D. Blair & Francine Lafontaine, *Understanding the Economics of Franchising and the Laws That Regulate It*, 26 FRANCHISE L.J. 55, 57 (Fall 2006).

franchise; the size of the territory offered; the franchise's length; and other fees to be charged by the franchisor.[55]

It is not unusual, particularly in emerging systems, for franchisees to object to the amount of the initial franchise fee and attempt to negotiate the fee. In a competitive landscape, some franchisors may be willing to entertain such negotiations in order to grow the system, though generally the initial fees are not negotiated unless there is a franchisor concern that makes negotiation more necessary.[56] This may cause the franchisor to put thought into how its initial franchise fee is actually calculated and what, if any, negotiation room there may be.

The initial fee will tend to increase in proportion to the term of the franchise agreement. It is more expensive for franchisees to obtain long-term rights because they will derive more value from using the franchisor's trademarks and system over a longer period of time. Further, the amount of the initial franchise fee may depend on the success and maturity of the franchise system. Established franchise systems are likely to charge a higher initial fee from their franchisees than newer franchise systems because they may have a more established value and ability to command such a fee. A new franchise system can still be very attractive to a potential franchisee because a lower cost of entry for a franchisee will allow for a greater reward if the venture succeeds.[57]

As illustrated in the second sample provision, some franchise systems break the total amount of initial fees into a series of smaller fees. Although this approach can have accounting benefits for the franchisor (discussed later in this chapter), franchisors should not think that breaking a single initial fee into smaller fees will make the system more attractive to franchisees. Franchisees performing a reasonable amount of due diligence will look at all the fees related to starting the franchise, whether titled "initial franchise fee" or something other, to determine the full amount of their required investment.

(iii) Refund of Fee

Drafters often state that the initial franchise fee is nonrefundable and deemed to be fully earned on execution of the franchise agreement. Franchisors do this in order to block the franchisee's potential argument that the franchisor's entitlement to the initial fee is conditioned on some further services being provided to the franchisee or that the fee should be refunded for lack of consideration. The nonrefundable nature of the initial franchise fee protects the franchisor in another way: it helps to ensure that a franchisee does not come to the system to "try it out" or to learn how to operate a system and business model without any intention of actually joining

55. Rupert Barkoff & Andrew Selden, eds., FUNDAMENTALS OF FRANCHISING 82 (2d ed. 2004).

56. Elizabeth S. Dillon, Leonard D. Vines, & Susan E. Tegt, *Drafting and Negotiating Challenging Provisions in Franchise and Development Agreements*, ABA 38th Annual Forum on Franchising W-13, at 7 (2015); Chernow, Olson, & Prince, *supra* note 53, at 13; Lawrence V. Ashe & Harris J. Chernow, *Negotiating Franchise Agreements: The Franchisee Perspective*, ABA 23rd Annual Forum on Franchising 13 (2000).

57. William L. Killion, *Putting Critical Decision Making Where It Belongs: Scouring the Franchise Agreement of the "D" Word*, 24 FRANCHISE L.J. 228 (Spring 2005).

the system. Having a franchisee irrevocably contribute money to the system can be especially important in jurisdictions where post-termination noncompetition clauses are either unenforceable or more difficult to enforce.

In certain instances the franchisor may specify in the franchise agreement situations where it will allow a portion of the fee to be refunded. For instance, this may arise if the franchised business does not materialize due to circumstances stated in the franchise agreement, such as if the franchisee fails to pass the initial training course or if the franchisee cannot find an acceptable site to open the location.[58] However, even in these situations, it is typical that the refund would be tiered or staggered, so that the franchisor will keep a portion of the initial franchise fee. Also, the agreement may specify that the franchisor's incurred expenses shall be deducted from any refund.

(iv) Accounting and New Financial Rules

Under prior accounting rules, the franchisor generally could not recognize initial franchise fees collected from the franchisees as income until "all material services or conditions relating to the sale have been substantially performed by the franchisor."[59] Generally, under these rules, substantial performance by the franchisor was not considered to be complete until the franchised location was open for business: "[t]he commencement of operations by the franchisee shall be presumed to be the earliest point at which substantial performance has occurred, unless it can be demonstrated that substantial performance of all obligations, including services rendered voluntarily, has occurred before that time."[60] All pre-opening and opening services for which the initial franchise fee is paid must be completed first.[61]

This point when initial franchise fees can be recognized as "collected" may be changing, however, under an accounting rule issued in 2016 by the Financial Accounting Standards Board. Under the revised Accounting Standards Codification Topic 606, the franchisor may be required to recognize the initial franchise fee over time—instead of at the franchise opening—so that it is amortized over the life of the franchise agreement.[62] This could change the window of recognition of the initial franchise fee over a period of years, instead of at a singular event.

The stated reasoning behind Topic 606 is "that an entity should recognize revenue to depict the transfer of promised goods or services to customers in an amount that reflects the consideration to which the entity expects to be entitled in exchange for those goods or services."[63] Much of the revised rule distinguishes between the effect of functional and symbolic licenses. It requires a franchisor to

---

58. Asbill, Barkoff, & Selden, *supra* note 4, at 27.

59. Fin. Accounting Standards Bd., Accounting for Franchise Fee Revenue, Original Pronouncements as Amended, Statement of Financial Accounting Standards No. 45, FAS45-3 (2010).

60. *Id.*

61. *Id.*

62. Fin. Accounting Standards Bd., Revenue from Contracts with Customers (Topic 606), Identifying Performance Obligations and Licensing, FASB Accounting Standards Update, No. 2016-10 (April 2016).

63. *Id.* at 2.

identify each of its performance obligations under the franchise agreement and to determine when those obligations happen. Importantly, the "when" can differ for various types of intellectual property, depending on whether the intellectual property is functional or symbolic. A symbolic license is "intellectual property that does not have significant standalone functionality," and is what many franchise systems offer via brand names, trade names, symbols, and franchise rights.[64] In contrast, intellectual property with "standalone functionality" allows the use of that property "at the point in time the license is granted," such as "the ability to process a transaction, perform a function or task."[65]

The revised rule considers the symbolic license to be satisfied over time because "the entity's obligation to support or maintain the intellectual property exists for the duration of the license period. . . ."[66] The license with standalone functionality is satisfied at a specific point in time—when "the customer is able to use and benefit from the license."[67]

In franchising, the trademark and trade name are central to the franchise promise, and the franchisor's obligation to support that intellectual property will remain during the entire franchise relationship. So, assuming a franchise term of ten years, when a symbolic license is transferred from the franchisor to the franchisee and the initial fee is based on payment for this symbolic license, the initial fee would be amortized and recognized on the franchisor's financial statements over a period of ten years.[68] If, however, items paid for by the initial fee are more functional, such as the sale of a piece of equipment or software at opening, then the revenue for that item can be recognized at that specific date.

The implications of this rule change on franchise licenses were only beginning to be tested at the time this book went to press. One position many franchise systems have articulated is that more than just tangible items of equipment or software have "standalone functionality." Often, franchise system training and operations manuals are designed "as if the franchisee has absolutely no experience in the industry and no prior skills."[69] They are structured so that a franchisee can buy a pizza restaurant under a particular system's brand even if they have no experience as a restauranteur and have never even worked in a restaurant. In addition to brand-specific education, such as how to make proprietary recipes or use exclusive software, a portion of the education they receive to prepare them to open their branded business is about the fundamentals of operating a restaurant, including managing staff, inventory, customer service, food safety issues, and bookkeeping matters. The latter part of the education, many systems argue, is transferable. Through training,

---

64. *Id.* at 4.

65. *Id.* at 3.

66. *Id.* at 76 (BC 57); *see also id.* Example 57 at 38–40, ¶¶ 606-10-55-375 through 606-10-55-382.

67. *Id.* at 4.

68. *Id.*

69. Mark Siebert, *Training Your Franchisees*, ENTREPRENEUR (May 23, 2005), https://www.entrepreneur.com/article/77928.

the inexperienced franchisee acquires the knowledge required to open and operate a competing business.

This suggests that franchisors seeking compliance with the new accounting standards will need to work closely with experienced auditors, knowledgeable in franchise matters, to analyze the portion of the entire initial fee that pays for brand-specific benefits, which must be amortized over the length of the franchise, and the portion that pays for transferable items or knowledge, which may be recognized immediately.

Some have suggested that under the new accounting rule a franchisor may want to consider charging separate amounts for specific services that are complete at opening of the franchise, in the event it would like to include some of the revenue received from the franchisees as income earlier as opposed to amortizing the entire fee over the life of the agreement. This same desire was present under the old rule too, in that a franchisor might want to recognize revenue before the opening date of a franchise, particularly where there may be a lengthy period of time between signing the franchise agreement and opening of the franchise or a lengthy franchise term. For example, the franchisor might divide a single initial fee into separate payments for such services as site selection, lease negotiation, and training, separate from its license of the brand, in order to be able to include these payments as income sooner than would otherwise be the case.

The question is whether such a division would be dispositive. This is likely to be a matter resolved on a case-by-case basis between each franchisor and its auditors. In some instances, auditors might not agree with the franchisor's designation of certain fees as brand-related or transferable.

In addition, the franchisor should consider whether it really wants to put too fine a point on how the fee is calculated dollar for dollar, because such specificity could incite franchisee claims of unfairness in what fee is required from the franchisee. For example, a franchisee who is experienced in the particular industry could claim that he does not require a certain training and thus should not be required to pay for it and, if that fee is included in the initial franchise fee, he may claim the fee should have been less or that he did not receive the full consideration for the fee. From the franchisor perspective, the franchise sales process is a business and an arms-length contractual process, and a franchisor should be able to negotiate the terms that are favorable to its interest, but such considerations do not prevent an adversarial franchisee from arguing the initial franchise fee was unfair. One way to try to head off the previous example could be to include language stating the items included in the initial franchise fee are offered and charged "whether or not utilized." The authors have not seen this litigated, but that kind of specific caveat may give the franchisor a tool in a fairness argument.

Careful practitioners will seek the latest guidance about revenue recognition standards when deciding how to articulate initial fees in a franchise agreement. They will also encourage the franchisor to work closely with its auditors and understand the auditors' perspective on this accounting rule so that the system is well-equipped for its audit process and not caught off guard by the impact of this rule on its financial statements.

B. Continuing Royalty

In return for the on-going rights and privileges granted to Franchisee hereunder, Franchisee shall pay to Franchisor, throughout the term of this agreement, a royalty of XX% percent of Gross Sales for each week (Monday to Sunday). All royalties are payable in arrears on or before the Tuesday of each week for the Gross Sales generated by Franchisee during the immediately preceding week.

Discussion:

As mentioned in Section V.A.(i), the franchisees are not expected to pay the full present value of future profits at the moment they enter the franchise relationship. In addition to the initial fee, the franchisors require the franchisees to make payments throughout the term of the agreement in the form of continuing royalties. The franchisors also elect to receive payments through royalties because it allows them to receive larger payments as the franchised business grows its revenues and to allow for a revenue stream from the franchisee as continuing services and benefits are provided by the franchisor. There are a myriad of different ways that franchisors calculate and assess royalties.

(i) Percentage Royalties

Many franchisors require the franchisees to pay royalties as a percentage of gross sales.[70] Sometimes the franchisor will base the percentage royalties on a sliding scale. In other words, the franchisor will increase the percentage of gross sales required for royalties at certain locations or overall, depending on the franchisee's range of sales or number of years in the system.[71] For example, a franchisee may have a 5 percent royalty rate for the first $500,000 in annual sales, but that rate could decrease to 4 percent for sales over that amount. This way the franchisee has an additional incentive to grow its business. Sometimes, too, the agreement will call for the royalty to increase or decrease over time. If a franchisee is just starting out, it may benefit the franchisee to have a lower royalty percentage for an initial time period and then have that percentage increase as the franchisee becomes more established. Or, to encourage longevity in the system, the franchisor could consider having the royalty percentage decrease at a certain milestone time.

The percentage rates can vary greatly between and even within industries. Retail franchise royalties do tend to be in the 4 to 6 percent range, while service franchise royalties can sometimes be somewhat higher. Specific industries, such as the coffee industry, tend to have higher royalty rates compared to other food service offerings, likely to offset the low cost of entry in the initial franchise fee. Some industries also have lower royalty rates, such as where expenses are higher.

Much like establishing an initial fee, setting royalty rates can be a blend of art and science: too high, and the potential franchisees are scared off; too low, and the franchisor may struggle to pay for its system. Rates often are set by looking

70. Blair & Lafontaine, *supra* note 54, at 57.

71. Andrew J. Sherman, Franchising & Licensing 111 (4th ed. 2011).

at market studies of the range of rates of competitor or similar systems, creating a financial analysis of cost projections and revenue estimates, and speaking with consultants and accountants. Whatever the method, the rates are not chosen cavalierly and are based on financial, rather than legal, advice.

Sometimes the rate is calculated through the franchisor's completion of a comprehensive business plan, while in other cases it is set based on the rates of other existing franchise systems in that industry. At minimum, the franchisor should include, as part of the continuing royalty rate, the estimated costs of continuing resources provided to the franchisee.[72] The franchisor should then evaluate this calculation of costs against the competitor's royalties to help gauge a ceiling rate.[73] Then, to ensure that the royalties calculated are sufficient to support the system, the franchisor should work closely with pro forma financial statements to estimate cash flows for a certain future period of time.[74] To perform a diligent review of the royalty amounts, sensitivity analyses should be conducted on the pro forma cash flow estimates in order to ensure that the royalties are satisfactory.[75] Calculating the royalty rate is one of the most important decisions a franchisor will make, as even a one percentage point difference can mean a significant amount of money over the long term of a franchise relationship, multiplied by many number of franchises.

It is significant to note that percentage-based royalties are often calculated on an accrual basis. In other words, the franchisee will have to pay royalties on all gross sales that have occurred, whether or not they are paid for by the consumer (i.e., this includes sales placed on credit that may not have been collected yet, rewards granted under customer loyalty programs, free and comped items, gift cards able to be used at multiple locations).[76] The sample clause requires that payment of continuing royalties be made weekly. Historically, it was common for payments to be made monthly, as the franchisors would be dependent on waiting for checks to arrive for payment. With the increase of electronic payment and reporting methods, the trend has moved toward more frequent payments, though many systems still call for monthly reporting and payment of continuing royalties.

(ii) Flat-Fee Royalties

Drafters should consider, however, that percentage-based royalties are not the sole method of calculating continuing royalties. For example, some systems have flat-fee royalties, such as a certain dollar amount per month or week, instead of a percentage of sales. By way of example, this could read:

> Franchisee will pay a monthly royalty of $XX.

This dollar amount can change over time. For example, the flat-fee royalty may increase as the franchisee becomes more established in the system and its business.

72. Darrow, Siebert, & Truby, *supra* note 52.
73. *Id.*
74. *Id.*
75. *Id.*
76. Asbill, Barkoff, & Selden, *supra* note 4, at 26.

A benefit to a flat-fee royalty is that it requires less oversight and potentially less reporting of the amounts of the franchisee's gross sales for royalty purposes, as the franchisor's own revenues are not dependent on the franchisee's revenues. There may, however, be other reasons to call for such reporting, such as the need for the franchisor to know the franchisee's sales volume in order to make disclosures to prospective franchisees. The downside of a flat-fee royalty is that the franchisor may not be able to as readily monitor franchisee success and know when a franchisee may be in financial straits—important to the system as a whole.[77] Moreover, the flat-fee amount will not rise to take into account inflation or a growing business, unless a mechanism is built into the franchise agreement that will permit such an increase.

(iii) Royalty Floors

Some continuing royalty provisions use a combination of these methods and will require that the franchisee pay a percentage subject to a floor or a minimum that must be paid to the franchisor. This operates to guarantee to the franchisor at least some compensation that the franchisee will pay to support the system and compensate the franchisor for the use of its name and marks.

(iv) Royalty Variances or Exclusions

In some systems, certain items like retail merchandise or a specific set of services are either excluded from the definition of gross sales and therefore are not subject to royalty payments, or are subject to a different royalty rate. This can be popular with franchisees who like the idea that they will pay a lower royalty on a portion of what they sell. It can encourage the sale of branded retail merchandise to consumers as a result.

On the other hand, these structures can also create accounting headaches, a heightened demand for audits, and subsequent disputes between franchisor and franchisee if there is not enough clarity about exactly what the franchisee sold and how it is classified. Drafters should consider hypothetical situations such as a franchisee offering a free sandwich (the higher royalty bearing item) with the purchase of a t-shirt (the no/low royalty item) and evaluate whether this royalty system is a good match for the franchisor's business objectives.

(v) No Royalty Systems

It should be noted that some franchisors charge no royalties whatsoever. These are often so-called product distribution franchises, where the franchisor is the primary or sole supplier of the product being sold. In these instances, the franchisor makes its revenues on the basis of the ongoing sales that it makes to the franchisee.[78]

77. Darrow, Siebert, & Truby, *supra* note 52, at 39.

78. These product distribution franchises should be distinguished from distributorships that are outside in the franchise regulations. In those cases, the supplier also makes its revenues from its sale of products, but it sells them

(vi) Importance of Clear Drafting in Royalties

Continuing royalty clauses should be drafted with a balance of simplicity and clarity in content and should utilize clear, defined terms. If a dispute over royalties arises, the parties and their counsel scrutinize the continuing royalty clause and often debate what the terms actually mean and what exceptions and carve-outs exist for the sales making up the royalties. The drafter's goal is to create language with as little ambiguity as possible about what is included in the royalty and how it is calculated.

Despite the wide variety of royalty options, most franchise systems charge royalties on a percentage basis. In terms of drafting, the percentage-based continuing royalty clause is the perfect example of why it is crucial to adequately define gross sales. If the franchisor drafts poorly, the franchisee might be able to earn income in connection with the franchised business without including the total sum of those earnings in the calculation of royalties. Thus, as discussed in Chapter 1, gross sales should be as all-encompassing as possible to ensure that all sums earned by the franchisee are considered in later fee calculations.

(vii) Additional Considerations

Although continuing royalties are usually non-negotiable, a franchisee may still try to negotiate, especially in situations where the franchisor feels significant pressure to open the franchise.[79] At the beginning of the franchise agreement, a franchisee might try to draft a clause stating that royalties will not exceed a certain percentage or will be otherwise capped or will not commence until after a start-up period.[80] The franchisees should remain aware that there are later situations that may allow them to renegotiate franchise fees, such as in a franchisor bankruptcy or where a franchisor's ability to provide services and growth of the brand has been impeded. These situations may not be common, but it benefits the franchisee to remember that change is possible in contract relationships.

C. Other Fees

1. Advertising Fees

> Franchisee must contribute XX% of Gross Sales to the National Advertising Fund for each week (Monday to Sunday). All advertising fees are payable in arrears on or before the Tuesday of each week for the Gross Sales generated by Franchisee during the immediately preceding week.

Discussion:

This sample clause is extremely simple, designed to do nothing more than define the amount and payment schedule for the advertising fund contribution. Depending

---

at a bona fide wholesale price and will not have charged a direct or indirect franchise fee or, depending on the jurisdiction, met other elements of the franchise definition under applicable law.

79. Chernow, Olson, & Prince, *supra* note 53, at 14; Ashe & Chernow, *supra* note 56, at 12.

80. Chernow, Olson, & Prince, *supra* note 53, at 14.

on the chosen structure for the agreement, drafters choosing to incorporate the advertising fees into a general fee summary may want to incorporate more information about how the advertising fund will operate, how the fees may be used, and other information discussed at length in Chapter 5. This clause references only contributions to a national advertising fund, but in systems with separate regional or local advertising requirements, it would be appropriate to also include provisions that outline those separate fees.

2. Relocation Fee

> Franchisee must not relocate the Franchised Business except with Franchisor's prior written consent. If Franchisor approves Franchisee's relocation, Franchisee must pay $XX as a relocation fee no later than XX days prior to opening the Franchised Business in the new location.

Discussion:
Relocation provisions are discussed in more detail in Chapter 3. While the sample clause suggests a flat amount as the relocation fee, some relocation fees are structured as percentages of the then-current initial fee, or occasionally tied to the franchisor's actual costs to review and approve the relocation. From the franchisor's perspective, relocation can involve many of the same elements of an initial franchise opening, including site review and approval, lease review, and review and approval of build-out and signage matters, so charging a fee is appropriate and will protect it from incurring significant unpaid costs.

From the franchisee's perspective, relocation is often an unwelcome event, which may have been triggered by losing its lease, destruction or condemnation of its premises, or a significant demographic or traffic shift that has made its current location no longer viable. Relocating franchisees are frequently in some financial distress. A relocation fee that is perceived as too high by the franchisee can contribute to acrimony between franchisor and franchisee or make it more difficult for the franchisee to afford its relocation. Consequently, a savvy drafter will encourage the franchisor to think carefully about its relocation fee amount and the timing of collecting the fee.

3. Transfer Fee

> Franchisee must not transfer the Franchised Business except with Franchisor's prior written consent. If Franchisor approves Franchisee's transfer as provided in Section XX, Franchisee must pay XX% of the then-current initial franchise fee as a transfer fee prior to completion of the transfer.

Discussion:
Transfers are complex and critical to handle correctly. Chapter 7 discusses transfer language and considerations in more detail. However, for drafters attempting to include all fees in a single section, it is a good idea to ensure that transfer fees are also covered.

Like all other fees, there is no single approach for setting the amount of the fee. They may be flat fees or percentages tied to some other fee as the franchisor prefers. One important consideration regarding amount turns on whether the franchisor will collect any initial fees or training fees from the incoming franchisee. In other words, must the transfer fee cover the cost of providing initial training and potentially new opening support to the incoming transferee, or is it only intended to cover the franchisor's costs in reviewing and helping to document the transfer?

It is quite common for the transferring franchisee to negotiate for the buyer to pay the transfer fee. Nevertheless, it is critical that the franchise agreement is drafted to impose this obligation on the current franchisee so the franchisor has assurance that the fee will be paid before the deal closes.

4. Renewal Fee

In order to renew this Franchise Agreement Franchisee must meet all conditions for renewal, and Franchisee must pay to Franchisor a renewal fee of XX% of Franchisor's then-current initial franchise fee.

Discussion:
Renewal is discussed in more detail later in this chapter at Section VI.B. A renewal fee can vary greatly, sometimes as a fixed amount, while other times an amount that can fluctuate, as in the sample clause. It is not uncommon for the renewal fee, if any, to be tied to the initial franchise fee, as then it can increase over time, which can be important when renewal will take place many years in the future. In some systems, the franchisor wishes to reward franchisees who are eligible to renew and encourage them to stay in the system, and so rather than charge a significant additional fee, they may choose to charge nothing. This is popular with franchisees, although practical franchisors will consider the amount of work they are likely to do in papering a new franchise agreement, site inspections to ensure that the franchisee's business meets current standards, and other expenses, before setting this fee at zero.

5. Additional Fees

[Additional system fees disclosed as necessary see note on page 150]

Discussion:
Any number of additional fees could be added to this section, depending on the franchise system. Drafters who wish to incorporate all fees into this section should carefully consider all the fees to be charged and add sections as appropriate for technology fees, additional training, convention fees, management fees, liquidated damages, fines in lieu of termination, and other items.

D. Late Payments

Any and all amounts owing to Franchisor or its affiliates by Franchisee shall bear interest at the rate of XX% per annum or the maximum contract rate of interest permitted by governing law, whichever is less, from and after the date of accrual thereof. In addition to interest charges on late continuing license fee and sales promotion program fee payments, Franchisor has the right to require Franchisee to pay to

Franchisor a service charge of up to $XX for each delinquent report or payment owed to Franchisor under this Agreement. A payment shall be deemed delinquent for any of the following reasons: (i) the payment is not received by Franchisor on or before the date due; (ii) the payment is received by Franchisor on or before the due date, but is not honored by Franchisee's bank or financial institution; or (iii) if Franchisee is required to pay by electronic transfer of funds or some other method of payment as described above, there are insufficient funds in Franchisee's bank account to collect the payment by a transfer of funds on or after the date due. The service charge is not interest or a penalty. It is only to compensate Franchisor for increased administrative and management costs due to late payment.

Discussion:

Many franchise agreements set a specific interest charge on late payments. As seen in the previous example, some franchisors also include a late fee (here called a "service charge") in addition to the interest charged for late payments.[81] Of course, drafters should ensure they are complying with the relevant maximum interest rates they are permitted to charge under applicable law. This sample clause includes this point by calling for the lesser of the stated interest rate or the maximum contract interest rate that is allowed by law. This type of phrasing is helpful for the franchise system because the maximum contract interest rate may well differ from state to state.

From a business perspective, the franchisor will want to institute higher interest charges to encourage and incentivize the franchisee to make payments on time. This is especially important when a franchisor relies heavily on the cash flow from such payments to maintain its own current operations. The franchisor wishes to discourage the franchisee from turning the franchisor into a lender.

It is helpful to include language in the late payment section to specify when a payment is late. One could assume that it is pretty simple to determine when a payment is late, that is, it is late after it was due. But in the context of a business that calls for continuing and repeated payments, it benefits all to detail some of the common situations that would make a payment late. For example, if the franchisee sends a payment on time, but the bank rejects the check because the account contains insufficient funds, the payment was not made timely. However, assuming the issue is eventually corrected and a payment is fully made, a dispute could arise about when the payment was made. This type of detail allows for clarity.

The late payment section of the franchise agreement is often overlooked by parties, perhaps because it is something that only becomes relevant at later times, when payments are late. However, it is important to ensure that this provision is carefully worded because these clauses are often implicated in the context of litigation and disputes. The interest rate and late payment clause should be drafted as clearly as possible so that the proper use and application is not a matter of dispute in a later litigation. When amounts are not being paid on time, the calculation of

81. Asbill, Barkoff, & Selden, *supra* note 4, at 27.

fees and penalties is inevitably an issue that is raised in a subsequent action, and it benefits all involved to have a clear interest rate.

Some forms of interest clauses in a franchise agreement call for interest rates that require calculation, such as an interest rate that is based on the annual rate of prime interest, plus a certain additional percentage. Although this is a valid approach, such a clause adds complexity to franchise operations, especially when the rate has to be calculated differently for different times. This approach is not recommended except perhaps for a sophisticated franchisor that can be trusted to make accurate calculations and keep up to date with rate changes. If the franchisor charges a rate in excess of what is permitted, the franchisee or its counsel is sure to raise this as either a defense or a potential claim against the franchisor.

While this provision is not typically negotiated, some franchisees may seek carve-outs or other sections that allow for a grace period of time before the interest rate or late fee becomes applicable. For example, a franchisee may seek to have the application of the interest rate or late fee delayed until five days after the underlying amount owed is actually due. This may not be attractive to the franchisor, as its interest is getting the fees paid in full and on time, to allow the system to operate properly.

E. Electronic Fund Transfers

> Franchisor has the right to require Franchisee to sign electronic transfer of funds authorizations, and/or such other documents as Franchisor designates from time to time, to authorize and direct Franchisee's bank or financial institution to transfer either electronically or through some other method of payment designated by Franchisor, directly to the account of Franchisor or its affiliates and to charge to the account of Franchisee all amounts due to Franchisor and/or its affiliates from Franchisee. Franchisee's authorizations shall permit Franchisor and/or its affiliates to designate the amount to be transferred from Franchisee's account. If Franchisor requires payment through the electronic transfer of funds or through some other method of payment, Franchisee shall thereafter maintain a balance in its account sufficient to allow Franchisor and its affiliates to collect the amounts owed to them when due. Franchisee shall be responsible for any penalties, fines or other similar expenses associated with the transfer of funds described in this subparagraph. Franchisee acknowledges and agrees that Franchisor has the right to require Franchisee to pay either by electronic transfer of funds or through some other method of payment designated by Franchisor, as described in this subparagraph, regardless of whether Franchisor imposes the same requirement on other Franchisees.

Discussion:

To make the transfer of funds as easy as possible, many modern franchise agreements allow for the electronic transfer of those funds. Other franchise agreements now take this one step further and require electronic transfer of funds flowing from the franchisee to the franchisor. These electronic funds transfers (EFTs) allow the franchisor to access an account funded by the franchisee to "sweep" or take fees that are due to the franchisor pursuant to the franchise agreement and the franchisee's reporting to the franchisor. EFT is used to allow the franchisor to pull all manner of fees, including, without limitation, continuing royalties, late fees, interest, and advertising fees. In this clause, the franchisee agrees to make deposits through electronic transfers if the franchisor exercises its right to require the franchisee to do so. Perhaps more importantly, the clause allows the franchisor to make withdrawals from such accounts if the franchisee is late or fails to make any payments.[82] The franchisees should take time to understand the rights of the franchisor to withdraw amounts.

EFT can become complicated when a franchisee has insufficient funds or closes the bank account approved for EFT. That said, most franchise agreements that have EFT provisions provide that late fees, interest, or insufficient funds charges will occur if the EFT does not work due to lack of funds or access. For example, the franchise agreement could read:

> Payments not honored due to insufficient funds will be subject to an insufficient funds charge of $XX.

Franchisees may object to the breadth of the EFT requirement.[83] That said, this is now a very common provision in franchise agreements and systems and will be hard to avoid. From a franchisee perspective, the franchisee may seek to limit what kinds of funds can be swept from the account.[84]

This sample clause is also drafted to provide the franchisor choice or discretion. This leaves the requirement open to complaints about the franchisees being singled out for EFT, as acknowledged by the last sentence in the sample clause stating "regardless of whether Franchisor imposes the same requirement on other Franchisees." The franchisor may consider making EFT mandatory for all in order to inoculate against this type of franchisee objection.[85]

F. Application of Payments

> All payments by Franchisee will be applied in such order as Franchisor may designate from time to time. Franchisee agrees that it may not designate an order for application of any fees different from that designated by Franchisor and expressly acknowledges and agrees that Franchisor may accept fees paid pursuant to different instructions without any obligation to follow such instructions, even if such payment is made by its terms conditional on such instructions being followed. This provision may be waived only by written agreement signed by Franchisor, which written agreement must be separate from the check or other document or medium constituting or transmitting payment.

82. *Id.*
83. Chernow, Olson, & Prince, *supra* note 53, at 14.
84. *Id.*
85. *Id.* (recommending that EFT be made a right for the franchisor, not a discretionary item).

Discussion:

This clause allows the franchisor to accept payments in any form, at any time, and apply them to such amounts owing by the franchisee as the franchisor sees fit. It is a way for the franchisor to maintain control over how the payments will be received, and it gives the franchisor the right to change those processes at any time. For instance, if the franchisee has missed a month's payment but makes a payment for the subsequent month, the franchisor might draft for the right to apply the later payment to the earlier default on payment. If the franchisor fails to speak to application of payments in the agreement, it might not be able to use a later month's payment to satisfy an earlier month's default on payment.

The application of payments clause can become significant in the context of a litigation dispute between the franchisor and the franchisee and can change what would otherwise be called for as a default by a particular state's law. For example, statutes of limitations can limit the amounts sought by the parties in a dispute, and some franchise agreements go so far as to augment the statute of limitations that would apply by law and create their own agreed-upon, and usually shorter, statute of limitations. In such a case, when payments of differing amounts flow from the franchisee to the franchisor, the timing of when the amounts are applied to the debt owing from the franchisee to the franchisor can become relevant. This clause clarifies that the franchisor has the ability to determine how payments are applied, instead of the franchisee making that determination.

VI. TERM

A. Initial Term

> The term of this Agreement (the "**Initial Term**") shall commence on the date hereof, and shall expire either at midnight on the day preceding the tenth (10th) anniversary thereof or on the date of expiration of Franchisee's lease or sublease for the Premises, whichever date shall be the earlier, unless terminated sooner in accordance with the provisions for termination of this agreement.

Discussion:

The term of the agreement is a relatively brief provision, but it is critical. It is the starting point from which the rights and obligations of the agreement begin, and it establishes the length of the relationship between the parties. From a business perspective, the parties want to institute a term long enough for each to benefit from the franchise relationship. It is in the best interests of the franchisor to give the franchisee enough time to recoup the initial investment.[86] If the franchisor does not give the franchisee enough time to recoup the investment, the franchisee might choose to pursue an alternative franchise. For instance, a large restaurant franchise with a significant build-out cost will typically require a term of at least ten years, if not more, to justify the investment being made. In contrast, a home-based, low-cost

86. *Id.*

service franchise, without a significant up-front investment, can and often does have a shorter initial term. Generally, there are average terms per industry.[87]

There are many factors that affect the parties' perspectives on the initial term. Some of the key factors are the market conditions, the flexibility desired by the franchisor to make system changes, the start-up costs, the lengths of associated agreements (i.e., lease agreements, bank loans), and consumer demand.[88] The time necessary for site selection and build out of the premises also may be a factor, as savvy franchisees will not want to start the clock ticking on the initial term prior to the franchised unit being open for business. If that is desired, the franchisee may want the term to commence on the signing of the agreement and end on a specified time period following opening of the business. The franchisors may need to be creative and draft so that the initial term begins earlier than the opening of the location but also takes into account the realities of build-out time, lease terms, and other factors. The approach to the term provision depends largely on the franchisor. Some franchisors might avoid a long-term agreement because it may signify less flexibility to adapt to the surrounding business environment. Others may want to attract the franchisees, or perhaps justify charging a larger initial fee, by offering a longer initial term. They may also want to ensure a longer term commitment by the franchisee and avoid the loss of a franchised location if a shorter term is granted.

Franchisees will typically want a longer initial term to make sure they can recoup their investment and to lengthen the time before they must pay a renewal fee. Longer initial terms can make the business more valuable, particularly if the franchise agreement provides that on a transfer of the franchise agreement the transferee's rights under the existing agreement continue only for the length of the initial term of the agreement. But a franchisee may want to negotiate a shorter initial term in situations where a franchisee wants to determine the suitability or viability of the franchise, particularly where the initial investment is relatively low. Franchisees who own multiple franchises may also want to consider having all of their franchise agreements expire at the same time so that if the franchise agreement does not prohibit them from operating a similar business they will be able to convert all of their business to a new brand at or about the same time.

Franchisors may want the initial term to be coterminous with the term of the lease or sublease for the premises of the franchise. This is to ensure that the franchisee will have possession of the premises for the duration of the term. From the franchisee's perspective, this may also be desirable since the franchisee may not want to make a lease commitment without the certainty of having a franchise for the length of the term of the lease. If the term of the franchise is longer than the lease term, both franchisor and the franchisee may find themselves in a position of having a franchise in place with no premises to conduct the business. In those states where post-term noncompetition covenants may be difficult to enforce, the

---

87. Scott A. Shane, From Ice Cream to the Internet: Using Franchising to Drive the Growth and Profits of your Company 133 (2005).

88. Sherman, *supra* note 71, at 106.

franchisor may want the term of the franchise to be coterminous with the lease so that the franchisee will be unable to continue to operate a competitive business at the location unless the franchisee is able to secure a new lease for the premises.

Franchisors favoring shorter terms should consider whether those terms will create conflict by accelerating the time frame for franchisees who may decide to exit the system or resist changes such as rebranding or refurbishing that franchisor may want to impose at the end of the initial term as a condition of renewing the franchise.

B. Renewal and Renewal Conditions

Franchisee may, at its option, renew this franchise for one (1) additional period of XX years or, if shorter, the renewal term of Franchisee's lease or sublease for the Premises, provided that, at the time of renewal:

1. the Franchisee gives the Franchisor written notice of such election to renew not less than six (6) months nor mor e than twelve (12) months prior to the end of the Term;
2. the Franchisee executes the Franchisor's then current standard form of Franchise Agreement, which may include, without limitation, a higher royalty fee and a higher advertising contribution than that contained in this agreement;
3. subject to any limitations imposed by applicable law, the Franchisee executes a general release in a form prescribed by the Franchisor of any and all claims against the Franchisor and its subsidiaries and affiliates, and their respective officers, directors, agents, and employees;
4. the Franchisee is not in default of any provision of this agreement, or any amendment hereof or successor hereto, or any other agreement between the Franchisee and the Franchisor, or any subsidiary or affiliate of the Franchisor, and the Franchisee has substantially performed all of the Franchisee's obligations throughout the Term;
5. the Franchisee has paid or otherwise satisfied all monetary obligations owed by the Franchisee to the Franchisor and its subsidiaries and affiliates and the Franchisee has timely paid or otherwise satisfied these obligations throughout the term of this Agreement;
6. the Franchisee agrees, at its sole cost and expense, to reimage, renovate, refurbish and modernize the Franchised Business, within the time frame required by the Franchisor, including the building design, parking lot, landscaping, equipment, signs, interior and exterior decor items, fixtures, furnishings, trade dress, color scheme, presentation of trademarks and service marks, supplies and other products and materials to meet the Franchisor's then current standards, specifications and design criteria for the Franchised Business, as contained in the then-current Franchise Agreement, Manual (as defined herein), or otherwise in writing, including, without limitation, such structural changes, remodeling and redecoration and such modifications to existing improvements as may be necessary to do so; and
7. the Franchisee shall have paid to the Franchisor a renewal fee of XX% of the Franchisor's then current initial franchise fee.

Discussion:

(i) Renewal Rights

Renewal has frequently been defined as "the opportunity to sign a new franchise agreement using the franchisor's 'then current form of agreement' if the conditions of 'renewal' are met."[89] However, renewal can happen without any of those things actually taking place. There are several approaches that the parties can take to the renewal provisions. First, the franchisor might prohibit renewal, if allowed by applicable law. Second, renewal might be allowed, but only under certain conditions and upon the approval of the franchisor. Third, renewal might be automatic upon expiration unless either party gives the other party written notice of an election not to renew. Fourth, the parties might agree that the agreement is perpetual ("evergreen").[90]

At the outset, the franchisee often seeks the broadest possible renewal rights, in the attempt to recapture the initial investment fully, and have a business to sell as a going concern.[91] On the other hand, the franchisor will want to draft for flexibility at the end of the term so that necessary changes can be made in the pursuit of system goals, profit, and financial success.[92] The franchisor will usually benefit from a franchisee with a long-term, vested interest in the franchised business.[93] However, the wise franchisor also understands that it will be best protected by restricting the renewal clauses to a certain extent so that it can deny renewal to the franchisees who have not lived up to the franchisor's expectations. If done properly from the franchisor's perspective, it can negotiate to treat "each franchisee uniquely and create its own calculus to determine whether renewal is desirable."[94] As such, the franchisor will try to ensure that the language regarding term and renewals allows for at least some flexibility. Much of the detail contained in the renewal provision relates to the conditions that a franchisee must satisfy to exercise his or her right to renew.

(ii) Successor Rights and Remodeling Issues

Rather than calling a continuation of the franchise a renewal, some franchisors refer to the process as the granting of a "successor" franchise. For example, a franchisor may include a provision that states:

> Provided Franchisee is in compliance with this Agreement at the end of the initial term, the Franchisor agrees to offer Franchisee a successor franchise on the terms and conditions of its then current form of Franchise Agreement, including the payment of

89. Robert M. Einhorn & Craig R. Tractenberg, *Renewals and Conditions on Renewal*, ABA 27th Annual Forum on Franchising 1 (2004).

90. *Id.* at 4.

91. *Id.* at 1.

92. *Id.*

93. Killion, *supra* note 57, at 228.

94. Craig R. Tractenberg, Robert B. Calihan, & Ann-Marie Luciano, *Practice Pointer: Up for Renewal? Disclosure, Drafting and Registration Tips*, 23 FRANCHISE L.J. 206 (Spring 2004).

> the initial franchise fee contained in such Franchise Agreement. The Franchisor may impose other terms and conditions in connection with its offer of a successor franchise, including, without limitation, requirements that the Franchisee refurbishes and remodels the premises to meet the Franchisor's then current standards and execute a release in favor of the Franchisor and its affiliates.

This is often done to support more extensive conditions on the right of the franchisee to continue operating the franchised business. Essentially, these franchisors consider the successor franchise as the grant of a new franchise subject to all of the terms and conditions applicable to a new franchisee entering the system. This frequently includes a requirement that the franchisee upgrade its business to incorporate all of the décor, equipment, and other indicia of a new unit, even if that means a significant construction project.

Before drafting such a clause, the franchisor should consider the implications. While this is a common and popular method to help the franchisor ensure that it does not end up with some units in its system that have 30-year-old styling, the most frequent objections at the time of renewal are to requirements that the franchisee remodel, upgrade, and refurbish the premises to current standards. These requirements may be costly and not supported by the profitability or cash flow of the franchise. Franchisees may want to place some limitations on the ability of franchisors to impose these requirements. These may include dollar limitations or the grant of an extended period of time to complete the requirements.

Although rare, there are some franchisors who do not offer renewal rights in their franchise agreements. They often adopt renewal policies that are applied on a case by case basis to expiring franchise agreements. This is intended to give the franchisor maximum flexibility in deciding whether to renew a franchise agreement and under what terms and conditions.

Essentially, the choice of renewal provisions, whether a single renewal period, an evergreen renewal, or no renewal, depends on the particular situation of the franchisor at the time of the agreement, including its business plans, bargaining power, and the law of the relevant jurisdictions.[95] The sample clause goes into specific details about the "then-current form," and drafters should consider doing the same to avoid future ambiguities about what the "then-current form" refers to. If the franchisor wishes to change one or more of the fundamental business terms, such as royalties, advertising, or other fees, in the then-current form, it is recommended that this be specifically stated. This is an area ripe for negotiation by experienced franchisees, who are likely to request that certain terms from the original agreement (generally relating to fees) are preserved in the new agreement.

Many renewal conditions are controversial with the franchisees. For example, a requirement that the franchisee refurbish the premises as a condition of renewal often causes difficulty, especially if the costs are going to be significant or if "refurbish" is not well defined. Most franchisors insist that the franchisee execute a

95. Asbill, Barkoff & Selden, *supra* note 4, at 29–30.

release as a condition of renewal. But in some states with franchise disclosure and/or relationship laws, such releases are void and unenforceable as violative of the provision in these state laws that prohibit the waiver of rights by the franchisees under such laws.[96]

It should be noted that each franchise system may include its own list of renewal criteria based upon the particular nature of the franchised business, and while the ones listed previously may be common, they are not necessarily boilerplate or standard.

Lastly, as noted previously in the discussion of renewal fees, any renewal, but particularly renewals requiring the signing of a new contract, will result in administrative implications for both parties. For instance, if the franchisee is required to sign a new agreement in connection with the renewal, the franchisor must comply with franchise disclosure laws, even though the franchisee likely knows of this information by virtue of its involvement in the system during the initial term.[97] Additionally, a new or renewed contract may be subject to laws and regulations that presently exist but did not exist or apply to the "old" agreement (because those laws were enacted after the original agreement was executed and did not apply retroactively). As a result, drafters should be clear on whether they intend to create a "new" agreement upon renewal and consider how the current regulatory landscape may affect the relationship and the costs and time associated with the renewal process.

(iii) State Relationship Laws

Drafters should consider applicable state laws when drafting the renewal provision or attempting to enforce a case-by-case renewal policy, as this is an area where the law may place certain restrictions on nonrenewal of a franchise agreement. Several state laws regulate the renewal process and frequently impose requirements that are more stringent than the provisions contained in the franchise agreement.[98] The franchise statutes in some jurisdictions, for example, require the franchisors to provide notice of and have "good cause" for nonrenewal notwithstanding contract terms to the contrary.[99] In other jurisdictions, even if good cause is not required, the franchisors must provide statutory minimum notice of nonrenewal and take other mandatory steps.[100] Depending on the jurisdiction and statute, the statutory notice period may be as long as 180 days. If the provision included in the franchise agreement is contrary to any such laws, attorneys need to advise clients that they should research

96. *See, e.g.*, IND. CODE ANN. § 23-2-2.7-1(5); REV. CODE WASH. § 19.100.180.

97. Einhorn & Tractenberg, *supra* note 89, at 2–3.

98. *See* CAL. BUS. & PROF. CODE §§ 20025, 20030; CONN. GEN. STAT. § 42-133f; HAW. REV. STAT. § 482E-6; 815 ILCS 705/20; IND. CODE §§ 23-2-2.7-1, -3; MICH. COMP. LAWS § 445.1527; MINN. STAT. § 80C.14; MISS. CODE ANN. § 75-24-53; MO. REV. STAT. § 407.405; NEB. REV. STAT. § 87-404; N.J. STAT. ANN. §§ 56:10-5, 6.1, 13.2-13.4; R.I. GEN. LAWS § 6-50-4; WASH. REV. CODE § 19.100.180; WIS. STAT. §§ 135.03, 135.04.

99. *See, e.g.*, MINN. STAT. § 80C14(4) wherein "good cause" is defined as the "failure by the franchisee to substantially comply with the material and reasonable franchise requirements imposed by the franchisor." *See also* IND. CODE § 23-2-2.71(8); ARK. CODE ANN. § 4-72-202(a)(2).

100. *See, e.g.*, ILL. STAT. § 705/20; *see also* Einhorn & Tractenberg, *supra* note 89.

applicable state law when contemplating nonrenewal of a franchise agreement, and should not merely rely on the contractual language.

(iv) Franchisee Associations Input

As noted previously, the renewal process can often be a source of conflict within franchise systems, particularly if onerous requirements are imposed upon the franchisees in order to renew the franchise. Damages for failure to comply with state relationship laws for an improper refusal to renew a franchise agreement can be severe. To avoid these conflicts, many franchisors consult with their franchisees through their advisory councils or other organizations formed for the purpose of providing input to franchisors before implementing or changing requirements on renewal.

While many franchisors and their counsel would like to make such decisions on their own, the system should consider whether there are long-term benefits to consulting with a franchisee association or advisory group and reaching a consensus about reasonable renewal language. In the long term, this may reduce the frequency and severity of disputes over renewal processes and secure more renewals for the system.

3

Training, Site Selection, Construction, and Opening

Harris Chernow and Beata Krakus

VII. TRAINING AND OPERATING ASSISTANCE

A. Initial Training by the Franchisor

Prior to the opening of the Franchised Business, Franchisor shall provide to Franchisee (or, in the case where Franchisee is a corporation or other legal entity, a principal or Designated Person (as defined herein) who has been approved in writing by Franchisor) and one (1) other key employee designated by Franchisee as the manager or assistant manager for the operation of the Franchised Business, a training course of such duration, content and at such location and in such format as Franchisor may deem necessary in its discretion, covering phases of the System as Franchisor deems necessary and may change from time to time. Franchisee and its trainee shall be obligated to attend, and successfully complete, Franchisor's training course to Franchisor's satisfaction. Franchisee shall be responsible for all travel and living expenses and all wages/compensation payable to any trainees. Franchisor further agrees to furnish one (1) person, experienced in the System, to assist Franchisee at the Premises for such period immediately preceding or following the opening of the Franchised

Business as Franchisor deems reasonable. Additional mandatory or optional training, start-up assistance or retraining or refresher courses may be provided by Franchisor (although Franchisor is not required to do so) at a cost to Franchisee based on Franchisor's then current fee, which may include a daily or hourly fee for Franchisor's personnel performing such training or assistance, plus other reasonable expenses, including all travel, meal and accommodation expenses. Any additional training, start-up assistance or retraining or refresher courses are subject to availability and shall be offered at Franchisor's sole discretion.

All required trainees must successfully complete the initial training before they may be involved in the operation of the Franchised Business. At least one of Franchisee's required trainees must successfully complete the initial training before the Franchised Business may open or operate. Franchisor has the right in its reasonable discretion to determine whether a trainee has successfully completed the initial training. If Franchisor concludes that a required trainee has failed to successfully complete the initial training, that person must re-enroll in Franchisor's next scheduled applicable initial training program at the current fee as determined by Franchisor. Franchisor will have the right to terminate this Franchise Agreement if, following the initial training and re-enrollment training, if any, none of Franchisee's required trainees have successfully completed the initial training. Scheduling of the initial training will be determined by Franchisor based on Franchisor's schedule and facility availability for training.

Discussion:

Most franchisors will require that franchisees attend and successfully complete an initial training course. The franchisor typically requires that the franchisee, if an individual, or its principals and designated manager (or other term used for a designated person to be the operational supervisor) learn and understand how to run the franchised business under the system. By requiring initial training, the franchisor is training all of its franchisees to operate the system in a uniform manner and ensure that the experience of the customer remains the same across all franchise locations (but for certain unique conditions that might exist as to certain franchisee locations), and that the system standards are maintained. Ideally, the franchisor will train the franchisee on all aspects of the system,[101] so that there are no unanswered questions before the franchisee begins operations.

Ultimately, the franchisor will decide the scope, content, location, and form of its training programs, including allowing for online and/or off-site training using technological advances. Given that training methods are constantly changing, a franchisor should draft a broad training clause to allow the franchisor to modify its training as necessary. Typically, the franchise agreement does not go into great detail about the training program (i.e., regarding topics, length, costs, and the like), although some drafters choose to provide specific details such as the number of hours and types of training. This on one hand allows for a franchisee to have the franchisor's commitment to certain specifics of training, but on the other

101. However, see discussion on joint employer liability in Section I.A.(iii) of this chapter and more thoroughly in Chapter 4.

hand places the franchisor in a position of committing to training details that could change from when the franchise agreement was signed and the time for training.

When drafting training provisions, the franchisor should be careful to accurately describe any details it chooses to include in the agreement. Failure to provide adequate training is a common claim by franchisees regardless of the language in the franchise agreement.[102] Franchisees will measure the adequacy of training primarily by how well it prepares them to competently operate their new franchised business. However, such claims would be augmented by franchise agreement language that shows that they did not receive all the training they were promised. Consequently, most drafters tend to structure training provisions using broad summaries and sometimes giving the franchisor discretionary power to modify training. At the same time, because the franchise disclosure document (FDD) requires the disclosure of certain details about the training regimen, if the language in the franchise agreement appears to contradict or disclaim the FDD's promised training this may present a red flag for franchisees.

(i) Fees for Attendance

The vast majority of franchise systems provide initial training to franchisees at no cost, except that the franchisee is required to pay for its own travel and lodging while attending training. In such systems the initial fee discussed in Chapter 2 is designed to cover this cost. At the same time, these systems typically limit the number of individuals who may attend training. This is an important element of this provision, which prevents the franchisee from requiring the franchisor to train scores of people at no cost.

The preceding sample clause provides that training will be provided for a maximum of two individuals: either the franchisee if he or she is a natural person or a "designated person" if the franchisee is an entity, plus one additional manager whom the franchisee has identified. These numbers should be modified as appropriate to ensure that a sufficient number of key personnel have the skills necessary to operate the franchised business pursuant to brand standards.

In some instances, the franchisee may wish to bring more personnel to initial training. In anticipation of this, drafters should consider whether to treat this as "additional training," covered in Section VII.B., or whether to include a different provision that is specifically for initial training for new or additional managers. A new manager provision might include language such as this:

> Should Franchisee name a new manager, Franchisee must notify Franchisor in writing of the identity of the new manager and Franchisor must approve in writing the new manager. The new manager must attend and complete the initial training program to Franchisor's satisfaction. Franchisee shall be responsible for all travel and living expenses and all wages/compensation due to the new manager in connection with

102. *See, e.g.*, Creative Am. Education v. Learning Experience Sys., LLC, No. 9:14-CV-80900, 2015 WL 4655087, at *36 (S.D. Fla. July 31, 2015) (claim for breach of franchise agreement for failure to train failed where agreement allowed franchisor to waive training requirement and any alleged alterations to training were at franchisee request).

> attendance at the initial training. Franchisor reserves the right to require Franchisee to pay Franchisor's then-current rates for additional training for managers, currently $XX, for providing initial training. These rates also apply per additional manager if Franchisee brings more than one manager to initial training.

This sample provision permits the franchisor to increase the cost of training so that the franchisee will pay a market rate for training a new manager hired many years after the franchisee's original training. Alternatively, drafters may choose a flat cost, which may be more popular with franchisees who anticipate high turnover in their managerial positions. In situations where particularly high turnover can be expected, such as businesses in which a manager is compensated at a relatively low rate, franchisors should expect franchisee objections to the cost of repeatedly sending new hires for training, potentially at a location that is remote from the franchised business. Some systems solve for this problem by providing an even higher level of training to the franchisee, which "certifies" the franchisee to then provide its own managerial training.

(ii) Training Employees

Virtually all franchisors provide initial training to franchisees and key managers who will be in control of the franchised business. With regard to providing training to employees, approaches differ. Many systems use a "train the trainer" philosophy in which the franchisor trains the franchisee and high level managers, and those individuals provide training to lower-level employees, often aided by training tools, which the franchisor provided during the initial managerial training. In some cases, these systems include a provision that grants permission for the franchisee to use training materials to perform this training:

> Employee Training. Franchisee and the initial required trainees are responsible for training Franchisee's other employees and other management personnel in connection with their respective roles/positions at the Franchised Business. Franchisee may utilize certain of Franchisor's confidential information and proprietary materials, including the Manual, when conducting training but only to the extent necessary to conduct such training and only pursuant to Franchisor's confidentiality terms and conditions.

Other systems consider it critical for the franchisor to provide some training relating to brand standards directly to at least some employees. Systems that provide an additional tier of training for a franchisee's employees often include a separate provision about required employee training provided by the franchisor. A sample provision could look like this:

> Franchisor will provide an initial training program in XX [subject matter]. Franchisee's XX [e.g. line cooks, lead therapist] must attend and successfully complete, to Franchisor's satisfaction, the XX training program prior to beginning work in the Franchised Business. Franchisee is responsible for all travel and living expenses and all wages/compensation due to Franchisee's XX in connection with attending this training.

The nature of this initial training for employees varies substantially, and many franchisors are increasingly using online videos as training tools to reduce the time and expense of in-person training sessions. The sample provision immediately preceding does not specify in what manner the franchisor will provide the training program, which could allow the franchisor to modify its program formats, as long as the critical training information is still conveyed.

(iii) Joint Employer Concerns

An important concern in both structuring and drafting training provisions is the issue of joint employer liability, which is discussed at length in Chapter 4. In essence, improperly drafted training provisions could contribute to a determination that the franchisor is the "joint employer" of the franchisee's employees, if such training provisions suggest that the franchisor exercises a sufficient degree of control over those employees.

It is critical for drafters to review the training provisions in light of this issue and, to the extent possible or feasible, revise them to reduce the risk of a joint employer problem. Naturally, this requires a careful evaluation of the system and its requirements, weighing the risks of making changes against the possibility of jeopardizing some protections of the system, and the business necessity of providing certain training. While there are no set guidelines as to when a franchisor may cross the line, the cases discussed in Chapter 4 may give some insight into the types of control that can be problematic. In order to avoid joint employer risks, many franchisors choose to reduce or eliminate training around general matters such as clocking in and out, and focus more exclusively on brand standard matters. These franchisors also emphasize during any training they provide that they are not the employer of the trainees, merely a third party trainer.

(iv) Anticipating Franchisee Concerns

In the midst of focusing on so many different provisions, many drafters underestimate how important training is to franchisees. Training can seem obvious and straightforward, but in particular to a franchisee it can be the cornerstone of what is being provided by the franchisor. In systems where the trademark is not yet famous, training is the crown jewel of what the franchisee receives, and from the franchisee's perspective the more details that are in the agreement about what will be provided, the better. Where possible, franchisors should anticipate and draft for franchisee concerns that training will not be robustly provided, while still balancing the system's interest in being able to modify and adjust training over the course of the franchise's entire term.

Franchisees are likely to focus on issues including how frequently training is scheduled, because infrequent trainings could delay the opening of the franchised business, where training will be held, because long distance travel can increase expense, and whether the franchisor will provide any on-site training at or after the franchised business's grand opening. As discussed previously, franchisees are also sensitive to the number of individuals who may be trained, and the number who must be trained. Training provisions that are seen as inadequate are likely to draw comment and requests for negotiation from franchisees.

(v) A Comment on "Discretion"

Many franchisors wish to provide training in their "discretion." Drafters should bear in mind that the term "discretion" has become a loaded term that tends to open franchisors to judicial review. While reserving matters to its sole discretion gives the franchisor greater power over its future actions, it has the potential to expose the franchisor to good faith and fair dealing claims.[103] However, some drafters who employ "discretion" in their agreements also include provisions whereby the franchisees acknowledge and agree that any discretion to be exercised by the franchisor is deemed to be exercised in good faith, and that such decisions will be made in the best interests of the franchisor and the franchise system and not necessarily in the best interests of the franchisee.

B. Ongoing Training by the Franchisor

> In addition to the initial training, Franchisee and any others that participated in the initial training, or others Franchisor designates, will be required to attend training programs specified by Franchisor regarding how to operate a Franchised Business generally or other subject matter that is designed to assist Franchisee in its Franchised Business. Franchisee will be required to pay the then-current training fee for those that attend this training, and Franchisee will be responsible for the costs and expenses associated with Franchisee and any other required trainees attending such training.

Discussion:

Ongoing training is important to the maintenance of the system and to ensuring that brand standards are met. Language that addresses ongoing training may be encapsulated in various other sections of the franchise agreement, such as in reference to system changes, the operations manuals, renewal, change in the ownership of the franchise or franchisee, and elsewhere, and drafters should make an effort to

---

103. See Killion, *supra* note 57, at 229–30; *but see* Burger King Corp. v. Ashland Equities, Inc., 217 F. Supp. 2d 1266, 1277–78 (S.D. Fla. 2002) (Where franchisor has retained complete discretion in a franchise agreement to determine whether a prospective purchaser meets its qualifications for new franchisees, the contract bars franchisees' breach of contract claim) (citing Burger King Corp. v. Hinton, Inc., 203 F. Supp. 2d 1357, 1362 (S.D. Fla. 2002) (holding provision that states BKC must provide support for marketing and advertising that BKC "deems necessary to continue to communicate and advise FRANCHISEE as to the Burger King System" as being within BKC's sole reasonable discretion, thus, barring Defendants' breach of contract claim); Ernie Haire Ford, Inc. v. Ford Motor Co., 260 F.3d 1285, 1290 (11th Cir. 2001) (affirming summary judgment denying dealer's breach of contract claim where dealership agreement required manufacturer's written consent for relocation of dealership based on manufacturer's "best judgment"); Perez v. McDonald's Corp., 60 F. Supp. 2d 1030, 1035 (E.D. Cal. 1998) (holding franchisor did not arbitrarily withhold its consent to transfer franchisee's interest in restaurant where prospective purchasers did not complete required training as set forth in the Franchise Agreement and where franchisor's written consent was required for sale)).

ensure that the various provisions do not contradict one another in a way that might create a later dispute. Franchisors typically balance the right to provide ongoing or additional training, their own interest in avoiding obligating themselves to provide a specific amount of additional training, and their interest in requiring the franchisee to comply with additional training and/or attend conventions or seminars as the franchisor determines.

Although the franchisor does not necessarily want to obligate itself to something that it may not be able to provide or does not wish to commit to at this time, this provision is still important because initial training and ongoing training are somewhat related. They both ensure consistency for the brand. Inadequate or improper training can be detrimental to the system as a whole. The ongoing training does not have to be in person, and the trend is for more and more to be online in one form or another, whether it be conference calls, webinars, or other uses of technology to provide and convey the ongoing training. Training can also be in the form of guidance and support. However, depending upon the type of franchised business, in-person training may still be the most effective and efficient method, or, at least combined with other methods, of delivering the training.

In addition, as discussed earlier in this chapter, there can be different training and requirements for different levels of positions within the franchised business, such as the franchisee (and/or its owners), the general manager, the regional manager, store manager, and frontline/hourly employees. The franchisor may have different ongoing training requirements of each group.

The preceding sample provision is intentionally very broad and simple. The goal is to allow the franchisor to have certain flexibility, and to provide more details and specifications in the operating manuals, which are further discussed in Chapter 5. The issues of concern in the franchise agreement from a franchisor perspective are to what extent the franchisor obligates itself to provide training and to what extent the training provision is too vague to allow for a franchisee to make a claim that certain ongoing training is required by the franchisor by virtue of the specific wording or based on claims of good faith and fair dealing.[104] As noted with initial training, this, too, is an area where failure to provide adequate training can be a common claim by the franchisees regardless of the language in the franchise agreement, even if such is broad and discretionary. The balance needs, at the end, to ensure that the franchisor does have the right to obligate a franchisee, along with its applicable representatives, to be subject to ongoing training at all times in order to maintain consistency within the system. It is also a benefit to the franchisee to know that there will be ongoing training, as it is one of the reasons for becoming a franchisee and being part of an ongoing and dynamic system.

(i) Solving Franchisee Concerns

The franchisee's concerns in connection with ongoing training can be very simple. Is or isn't it being provided, and to what extent? As discussed previously, a

---

104. *Id.*

franchisor does not necessarily want to obligate itself to certain specifics, but on the other hand, the franchisee desires specifics so that it knows what it is receiving for its investment and it is assured that it will be current with all training. Training is an essential component of a franchise system and the balance for the franchisee is having access to ongoing training while, at the same time, not being inundated with such so that it is taken away from its operations and incurring significant costs in constant/ongoing training.

Drafters anticipating franchisee responses to this language will consider franchisee concerns about where additional training will be held and how disruptive it will be. Franchisees will have concerns about sending frontline employees to training out of town and the costs associated therewith. Although most franchisees welcome additional training, they will be more amenable to requirements that are unlikely to interfere with their operations and that are provided at no additional cost.

Another aspect of training concerns is the constant advances in technology, and that the franchisee may need to be trained in how to use certain technology in order to access the ongoing training. This sometimes is overlooked by the franchisor, who may assume that everyone is technologically savvy. Particularly in a system with less sophisticated franchisees and an aging franchisee population, this can be a hurdle. Accessibility to the training tools and techniques should not be assumed or overlooked, and the franchisor may need to provide technology training prior to the actual ongoing system training (or along with it).

(ii) Training in Response to Poor Operations

Some franchise agreements include a specific provision that gives the franchisor authority to mandate training if it determines that the franchisee is not complying with brand standards. An example of this language is:

> If Franchisor determines that Franchisee is operating the Franchise Business in a manner that is not consistent with the terms of this Franchise Agreement or the Manuals, or if Franchisee is otherwise in material default of this Franchise Agreement, Franchisor may require that Franchisee and/or Franchisee's management personnel attend and complete up to XX [days/hours] of training at (a) Franchisor's designated training facility, (b) Franchisee's Franchised Business or (c) other location Franchisor designates, that is designed to address the default or other noncompliance issue. Franchisor reserve the right to charge Franchisee its then-current training fee for Franchisee and any other person that is required to attend such training, and Franchisee will be responsible for the costs and expenses associated with Franchisee and any other required trainees attending such training.

While this requirement may be subsumed in a broader provision that allows the franchisor to require any amount of additional training, some drafters feel that this type of provision may give the franchisor more specific authority to require the franchisee and its key managers to attend the entirety of initial training, at the franchisee's cost, where the franchisor can show that the franchised business is materially out of compliance.

This provision should not be used in lieu of a broader additional training provision, only in addition to it.

(iii) Franchise Conventions

Many franchisors require that the franchisees attend the franchisor's annual convention due to the prior experiences of the franchisees not voluntarily attending. An annual convention can be good for the system and for the franchisees, by bringing the system together for educational and social activities. It also allows the franchisor to provide additional training and roll out new concepts with all in attendance, and provides for instant feedback and collaboration among the franchisees in person.

Drafters have many different approaches for where in the franchise agreement to put a provision for franchise convention attendance. Some systems treat it like training, some consider it closer to marketing if the convention will focus on introducing franchisees to new promotions and sales tools, some include it with the list of fees the franchisee must pay, and some franchise agreements group it in a section on franchisor obligations. Regardless of how the franchisor wishes to characterize it, it is important to have language that explains whether the franchisee is required to attend and required to pay for it.

> Annual Convention. Franchisor may hold and require Franchisee (or at least one of Franchisee's owners if Franchisee is an entity), Franchisee's manager, and assistant manager to attend an annual convention or meeting of franchisees (the "**Annual Convention**"). In addition to being responsible for any travel, accommodations, wages, and all other expenses for Franchisee's representatives attending the Annual Convention, Franchisee will pay Franchisor, at Franchisor's option, the fee that Franchisor designates for each attendee at the Annual Convention. The fee will generally reflect Franchisor's direct and administrative costs of organizing and providing the programs and materials for the Annual Convention. If Franchisee (or a required representative) fails to attend a mandatory Annual Convention, in addition to any other remedies available to Franchisor pursuant to this Franchise Agreement, Franchisor reserves the right to charge Franchisee a nonattendance fee in an amount Franchisor determines, in its sole discretion, to be the costs attributed to Franchisee's failure to attend.

The preceding sample provision allows the franchisor to make attendance at the convention mandatory, to make payment mandatory, and allows the franchisor to pass the full cost of putting on the convention on to franchisees. Significantly, this provision also specifies what fees the franchisor can assess if the franchisee does not attend. Nonattendance by a percentage of franchisees should be anticipated both because of the cost of attending and because of the challenges of business coverage while the franchisee and its key managers travel to attend the event. Many franchisors include a nonattendance fee both to ensure that every franchisee shares the cost of the convention and to encourage franchisees to attend by making them pay for it regardless of whether they attend. The "cost" to the system of nonattendance is that those franchisees do not receive the same training on new initiatives and systems, and their compliance may lag behind other franchisees as a result.

C. Franchisor's Operating Assistance

1. Additional Discretionary Assistance. Franchisor may, in its sole discretion, provide the following:

(a) Additional training programs, after the opening of the Franchised Business, as Franchisor, in its sole discretion, deems appropriate.

(b) Continuing advisory assistance in the operation of the Franchised Business, after the opening of the Franchised Business, as Franchisor, in its sole discretion, deems advisable.

(c) Advice and written materials concerning techniques of managing and operating the Franchised Business including required and suggested inventory and sales instructions, new developments and improvements in Franchised Business layout and design, and new developments in services, merchandising and packaging of services and products.

Franchisor may, in its sole discretion, elect to outsource, and/or subcontract certain of Franchisor's obligations under this Franchise Agreement to subsidiaries, affiliates, contract employees, third-party vendors, and/or other third-party suppliers; provided (i) any such outsourcing and/or subcontracting shall not discharge Franchisor from its obligations under this Franchise Agreement, and (ii) any such outsourced or subcontracted obligations shall be performed in accordance with the terms of this Agreement.

Discussion:

A franchisor typically drafts the franchise agreement so that it is not required to do more than what it deems absolutely necessary for the success of the franchised business. Oftentimes, franchise agreements sparsely assign obligations to the franchisor.[105] Their provisions tend to state that the franchisor has the option to do certain things if and when it decides that it wants to do them. The clause concerning the franchisor's operating assistance (training) is a typical example of this very broad "obligation." Notably, it is not always clear that the franchisor has obligated itself to anything under this provision. Generally, these sections are relatively brief and somewhat vague, with the purpose to allow the franchisor to keep ultimate discretion on what, if any, operating assistance/training it will provide. As with many of the provisions within the franchise agreement, it should be forward looking with the need to cover a 5- to 20-year term and allow for the franchisor to have flexibility to address the system and its franchisees over the course of the term. However, the franchisor needs to balance being too vague, or too detailed, and the potential

105. For the perspective of franchisee counsel on this topic, *see* Peter C. Lagarias & Robert S. Boulter, *The Modern Reality of the Controlling Franchisor: The Case for More, Not Less, Franchisee Protections*, 29 FRANCHISE L.J. 139 (Winter 2010).

to invite disputes about the franchisor's exercise of this contractual discretion or obligations.

Other chapters, including Chapters 4 and 5, include in-depth discussion concerning the operation manuals, compliance with the system standards, and overall changes to the standards and specifications. What is important to note here is that many times these terms are confused or commingled, and sometimes intentionally, to also be the provisions that deal with ongoing training, since there are many overlapping similarities to ongoing assistance and training. Again, from the franchisor perspective, the issue is providing enough so that the franchisee has some comfort that there will be some form of ongoing training or assistance, while avoiding so many specifics that the franchisor is definitively obligated to provide something it may not want to provide, or may be incapable of providing, at the time the franchise agreement is executed. Given that the franchise relationship is a long-term agreement and that training and assistance are very dynamic and need to adjust to then-current situations such as competition, new technology, new services, new products, and new methods and procedures for performing the operations of the franchised business, the agreement, by nature, needs to be flexible.

Drafters of these provisions should be mindful that franchisees may actively try to negotiate for more assistance if the provision appears to be so vague as to obligate a franchisor to no assistance. Franchisee counsel will push for the franchise agreement to show some reasonableness on the part of the franchisor by committing the franchisor to at least a minimal amount of advice, guidance, or some other type of support on an ongoing basis, given the fact that the term will last many years and likely see a variety of stresses and challenges occur during that period of time.

At the same time, franchisees need to understand that by the nature of the franchise structure most of the specifications regarding what the franchisor may provide could be contained in the operations manuals rather than the franchise agreement, and most franchisors will resist adding a detailed level of specificity to the franchise agreement, even if they may be willing to state some broad categories where they will agree to put a minimum amount of attention during the term of the agreement. This definitely is an area of broad and vague provisions, which may not satisfy a franchisee's concerns, but one where the franchisee may need to "trust the process."

VIII. Location and Premises

A. Choice of Location and Franchisor's Approval

Franchisee must operate its Franchised Business at and only at the location that is described on Exhibit 1. Franchisee may not change the location of the Franchised Business without Franchisor's prior written approval, which Franchisor may grant or withhold in its sole discretion. Franchisee acknowledges that, within [number of days] days following the signing of this agreement, Franchisee will find and submit to Franchisor, for Franchisor's approval, a location for the Franchised Business, and such information regarding the location as Franchisor may require. Franchisor has the right to require that Franchisee, at Franchisee's expense, use a real estate broker or other site selection services provider to assist Franchise in finding a location.

Franchisor will have XX days from receipt of all the requested information to approve or disapprove the location. Franchisor has the right to grant or withhold approval of any proposed location in its business judgment. Franchisee acknowledges and agrees that Franchisor's consent to the location, and any information regarding the location communicated to Franchisee regarding the standard site selection criteria for Franchised Businesses, does not constitute a representation or warranty of any kind, express or implied, as to the suitability of the location for a Business or for any other purpose. Franchisor's recommendation of or consent to the location indicates only that Franchisor believes that the location falls within the acceptable criteria for locations that Franchisor has established as of the time of the consent to the location. Franchisee acknowledges and agrees that Franchisee's selection of the location is based on Franchisee's own independent investigation of the suitability of the location and that Franchisor's approval is not a guarantee or promise of success.

Discussion:

The franchisor's involvement in site selection varies significantly from franchise system to franchise system, often depending on the type of industry. Accordingly, the provisions in the franchise agreement related to location and premises can vary significantly. However, as most franchises require a brick-and-mortar location, following the basic terms of the sample provision is common.

Assuming that the franchise system requires the franchisee to operate out of a physical, brick-and-mortar location, there is still significant discrepancy between how different franchisors will approach and draft this provision and how involved the franchisors will be in the site selection process. Historically, many franchisors would own or lease the real estate for franchised locations and then lease or sublease the location to their franchisees.[106] When the franchisor selects the location

106. Darrow, Siebert, & Truby, *supra* note 52, at 23. The practice of franchisors leasing or subleasing locations to franchisees has given way to requiring that the franchisee's landlord agree to certain lease riders that give the franchisor rights upon franchisee's default under the lease or franchise agreement. From a financial perspective, this often makes sense to the franchisor, as there will either be a significant financial investment up front for a franchisor who owns the real estate it leases to its franchisees, or a significant potential risk for future lease payments in the case of franchisee default if the franchisor leases the real estate and subleases it to its franchisee. That said, some franchisors still maintain this model. For example, the 2016 annual report for McDonald's indicates that the franchisor owns 70 percent of the property (and 45 percent of the land) of all its locations, and property and equipment make up a vast majority of the franchisor's balance sheet assets. *See* http://corporate.mcdonalds.com/content/dam/AboutMcDonalds/Investors/2016%20Annual%20Report.pdf. Franchisors often assign great value to specific locations and want to maintain more control over the location but without the financial and man-hour requirement that actually owning or leasing franchised locations requires. The previously-mentioned lease rider can be a good solution. The reason for maintaining control is often that they may want to ensure that the location will continue to operate as a system location, even if the franchisee would default or decide to leave the system. To do this, some will mandate a sublease from the franchisee, where the franchisor becomes the landlord of the premises. More commonly though, a franchisor could mandate an automatic assignment of the lease upon termination of the franchise agreement (either through expiration or default). Those types of mandates are either enumerated in the franchise agreement or included in a lease rider that the franchisor attaches as a standard exhibit to its form of franchise agreement, which is discussed in the following. In addition to mandating automatic assignment of the lease to the franchisor if the franchise agreement terminates lease riders often include other provisions, such as giving the franchisor

there is no need for the sample provision, other than the acknowledgment that the franchisee may only operate out of that location and the disclaimer of the franchisor's responsibility for the selection of the location. While more and more franchisors have abandoned that model, there has been an increasing movement in recent years toward franchisors requiring the franchisees to use the franchisor-approved third party site selection services. The preceding example reflects a happy medium: the franchisee is required to find its own location, but the franchisor has the right to require the involvement of a real estate broker who will help.[107]

(i) Franchisor's Risk Exposure for Site Selection Assistance

Even though there usually are good reasons for why a franchisor wishes to help its franchisee find a location, the franchisor should be aware that an increased involvement in site selection often increases exposure to claims by the franchisee if the business fails. For example, franchisees have claimed that the franchisor's approval of the site of the franchisee's failed location was a breach of the franchisor's common law duty of competence; that the franchisor knowingly let the franchisee operate in a location the franchisor knew would fail, thereby committing fraud or misrepresentation; or, more generally, that the franchisor's approval of a site implies financial viability and therefore the franchisee's failure must be due to the franchisor's site approval.[108]

While these claims are typically unsuccessful, the drafter should keep this type of claims in mind when phrasing the franchisor's support. Courts that have considered this issue have been persuaded by disclaimers in the agreement that place sole responsibility for site selection in the franchisee's hands and disclaim any negative effects on the franchisee's performance that may be attributable to the location.[109] For this reason, the careful drafter will ensure that sufficient disclaimer language is present to protect the franchisor from such claims.

---

the right to cure the franchisee's default under the lease. If the lease is for a mall location, the rider may also include restrictions on what other tenants the landlord may lease to during the lease term.

107. The reason given for requiring the use of a franchisor-approved real estate broker is typically that by using a real estate broker who is familiar with the requirements of the franchise system, it will be easier to find good locations and consequently the site location process will be both easier and hopefully result in a better location than the franchisee could find on its own, or using a broker who is not familiar with the franchise system. Using a third party may also alleviate concerns about the franchisor imposing itself into an important aspect of the franchisee's business, thereby reducing potential allegations that the franchisor has been so involved in the franchisee's business that it has opened itself up to vicarious liability or joint employer liability.

108. *See, e.g.*, RHC, LLC v. Quizno's Franchising, LLC, No. 04CV985, 2005 WL 1799536 (D. Colo. July 19, 2005) (franchisees alleged that their failure was due to poor locations, which the franchisor had approved, which was a breach of its duty of competence); Zeidler v. A & W Restaurants, Inc., 219 Fed. Appx. 495 (7th Cir. Feb. 15, 2007) (franchisee alleged that the type of building approved by franchisor would, to franchisor's knowledge, not be profitable); Overturf v. Rocky Mountain Chocolate Factory, Inc., No. SACV 08-0365 AG, 2008 WL 11334981 (C.D. Cal. July 21, 2008) (plaintiff alleged that the franchisor's approval of a site implied it would be economically viable). In each of these cases, the courts rejected the franchisee's claims, typically pointing to express language in the franchise agreements that there was no guarantee of financial viability.

109. RHC, LLC v. Quizno's Franchising, LLC, No. 04CV985, 2005 WL 1799536 (D. Colo. July 19, 2005); Overturf v. Rocky Mountain Chocolate Factory, Inc., No. SACV 08-0365 AG, 2008 WL 11334981 (C.D. Cal. July 21, 2008).

(ii) Mobile or On-Site Service Businesses

Some franchised systems do not require a brick-and-mortar location at all, or they are structured so that the franchisee's physical location mostly is for back office use. Examples of this type of business are handyman services, mobile dog grooming, or in-home senior care businesses. For these types of franchises, location-related provisions will read very differently from the preceding example. If included at all in the franchise agreement, they may simply specify that the franchisee may operate its franchised business from anywhere and that the franchisor does not need to approve the location. One example of such language is as follows:

> Franchisee must identify and lease a warehouse for storage within XX days after opening for business. Franchisor will provide general guidance concerning site selection. Franchisee must select and lease premises for the Franchised Business consistent with the standards and requirements provided by Franchisor. Franchisee is solely responsible for identifying and securing suitable premises for the Franchised Business.

This clause is notably different from the sample provision for a brick-and-mortar location in that the franchisor has no prior right of approval for the space. In a "back office" or "storage" type premises, the franchisor should consider whether it would ever want to take over the physical space. If it might, the agreement should require lease assignment language and the franchisor's approval of the lease. In other circumstances, the franchisor might be confident that a replacement franchisee could find their own office or warehouse space. Because customers do not visit the leased space, it typically has no branded signage and there is consequently little value in that specific premises for the brand.

In other instances, mobile businesses simply omit provisions about a physical premises but sometimes substitute requirements regarding vehicles used for the franchised business.

B. Purchase or Lease of the Location

> Franchisee must purchase or lease the location within XX months after signing this Agreement. Failure to sign a lease within this timeframe constitutes grounds for immediate termination of this Agreement and the loss of Franchisee's nonrefundable Initial Franchise Fee. Franchisor has the right, but not the obligation, to review and approve the terms of any lease or purchase contract for the location, and Franchisee agrees to deliver a copy to Franchisor for approval before it is signed. Franchisee agrees that any lease for the location must be in form and substance satisfactory to Franchisor and must include all of the following provisions: (i) Franchisor's right to, at its option, cure Franchisee's default under the lease; (ii) Franchisor's right to, at its option, to assume the lease in the event of Franchisee's default under the lease; (iii) the landlord's obligation to provide Franchisor with notice of Franchisee's default under the lease; (iv) Franchisor's right to enter the leased premises without landlord's

interference; and (v) the landlord's consent to Franchisee and Franchisor to take the necessary action to comply with post-termination obligations under this Agreement and to exercise post-termination rights hereunder.

Franchisee may not execute a lease, sublease, purchase contract or any modification thereof without Franchisor's approval. Franchisor's approval of the lease, sublease or purchase contract does not constitute a warranty or representation of any kind, express or implied, as to its fairness or suitability or as to Franchisee's ability to comply with its terms. Franchisor does not, by virtue of approving the lease, sublease or purchase contract, assume any liability or responsibility to Franchisee or to any third parties. Such approval indicates only that Franchisor believes that the location and certain terms of the lease, sublease or purchase contract fall within the acceptable criteria established as of the time of approval. Franchisee further acknowledges that Franchisor has advised Franchisee to seek legal counsel to review and evaluate the lease. Franchisee must deliver a copy of the fully signed lease, sublease or purchase contract to Franchisor within XX days after its execution.

Discussion:

The franchisor often requires a deadline for a site lease or purchase to ensure that the business is going to be up and running as soon as possible after the franchise agreement is finalized. Without such deadlines a franchisor may find it hard to enforce expected development schedules on the franchisees, and the franchisees who are dragging their feet may tie up locations and markets that could otherwise be operational. From the franchisee's perspective, if a franchisee believes it may not be able to satisfy this timing requirement, it should try to negotiate the deadline since the consequence of missing it is complete termination of the agreement. Franchisors selling franchise opportunities in locations where real estate prices are high and good opportunities are scarce may want to negotiate for a longer period of time to permit a franchisee to wait for a better location to become available.

The remedy reserved by the franchisor in the sample provision of being able to terminate the franchise agreement and keep the initial fee if the franchisee fails to sign a lease within the required time frame is harsh but fairly typical. In structuring the agreement, the franchisor should consider the reasonableness of this provision.

(i) Lease Review and Riders

While it is typical to have a deadline by which the franchisee must have signed a lease or purchased a location, the specific content of this type of provision will vary. Some franchisors will require review of the lease and will be very involved in the lease negotiations, but frequently, instead, the franchise agreement will require the inclusion in the lease of specific provisions protecting the franchisor in the case of a franchisee default. Sometimes the provision will enumerate the specific provisions, as is done in the sample provision. In other instances, the franchisor will require that the franchisee and landlord execute a lease rider, the form of which is attached to the form of franchise agreement. Another option is that the franchisor requires the franchisee to hire an attorney to help them negotiate the lease.

Lease riders for the franchisor's benefit are very common requirements and typically include provisions covering the types of issues that are described in the provision above and are intended to function much like comfort letters often entered into between the franchisor and the franchisee's lender. They regulate what happens if there is a default under the lease or under the franchise agreement, often giving the franchisor the right to step in to the franchisee's shoes under the lease. The franchisees need to keep in mind that landlords will not always agree to these types of riders, or that significant negotiations may be required. Consequently, the franchisees should learn up front from the franchisor how willing the franchisor is to negotiate the rider with landlords, as it may limit the franchisee's location options.

(ii) Lease Tracking

Whether or not the franchisor gets involved in the lease review, it is very common for franchisors to require a copy of the franchisee's lease. Whether through active involvement in the lease negotiations or through requiring that the franchisee negotiates certain rights for the franchisee under the lease, it is prudent on the franchisor's part to have a copy of the lease outlining those rights. Furthermore, there may be other provisions in the lease that the franchisor wants to be aware of. For example, oftentimes a lease is not coterminous with the franchise agreement and the franchisor may wish to keep track of the lease term to understand what impact it may have on the franchise agreement term.

In any event, the franchisor should state that the terms and conditions of the lease are the responsibility of the franchisee. To the extent the franchisor wishes to be involved in the lease negotiations and the details of the lease, the franchisor needs to consider the impact such involvement may have on potential vicarious or joint liability claims. Typically, the franchisor should limit its involvement to matters that will have an impact on the franchisor and the franchise system. For example, the franchisor may wish to retain a right to enter the premises upon the franchisee's default to remove signage and other brand-specific elements. To contrast, the franchisor will typically not involve itself in the financial aspects of the franchisee's lease. As already mentioned, a less-invasive approach may be for the franchisor to require in the franchise agreement that specific terms be included in the lease or to require a lease rider be executed.

C. Relocation

1. Relocation of the Franchised Business.

(a) Relocation Request. Franchisee may relocate the accepted location of the Franchised Business at Franchisee's expense, only if, prior to closing the Franchised Business, Franchisee submits a site acceptance request (in the form Franchisor provides to Franchisee) for Franchisee's new proposed location and obtains Franchisor's written acceptance of the relocation to the proposed location. A relocation includes any change of the location of the Franchised Business within a mall, facility, pad-site, building or anywhere to a new location within the same mall, facility, building or area.

Franchisor is under no obligation to approve a relocation of the Franchised Business. Approval under this Section will be within Franchisor's sole discretion, and such approval, should Franchisor decide to approve such request, shall not be granted unless Franchisee is in compliance with all terms and conditions of this Franchise Agreement and Franchisee has the funds available to relocate the Franchised Business, construct a new Franchised Business according to Franchisor's then-current design standards and do so within a time period acceptable to Franchisor.

(b) Relocation Conditions. If Franchisor approves the relocation of the Franchised Business under this Section, the new location will be considered the "Accepted Location" as used in this Franchise Agreement. All site agreements Franchisee enters into to secure the new location must comply with the site acquisition terms of this Franchise Agreement. In addition, you will be required to make or cause to be made to the former Accepted Location such changes in the signs and interior and exterior of the former Accepted Location so as to effectively distinguish such location from any other Franchised Business. If Franchisor consents to a relocation of the Franchised Business, Franchisor will have the right to (i) charge Franchisee a relocation fee as specified in XX (the "Relocation Fee") to cover costs incurred by Franchisor in connection with any such acceptance, evaluation, and relocation of the Franchised Business, (ii) condition Franchisor's consent upon the payment of an agreed minimum royalty to Franchisor by Franchisee during the period in which the Franchised Business is not in operation (if any), and (iii) require Franchisee to sign Franchisor's then-current form of franchise agreement to replace this Franchise Agreement or any other documents Franchisor may require, including a general release in favor of Franchisor.

Discussion:

It is typical for the franchisor to limit the franchisee's operations to a certain preapproved location for a number of reasons, including territorial rights granted to other franchisees or corporate stores. Business realities dictate that the franchised business might need to move at some point during the term of the franchise agreement due to a variety of reasons, including loss of possession of the location (due to lease issue, destruction of premises, condemnation); the need for a better, more competitive location; or the need for a larger or smaller location. Thus, it is not uncommon for franchisors to include a provision on relocation, but with certain restrictions.[110] The franchisor typically starts with a general prohibition, but will allow relocation in certain circumstances, and/or allow relocation with added conditions.[111] The franchisor will typically take into account the specific circumstance and location of the franchised business and provide for relocation as appropriate. In some cases, the causes of relocation might be cause for termination of the agreement. This typically would only occur in situations where the location is a fundamental factor in the success of the franchised business and the franchisee closed or relocated without permission. In any relocation, it is important for a franchisor to

110. Douglas L. Carden & Peter L. Klarfeld, *"We Have to Live with It": Tips from the Litigators' Perspective on Advanced Drafting,* ABA 28th Annual Forum on Franchising 34 (2005).

111. *Id.* at 34–35.

avoid a relocated franchisee encroaching upon the territory and/or sales of another franchisee already operating or in development.

An issue that is sometimes overlooked by a franchisor in connection with a relocation is making sure that the relocation does not encroach or impede upon another franchisee's territory or that of a corporate location. Allowing a relocation to be within another franchisee's territory, even if unintentional, is a recipe for disaster, which would then have the franchisor incurring potential claims from two franchisees.

Franchisees will expect the right to relocate within its territory (assuming it is not a spot location territory) in connection with (1) a force majeure situation that compels franchisee to lose its current location, (2) a lease issue that is not a result of franchisee/tenant's fault, (3) a significant economic situation affecting the current location, and (4) matters outside the control of franchisee. Franchisors operating in areas like the Gulf Coast where hurricanes have destroyed other businesses can expect prospective franchisees to be particularly attuned to this issue. Franchisees may object to a franchisor retaining "sole discretion" over approval of a relocation.

The franchisee's ultimate concern may be that it does not have any rights to relocate, even in a situation where it has a given territory. As noted previously, it should be recognized by the franchisee that it cannot necessarily have unfettered rights to relocate wherever and whenever without franchisor approval. Such rights could be disastrous to not only the franchisee but also to the system, and cause issues, such as encroachment claims. In addition, having a set location tends to help establish the brand for that location and territory. Certain conditions in the sample relocation provision may be especially troublesome for a franchisee, in particular the requirement to sign the then-current franchise agreement. From the franchisee perspective, there should be no need to sign a new franchise agreement; the agreement can simply be modified to reflect the new location. Nothing has changed and, typically for relocation, it is not a result of any franchisee fault or default and, therefore, the franchisee should not be penalized. Nothing changes but for the location. In a similar vein is the issue of a release and why a franchisee should have to sign a release waiving or barring any and all claims that it might have against the franchisor simply because it needs to relocate. The franchisor position in connection with a release is that there is a change being requested by the franchisee that is not permitted but for franchisor approval and if the franchisor is to provide its approval for relocation, it should be entitled to a release in return for such. A possible compromise to the positions would be a release dealing specifically with the new location, in that the franchisee will not make any claims concerning franchisor's approval of franchisee's request to relocate.

D. Modernization or Replacement

Within the time periods specified in XX, Franchisee must, at Franchisee's sole expense, remodel, modernize, and redecorate the Franchised Business, including the Franchised Business' internal and external construction, design, furniture, fixtures, equipment, and décor, so that the Franchised Business reflects Franchisor's then-current Standards as to image and quality. Franchisee acknowledges that this obligation could result in Franchisee making extensive structural changes to, and significantly remodeling and renovating of, the Franchised Business, and/or in Franchisee spending substantial amounts for such remodeling. Franchisee agrees to incur, without limitation, any capital expenditures required in order to comply with this obligation and Franchisor's requirements (even if those expenditures cannot be amortized over the remaining Term). Franchisee will perform all remodeling in compliance with the Standards, using a general contractor Franchisor reasonably accepts in writing. Franchisor's acceptance of Franchisee's general contractor will not in any way be Franchisor's endorsement of Franchisee's general contractor or render Franchisor liable for such general contractor's performance. All replacement designs, furniture, fixtures, equipment, and décor must be approved by Franchisor in writing; must conform to Franchisor's then-current Standards; and, where Franchisor so requires, must be purchased from Approved Suppliers Franchisor designates or approves in writing. Franchisee must complete all remodeling within a reasonable time after its beginning, but in no event longer than XX months after Franchisee begins remodeling. The requirements of this Section are in addition to the requirements for continuing maintenance and minor refurbishments.

Discussion:
Brand recognition and maintaining the brand standards are important ingredients to any successful franchise system. As franchise agreements span a considerable period of time, the franchisor will include an obligation for the franchisee to upgrade the franchised business throughout that time period or as triggered by a particular event, such as renewal or transfer (which is not referred to in the preceding example and is typically part of the transfer and renewal sections).

(i) Terminology

The terms modernization, replacement, remodel, and the like are, at times, interchangeable and blurred in terms of their definition and meaning. Although they are not used uniformly from one system to the next, "modernization" most typically means replacing an older item for a different and updated item that serves the same purpose. "Replacement" is simply purchasing a new item to replace the old item without necessarily upgrading (although for some equipment like computers the new item may necessarily also be an upgrade because of technological advances). "Remodeling" or sometimes "renovating" encompasses a completely new look and is typically the most expensive of the requirements a franchisor may impose.

Drafters should consider that franchisors typically impose ongoing requirements to maintain the condition of the location, but less frequently they may want to impose additional requirements to upgrade the look and feel of the franchised business. Most common is a three-part process: (1) the ongoing maintenance, such as repainting scuffed walls; (2) refurbishing somewhere in the midterm including replacing certain items with newer modernized versions; and, (3) the ultimate replacement and rebuilding of the location which, depending upon the length of the term, can occur midstream and also upon a renewal or a transfer/sale. There are franchise agreements that, by their literal wording, require the ultimate refurbishment/rebuild at any given time.

(ii) Franchisor and Franchisee Perspectives

The franchisor should be mindful of this clause so that the general image of the trademarks is being adequately preserved and improved throughout the term of the franchise agreement.[112] If this provision is inadequately drafted, the franchisor might risk not being able to require that the franchisees keep their locations up to current standards, which in turn might end up damaging the goodwill of the system or that particular location (and harm the franchisee). Franchisors also have a strong interest in being able to require that franchised businesses not only maintain basic cleanliness and good condition but also periodically update to keep pace with updated branding, which may be required for the brand to continue to appeal to customers.

Perhaps unsurprisingly, this is a term that franchisees frequently attempt to negotiate. Franchisees may balk at the notion of these types of provisions, especially if this clause provides the franchisor with a "blank check" in terms of what renovations the franchisee is required to undertake.[113] These types of provisions can provide a franchisor with a powerful tool of requiring a franchisee to remodel/rebuild, and franchisees frequently seek modest revisions to make them more reasonable from the franchisee perspective. Among the relief that is frequently sought are limits on when such requests can be made (e.g., neither within the first two years, nor within the last three years, unless the franchisee has already elected renewal); limits on the type of remodeling; caps on total expense of the project; and assurances that remodel requests are regional or systemwide requirements, include corporate locations, and are not so frequent that they eliminate profit.

The ultimate concern for the franchisees tends to be the costs and disruption that are involved with any type of upgrade, remodeling, or rebuild, however described. In connection with the cost, it is how and when such are implemented and the exact requirements of the remodel. As noted previously, a number of franchise agreements do not clearly differentiate between the various types of maintenance or upgrade requirements.

Franchisors should also consider the impact of these provisions on shorter-term franchise agreements. A franchisee may be willing to remodel its franchised business after 10 or 20 years, but if asked to do so after five years, it is more likely for the franchisee to object that this is an unfair expectation. This is an area that does cause a lot of anguish and frustration for the franchisees and potential claims against the franchisor for what may be referred to as a de facto termination by forcing a franchisee to either sell or terminate its franchise or go into some form of insolvency if the requirements are overreaching.[114] A franchisee, on the other hand, needs to also recognize that it is important for the brand to maintain its competitive edge, which may require certain upgrades and refurbishing of the locations.

112. Hurwitz & Schnell, *supra* note 36, at 73–74.

113. For a discussion of such wariness from the perspective of counsel representing franchisees, *see* Lagarias & Boulter, *supra* note 105, at 145 & n.84.

114. *See, e.g.*, Burger King Corp. v. Cabrera, No. 10-20480-Civ, 2010 WL 5834869 (S.D. Fla. Dec. 29, 2010) (dispute involving replacement of POS system).

IX. Design and Construction

A. Development of Premises by the Franchisee

Franchisee shall construct and equip the Premises in conformity with the System standard layout plans, specifications and drawings approved by Franchisor. The standard layout plans, specifications and drawings may not contain the requirements of federal, state or local laws, codes or regulation and it is Franchisee's responsibility to prepare, at its expense, all required construction plans and specifications to suit the shape and dimension of Franchisee's location and to ensure that such plans and specifications comply with all applicable state, federal or local laws, codes, regulations, ordinances, building codes and permit requirements and with lease requirements and restrictions. Franchisor's review and approval is only with respect to System standards and requirements and Franchisor will not review the plans, specifications and drawings for compliance with law. Franchisor shall have the right to inspect the construction and development of the Premises at all reasonable times. Franchisor does not by approving Franchisee's plans or specifications or inspecting the location assume any liability or responsibility to Franchisee or to any third parties. Such approvals and inspections are solely for the purpose of assuring compliance with System standards. The cost of plans, designs, drawings, and specifications, any commissions or broker's fee payable by Franchisor to find or secure the Premises and/or Franchisee, and all costs and expenses pertaining to the construction and equipping of the Premises shall be borne exclusively by Franchisee. Franchisor shall provide such advice and assistance to Franchisee in constructing and equipping the Premises as may reasonably be required. Franchisee agrees to do or cause to be done the following at its sole cost and expense:

1. ensure that all applicable laws, building codes, permit requirements and lease requirements and restrictions are complied with in connection with such construction;
2. obtain all required building, utility, sign, sanitation and business permits and licenses and any other required permits and licenses;
3. construct all required improvements to the Premises and decorate the Premises in compliance with plans and specifications approved by Franchisor;
4. subject to the provisions hereof, purchase or lease and install all fixtures, equipment and signs required for the Premises by Franchisor; and
5. present a chosen contractor and contractor's tender for approval by Franchisor and retain and compensate all contractors, subcontractors or other professionals required in connection with the construction and development of the Premises.

Discussion:

No matter whether the build-out of the franchisee's location is extensive, such as requiring the construction of a new building, or more cosmetic, it is common for the franchisor to place all construction-related obligations solely on the franchisee.[115]

115. This analysis assumes that the franchisor sets requirements for the franchisee's location and premises. As discussed in the section on site location, not all franchise systems require franchisees to operate out of a specific

To maintain some control over the building and construction, the franchisor will often include a requirement in the franchise agreement for the franchisee to seek franchisor approval of building plans and designs.

When the construction and design of the franchisee's location is complex, such as in the build-out of a new hotel, it is common for this provision to be significantly more detailed than the sample provision. For example, instead of giving the franchisor a general right to inspect the construction site, there may be specific points in time during the construction process at which the franchisor's approval is required before the franchisee is allowed to continue its construction. As more complex construction usually takes longer, there may be deadlines for reaching certain points in the construction process, which will be tied to the termination provision in the agreement.

It is also important that this section includes enough details for the franchisee to be aware of its specific obligations (i.e., regarding permits, fixtures, contractors, design, among others) and to understand how these obligations will impact the cost of construction. In a similar vein, while it may be important for the franchisor to approve who the general contractor for the building project is, in order to ensure building quality and compliance with system building standards, it may be important to franchisees to understand how having to use an approved general contractor may affect its construction cost.[116] Most often, the franchisor will stay removed from the day-to-day construction process so as to avoid or limit any vicarious liability claims or claims by the franchisee.[117]

B. Licenses and Permits

> Franchisee must at all times maintain Franchisee's premises and conduct operations in compliance with all applicable laws, regulations, codes and ordinances. Franchisee must secure and maintain in force all required licenses, permits and certificates relating to the Franchised Business.

Discussion:

The clause regarding licenses and permits ties directly into the previous clause regarding development of the premises by the franchisee. Consistent with the allocation of obligations in that clause, it is the franchisee's obligation to ensure compliance with laws during the construction process and obtain necessary permits.

---

location, or the location may just be used for back office services. In those situations, typically the franchise agreement will not contain provisions about build-out and construction.

116. It should be noted that there may be many benefits to franchisees from using approved general contractors. Especially if the build-out is more complex or there are some very specific construction standards, using a contractor who is experienced in building out locations for the franchise system may save the franchisee both cost and time.

117. Some franchisors offer franchisees turnkey franchises. This model tends to be more common in other countries, such as Canada, but it is not unheard of in the United States. For turnkey offerings, this provision would not be in the agreement at all. In the case a franchisee is negotiating for a turnkey franchise with a franchisor that doesn't typically offer them, it is important for the franchisee to make sure that this type of provision in the franchise agreement is amended to reflect the allocation of responsibility for the construction process, or removed completely.

The preceding example is relatively broad and general. If the build-out of the franchised business is complex or requires compliance with specific laws and regulations, the franchisor should consider including more detailed information about the applicable laws and regulations in this provision. In the opposite situation, where the franchisee's build-out is minimal and limited to cosmetic changes, this provision may not be necessary at all. In either situation, it is important that the provision stresses the franchisee's responsibility for the construction and build-out process, as the sample provision does. In drafting this clause, the franchisor is explicitly removing itself from the responsibility of ensuring compliance with relevant laws, and licenses, permits, and certificates. Note that, though not specifically stated in the provision, it is only intended to apply to the construction process. The general provision regulating compliance with law, including maintenance of the proper licenses and permits, is discussed in Chapter 4.

C. Fixtures, Equipment, Signs, and Computer Systems

> Franchisee agrees to use in the operation of the Franchised Business only those brands or types of fixtures, furnishings, equipment (including without limitation, computers, cash registers and point of sales systems), and signs that Franchisor has approved as meeting its specifications and standards for design, appearance, function, performance quality and serviceability. Franchisee may purchase and lease approved brands or types of fixtures, furnishings, equipment and signs only from suppliers approved by Franchisor, which may include Franchisor or its affiliates. Franchisee further agrees to only place or display at the Premises (interior and exterior) such signs, emblems, lettering, logos and display materials that are from time to time approved in writing by Franchisor.
>
> Franchisee acknowledges and agrees that from time to time, Franchisor may modify the list of approved types, brands, models and/or suppliers, and Franchisee may not, after receipt of notice of such modification, reorder any type, brand or model from any supplier, which is no longer approved. If Franchisee proposes to purchase any fixtures, furniture, equipment, signs or supplies of a type, brand or model, or propose to purchase from a supplier that Franchisor has not previously approved, Franchisee must notify Franchisor and submit to it such information as Franchisor may request. Franchisor may impose reasonable inspection and supervision fees on approved suppliers to cover its costs. Franchisor and its affiliates may receive revenue or other consideration as a result of Franchisee's purchases of goods or services from Franchisor, its affiliates, or third party suppliers. Franchisor and its affiliates have the right to retain any revenue that Franchisor or they receive as a result of Franchisee's purchases of goods and services.

Discussion:

It is important to note that this provision covers two different types of requirements relating to fixtures, equipment, signs, and computer equipment (FF&E). First, it requires that the franchisees purchase a specific, or approved, type or brand of FF&E. Second, it requires that the FF&E be purchased from specific, approved suppliers. The two requirements are often presented hand in hand in franchise agreements, but they are still separate requirements. For example, the franchisor may mandate a restaurant franchisee to obtain a specific brand and model of stoves for the kitchen, but it may allow the franchisee to buy the stoves from any supplier (an approved product requirement). On the other hand, the franchisor may also require the franchisee to buy the stove from a particular supplier (an approved supplier requirement). To some extent, the motivation behind the two requirements is different. As emphasized throughout this book, the franchisor drafts clauses to protect the goodwill and reputation of its trademarks and system. Franchisors often put in place minimum quality requirements for the fixtures, equipment, signs, and computer systems. At its root, the intention behind the requirement of specific FF&E is to ensure a satisfactory and consistent customer experience across all franchise locations. The larger the franchisor becomes, the more likely it is to require that the franchised locations use specific materials or FF&E. This is because the larger the system, the harder it is for the franchisor to manage discrepancies across the system while maintaining a consistent look and feel.

The requirement that the franchisees use approved suppliers may be motivated by a desire to achieve brand consistency, thus the same driver as is behind the approved types and brands of FF&E, but there are additional reasons to require the use of approved suppliers. It is easier for the franchisor to ensure that the franchisees are complying with the mandatory FF&E requirements if the franchisees must buy from approved suppliers. Just as importantly though, cumulating all the franchisee purchases from specific suppliers will often result in better pricing for all, and possibly payments directly from the supplier to the franchisor. Negotiated volume discounts are more common in relation to ongoing purchases by the franchisees (e.g., food products by a restaurant franchisee) but can also apply to FF&E purchases. The discounts can take many different forms, and it is not unusual for suppliers to contribute funds toward the franchise system annual conference, or pay the funds into the system marketing fund. In some instances though, the payment will go directly to the franchisor without being earmarked for any particular purpose.[118] Where the franchisor or its affiliates acts as the approved supplier, the FF&E may also be an important income source for the franchisor.

The degree to which a franchisor chooses to regulate FF&E purchases varies significantly between systems. In some cases, the franchisor acts as the supplier, while in other cases the franchisor merely establishes minimum requirements for the supplies. Sometimes the franchisor also will recommend or require use of one or several approved suppliers. The specifications of this clause depend on the nature of the franchise and the franchisor's desire to put out a unified message to its customers.

Often, the franchisor's interest in controlling the source for FF&E purchases is in harmony with the franchisee's interests. The franchisor may get a rebate or other consideration from the designated suppliers and therefore desire the use of

---

118. Note, however, that some states restrict franchisors' right to receive payments from franchisee suppliers. *See, e.g.*, IND. CODE § 23-2-2.1(4).

a particular supplier.[119] While supplier rebates may motivate some franchisors, in most instances the driver is that volume purchasing results in lower prices for the franchisees than they could get on their own, which in turn will likely lead to more successful franchisees, less turnover in the franchise system, and therefore less hassle and more royalties to the franchisors. However, since the franchisee perception might be that the franchisees are paying extra for supplies because they have to use a particular supplier, the franchisor will want to explicitly outline the possibility of such rebates and payments so that the franchisee is not surprised by it during the term of the agreement. The franchisor also must check the statutory regulations with respect to rebates in relevant jurisdictions. Hawaii, Indiana, and Washington are among the states that set restrictions on the franchisors' ability to require the franchisees to use particular suppliers or otherwise set restrictions on supplier relationships. Hawaii only permits limitations on who franchisees can purchase goods or services from if the restrictions are reasonably necessary "for a lawful purpose justified on business grounds."[120] Indiana limits the franchisors' rights to get rebates from suppliers purely based on franchisee purchases.[121] Washington has a statutory provision very similar to the Hawaii statute.[122]

Because most franchisees conduct a lot of due diligence on their initial costs before agreeing to become a franchise, beyond the rebate issue, the average franchisee is not too concerned about this provision. However, this provision relates back to the discussion of modernization and replacements discussed earlier in this chapter. In franchise systems with frequent and expensive updates, it should not be disregarded by the franchisee (see Chapter 4 for a discussion of the franchisee's ongoing obligation to maintain FF&E in accordance with the franchisor's requirements). For ongoing obligations relating to approved FF&E and approved suppliers, however, a franchisee may want to negotiate certain aspects of this provision. For example, it may wish to limit the types of FF&E that the franchisor can approve to those that are at the core of the franchise system, or require that there always be more than one approved supplier for FF&E items. Franchisors will typically resist such changes, as agreeing to it for one franchisee indirectly will affect its ability to make changes to the system as a whole.

This provision also covers a third point not discussed previously—limitations on signage at the location. The franchisee's obligations relating to the franchisor's intellectual property is discussed at length in Chapter 5, but this provision relates more specifically to what is not allowed to be displayed at the franchisee's location. This is an important part of the provision from the franchisor's perspective,

---

119. Joyce Mazero & Suzie Loonam, *Purchasing Cooperatives: Leveraging a Supply Chain for Competitive Advantage* 29 Franchise L.J. 148 (Winter 2010). Note that supplier rebates being paid to a franchisor and best pricing to the franchisees are not mutually exclusive concepts. A supplier may give a franchisor a rebate and the supplier's pricing to the franchisees may still be well below what the franchisee could have negotiated on its own. Further, many franchisors will use supplier rebates to pay for marketing and other activities that benefit the entire franchise system.

120. Haw. Rev. Stat. § 482E-6(2)(B).

121. Ind. Code § 23-2-2.7-1 (4).

122. 6 Wash. Rev. Code § 19.100.180(2)(b).

as signage displayed at a franchisee's location that is *not* related to the franchise system may be distracting and detracting as much from the brand and the goodwill as incorrect franchise branding. Typically this part of the provision should not be an issue to the franchisee, except in the situation where the franchise is going to be operated out of the same premises as another business.

D. Commencement of Operations

Franchisee agrees not to open the Franchised Business until: Franchisee is notified by Franchisor that the Franchised Business meets Franchisor's standards and specifications; Franchisee is fully-staffed; Franchisee has successfully completed training to Franchisor's satisfaction; Franchisee has an approved marketing plan; Franchisee has given Franchisor a copy of the lease, sublease or purchase contract for the location; Franchisor has been furnished with copies of all insurance policies required by the agreement, or such other evidence of insurance coverage and payment of premiums as Franchisor requests or accepts them; Franchisee has obtained all required permits, licenses, and certifications for operating the Franchised Business, and the location is in compliance with all laws, rules and regulations; and all applicable franchise fees and other amounts owing to Franchisor have been paid.

Franchisee agrees to commence the Franchised Business operations within XX months after the execution of this agreement and within [number of days] days after Franchisor notifies Franchisee that the conditions set forth in this Article have been satisfied.

Discussion:
The franchisor will generally not allow the franchised business to open without prior approval and confirmation that all necessary work prior to opening has been completed. The franchisee is usually required to do all of the preparatory work, and once this work is completed the franchisor will inspect the physical premises or other aspects of the business.[123] As mentioned previously, this approval ensures that the franchisor does a last review before the franchised business begins to represent the system in a new location. The intent behind this clause is to ensure that there is no harm done to the value of the trademarks or system by prematurely opening and operating under the franchisor's name.

For a franchisor, it is often advisable to set a deadline for when the franchisee must open the business. This puts pressure on the franchisee to complete its build-out and other pre-opening obligations in a timely fashion, as failure to meet the deadline may lead to termination of the franchise agreement. From a franchisee's perspective, it is important to ensure that there is sufficient time to complete all the required obligations. A franchisor, on the other hand, is usually eager for the location to be completed and open as soon as possible. The sooner the location opens, the sooner the franchisee will start making money and start paying royalties and other ongoing fees to the franchisor.

123. Julie Bennet & Cheryl Babcock, Franchise Times: Guides to Selecting, Buying & Owning a Franchise 237 (2008).

4

Operation of the Business

Kathryn Kotel and Will K. Woods

X. General Ongoing Obligations of Franchisee

A. Maximum Operation of the Franchised Business

During the Initial Term, Franchisee must use the Premises solely for the operation of the Franchised Business. Franchisee must maintain sufficient inventories and continuously operate the Franchised Business at its maximum capacity and efficiency for the minimum number of days and hours set forth in the Manuals or as Franchisor otherwise prescribes in writing (subject to the requirements of local laws and licensing requirements).

Discussion:

As the franchisor's primary objective is to have consistent operations across all locations within the franchise system, some franchisors will require the franchisees to operate the franchised business on certain days and during specific hours. Franchise agreements may provide the required hours of operation within the franchise agreement, while others reference the operations manuals, thereby providing flexibility to the franchisor to change the required hours of operation during the franchise term as market conditions or product offerings change over time. Occasionally, third parties will argue that the franchisor's requirement that the franchisee operate on specific days or hours is sufficient to prove vicarious liability of the franchisor for acts or omissions of the franchisee. The franchisors must, therefore, consider this requirement carefully. If requiring all franchisees to be open at certain times or on specific days is an essential element of the franchise system and brand consistency, then the franchise agreement should contain language like the sample language in the preceding text. If it is not essential to the overall operation of the brand, it may be prudent to forego this language in the franchise agreement.

B. Customer Relations

> Except as otherwise specified by Franchisor in the Manuals or otherwise, Franchisee must immediately resolve any customer complaints regarding the quality of products, service and/or cleanliness of the Franchised Business or any similar complaints. When any customer complaints cannot be immediately resolved, Franchisee must use reasonable efforts to resolve the customer complaints as soon as practical and must, whenever feasible, give the customer the benefit of the doubt. If Franchisor determines that its intervention is necessary or desirable to protect the System or the goodwill associated with the System, or if Franchisor believes that Franchisee has failed adequately to address or resolve any customer complaints, Franchisor may, without Franchisee's consent, resolve any complaints and charge Franchisee an amount sufficient to cover Franchisor's reasonable costs and expenses in resolving the customer complaints, which amount Franchisee must pay Franchisor immediately on demand. Franchisee must participate in all customer relations programs initiated by Franchisor, including but not limited to, visibly posting any 800 numbers, email or other contact information for customers to contact Franchisor's customer relations providers. Franchisee agrees to pay for all costs associated with Franchisor's customer relations providers relating to customer complaints or issues arising from its operation of the Franchised Business, including but not limited to the costs of gift cards or other remuneration given to customers needed to resolve the complaint.

Discussion:

With today's social media and Internet environment, one customer's negative review of a franchised location can immediately impact not only the franchisor's goodwill but also revenue at other franchised locations. The franchisors should consider, therefore, including specific language in their franchise agreements that requires franchisees to immediately respond to any customer complaint and resolve that complaint to the customer's satisfaction. Additionally, the franchisor reserves the right to step in and respond to a customer complaint if the franchisee fails to do so promptly and properly. Since the resolution of a customer complaint often includes providing the customer with some form of remuneration, typically in the form of a gift card or discount on future visits to the franchised location, the franchisor must include language requiring the franchisee to reimburse the franchisor for any form of remuneration it incurs to resolve a customer complaint relating to the franchised location. Many large franchisors establish an internal customer satisfaction department to handle all customer complaints in a consistent manner across the system. This work may also be outsourced to a vendor to handle for the system.

The franchisors that have a systemwide customer satisfaction program must address this in the franchise agreement or in their operations manual. The franchisors that do not currently have such a program would be wise to reserve the right to provide for a future program and require full participation by all franchisees.

C. Health Standards

Franchisee must meet and maintain the highest health standards and ratings applicable to the operation of the Franchised Business. Franchisee must participate in any food safety and brand standard audit program specified by Franchisor and the Franchised Business must undergo the then current number of audits per year as required by Franchisor, which will all be at Franchisee's expense. Franchisee must furnish to Franchisor, within five days after receipt thereof, a copy of all inspection reports, warnings, citations, certificates, and/or ratings resulting from inspections conducted by any federal, state or municipal agency with jurisdiction over the Franchised Business. Without limiting the foregoing, Franchisee and all required personnel must obtain and maintain all necessary and required licenses and certificates for food service and food handling as may be required by applicable local rules and regulations and/or the Manuals.

Discussion:
Restaurant, hotel, and certain other franchise systems are all subject to local health code requirements, as well as the franchisor's standards for food safety. Since compliance with all health code and food safety standards is critical for the successful operation of restaurant franchises (and the protection of the goodwill associated with the franchisor's trademarks), franchisors often address this requirement separately in lieu of relying solely on the more general "compliance with all laws" section of the franchise agreement. Franchise systems that operate businesses subject to other local, state, or federal laws should consider addressing compliance with those laws in a separate section similar to the sample language provided in the preceding text. Note that while this provision creates the franchisee's obligation to comply with all applicable health codes and the franchisor's standards, it is prudent for the franchisor to also include a provision in the franchise agreement that gives it the right to take actions, up to and including declaring a default, if the franchisee fails to meet any of these requirements. See Section X.F., Inspection of the Franchised Business, in this chapter for sample language addressing the franchisor's rights.

D. Maintenance and Equipment Upgrades

1. Franchisee must constantly maintain and continuously operate the Franchised Business and all furniture, fixtures, equipment, furnishings, floor coverings, interior and exterior signage, the building interior and exterior, interior and exterior lighting, landscaping and parking lot surfaces in first-class condition and repair in accordance with the requirements of the System, including all ongoing necessary remodeling, redecorating, refurbishing and repairs. In addition, Franchisee must promptly and

diligently perform all necessary maintenance, repairs and replacements to the Franchised Business as Franchisor may prescribe from time to time, including periodic interior and exterior painting; resurfacing of the parking lot; roof repairs; and replacement of obsolete or worn out signage, floor coverings, furnishings, equipment and decor. Franchisee must not make any material alterations to the Franchised Business that affect operations or the image of the System without Franchisor's prior written approval. Franchisee acknowledges and agrees that the requirements of this Section are both reasonable and necessary to ensure continued public acceptance and patronage of all restaurants in the System, to assist the Franchised Business to compete effectively in the marketplace and to avoid deterioration or obsolescence of the operation of the Franchised Business.

2. In addition to Facilities Remodeling (defined below), Franchisee must make, from time to time, such upgrades and other changes to the equipment utilized in the Franchised Business (other than the Computer System) as Franchisor may request in writing (collectively, "**Equipment Upgrades**"). Franchisor will have the right to require any Equipment Upgrades it deems necessary for the Franchised Business.

Discussion:

To ensure that the franchised business continually operates according to the system standards, the franchisors include language requiring the franchisee to continually maintain and repair the premises during the term of the franchise agreement. Some agreements limit the annual costs of such maintenance and repair; however, from the franchisor perspective, it is a best practice to avoid such limitations and instead require all necessary work be done as needed over the term of the agreement.

The franchisors should also consider using a provision that requires franchisees to update equipment used in the operation of the franchised business over the term of the agreement. This language may include a cap on the costs of the new equipment, as well as time restrictions on how often the franchisor may require such upgrades. The franchisor must have a good understanding of its industry and the development of potential new equipment to properly draft this provision.

This provision is relevant not only for updates of existing equipment as technology and equipment design changes over the term of the franchise agreement but also addresses any changes in the equipment needed to operate the franchised business, as the products offered may change over time or if the franchisor determines that a business line extension is necessary to grow the business. Consider those restaurant franchises that offered only regular coffee for many years and then expanded their coffee lines to include the multitude of coffee-related products now routinely offered by most restaurants. If the franchisor did not have the ability to require its franchisees to purchase the new equipment needed to make those new coffee products, the franchisor would have to wait until each franchise agreement was renewed to require these changes, thereby preventing the system from quickly adopting the new products systemwide and likely would never be able to regain market share lost to competitors who could more quickly require systemwide changes to required equipment.

E. Modernization

1. Franchisee must cause to be completed extensive structural changes, major construction, and substantial modifications to existing furniture, fixtures, equipment and improvements to modernize and conform the Franchised Business to the existing or a new image of the System for new franchised and company businesses ("**Facilities Remodeling**") at Franchisor's request, which may not be made sooner than XX years after the later of (a) the date that Franchisee commenced construction-related work for the initial construction of the Franchised Business; and (b) the date that Franchisor required the most recent Facilities Remodeling to be completed at the Franchised Business, provided that, if Franchisor did not set such a date or if Franchisee completed the Facilities Remodeling prior to the date set by Franchisor, the date that Franchisee commenced work at the Franchised Business to complete that Facilities Remodeling, as applicable. For the avoidance of doubt, (i) Sections [Construction] and [Opening] of this Agreement must apply to all Facilities Remodeling; (ii) there must be no cap on the cost of the Facilities Remodeling; and (iii) capital expenses necessary for the repair and maintenance of the Premises are not subject to the time limitations described in the preceding sentence. Within XX days after receipt of Franchisor's written notice regarding the required Facilities Remodeling, Franchisee must prepare and complete the corresponding Plans. These Plans must be submitted to, and their use approved by, Franchisor prior to the commencement of construction. Franchisee must complete the required Facilities Remodeling within XX months after receipt of Franchisor's written notice, or such other time reasonably specified by Franchisor in its written notice.

2. The limitation on the frequency or scope of Facilities Remodeling will not include repair to, or the normal upkeep of, the Franchised Business, nor will it include Equipment Upgrades (as defined above).

Discussion:

Perhaps more important than ongoing maintenance requirements, the franchisor must also require the franchisee to remodel or upgrade the franchised location during the term of the agreement.[124] This language allows the franchisor's brand to stay current in the market as other competitors open or as the franchise system evolves over time. Redesigns of the standard franchised location occur within each system over the years; requiring the existing franchisees to update their locations to the new design results in consistency across all locations regardless of when the franchise agreement was signed. Without this language, the franchisors risk that the franchisees will not update their locations and the goodwill associated with the franchisor's trademarks will erode. Developing the appropriate language for a particular system requires the franchisor to carefully balance the length of the franchise term with the relevant "life" of the initial construction and design of a franchised location.

124. *See* Chapter 2 for a discussion of remodeling requirements applicable to franchise renewal.

In restaurant systems, the typical remodeling requirement is every seven years, given the expected life of many physical components of a restaurant as well as the costs associated with the initial construction and any major remodel. Other systems must determine a reasonable timeframe for required remodels. Franchisors also must determine if they will cap the amount the franchisee must spend on each remodel or leave the amount open to provide for greater flexibility in design changes. While an open-ended amount may seem ideal for the franchisor, this must be balanced with the franchisees' concerns about the required timeframes and costs. Franchisees will be looking for more certainty in this provision, including (1) maximum expenditures, (2) an initial period of time when no upgrades will be required, (3) an ability to avoid a remodel if the franchisee's existing lease term is too short to recoup the expense of the remodel, and (4) a reasonable amount of time to complete a remodel.[125]

F. Inspection of the Franchised Business

1. To determine whether Franchisee and the Franchised Business are in compliance with this Agreement and with all System Standards, Franchisor or its designees shall have the right at any reasonable time and without prior notice to Franchisee to: (a) inspect the Premises; (b) observe, photograph and videotape the operations of the Franchised Business for such consecutive or intermittent periods as Franchisor deems necessary; (c) remove samples of any food and beverage products, material or other inventory items for testing to determine if such samples meet the System Standards (without paying for the samples) and Franchisor may require Franchisee to bear the cost of such testing if Franchisor has not given consent to the supplier or if the sample fails to conform to Franchisor's specifications; (d) interview personnel and customers of the Franchised Business; and (e) inspect and copy any books, records and documents relating to the operation of the Franchised Business or, upon the request of Franchisor or its designee, require Franchisee to send copies thereof to Franchisor or its designee.

2. Franchisee agrees to cooperate fully with Franchisor or its designee in connection with any such inspections, observations, videotaping, product removal and interviews. Following each inspection, Franchisor will provide Franchisee an inspection report listing Franchisee's score on the inspection and those conditions at the Franchised Business that must be rectified. Franchisee must take all necessary steps to immediately correct any deficiencies detected during these inspections, including, without limitation, ceasing further sale of unauthorized menu items (regardless of Franchisee's inventory) and ceasing further use of any equipment, advertising materials or supplies that do not conform with the System Standards.

3. Recognizing that the failure of Franchisee to meet the System Standards may endanger the reputation and operations of other restaurants operated under the System and/or potentially endanger the general public, Franchisee and Franchisor agree

125. Chernow, Olson, & Prince, *supra* note 53, at 20.

that in the event operations at the Franchised Business fall below the System Standards, Franchisor has the right to, in addition to and not in lieu of its right to terminate this Agreement pursuant to Section XX, require that Franchisee discontinue all operations at the Franchised Business and close the Franchised Business to the public until Franchisee is able to establish to Franchisor's reasonable satisfaction that operations at the Franchised Business meet or exceed the System Standards.

4. If Franchisee fails to achieve a passing score on an inspection, Franchisor has the right to require that Franchisee, the Operating Principal and/or one or more managerial employees of the Franchised Business attend and successfully complete an additional training to be held at a location designated by Franchisor. Franchisee must pay a tuition charge as established by Franchisor from time to time for this training program and the travel, living, food and other incidental expenses incurred by Franchisee's employees while attending this training program.

5. In addition, if Franchisee fails to achieve a passing score on an inspection, the inspection report shall constitute a notice of default. If Franchisee fails to achieve a passing score on the next inspection (which will be conducted at least XX days after Franchisee's receipt of the inspection report for the prior inspection), Franchisor may terminate this Agreement, without opportunity to cure, by providing Franchisee written notice of termination along with a copy of the inspection report.

Discussion:

Language regarding the inspection of a franchised location can be included in the operations section of the franchise agreement or may be included in the default and termination section. The franchisor must create a right to perform ongoing inspections at the franchised location to ensure compliance with system standards and protect its trademarks. This language gives the franchisor the right to enter the franchised location at any time to assess compliance with its standards, including the right to take pictures or videos, remove samples of products offered to customers, talk with the franchisee's employees or customers, and review all books and records of the business. While the specifics of such a program, including timing of inspections and consequences of failed inspections, may be included in the franchise agreement, often these details are instead included in the system standards and manuals, thereby allowing the franchisor flexibility to change its inspection process over the term of the franchise agreement.

Note that the failure to comply with system standards, as measured by these inspections, can result in the franchisor terminating the franchise agreement. In some franchise systems, the franchise agreement (or the operations manual or system standards) may also provide other remedies prior to the termination of the franchise agreement. The sample language gives the franchisor the right to have the franchised business close for a period of days so the franchisee can bring the franchised business into compliance with system standards. This right correlates to the franchisee's obligation to comply with local health codes and the franchisor's food safety standards (see Section X.C., Health Standards). For restaurant systems, this can be an effective tool if the franchised restaurant is not meeting food safety or other health standards, but these failures can be fixed, either with new equipment, training, or deep cleaning the restaurant. Providing interim remedies for sporadic failures of system standards can be beneficial to both the franchisor and the franchisee.

The sample provision provided here references "passing scores" from inspections. This is typical language for mature systems with well-developed inspection protocols that include a specific list of items to be inspected and scored. In a smaller system that does not have an established inspection checklist and is not prepared to create one, drafters should modify this language to suit the type of inspection that the franchisor will conduct.

While drafters should consider obtaining a litigator's perspective on the entire franchise agreement, this particular provision and any related operations manual provision or system standard should be reviewed with a litigator during drafting. Any default or termination action taken by the franchisor may result in litigation. Even if the franchise agreement provides for interim remedies in lieu of a default, the franchisee may not agree to implement the interim remedy or may take preemptive action against the franchisor to prevent the franchisor from pursuing the interim remedy. In a restaurant system with the sample language in the preceding text, the franchisee may refuse to close the restaurant or take all the actions required by the franchisor to fix the issues. Therefore, obtaining a litigator's perspective of the language of this provision (or related system standard or operations manual provision) is essential to ensure the franchisor can properly enforce the rights created by this section.

G. Compliance with All Laws and Good Business Practices; Taxes

1. Franchisee must secure and maintain in force in its name all required licenses, permits and certificates relating to the operation of the Franchised Business. Franchisee must operate the Franchised Business in full compliance with all applicable laws, ordinances and regulations including, without limitation, all laws or regulations governing or relating to the handling of food products, immigration and discrimination, occupational hazards and health insurance, employment and labor laws, including, without limitation, workers' compensation insurance, unemployment insurance, and the withholding and payment of federal and state income taxes, social security taxes and sales taxes. All advertising and promotion by Franchisee must be completely factual and must conform to the highest standards of ethical advertising. Franchisee must, in all dealings with Franchisee's customers, suppliers and the public, adhere to the highest standards of honesty, integrity, fair dealing and ethical conduct. Franchisee agrees to refrain from any business or advertising practice that may be injurious to the goodwill associated with the Proprietary Marks or the business of Franchisor or its affiliates, the System or other restaurants operated or franchised by Franchisor or its affiliates.

2. Franchisee must promptly pay when due all taxes levied or assessed, including, without limitation, income, unemployment, and sales taxes, and all accounts and other indebtedness of every kind incurred by Franchisee in the conduct of the business

franchised under this Agreement. Franchisee must pay Franchisor an amount equal to any sales tax, gross receipts tax, or similar tax (other than income tax) imposed on Franchisor with respect to any payments to Franchisor required under this Agreement, unless the tax is credited against income tax otherwise payable by Franchisor.

3. In the event of any bona fide dispute as to Franchisee's liability for taxes assessed or other indebtedness, Franchisee may contest the validity or the amount of the tax or indebtedness in accordance with procedures of the taxing authority or applicable law; however, in no event shall Franchisee permit a tax sale or seizure by levy of execution or similar writ or warrant, or attachment by a creditor, to occur against the premises of the Franchised Business, or any improvements thereon.

4. Franchisee must notify Franchisor in writing within XX days after the commencement of: (a) any action, suit or proceeding, or the issuance of any order, writ, injunction, award or decree of any court, agency or other governmental instrumentality, which may adversely affect the operation or financial condition of Franchisee or the Franchised Business; or (b) of any notice of violation of any law, ordinance or regulation relating to health or sanitation at the Franchised Business.

Discussion:

Franchise agreements typically contain a provision that requires the franchisee to comply with all laws applicable to the franchised business. This provision can be short and generally requires compliance with all local, state, and federal laws.[126] Alternatively, additional language can be included to specifically reference certain laws of particular importance to the franchised business. The sample language goes further and requires the franchisee to also comply with good business practices, specifically describing certain behavior important to the franchisor and the franchise system.

The franchisee's requirement to pay all taxes assessed against the franchised business is critical to the franchise agreement, and must be included, if not in the operations section then in the accounting and records provisions. Failure of the franchisee to pay any taxes can then be asserted by the franchisor as a default under the franchise agreement. Likewise, the provision that requires the franchisee to maintain all licenses and permits relevant to the business is crucial. In some systems, such as senior care or preschool/daycare systems, the franchisee may be required to have specific approvals or certifications in order to operate the business, and the lack, or lapse, of these permits can shut down the business and create a public relations problem.

---

126. *See* Section XIV in the following text regarding the importance of including a requirement to comply with all employment laws.

XI. System Standards and Modification of System

A. Modifications of the System

1. System Modifications

Franchisor will be entitled from time to time to change or modify the System, including modifications to the Manuals, the System Standards, the menu and menu formats, the required equipment, the signage, the building and premises of the Franchised Business (including the trade dress, decor, and color schemes), the presentation of the Proprietary Marks, the adoption of new administrative forms and methods of reporting and of payment of any monies owed to Franchisor (including electronic means of reporting and payment), and the adoption and use of new or modified Proprietary Marks or copyrighted materials. Franchisee must accept and use or display in the Franchised Business any such changes or modifications to the System as if they were a part of the System at the time this Agreement was executed, and Franchisee will make such expenditures as the changes or modifications in the System may require.

2. Variations from System Standards

Franchisor has the right to waive, defer, or permit variations from the System Standards or the applicable agreement to any franchisee or prospective franchisee based on the peculiarities of a particular site, existing building configuration or circumstance, density of population, business potential, trade area population, or any other condition or circumstance without providing the same or any variations to Franchisee. Franchisor shall have the right to deny any such request.

3. Franchisee's Development of System Improvements

If Franchisee develops any new concepts, processes, or improvements relating to the System, whether or not pursuant to a Franchisor's authorized test, Franchisee promptly must notify Franchisor and provide Franchisor with all information regarding the new concept, process, or improvement, all of which shall, at Franchisor's option, automatically become the property of Franchisor and its affiliates and which may be incorporated, in Franchisor's sole discretion, into the System without any payment to Franchisee. If Franchisor so elects, Franchisee, at its expense, promptly must take all actions deemed necessary or desirable by Franchisor to vest in Franchisor's ownership of such concepts, processes, or improvements.

Discussion:

Fundamentally, the purpose of a franchise agreement's operational provisions is to provide the franchisor with the ability to implement and enforce standards and other operating requirements that are needed in order to maintain consistency and quality operations in its franchise system. Ensuring that the franchise agreement's provisions related to the operation of the franchised business are sufficiently detailed to address key operational issues and, at the same time, general enough to provide the franchisor with flexibility to adapt to market and other changes during the relatively lengthy term of the franchise agreement is crucial in the drafting of any franchise agreement.

Virtually every modern franchise agreement obligates the franchisee to comply with the franchisor's standards to ensure uniformity in the system and to protect the franchisor's trademarks and related goodwill. Further, franchise agreements generally permit the franchisor to modify the standards and require that the franchisees comply with those modified standards, even if the franchisees' compliance with such modified standards would result in (sometimes substantial) expenditures by the franchisees. But, how far can a franchisor go in changing the system and standards and requiring franchisees to comply?[127]

As a general matter, courts have recognized that franchisors may make changes to their franchise systems by modifying the brand (or system) standards under which the franchisees are contractually obligated to operate. Franchise agreements are long-term contracts, and changes to standards provide a mechanism for the franchisors to adjust to market changes and competitive challenges that occur over the term of the franchise agreement.

However, there are limitations on the franchisor's ability to require system changes through modifications to standards. Those limitations include:

- The language of the franchise agreement. The franchise agreement should permit the franchisor to act through standards in the area of the business at issue, and the change in operating procedures mandated by the change in standards must not contradict an express term of the franchise agreement. The franchisees challenging a change in standards also may argue that other system documents (e.g., the franchise disclosure document (FDD) or agreements ancillary to the franchise agreement) contain terms of the parties' agreement that would be breached if the franchisor were permitted to require compliance with the proposed change in brand standards. Additionally, notwithstanding the presence of integration clauses in most franchise agreements, oral or other extra-contractual communications with the franchisees can be a factor in the outcome of disputes related to system changes.
- Common law principles, such as the covenant of good faith and fair dealing and similar theories.
- Where applicable, state statutes designed to protect the interests of the franchisees.

While the outcomes of the various cases range from good to bad from the perspective of franchisors, most decisions are highly fact-specific and are impacted by specific contractual language, application of particular state statutes, the degree of financial impact on the franchisees, and, to some extent, jurisdictional biases.

---

127. *See generally* David A. Beyer, Himanshu M. Patel, & John Dent, *Changes in System Standards: What Is the Extent of the Franchisor's Latitude?*, ABA 35th Annual Forum on Franchising (2012).

A number of the decisions in this area suggest that the courts often struggle to balance the equities at issue in a particular case.[128] The franchisor's chances of success are arguably better where it can show that a change in brand standards is necessary for the franchise system to remain competitive and that the change is made for the purpose of benefiting the franchise system as a whole and not primarily to generate additional revenue for, or otherwise benefit, only the franchisor.[129] Chances of success are arguably less where the change requires a significant financial investment by the franchisees or where the franchisees have a credible position that the change may result in operating losses.[130] However, market-driven factors favoring the change may not be sufficient to overcome express language of the franchise agreement limiting the franchisor's right to make the desired change.

If franchisees sue to challenge a franchisor's right to make changes, even if the franchisor is ultimately successful in mandating system changes through modifications to brand standards, the issues are not easily resolved at the early stages through summary judgment or motions to dismiss and may be fully litigated.

XII. Sourcing Restrictions and Supplier Rebates/Bonuses

A. Approved Suppliers

> Franchisee must purchase all products, ingredients, supplies, materials, furnishings (including décor), fixtures and equipment, merchandise and other products used in the construction and development of the Franchised Business and/or offered for sale at the Franchised Business solely from suppliers that Franchisor has approved in writing, which may be Franchisor or its affiliates or a buying cooperative that Franchisor organizes. In determining whether it will approve any

128. *See, e.g.*, Bores v. Domino's Pizza, LLC, 530 F.3d 671 (8th Cir. 2008) (Through an arguably tortured interpretation of the franchise agreement, which appeared to provide that franchisees could use a computer system from any source so long as it met the franchisor's specifications, the Eighth Circuit held that the franchisor could require franchisees to purchase and use only the franchisor's custom-designed integrated computer system.).

129. *See, e.g.*, Remus v. Amoco Oil Co., 794 F.2d 1238 (7th Cir. 1986) (Where franchisee argued that a discount program implemented by the franchisor under which franchisees who attracted more credit card business would experience negative financial impact constituted fraud, breach of contract, and a violation of the Wisconsin Fair Dealership Law, since the law required that the franchisor obtain unanimous consent to implement a system-wide change, Seventh Circuit disagreed and held that such an interpretation would not serve franchisees as a whole because a proposed change that would benefit most franchisees could be blocked by a handful of dissenters.); Trail Burger King, Inc. v. Burger King of Miami, Inc., 187 So. 2d 55 (Fla. Dist. Ct. App. 1966) (Court held that one of the objects of the franchise agreement was to achieve uniformity among franchisees, and that to accomplish such uniformity the agreement permitted franchisor to dictate the standards and specifications that franchisees were required to follow; thus, changes to the standards or specifications were not modifications or amendments to the agreement, but were provided for in the franchise agreement.).

130. *See, e.g.*, Beilowitz v. Gen. Motors Corp., 233 F. Supp. 2d 631 (D.N.J. 2002) (The franchisor revised its business strategy, imposing a new territorial limit that required franchisee to stop selling automobile parts outside of a specified area, which would have resulted in franchisee losing $11 million (40 percent) of its sales. In responding to the franchisee's request for injunctive relief to stop the implementation of the strategy, the Federal District Court for New Jersey granted the injunction, stating that "[i]t is clearly an 'unreasonable standard of performance' within the meaning of the [NJFPA] to require a franchisee to operate at a substantial financial loss while the franchisor attempts to implement a new and unproven marketing strategy.").

particular supplier, Franchisor shall consider various factors, including a supplier who can demonstrate, to Franchisor's continuing reasonable satisfaction, the ability to meet Franchisor's then-current standards and specifications for such items; who possesses adequate quality controls and capacity to supply Franchisee's needs promptly and reliably; who would enable the System, in Franchisor's sole opinion, to take advantage of marketplace efficiencies; and who has been approved in writing by Franchisor prior to any purchases by Franchisee from any such supplier, and has not thereafter been disapproved. For the purpose of this Agreement, the term "supplier" shall include, but not be limited to, manufacturers, distributors, resellers, and other vendors. Franchisee recognizes that Franchisor shall have the right to appoint only one manufacturer, distributor, reseller, and/or another vendor for any particular item, and that Franchisor may so designate itself or its affiliate. Franchisee acknowledges that Franchisor may profit from its sale of such items to Franchisee or receive rebates or other consideration from the third party supplier with respect to Franchisee's purchases of such items.

B. Approval of Alternative Suppliers

If Franchisee wishes to purchase any products or any items from an unapproved supplier, Franchisee must first submit to Franchisor a written request for such approval. Franchisee must not purchase any products or services from any supplier until, and unless, such supplier has been approved in writing by Franchisor. Franchisor shall have the right to require that its representatives be permitted to inspect the supplier's facilities, and that samples from the supplier be delivered, either to Franchisor or to an independent laboratory designated by Franchisor for testing. A charge not to exceed the reasonable cost of the inspection and the actual cost of the test must be paid by Franchisee or the supplier. Franchisor may also require that the supplier comply with such other requirements as Franchisor may deem appropriate, including payment of reasonable continuing inspection fees and administrative costs, or other payment to Franchisor by the supplier on account of their dealings with Franchisee or other franchisees, for use, without restriction (unless otherwise instructed by the supplier) and for services that Franchisor may render to such suppliers. Franchisor reserves the right, at its option, to reinspect from time to time the facilities and products of any such approved supplier and to revoke its approval upon the supplier's failure to continue to meet any of Franchisor's then-current criteria. Nothing in the foregoing shall be construed to require Franchisor to approve any particular supplier, nor to require Franchisor to make available to prospective suppliers, standards and specifications for formulas, which Franchisor shall have the right to deem confidential.

C. Purchasing Arrangements

Notwithstanding anything to the contrary contained in this Agreement, Franchisee acknowledges and agrees that, at Franchisor's sole option, Franchisor may establish one or more strategic alliances, purchasing and/or distribution cooperatives or preferred vendor programs with one or more nationally or regionally-known suppliers who are willing to supply all or some of the Restaurants with some or all of the products and/or services that Franchisor requires for use and/or sale in the development and/or operation of the Restaurants. In this event, Franchisor may limit the number of approved suppliers with whom Franchisee may deal, designate sources that Franchisee must use for some or all products and other products and services, and/or refuse any of Franchisee's requests if Franchisor believes that this action is in the best interests of the System. Franchisor shall have unlimited discretion to approve or disapprove of the suppliers who may be permitted to sell products to Franchisee. Franchisor may charge a surcharge to Franchisee on any items purchased from approved suppliers for Franchisor's role in managing the purchasing and distribution contracts for the System.

D. Allowances

Franchisee acknowledges and agrees that Franchisor shall have the right to collect and retain all manufacturing allowances, marketing allowances, rebates, credits, monies, payments or benefits (collectively, "Allowances") offered by suppliers to Franchisee or to Franchisor or its affiliates based upon Franchisee's purchases of products and other goods and services. These Allowances are based on System-wide purchases of food, beverages, alcohol, paper goods, merchandise and other items. Franchisee assigns to Franchisor or its designee all of Franchisee's right, title and interest in and to any and all such Allowances and authorizes Franchisor or its designee to collect and retain any or all such Allowances without restriction (unless otherwise instructed by the supplier); provided, however, that Franchisor's current policy is to utilize such funds for purposes that Franchisor believes may enhance the System and the Proprietary Marks and/or public awareness of the Restaurants.

E. Obligations to Suppliers

Franchisee must comply with all terms, conditions, and obligations of all contracts and arrangements with suppliers, including contracts and arrangements negotiated by Franchisor or third parties as part of a network or multiple-franchise or multiple-restaurant supply and distribution arrangement, and Franchisee's contracts with and obligations to suppliers. Franchisee must promptly pay all suppliers in accordance with the agreed-upon terms. In the event Franchisee fails to promptly pay one or more suppliers as required, Franchisor may, but is not required to, pay such supplier(s) on behalf of Franchisee, and Franchisee must promptly reimburse Franchisor for such payment following notice from Franchisor, or Franchisor may obtain payment through the electronic process described in Section XX above and the Manuals.

Discussion:

Franchisors typically require franchisees to purchase goods, services, and supplies from suppliers that have been approved by the franchisor. There are a number of benefits to both the franchisor and the franchisees from this practice, including

> (a) maintaining product quality, standardization and uniformity that are important to the image and integrity of the franchise system; (b) assuring regular sources of supply at relatively stable and predictable prices; (c) enabling the franchisor to reduce the cost of delivering supplies to the franchisees because of the leverage created by the franchisees' collective purchases, allowing the franchisor to negotiate lower prices; and (d) increasing accountability for the safety of the products distributed.[131]

In addition to these benefits, many franchisors receive a significant amount of revenue from either the direct sale of goods and services to the franchisees or from rebates or other payments from approved vendors based on the franchisees' purchases from such vendors. As a result, sourcing restrictions and vendor rebates are a significant point of contention between a franchisor and its franchisees, which can lead to litigation as discussed in the following.[132]

Sourcing restrictions vary across franchise systems, depending on the type and size of the system. The franchisors may (1) provide required specifications for the goods and supplies but not the vendors from which the franchisees can purchase these items, (2) require the franchisees purchase only from approved vendors but not provide specifications for the items purchased, (3) require the franchisees purchase goods and supplies that meet the franchisor's specifications only from approved vendors, or (4) require the franchisees purchase some or all goods and supplies directly from the franchisor or its affiliate.[133] Many systems require the franchisees to use inventory items or supplies that are proprietary to the franchisor, and such items are often sold to the franchisees directly by the franchisor or its affiliate. In restaurant systems, the source of many of the food items is of critical importance given the food safety risks associated with the supply chain. Not only will the franchisor want the suppliers to meet the franchisor's specifications, it will also want to ensure that each supplier complies with all applicable food safety requirements.

To effectively draft language for sourcing restrictions, the franchisor must first decide whether it will approve inventory items, supplies, and other goods the franchisee must use but allow the franchisee to purchase inventory and supplies from any vendor, or whether it will approve inventory items and approve specific vendors from which the franchisee must purchase those items.[134] Does the franchisor have proprietary items it requires the franchisees to use? Is the franchisor or its affiliate a supplier of the proprietary products or other approved products? This analy-

131. Lee N. Abrams & Robert T. Joseph, *Vendor Rebates: Considerations in Drafting and Litigating*, ABA 34th Annual Forum on Franchising 1 (2011); *see also* Chesley K. "Bud" Culp III & Rochelle B. Spandorf, *Sourcing Products and Services for the System: Efficiencies and Traps in Supply Chain Management*, ABA 32nd Annual Forum on Franchising (2009).

132. *See* Gregg A. Rubenstein & Robert Salkowski, *The Five Most Litigated Provisions in the Franchise Disclosure Document*, ABA 34th Annual Forum on Franchising 8–10 (2011); Dillon, Vines, & Tegt, *supra* note 56, at 13–14.

133. Kerry Olson, Robin M. Spencer, & Larry Weinberg, *The Annotated Franchise Agreement*, ABA 33rd Annual Forum on Franchising 37 (2010).

134. Jamila B. Granger, David W. Oppenheim, & Brian B. Schnell, *Fundamentals 201: Advanced Drafting of Franchise Agreements*, ABA 36th Annual Forum on Franchising 45 (2013).

sis will differ depending on whether the franchise system is a product or service franchise. If the franchise system is still young and the franchisor does not have a robust sourcing program, the franchisor should reserve the right in the franchise agreement to change the supply chain as the system matures, thereby allowing the franchisor in the future to require the franchisees to purchase inventory directly from the franchisor or only from approved vendors, as well as reserving the right to retain any rebates or other payments the franchisor may receive in the future from approved vendors.[135] After this analysis is complete, the franchisor must also determine if it will include the more detailed language of its sourcing restrictions in the franchise agreement as the sample language reflects, or if it prefers to keep the franchise agreement language brief and include the specific requirements in its operations manual. In either case, the operations manual will undoubtedly include the specific inventory items and vendors approved by the franchisor and any forms or processes established by the franchisor to approve vendors or inventory items over time. This provides the franchisor with greater flexibility during the term of the franchise agreement, as products or vendors may change. Deciding whether to include the longer provisions about its sourcing requirements in the franchise agreement may depend on the franchisor's concerns about the overall length of the franchise agreement. At a minimum, the franchisor must include language that creates its right to impose sourcing restrictions on its franchisees.

As noted previously, sourcing restrictions and vendor rebates can create friction between the franchisor and its franchisees. While systemwide approved vendors often provide required items to the franchisees at a lower cost based on volume purchases across the system, many franchisees complain that they could obtain similar products at a lower cost from other vendors. Franchise agreements typically contain language like the sample language in the preceding text to give the franchisee a mechanism to request that a specific vendor become an approved supplier. If a vendor can meet the franchisor's specifications for a product and can ensure the continued quality and quantity of the item as required by the franchisor, the franchisor can approve the vendor for use by the franchisee. This can create goodwill between the franchisor and the franchisee, as well as reduce the franchisee's costs for certain inventory items or supplies. If the franchisor is receiving any rebates or bonuses from existing approved vendors, or is supplying the product directly, its revenues will be directly impacted by approving another vendor to supply one or more franchisees and therefore the franchisor will likely not approve such vendor. The franchise agreement should expressly state that the franchisor is not obligated to approve any such vendor request and any such approval is at the franchisor's sole discretion. This is essential for the franchisor to avoid any claim of a breach of the covenant of good faith and fair dealing if it denies approval to a franchisee's proposed vendor.[136]

---

135. *Id.*

136. *See* DavCo Acquisition Holding, Inc. v. Wendy's Int'l, Inc., 2008 WL 755283 (S.D. Ohio Mar. 19, 2008); *see also* Timothy J. Bryant, Susan Grueneberg, & Jane W. LaFranchi, *Keep It Simple! Drafting a Pragmatic Franchise Agreement Against the Backdrop of Over Fifty Years of Franchise Law Precedent*, ABA 35th Annual Forum on Franchising 6–11 (2012).

Given the potential conflicts that can arise when the franchisor requires its franchisees to purchase goods and services that meet the franchisor's specifications only from vendors approved by the franchisor, as well as the franchisor receiving any rebates or other payments from such purchases, the Federal Trade Commission (FTC) has long required that the franchisor make specific disclosures about its sourcing program and restrictions in Item 8 of its FDD.[137]

These disclosures include details about the restrictions imposed on the franchisees on their purchases of goods and supplies, as well as details about the rebates and other amounts received by the franchisor from system vendors and revenue received by the franchisor and its affiliates based on purchases of products and services by its franchisees. When drafting the franchise agreement and FDD, it is important that the language in the franchise agreement (and related operations manual provisions) is consistent with the disclosures made in Item 8.

While the proper disclosures in Item 8 provide a prospective franchisee with information regarding the franchisor's sourcing requirements, it does not eliminate the conflicts that often arise when the franchisees believe that they are being charged noncompetitive prices by the franchisor's approved vendors. The franchisor's receipt of revenue from these approved vendors only adds fuel to the franchisees' discontent. If the relationship is already troubled, franchisees have attacked the franchisor's sourcing requirements among other claims brought against a franchisor. The franchisees have used a variety of claims to attack the franchisor's sourcing requirements, in particular its vendor rebates, most notably by arguing that these restrictions violate state and federal antitrust laws.[138] One of the most frequently asserted antitrust claims is that the franchisor has improperly "tied" the purchase of a product in a market where the franchisor has market power with the purchase of goods sold by the approved vendor.[139] In a franchise context, the tying product is alleged to be the purchase of the franchise and the tied product is the item(s) the franchisor requires the franchisee to purchase. Franchisees then allege that the franchisor benefits from the rebates (often described as "kickbacks") from the vendors.

To establish a tying claim, plaintiffs must prove that the defendant has "appreciable economic power in the tying product market. Market power is the power 'to force a purchaser to do something that he would not do in a competitive market.'"[140] While early franchise-related antitrust cases pursued this theory based on the *Kodak*

137. 16 C.F.R. § 436.5(h) (2007); *see also* North American Securities Administrators Association (NASAA) 2008 Franchise Registration and Disclosure Guidelines, http://www.nasaa.org/wp-content/uploads/2011/08/6-2008 UFOC.pdf.

138. A full discussion of the antitrust theories applicable to franchising and franchisors' sourcing requirements is beyond the scope of this chapter. For more in-depth analysis of these issues, *see* Abrams & Joseph, *supra* note 131; Kay Lynn Brumbaugh & Allan P. Hillman, *Fundamentals 201: Antitrust Essentials for Franchise Lawyers*, ABA 35th Annual Forum on Franchising (2012); Robert T. Joseph, *Antitrust Law, Franchising, and Vertical Restraints*, 31 FRANCHISE L.J. (2011); James L. Petersen & Angela M. Fifelski, *State Tying Claims: Do You Know What Might Be Lurking?*, 21 FRANCHISE L.J. (2001).

139. Abrams & Joseph, *supra* note 131, at 4.

140. Eastman Kodak v. Image Technical Services, Inc., 504 U.S. 451, 464 (1992), citing to Jefferson Parish Hosp. Dist. No. 2 v. Hyde, 466 U.S. 2, 21 (1984).

decision, the Third Circuit later held that *Kodak* does not apply in a franchise context when the franchisee's obligation to purchase goods and supplies only from the franchisor or approved vendors arises contractually in the franchise agreement and these obligations are properly disclosed prior to the franchisee entering into the franchise agreement.[141] Since the Third Circuit's opinion in *Queen City*, "courts generally have been unreceptive to arguments from the franchisees that they were 'locked in' to an aftermarket of the franchisor's approved supplies, at least where there was no change in the franchisor's supply policy and the policy was fully disclosed to franchisees in the FDD or the franchise agreement."[142] However, as noted previously, failing to properly draft these provisions in the franchise agreement and fully disclose details of the franchisor's sourcing requirements in Item 8 may result in a franchisee making a successful tying claim, alleging it was not aware of these requirements prior to entering into the franchise agreement.[143] Careful drafting of the provisions regarding rebates is needed, in particular for emerging and growing franchise systems. The franchise agreement terms must be specific enough to give the prospective franchisee notice of the franchisor's right to collect rebates, while leaving flexibility for the franchisor to make changes to its sourcing requirements and rebate practices if the franchisor's or the system's needs change over time.[144]

Franchisees have brought vendor rebate-related claims against franchisors under other legal theories. Some have relied upon Section 2(c) of the Robinson-Patman Act[145] to allege commercial bribery.[146] Others have used a wide variety of federal and state fraud and misrepresentation theories or have alleged breach of contract.[147] While most of these matters have ultimately been resolved in the franchisor's favor, these cases are very fact intensive and time consuming. Proper drafting of the franchise agreement language and FDD, as well as compliance with the franchisor's own policies during the term of the franchise agreement, are essential to defeat these claims.

It is also important to note that several state franchise relationship laws place limitations on a franchisor's sourcing requirements.[148] While these relationship laws make it an unfair or deceptive act or practice to require a franchisee to buy or lease goods from the franchisor or designated suppliers unless the purchasing requirements are reasonably necessary for a lawful purpose, the franchisor is typically permitted to set required specifications for the goods and services used in the franchised business and publish a list of approved suppliers. Franchise counsel

---

141. Queen City Pizza, Inc. v. Domino's Pizza, Inc., 124 F.3d 430 (1997).

142. Abrams & Joseph, *supra* note 131, at 11. *See also* Window World of Baton Rouge, LLC v. Window World, Inc., Nos. 15 CVS 1, 2, 2016 NCBC 80, Bus. Franchise Guide (CCH) ¶ 54,880, 2016 WL 6242945 (N.C. Super. Ct. Oct. 25, 2016).

143. *See* Little Caesars Enterprises, Inc. v. Smith, 34 F. Supp. 459 (E.D. Mich. 1998).

144. Abrams & Joseph, *supra* note 131, at 37.

145. 15 U.S.C. § 13(c) (1936).

146. *See* 2660 Woodley Rd. Joint Venture v. ITT Sheraton Corp., 369 F.3d 732 (3d Cir. 2004) and In Town Hotels Ltd. P'ship v. Marriott Intern., Inc., 246 F. Supp. 2d 469 (S.D. W. Va. 2003).

147. For an in-depth discussion of these claims, *see* Abrams & Joseph, *supra* note 131.

148. *See* HAW. REV. STAT. § 482E-6(2)(B); IND. CODE § 23-2-2.7-1(1), and RCW 19.100.180(2)(b).

must be aware of these state relationship laws and the impact they may have on a franchisor's proposed sourcing requirements.

Finally, while the sample language provided does not contemplate that the franchise system has formed a purchasing co-op, many systems today do operate a purchasing co-op and require their franchisees to join the co-op. If such a co-op exists, the franchise agreement language must provide for this and the requirement that the franchisee participate in the co-op. If the system does not currently operate a co-op, the franchisor may wish to reserve the right to form a co-op in the future.[149]

XIII. Restrictions on Products and Services Offered by the Franchised Business and Pricing Considerations

A. Product and Service Standards and Uniformity of Operation

Products sold and services performed under the Proprietary Marks have a reputation for quality. This reputation has been developed and maintained by Franchisor, and it is of the utmost importance to Franchisor, Franchisee, and all other franchisees of Franchisor that this reputation be maintained. In recognition of the mutual benefits that come from maintaining the reputation for quality enjoyed by the System, Franchisee covenants and agrees, with respect to the operation of the Franchised Business, that Franchisee and its employees must comply with all of the requirements of the System as set forth in the Manuals or otherwise, and Franchisee additionally must comply with the following:

To ensure that the highest degree of quality and service is maintained, Franchisee must operate the Franchised Business in strict conformity with such methods, standards, and specifications as Franchisor may from time to time prescribe in the Manuals or otherwise in writing. Therefore, Franchisee will:

1. Maintain in sufficient supply, and use and/or sell at all times, only such products, ingredients, materials, supplies, merchandise, and paper goods as conform to Franchisor's written standards and specifications, and to refrain from deviating therefrom by the use or offer of any nonconforming items without Franchisor's specific, prior, written consent.
2. Sell or offer for sale only such products as have been expressly approved for sale in writing by Franchisor; sell or offer for sale all such products, utilizing the ingredients and employing the preparation standards and techniques, as specified by Franchisor; refrain from any deviation from Franchisor's standards and specifications, including the manner of preparation of products, without Franchisor's prior written consent; and discontinue selling and offering for sale any products which Franchisor shall have the right to disapprove, in writing, at any time. If Franchisee deviates or proposes to deviate from Franchisor's standards

149. For more in-depth discussion of purchasing co-ops, *see* Joyce Mazero & Suzie Loonam, *Purchasing Cooperatives: Leveraging a Supply Chain for Competitive Advantage*, 29 Franchise L.J. 148 (2010) and Gina Romo, R. James Straus, & Suzanne Trigg, *Building an Effective Supply Chain and Distribution System*, 35th ABA Annual Forum on Franchising (2012).

and specifications, whether or not such deviation is approved by Franchisor, such deviation will become the property of Franchisor.

3. Permit Franchisor or its agents, at any reasonable time, to remove samples of products, without payment therefor, in amounts reasonably necessary for testing by Franchisor or an independent laboratory to determine whether such samples meet Franchisor's then-current standards and specifications. In addition to any other remedies it may have under this Agreement, Franchisor may require Franchisee to bear the cost of such testing if the supplier of the item has not previously been approved by Franchisor or if the sample fails to conform to Franchisor's specifications.
4. Purchase and install, at Franchisee's expense, all fixtures, furnishings, equipment, decor, and signs as Franchisor shall specify; and refrain from installing or permitting to be installed on or about the Franchised Business premises, without Franchisor's prior written consent, any fixtures, furnishings, equipment, decor, signs, or other items not previously approved as meeting Franchisor's standards and specifications.
5. Fully and faithfully comply with all applicable governing authorities, laws and regulations. Franchisee must immediately close the Franchised Business and terminate operations in the event that: (a) any products sold at the Franchised Business evidence adulteration or deviation from the standards set for products by Franchisor; (b) any products sold at the Franchised Business fail to comply with applicable laws or regulations; or (c) Franchisee fails to maintain the products, Franchised Business premises, equipment, personnel, or operation of the Franchised Business in accordance with any applicable law or regulations. In the event of such closing, Franchisee must immediately notify Franchisor in writing, and Franchisee must immediately undertake all action required by Franchisor or any regulatory authority having jurisdiction to either remove or destroy such products from the premises or preserve such products. Franchisee must not reopen the Franchised Business until after Franchisor has inspected the Franchised Business premises and Franchisor has determined that Franchisee has corrected the condition and that all products sold at the Franchised Business comply with Franchisor's standards.

Discussion:

A core element of virtually every franchise system is the desire for uniformity of the products and services experienced by customers at franchised units of a particular system, regardless of location.[150] The ability to mandate the products and services that

150. Although uniformity is still the rule in most franchise systems, in an effort to address changing consumer tastes, there is an increasing trend toward "localization" of products and services offered by non-franchised and franchised businesses alike; *see, e.g.*, Teresa Gubbins, *Shake Shack Dallas Menu Incorporates Goods from 3 Local Food Favorites*, CultureMap Dallas (Aug. 29, 2016, 9:55 AM), http://dallas.culturemap.com/news/restaurants-bars/08-29-16-shake-shack-secret-dallas-menu-pecan-lodge/#slide=0. Similarly, the lack of uniformity is driving growth of "collection" brands in the hotel industry; *see, e.g.*, Julie Sickel, *The Rise of Hotel "Collection" Brands*, Business Travel News (July 7, 2017), http://www.businesstravelnews.com/Procurement/The-Rise-of-Hotel-Collection-Brands.

franchisees can offer (and must offer) is present in virtually every modern franchise agreement. These provisions are different from, but closely related to, the supplier-related provisions of the franchise agreement discussed previously. Although sometimes confused, the provisions that are the subject of this section address the products and services that the franchisee is permitted and is required to offer and sell, while the supplier provisions relate to the source from which franchisees are permitted to purchase products and services.[151]

These sections of the franchise agreement will most often contain very broad and general requirements that the franchisee offer and sell all of the products and services that the franchisor requires and not offer any other products or services, with the specific requirements and prohibitions conveyed in the standards and other system communications. Depending on the industry, the franchise agreement itself may contain more specific requirements in this regard, for example, a restaurant franchise agreement may specifically require that the franchisee implement new menu items within a certain period of time after receiving notice from the franchisor that the item must be offered, or a hotel franchise agreement might specifically prohibit the franchisees from operating a casino or other gaming facilities, or offering "adult" in-room movies.

In addition to ensuring uniformity, these provisions also have the important function of protecting the franchisor's trademarks and the associated goodwill, which is, of course, a (if not *the*) core asset of any franchise system. Further, these provisions support the underlying, general obligation of the franchisee to operate in accordance with system standards, including compliance with applicable laws in the operation of franchised units.

B. Prices

> With respect to the sale of all menu items, products, merchandise, or services, Franchisee must be solely responsible for determining the prices of products offered at the Franchised Business; however, Franchisee is required to comply with any maximum or minimum resale pricing restrictions Franchisor may implement so long as such pricing does not violate applicable law.

Discussion:

Pricing restrictions on the products and services that franchisees offer is an issue that often arises in the context of the restrictions the franchisor imposes on the franchisee, and resale price maintenance is a particular concern in franchising given the "vertical" nature of the relationship.[152] Resale price maintenance (RPM, or vertical

---

151. The disclosures related to these aspects of the franchise relationship appear in different Items, with Item 8 addressing supplier matters and Item 16 addressing restrictions on products and services that franchisee may offer and sell through their franchised units.

152. Section 1 of the Sherman Act is the federal antitrust statute that prohibits every "contract, combination or conspiracy in restraint of trade." Aspects of certain franchise relationships may be "horizontal" for antitrust purposes as well, for example, where the franchisor's company-owned outlets compete against franchised outlets. *See, e.g.*, Quentin R. Wittrock & Jeremy L. Johnson, *Can Franchisors Control Franchisee Prices?*, 28 FRANCHISE

price fixing) is an agreement between a seller and a buyer as to the buyer's resale price, including either an actual or advertised resale price.[153]

It is important to understand the history of RPM issues with *some* historical context. In 1911, the U.S. Supreme Court held that *all* RPM agreements (maximum pricing and minimum pricing) were per se illegal; the only thing necessary for liability was proof that the parties had reached an express or tacit understanding as to resale price.[154] Then, in 1997, in the case of *State Oil v. Khan*,[155] the U.S. Supreme Court held that maximum resale price maintenance (that is, the requirement that a franchisee charge *no more* than a certain amount for a product or service) was no longer per se illegal and would be judged under the rule of reason. This ruling was viewed as pro-consumer, and maximum resale price maintenance is now generally accepted, subject to the rule of reason test.

Until 2007, minimum RPM (that is, the requirement that a franchisee charge *no less* than a certain amount for a product or service) continued to be per se illegal in the United States. In 2007, in the case of *Leegin Creative Leather Products, Inc. v. PSKS, Inc.*,[156] the U.S. Supreme Court held that minimum RPM was no longer per se illegal and that these arrangements would also be judged under the rule of reason. However, the ruling did not prevent states from continuing to prohibit minimum RPM under state antitrust laws, and a number of states continue to do so (including California, Maryland, New York, New Jersey, and Illinois). There have also been legislative moves at the federal level to attempt to override *Leegin*, none of which have yet been successful.

In an effort to avoid any agreements with the franchisees as to resale price or, at least, minimum resale price (in the franchise agreement and elsewhere), many franchisors continue to employ "brand equity programs" under which the franchisors only suggest prices and that the franchisee's "resale prices remain unilaterally its own, without economic discrimination or coercion."[157]

Given the continued uncertainty with respect to minimum RPM, provisions related to pricing restrictions must be drafted (and the implementation and enforcement of such pricing programs must be conducted) carefully in order to avoid

---

L.J. 199 (Spring 2009). Horizontal agreements may present the "classic case of a per se illegal agreement"—"one between competitors . . . to fix prices or divide customers between themselves, which is subject to criminal prosecution as well as civil liability." Richard J. Hoskins, Resale Price Maintenance under the Federal and State Antitrust Laws 1 (2010).

153. It is important to note that under a cooperative advertising program, a seller is permitted to condition participation in the program on the buyer's agreement to advertise at a certain price. In other words, even where a seller and buyer are prohibited from agreeing on buyer's actual or advertised resale price, the seller is not required to extend its co-op advertising support to a buyer who chooses to advertise at a price below (or above) the suggested resale price. *See, e.g.*, Hoskins, *supra* note 152, at 1.

154. Dr. Miles Med. Co. v. John D. Park & Sons Co., 220 U.S. 373 (1911).

155. State Oil Company v. Khan, 522 U.S. 3 (1997). Ordinarily, under the Rule of Reason analysis, a plaintiff alleging an antitrust violation must show (a) the existence of a contract, combination or conspiracy ("agreement") between the defendant and at least one other person, that (b) had an adverse effect on competition in a properly defined geographic and product market.

156. 551 U.S. 877, 127 S. Ct. 2705 (2007).

157. Hoskins, *supra* note 152, at 2. *See also* Wittrock, & Johnson, *supra* note 152.

running afoul of federal and state antitrust laws. In addition to antitrust concerns, drafters should be mindful that once a franchisor states in the franchise agreement that it will not mandate franchisee retail prices, it is contractually bound by that agreement, notwithstanding any later change in state antitrust law that might permit it to do so. Therefore, franchise agreements should be drafted flexibly to require the franchisees to comply with any pricing restrictions imposed by the franchisors that are permitted under applicable law.

XIV. Personnel and Management

A. Management and Personnel

1. The Franchised Business must, at all times, be under the on-site supervision of the Operating Principal or a Validated Manager who must meet, to the satisfaction of Franchisor, Franchisor's applicable training qualifications for their designated position. Franchisee must, at all times, employ at least XX Validated Managers for the Franchised Business. At Franchisee's option, the Operating Principal can be one of the Validated Managers. Franchisor shall have the right to interview and consent to each Operating Principal and each Multi-Unit Manager (as described in Section XX). Franchisor shall endeavor to conduct such interviews at the Franchised Business but may require that such interviews occur at Franchisor's corporate headquarters. Franchisee will bear all costs and expenses related to making these individuals available for such interviews.

2. Franchisee (or, if applicable, the Operating Principal) must remain active in overseeing the operations of the Franchised Business, including, without limitation, regular, periodic visits to the Franchised Business and sufficient communications with Franchisor to ensure that the Franchised Business's operations comply with the System Standards as promulgated by Franchisor from time to time in the Manuals or otherwise in written or oral communications.

3. Franchisee will have the sole authority and control over the day-to-day operations of the Franchised Business and its employees. Franchisee must hire all employees of the Franchised Business and be exclusively responsible for the terms of their employment, including but not limited to their compensation, taxes, benefits, safety, work schedules, work conditions, assignments, discipline and termination, and for the proper training of such employees in the operation of the Franchised Business. Franchisee must establish at the Franchised Business a Team Member Training Program for all employees that covers training for all System Standards as relevant to the employees' positions. At no time will Franchisee or Franchisee's employees be deemed to be employees of Franchisor. Franchisor has no right or obligation to direct Franchisee's employees or to operate the Franchised Business.

Discussion:

(i) Responsible Persons

All franchisors have criteria for selecting their franchisees to ensure their franchisees possess the appropriate skills, experience, and financial net worth or financial ability to operate a successful franchised business. Once a franchisee is approved, the franchisor requires the franchisee be involved in the operation of the franchised business. In many systems today, the franchisees own more than one location, thereby making it difficult for the franchisee to be involved in the day-to-day operation of each location. In those systems, the franchisors allow an operations principal or a multi-unit manager (various systems use different terms with the same intent) to operate the day-to-day business. Given the due diligence that the franchisor uses to initially select the franchisee, the franchisors typically retain approval rights over the individuals who will be responsible for the daily operations, making sure that each individual also possesses the necessary skills and experience to successfully operate the franchised business.[158] This often is extended to the managerial staff responsible for the operation of the franchised business.

Once those individuals are approved, the franchise agreement requires them to be present at the franchised location and operate the business. If the franchisee is not the individual operating the business on a daily basis, the franchisor wants to ensure that the individuals who are operating the business do so in accordance with the franchisor's standards. However, since the franchisee is ultimately responsible for compliance with the franchisor's standards and the terms of the franchise agreement, language is typically included in the franchise agreement that requires the franchisee to be active in the business and remain in contact with the franchisor.

The sample language provided in sections (1) and (2) in the preceding text are used in systems where the franchisee owns more than one location. For those systems in which the franchisee owns just one location, the franchise agreement will typically require the franchisee to be active in the day to day operation of the business and even prohibit the franchisee from participating in any other business. This language can be as simple as "the franchisee must devote its full time and attention to the establishment, development and operation of the franchised business."[159]

Historically, many forms of franchise agreement went further and required the franchisee to have a specified number of managers and employees. Some franchisors have also historically provided assistance to franchisees with employment-related issues. While these requirements or practices have been used to protect the goodwill associated with the franchisor's trademarks and to assist the franchisees, conflicts have often arisen with the principles of vicarious liability and the franchisor's intent to limit its liability for the franchisee's acts or omissions. The franchise agreement will typically include language that clearly states that the franchisee is an independent contractor.[160] This language, along with a properly drafted operations manual and the franchisor's operational practices, can often defeat a third party's claim that the franchisor is vicariously liable for the actions of the franchisee or its employees.

158. *See* Chapter 1 for a discussion of franchisor's approval rights.

159. Olson, Spencer, & Weinberg, *supra* note 133, at 33.

160. *See* Chapter 10.

(ii) Joint Employer

In recent years, there has been an increased focus on whether the franchisor is vicariously liable for employment law violations brought by employees of the franchisee or by various state or federal agencies under a joint employer theory. While plaintiffs' lawyers have historically attempted to hold the franchisor liable for its franchisee's alleged employment law violations, recent actions taken by the U.S. National Labor Relations Board (the NLRB) and the U.S. Department of Labor (the DOL) have increased the scrutiny on the franchisor's ability to control the terms and conditions of the franchisee's employees' employment.[161] To find a franchisor liable as a joint employer of its franchisee's employees, the long-held standard required a showing that the franchisor and the franchisee shared or codetermined matters governing the essential terms and conditions of the franchisee's employees employment.[162] This analysis was focused on whether the franchisor had direct and immediate control of such matters as the hiring, firing, discipline, and supervision of those employees. With its 2015 decision in *Browning-Ferris*,[163] the NLRB expanded the scope of the matters to be considered to include wages and hours, scheduling, overtime, and determining the manner and method of work performance. More importantly, the NLRB ruled that the control did not need to be direct or immediate but indirect control could be sufficient.[164]

Prior to its *Browning-Ferris* ruling, the NLRB began joint employment litigation against McDonald's USA, LLC, alleging that McDonald's is a joint employer with its franchisees.[165] In pursuing its joint employer argument, the NLRB has engaged in an extensive analysis of the McDonald's system. A settlement of this case was announced on March 19, 2018.[166] While the terms of the settlement were not disclosed, the settlement does not address whether or not McDonald's is a joint employer of its franchisees' employees,[167] leaving this issue open for ongoing analysis by the courts and state and federal legislation.

---

161. An in-depth discussion of these issues is beyond the scope of this book. For more details, *see* Joe Fittante, Justin Klein, & Karen Marchiano, *Griffin and Weil One Year Later: Has a Clearer Picture of the Joint Employer Conundrum Come into Focus?*, ABA 39th Annual Forum on Franchising (2016); Susan A. Grueneberg, Joshua Schneiderman, & Lulu Y. Chiu, *Drafting Franchise Agreements After* Patterson v. Domino's: *Avoiding the Minefield of Vicarious Liability and Joint Employment*, 36 Franchise L.J. 189–218 (2016); Christopher J. Wallace, James B. Shrimp, & Susan Grueneberg, *Walking the Line: Best Practices for Advising Franchise Clients on Avoiding Employment Risks*, ABA 38th Annual Forum on Franchising (2015).

162. Fittante, Klein & Marchiano, *supra* note 161, at 2.

163. Browning-Ferris Industries of California, Inc., 362 N.L.R.B. 186 (2015). While not a franchise-related case, the NLRB's ruling in this case has been anticipated to be extended to franchise-related cases. *But see* Advice Memorandum, N.L.R.B., Office of the General Counsel, Nutritionality, Inc. d/b/a Freshii, Case 12-CA-134294 (Apr. 28, 2015), in which the NLRB found no evidence in the Freshii system that the franchisor affected the employment relationship between the franchisee and its employees.

164. *Browning-Ferris*, 362 N.L.R.B. 186 (2015), at 2.

165. *McDonald's USA, LLC.*, 02-CA-093893, https://www.nlrb.gov/case/02-CA-093893.

166. Daniel Wiessner, *McDonald's Agrees Settlement in Franchisees' U.S. Labor Case*, REUTERS (Mar. 19, 2018, 1:28 PM), https://www.reuters.com/article/us-mcdonalds-nlrb/mcdonalds-agrees-settlement-in-franchisees-u-s-labor-case-idUSKBN1GV2BL.

167. *Id.*

In early 2016, the DOL issued an interpretation opinion that arguably broadened the joint employer analysis even further.[168] The DOL guidance stated it would "not only analyze the control present in the relationship, but also the economic realities of the relationship, and specifically the economic dependence of the workers on the putative employer."[169] The DOL provided seven broad factors it would use as guides in analyzing the level of economic dependence.[170]

The changing political environment in 2017 led to the DOL's withdrawal of this 2016 guidance. The U.S. Congress is actively working to pass federal legislation that would rescind the NLRB's ruling by changing the definition of "employer" in both the National Labor Relations Act and the Fair Labor Standards Act. Under The Save Local Business Act,[171] a company could only be considered a joint employer with another employer if it directly, actually, and immediately has control over essential terms and conditions of employment.

Additionally, a number of states have passed laws that limit, to varying degrees, a franchisor's liability as a joint employer of its franchisees' employees.[172] These laws help clarify the franchisor's liability as to the relevant state employment laws, but do not address liability under the federal employment laws.[173]

While the legislative and regulatory landscape relating to joint employment continues to evolve, the courts have continued to use differing theories to analyze joint employer claims brought by the franchisees' employees against the franchisor. One of the most noteworthy cases in recent years is the California Supreme Court's ruling in *Patterson v. Domino's Pizza*.[174] The California Supreme Court ruled that a franchisor could potentially be liable as a joint employer of the franchisee only if "it has retained or assumed a general right of control over factors such as hiring, direction, supervision, discipline, discharge, and relevant day-to-day aspects of the workplace behavior of the franchisee's employees."[175] The court found that Domino's system standards did not create this level of control but rather were necessary to protect Domino's trademarks and goodwill. Subsequent cases have pro-

---

168. Administrator's Interpretation No. 2016-1, U.S. Department of Labor: Wage and Hour Division, http://www.dol.gov/whd/opinion/adminIntrptnFLSA.htm. This informal guidance was withdrawn by the DOL effective June 7, 2017.

169. Fittante, Klein, & Marchiano, *supra* note 161, at 5.

170. *Id.*

171. H.R. 3441-115 Congress (2017–2018). This bill was passed in the U.S. House of Representatives on November 7, 2017, and sent to the U.S. Senate where it remains pending as of the writing of this chapter.

172. ALA. CODE § 25-6-5; ARIZ. REV. STAT. § 23-1604; ARK. CODE § 11-2-125; GA. CODE ANN. § 34-1-9; IND. CODE § 23-2-2.5-0.5; KY. REV. STAT. §§ 337.010(1)(e)(1), 338.021(2), 341.070(14), 342.690(4), 344.030(5); LA. STAT. § 23:921; MICH. COMP. LAWS §§ 408.1005, 408.471, 408.412, 421.41, 445.1504B; N.C. GEN. STAT. § 95-25.24A; N.D. CENT. CODE § 51-19-18; N.H. REV. STAT. § 275:4; OKLA. ST. ANN tit. 59 § 6005; S.D. CODIFIED LAWS § 60-1-6; TENN. CODE ANN. § 50-1-208; TEX. LABOR CODE ANN. §§ 21.0022, 61.0031, 62.0006, 91.0013, 201.021, 401.014, 411.005; UTAH CODE ANN. §§ 31A-40-102, 31A-40-212, 34-20-2, 34-20-14, 34-28-2, 34-40-102, 34A-2-103, 34A-5-102, 34A-6-103, 35A-4-203; WIS. STAT. ANN. §§ 102.04, 104.015, 108.065, 109-015, 111.3205; WYO. STAT. § 27-1-116.

173. *See* Allison R. Grow & Adrienne L. Saltz, *Effectiveness of the Legislative Response to Joint Employer Liability*, 37 FRANCHISE L.J. 349–77 (2018).

174. Patterson v. Domino's Pizza, LLC., 333 P.3d 723 (Cal. 2014).

175. *Id.* at 726.

vided a mix of results. Courts have granted the franchisors' motions to dismiss or summary judgment, declaring the franchisor did not have sufficient control over the franchisees' employees.[176] However, other courts have found at least plausible claims that the franchisors exerted sufficient control over franchisees' employees and have denied franchisors' motions to dismiss.[177]

Given the uncertainty about the state of the law relative to a franchisor's joint employer liability, franchise agreements have been modified as the sample language in (3) of the preceding text reflects. The franchise agreement must make it clear that the franchisee alone is responsible for all aspects of the employment relationship with its employees. If former versions of a franchise agreement were silent on this issue, language should be added so there is no uncertainty about who controls the franchisee's employees. This language should be specific in describing the areas in which the franchisee has sole control, such as hiring, firing, discipline, rates of pay, and scheduling. Additionally, language regarding the training of the franchisee's employees should be added (or modified) to make it clear that the franchisor will train the franchisee and its managers, but that the franchisee is then responsible for training its employees. The focus of this provision, as with other related provisions in the franchise agreement, must be on the protections the franchisor requires to protect the goodwill associated with its trademarks while clearly providing that the franchisee is responsible for the day-to-day operation of the business and for all employment-related matters.

(iii) Employee Acknowledgment

Even with this language in the franchise agreement, franchisors must be aware that the franchisees' employees often do not understand that they work for the franchisee and not the franchisor. The franchise agreement should provide that the franchisee must use its own name on its paychecks and hiring and employment materials, and take ongoing actions to ensure that its employees understand that they work for the franchisee.[178] Concerned franchisors may consider including additional language within this operations section requiring the franchisee to obtain acknowledgments from its employees that the employee understands it works for the franchisee. The following language could be included:

---

176. *See* Gessele v. Jack in the Box, Inc., Bus. Franchise Guide (CCH) ¶ 15,887, 2016 WL 7223324 (D. Or. Dec. 13, 2016); Salazar v. McDonald's Corp., Bus. Franchise Guide (CCH) ¶ 15,818, 2017 WL 950986 (N.D. Cal. Mar. 10, 2017) and Bus. Franchise Guide (CCH) ¶ 15,818, 2016 WL 4394165 (N.D. Cal. Aug. 16, 2016); Pope v. Espeseth, Inc., No. 15-cv-486, 2017 WL 108081 (W.D. Wis. Jan. 11, 2017); Beckley v. McDonald's USA, LLC., No. 16-cv-00054, Bus. Franchise Guide (CCH) ¶ 15,952, 2017 WL 508587 (M.D. Ala. Feb. 7, 2017); Wright v. Mt. View Lawn Care, LLC., Bus. Franchise Guide (CCH) ¶ 15,741, 2016 WL 1060341 (W.D. Va. Mar. 11, 2016).

177. *See* Ocampo v. 455 Hospitality LLC., No. 14-cv-9614, Bus. Franchise Guide ¶ 15,835, 2016 WL 4926204 (S.D.N.Y. Sept. 14, 2016); Lora v. Ledo Pizza System, Inc., No. 16-4002, 2017 WL 3189406 (D. Md. July 27, 2017); and Reed v. Friendly's Ice Cream, LLC., Bus. Franchise Guide (CCH) ¶ 15,777, No. 15-cv-0298, 2016 WL 2736049 (M.D. Pa. May 11, 2016).

178. *See* Chapter 5.

Employer Acknowledgment – Franchisee must obtain from each of its personnel an acknowledgment signed by such personnel providing that such individual understands, acknowledges, and agrees that he or she is an employee of Franchisee and not Franchisor and that such individual must look solely to Franchisee for his or her compensation and for all other matters related to their relationship with Franchisee.

Employment Notices – Franchisee must post a notice on the employee bulletin board clearly visible to employees at the [franchised business], notifying all employees of their employer and clearly stating that neither Franchisor nor its affiliates are the employer of the employees.[179]

Given the heightened awareness of the joint employer issue over the last several years and the virtual certainty it will not diminish, it will remain good practice for the franchisors to use language similar to the sample language provided and remain clear in the franchise agreement, as well as in their operations manual and in practice, that the franchisee alone has control over all employment-related matters.

XV. Customer Satisfaction Programs

Alternative One (Restaurant System)

A. Operation of the Franchised Business

In order to (among other things) maintain and enhance the goodwill associated with the Proprietary Marks, the System, and each Franchised Business, Franchisee will participate and request its customers to participate, at Franchisee's expense, in programs initiated by Franchisor to verify customer satisfaction and/or Franchisee's compliance with all operational and other aspects of the System, including (but not limited to) an 800 number, Franchisor's customer feedback and satisfaction programs, secret shoppers, or other programs as Franchisor may require. Franchisor will share the results of these programs, as they pertain to the Restaurant, with Franchisee.

Alternative Two (Hotel System)

B. Compliance with the Standards

"Quality Assurance Program" means the program that Franchisor uses to monitor guest satisfaction and the operations, facilities, and services at System Hotels.

1. Required Activities. Franchisee will: (a) operate the Hotel at all times in compliance with the Standards; (b) fully participate in the Quality Assurance Program and all mandatory programs for System Hotels (which may require providing complimentary guestrooms and refunds); (c) offer all guest services required for System Hotels (which may include complimentary services); (d) make all payments due in

179. Fittante, Klein, & Marchiano, *supra* note 161, at 9.

accordance with the terms of all contracts and invoices related to the Hotel, except for payments that are disputed in good faith; and (e) provide all food and beverage service in the Hotel in compliance with the Standards and Applicable Law.

Discussion:

The franchisors typically monitor franchised unit operations in two primary ways: unit inspections (either through formal visits conducted by the franchisor or its agent or other mechanisms like "secret shoppers") and customer feedback. Generally, inspections are more likely to be focused on standards compliance and system consistency. Measuring customer satisfaction through feedback is focused more on the actual perception of customers and their experience at franchised units.

Obtaining and analyzing customer feedback is, therefore, critical both in reviewing individual unit performance and in analyzing the overall picture of a franchise system's market position and health. Customer feedback can be used as a tool to improve operations as well as a mechanism for enforcement of system standards.[180] Customer feedback can come in many forms, for example, surveys mailed to customers (or more likely e-mailed or accessed through a mobile app) after a hotel stay, a point-of-sale quick survey at a restaurant, and the now-ubiquitous feedback posted on websites and through social media, whether controlled by the brand owner or third parties. The methods and manner for obtaining customer feedback continue to expand and evolve regardless of the nature of the interaction between the franchised unit and the customer.

The franchise agreement provisions related to customer satisfaction and participation in related programs will vary depending on the intended use of the customer feedback by the franchisor. If, on the one hand, the franchisor intends to use feedback obtained from customers solely for operational purposes (training, remediation of operational issues, etc.), then a more general provision requiring the franchisee to participate in customer satisfaction programs may be sufficient. If, on the other hand, the franchisor wants the ability to condition renewal or consent to transfer on obtaining "passing" customer satisfaction scores or to be able to use "failing" customer satisfaction scores as a basis for termination, then more explicit provisions in this regard (such as the sample included in the preceding text) would be advisable. Additionally, given the pace of changing technology, coupled with the relatively lengthy terms of most franchise agreements, including more general language regarding the nature of customer satisfaction programs should be considered in order to provide for flexibility to adjust the program in the future.

As discussed previously with respect to standards of enforcement more generally, courts will typically enforce express provisions included in the franchise agreement related to customer satisfaction standards. In a case involving the Hampton by Hilton system, *HLT Existing Franchising Holding LLC v. Worcester Hospitality Group LLC*,[181] the Second Circuit upheld the district court's grant of summary judg-

180. *See generally* Coleman, Einhorn, & Winkler, *Fair or Foul? Use of Guest Surveys and Customer Feedback*, ABA 38th Annual Forum on Franchising (2015).

181. 2015 U.S. App. LEXIS 5710 (2d Cir. Apr. 9, 2015).

ment in favor of Hilton, holding that Hilton's use of guest surveys that demonstrated customer dissatisfaction as a basis for terminating the franchise agreement was not arbitrary, irrational, or in violation of the implied covenant of good faith and fair dealing and that the guest surveys were not inadmissible hearsay.[182]

XVI. Franchised Business Telephone Numbers and E-Mail Addresses; Websites and Other Online Communications

Franchisee acknowledges that, at all times, the Franchised Business telephone number(s) and listing(s) will remain in the name, and the sole property, of Franchisor, provided that Franchisee will be responsible for any and all costs, expenses and deposits associated with the Franchised Business telephone number(s) and listing(s) including, without limitation, any telephone company deposits and all local, long distance, installation and connection charges.

Franchisee agrees to advertise the Franchised Business (at Franchisee's expense) in all telephone directories or other directories as Franchisor designates, using only such advertisements as may be approved by Franchisor.

Franchisor retains all rights relating to Franchisor's website, e-mail address, and intranet system or other online communications and specifically Franchisee's use of Franchisor's Trademarks or any advertising subject to this agreement. Franchisor reserves the right to establish and modify rules which will govern Franchisee's use of the Trademarks on the Internet and in domain names and Franchisee agrees to abide by such rules. Franchisee's right to use the Trademarks on the Internet will terminate immediately upon the expiration or termination of this agreement. Franchisee must maintain (i) an e-mail account for Franchisor's direct correspondence with Franchisee and (ii) a separate e-mail account for the Franchised Business.

Discussion:

Customers locate and communicate with the franchised business through various means. Historically, the primary method was by telephone. More recently, this has shifted to e-mail, websites, and various forms of social media. Each franchise system must determine the manner by which its customers locate and communicate with its various locations and address those in the franchise agreement. Some forms of franchise agreement no longer reference telephone numbers or white/yellow pages as these forms of communication and advertising are no longer relevant to the industry. Instead, they focus on e-mail, website, and social media.

---

182. *See also* Gray v. Toyota Motor Sales, USA, Inc., 806 F. Supp. 2d 619 (E.D.N.Y. 2011) (Toyota's refusal to approve a transfer due to the proposed transferee's (an existing Toyota dealer) unsatisfactory customer satisfaction scores was not an improper basis for withholding consent to transfer); Midwest Automotive III, LLC v. Iowa Dept. of Transp., 646 N.W.2d 417 (2002) (Jaguar's refusal to permit the transfer of a dealership to a dealer that had below average customer satisfaction scores from other dealerships it held was not improper); and Ford Motor Co. v. West Seneca Fort, Inc., No. 91-CV-0784E(F), 1996 U.S. Dist. LEXIS 17616 (W.D.N.Y. Nov. 21, 1996) (Ford was justified in terminating the dealer for its failure to achieve sufficient levels of customer satisfaction and service scores).

Regardless of the forms of communications used in a particular industry, these links to the franchised business's customers are a vital part of the business. Since all forms of communication use the franchisor's trademarks and ultimately impact the goodwill of the system, franchisors want to have the ability to control each of these forms of communication if the franchised business should close or be converted to another brand. Language that either requires that the franchisor own these channels of communication from their inception, or requires the franchisee to assign them to the franchisor upon the expiration or termination of the franchise agreement, is crucial.

As social media and websites become the primary method of communicating and advertising with customers, the franchisors are adding language specifically addressing the concerns associated with these channels. The franchisors often prohibit the franchisee from establishing domain names using the franchisor's trademarks, or require that any domain names registered to the franchisee are assigned to the franchisor at the end of the franchise term.[183] Most franchisors have developed social media policies that limit how a franchisee can use any social media associated with the franchisor's trademarks. As this area continues to evolve with new forms of electronic communications being developed, franchise agreements should at a minimum contain language requiring the franchisees to comply with policies established by the franchisor from time to time as contained in the operations manual and system standards.

XVII. Technology Requirements and Participation in Websites and Other Online Channels

A. Technology and Computer Systems

> Franchisor has the right to specify or require that certain brands, types, makes, and/or models of communications, computer systems, and hardware be used by, between, or among the Franchised Business, including without limitation: (1) back office and point of sale systems, mobile devices, data, audio, video, and voice storage, retrieval, and transmission systems for use at the Franchised Business, between or among Franchised Businesses, and between and among Franchisee's Franchised Business and Franchisor, our designee, and/or Franchisee; (2) physical, electronic, and other security systems; (3) printers and other peripheral devices; (4) archival back-up systems; and (5) Internet access mode (e.g., form of telecommunications connection) and speed (collectively, the "Computer System"). Franchisee must purchase or lease, and thereafter maintain, the Computer System, and comply with Franchisor's requirements, specifications, and policies concerning the use of technology, as they may be specified in this Agreement, or specified or modified in the Manuals or otherwise in writing.

183. *See* Section XVII in the following text.

1. Franchisor's Use of Data

Franchisor shall have the right at any time to retrieve and use such data and information from Franchisee's Computer System that Franchisor deems necessary or desirable, including, without limitation, the uses identified in Section XX above. In view of the contemplated interconnection of computer systems and the necessity that such systems be compatible with each other, Franchisee expressly agrees that it must strictly comply with Franchisor's standards and specifications for all item(s) associated with Franchisee's Computer System and will otherwise operate its Computer System in accordance with Franchisor's standards and specifications. To ensure full operational efficiency and optimum communication capability between and among equipment and computer systems installed by Franchisee, Franchisor, and other franchisees, Franchisee agrees, at its expense, that Franchisee must keep its Computer System in good maintenance and repair, and, at its expense, and following the determination that Franchisor shall have the right to make, to the effect that same will prove economically or otherwise beneficial to all System franchisees, that Franchisee must promptly install such additions, changes, modifications, substitutions, and/or replacement to Franchisee's computer hardware, software, telephone, and power lines, and other related facilities, as Franchisor directs periodically in writing. Franchisee must provide to Franchisor, upon Franchisor's request, all e-mail lists and customer lists used or maintained by Franchisee on the Computer System or elsewhere.

2. Required Programs

Franchisor has the right, but not the obligation, to develop or have developed for it, or to designate, any or all of the following: (a) computer software programs and accounting system software that Franchisee must use in connection with the Computer System ("Required Software"), which Franchisee must install; (b) updates, supplements, modifications, or enhancements to the Required Software, which Franchisee must install; (c) the tangible media upon which such Franchisee must record or receive data; (d) the database file structure of Franchisee's Computer System; (e) an Extranet for informational assistance, which may include, without limitation, the Manuals, training, other assistance materials, and management reporting solutions; and (f) answering service requirements and/or system-wide phone, online, or mobile order processing of all delivery orders, and/or to designate vendors that will provide such order processing.

3. Upgrades and Access

Franchisee agrees to install and use the Computer System and Required Software in the manner that Franchisor requires. Franchisor may charge a reasonable software license fee for any Required Software. Franchise agrees to implement and periodically upgrade and make other changes to the Computer System and Required

Software as Franchisor requests in writing, which shall not be more often than one upgrade per year (collectively, "Computer Upgrades"). Franchisee will comply with Franchisor's written specifications (whether in the Manuals or otherwise) with respect to the Computer System and the Required Software, and with respect to Computer Upgrades, at Franchisee's own expense.

Franchisee agrees to afford Franchisor unimpeded access to its Computer System and Required Software in the manner, form, and at the times that Franchisor requests. Franchisee must provide Franchisor with user identifications and passwords required to access files and other information contained on the Computer System.

Because changes to technology are dynamic and not predictable within the Initial Term, and in order to provide for inevitable but unpredictable changes to technological needs and opportunities, Franchisee agrees: (a) that Franchisor will have the right to establish, in writing, reasonable new standards to address new technologies and data security, whether published in the Manuals or otherwise in writing, and that Franchisor has the right to implement those changes in technology into the System; and (b) to abide by Franchisor's new standards (and with Franchised Business audits conducted by Franchisor or its designee to confirm Franchisee's compliance) as if this Section, and other technology provisions in this Agreement, were periodically revised for that purpose.

B. Extranet

Franchisee must comply with Franchisor's requirements (as set forth in the Manuals or otherwise in writing) with respect to establishing and maintaining telecommunications connections between Franchisee's Computer System and Franchisor's Extranet and/or such other computer systems as Franchisor may reasonably require. The term "Extranet" means a private network based upon Internet protocols that will allow users inside and outside of Franchisor's headquarters to access certain parts of Franchisor's computer network via the Internet. Franchisor may establish an Extranet (but is not required to do so or to maintain an Extranet). Franchisee must comply with Franchisor's requirements (as set forth in the Manuals or otherwise in writing) with respect to connecting to the Extranet, and utilizing the Extranet in connection with the operation of the Franchised Business. The Extranet may include, without limitation, the Manuals, training and other assistance materials, and management reporting solutions (both upstream and downstream, as Franchisor may direct).

Franchisee must purchase and maintain such computer software and hardware (including but not limited to telecommunications capacity) as may be required to connect to and utilize the Extranet. Franchisor reserves the right to require Franchisee to contribute a reasonable amount toward the cost of the Extranet's maintenance and further development. If Franchisee fails to comply with any policy or procedure governing the Extranet, Franchisor may temporarily suspend Franchisee's access to all or any aspect of the Extranet (such as a chat room, bulletin board, list serve, or similar feature) until Franchisee fully cures the breach. Franchisee will not have any claim against Franchisor or any affiliate arising from such suspension from the Extranet pursuant to this Section [], and Franchisee hereby waives any such claim it may at any time have and releases Franchisor and its affiliates from any liability arising therefrom.

Franchisee and Franchisor shall each be responsible for protecting their own interests in relation to electronic communications. Franchisor shall have no liability to Franchisee on any basis, whether in contract, tort (including negligence) or otherwise, in respect of any error, damage, loss, or omission arising from or in connection with electronic communication of information.

C. Computer Systems

Franchisee shall at its expense install and maintain the computer hardware and software Franchisor requires for the operation of the Franchised Business (including systems that permit Franchisor to access and retrieve electronically, any information stored in Franchisee's computer systems) and shall follow the procedures Franchisor specifies in the Manuals or otherwise in writing. Franchisee acknowledges that Franchisor may, during the term of this Agreement, require Franchisee to modify, enhance and/or replace all or any part of the computer hardware and software comprising the computer system at Franchisee's expense. Any such modifications, enhancements, and replacements may require Franchisee to incur costs to purchase, lease and/or license new or modified equipment and to obtain different and/or additional service and support services during the term of this Agreement.

D. Internet Website

Franchisee shall have and maintain adequate hardware and software in order to access the Internet at the bit speed required by Franchisor from time to time. Franchisee shall not establish or participate in any website or other listing on the Internet except as provided herein.

1. Franchisor has established, or may establish, an Internet Website that provides information about the System and the products and services offered by the Franchised Businesses. Franchisor has sole discretion and control over the Website (including timing, design, contents and continuation).

2. Franchisor may (but is not required to) include at the Website an interior page containing information about Franchisee's Franchised Business ("Franchisee's Page"). If Franchisor includes such information on the Website, Franchisor may require Franchisee to prepare all or a portion of Franchisee's Page, at Franchisee's expense, using a template that Franchisor provides. All such information will be subject to Franchisor's approval prior to posting. Any modifications (including customizations, alterations, submissions or updates) to the template made by Franchisee for

any purpose will be deemed to be a "work made for hire" under the copyright laws, and therefore, Franchisor shall own the intellectual property rights in and to such modifications. To the extent any modification does not qualify as a work made for hire as stated above, Franchisee hereby assigns those modifications to Franchisor for no additional consideration and with no further action required and shall execute such further assignments(s) as Franchisor may request.

3. Franchisor also shall have the sole right (but no obligation) to develop an Intranet through which Franchisor and its franchisees can communicate by e-mail or similar electronic means. If Franchisor develops such an Intranet, Franchisee agrees to use the facilities of the Intranet in strict compliance with the standards, protocols and restrictions that Franchisor includes in the Manual (including, without limitation, standards, protocols and restrictions relating to the encryption of confidential information and prohibitions against the transmission of libelous, derogatory or defamatory statements). Franchisee will be solely responsible for compliance with any laws pertaining to sending e-mails, including but not limited to the Controlling the Assault of Non Solicited Pornography and Marketing Act of 2003 ("CAN-SPAM Act of 2003").

Discussion:

Given technological developments and the ubiquity of technology in franchised businesses, franchise agreement provisions related to technology systems used at franchised locations have taken on heightened importance. Virtually every franchisor has an interest in ensuring that their franchisees use appropriate technology in their franchised businesses.

While many franchise agreements contain shorter, more general provisions regarding technology and online matters with the details left to the operations manuals and standards like the alternative provision included in the preceding text, these provisions in some franchise agreements are becoming much more detailed, while still preserving the right to impose more specific or supplemental requirements in the standards, like the sample provision included in the preceding text. Regardless of the level of detail contained in the franchise agreement, there are some key elements that these provisions should address.

With respect to technology-related provisions, for most franchise systems it is important, at a minimum, to require the franchisees to purchase, install, and maintain the computer hardware and software, including both back-office systems and customer-facing systems like POS systems and noncash payment systems, that are used in the franchised business or to communicate with the franchisor. In addition, the franchisor should have the express right to require the franchisees to modify, upgrade, and supplement the technology systems and software used in the franchised business at the franchisees' expense. These requirements are needed in order to ensure, among other things, consistency in the franchise system, the ability to communicate efficiently with the franchisor, and the security of both the franchisor's confidential and proprietary information and customer information.

E. Customer Data

Franchisee agrees that all data and personally identifiable information (including, but not limited to, name, birth date, mailing address, phone number, and email address) that it collects from customers and potential customers in connection with the Franchised Business ("Customer Data") is deemed to be owned exclusively by Franchisor, and Franchisee also agrees to provide the Customer Data to Franchisor at any time that Franchisor requests. Franchisee has the right to use Customer Data during the Initial Term, but only as authorized by Franchisor in connection with operating the Franchised Business and only in accordance with the policies that Franchisor establishes from time to time. Franchisee may not sell, transfer, or use Customer Data for any purpose other than operating the Franchised Business and marketing Franchisor's products and services.

Discussion:
Franchise agreements should be clear as to who owns customer data obtained through the operation of the franchised business (typically, the franchisor will claim ownership of such customer information) and that the franchisee must permit the franchisor access to appropriate information stored in the franchisee's systems, including sales information and customer data, including valuable customer loyalty information. While ownership of data by the franchisor may be a factor in a control/joint employer analysis, given the link to customer data and a franchisor's trade secrets and noncompetition requirements, many franchisors consider the reward in claiming ownership of the data to outweigh the risk.

F. Privacy Laws

Franchisee agrees to abide by all applicable laws pertaining to the privacy of consumer, employee, and transactional information ("Privacy Laws"). Franchisee agrees to comply with Franchisor's standards and policies pertaining to Privacy Laws. If there is a conflict between Franchisor's standards and policies pertaining to Privacy Laws and applicable law, Franchisee must: (1) comply with the requirements of applicable law; (2) immediately give Franchisor written notice of such conflict; and (3) promptly and fully cooperate with Franchisor and its counsel in determining the most effective way, if possible, to meet Franchisor's standards and policies pertaining to Privacy Laws within the bounds of applicable law. Franchisee agrees not to publish, disseminate, implement, revise, or rescind a data privacy policy without Franchisor's prior written consent.

G. POS or Cash Register Systems

Franchisee agrees to record all sales on computer-based point of sale systems or such other types of cash register systems that Franchisor has the right to designate or approve in the Manuals or otherwise in writing ("POS System"). The POS

System is deemed to be part of Franchisee's Computer System. Franchisee agrees that only trained and qualified personnel will be assigned the responsibility for conducting transactions on the POS System.

H. Noncash Payment Systems

Franchisee must accept debit cards, credit cards, stored value gift cards, or other noncash systems specified by Franchisor to enable customers to purchase authorized products and must obtain at Franchisee's expense all necessary hardware and/or software used in connection with these noncash systems. At all times, Franchisee must maintain credit card relationships with the credit and debit card issuers or sponsors, check or credit verification services, financial center services, and electronic-fund-transfer systems that Franchisor designates as mandatory, and Franchisee must not use any such services or providers that Franchisor has not approved in writing or for which Franchisor has revoked its approval. Franchisor has the right to modify its requirements and designate additional approved or required methods of payment and vendors for processing such payments and to revoke its approval of any service provider. Franchisee must comply with Franchisor's credit card policies, including minimum purchase requirements for a customer's use of a credit card as prescribed in the Manuals. Franchisee must comply with the Payment Card Industry Data Security Standards (PCI DSS) as these standards may be revised and modified by the Payment Card Industry Security Standards Council (PCISSC) or such successor or replacement organization, and/or in accordance with other standards as Franchisor may specify. In addition, Franchisee must submit annually to Franchisor a fully completed copy of Franchisee's PCI Attestation of Compliance on the then current PCISSC form via email at XX or such successor or replacement form(s) and/or processes.

Franchisee will participate in any gift card program(s) that Franchisor specifies. For this purpose, Franchisee must purchase the software, hardware, blank cards, and other items needed to sell and process gift cards or stored value cards, which Franchisor may specify in writing in the Manuals or otherwise. Franchisee also agrees to pay such monthly and per-swipe transaction fees as may be required by the vendor of the gift card system. Franchisee must sell or honor gift cards only in accordance with Franchisor's written standards. Franchisee must account for all gift card sales, gift card redemptions, and other gift card transactions in the manner Franchisor specifies in the Manuals. Franchisee must maintain sufficient cash reserves to pay Franchisor or other franchisees as part of any network-wide periodic reconciliation of the gift card program. Franchisee must pay Franchisor or make payments as specified by Franchisor, in such amounts and at such times as directed by Franchisor, in accordance with Franchisor's gift card rules, programs and policies. Franchisee agrees not to sell, issue, or redeem gift certificates other than gift cards that Franchisor has approved in writing. Concurrent with the execution of this Agreement, Franchisee must sign and deliver to Franchisor the Gift Card Participation Agreement attached to this Agreement as Exhibit XX.

Discussion:
Cybersecurity threats, including data breaches, continue to plague businesses of all sizes. Therefore, having in place updated and comprehensive standards and protocols related to privacy and data protection is critical for virtually every franchise system. Including specific provisions in franchise agreements related to compliance with those standards and protocols is becoming commonplace. Even though cyber insurance coverage is still in its formative stages and coverage varies greatly between policies, the franchisors should consider adding the requirement for cyber insurance to their insurance requirements.[184]

I. Websites

1. Ownership of Brand Website

Franchisor may establish and maintain one or more websites and/or mobile applications (collectively, "**Franchisor's Websites**") that provide information about the System and the products and services offered and sold by Franchisor's Businesses. Franchisor's Websites may also offer reservations, online and mobile ordering, mobile payments, or similar services or sales of items bearing the Proprietary Marks, including, but not limited to, Franchisor's memorabilia, clothing, and pre-packaged food and beverage products. Franchisor has absolute control over Franchisor's Websites' design and content. Franchisor will attempt to configure Franchisor's Websites to accommodate individual Franchised Business pages described in Section XX. Franchisor will have no obligation to maintain Franchisor's Websites indefinitely, but may discontinue them at any time without liability to Franchisee. Further, as Franchisor has no control over the stability or maintenance of the Internet generally, Franchisor is not responsible for damage or loss caused by errors of the Internet. Franchisor is not liable for any direct, indirect, special, incidental, exemplary, or consequential damages arising out of the use of the Internet or the inability to use the Internet including loss of profits, goodwill or savings, downtime, or damage to or replacement of programs and data, whether based in contract or tort, product liability, or otherwise.

2. Franchisee Modifications

Franchisor's Websites may include a series of interior pages developed by Franchisor (and, at Franchisor's sole discretion, using content provided by Franchisee as requested by Franchisor) that identify participating Businesses by address, telephone number, and e-mail address. At Franchisee's request, Franchisor will endeavor (technology permitting) to include on Franchisor's Websites one or a series of interior pages devoted to information about the Franchised Business. Franchisee will not have the capability to modify such page(s) except in coordination with Franchisor and in compliance with Franchisor's policies and procedures as such may change from time to time.

---

184. For example, "Franchisee shall also maintain, at its cost, cyber liability insurance with limits and coverages reasonably required by Franchisor."

3. Digital Fee

Franchisor may require Franchisee to contribute an amount, as determined by Franchisor ("Digital Marketing Fee"), toward the cost of the development and maintenance of Digital Media (including, but not limited to, Franchisor's Websites) to be used for advertising, marketing, promotional, technology, or other purposes in Franchisor's sole discretion. Franchisor will collect the Digital Marketing Fee monthly and will notify Franchisee in or before January of each year the amount of the Digital Marketing Fee for that calendar year, provided that the Digital Marketing Fee will remain the same for that calendar year if Franchisor does not notify Franchisee before January 31 of each year of a change in the amount of the Digital Marketing Fee. In addition or alternatively, Franchisor may use part of the National Advertising Fund contributions that Franchisor collects under this Section [] to maintain and further develop the Digital Media and may elect in conjunction therewith to establish a separate fund for the Digital Marketing Fee and such contribution amounts apart from the National Advertising Fund.

4. Remedies for Franchisee Default

If Franchisee fails to pay when due any fees or other amounts payable to Franchisor under this Agreement or otherwise fails to comply with any policy or procedure governing the Digital Media, in addition to other remedies, Franchisor may, at its option, temporarily disable Franchisee's interior page(s) on Franchisor's Websites (or other Digital Media) and/or Franchisee's ability to accept online or mobile orders and/or mobile payments for the Franchised Business, until Franchisee pays its outstanding obligations in full and/or Franchisee fully cures the breach. Franchisee will not have any claim against Franchisor or any affiliate arising from Franchisor's actions pursuant to this Section XX, and Franchisee hereby waives any such claim it may at any time have and releases Franchisor and its affiliates from any liability arising therefrom.

J. E-mail, Internet, Social Media, and Other Media

Franchisee must comply with Franchisor's requirements and policies (as described in the Manuals or otherwise in writing) with respect to all Digital Media in connection with the Franchised Business and in connection with discussing, advertising, or disseminating any information, or otherwise having a presence, on the Internet, in Social Media, or in any other media, regarding the Franchised Business. Such activities include, without limitation, participation in any Internet "blogs" or Social Media sites. Any such activities which are not expressly permitted in the Manuals or otherwise in writing, or for which Franchisee has not previously received approval from Franchisor, will be subject to Franchisor's approval as Local Store Marketing.

1. Franchisee may advertise and promote the Franchised Business via Social Media, which must be comprised of pages, communications, and content located on third-party platforms using the Proprietary Marks as specified by Franchisor (collectively, "Franchisee's Social Media"), provided that Franchisor is granted administrator

access to Franchisee's Social Media. All uses of Franchisee's Social Media pages and communication channels and uses must be established in accordance, and at all time be in compliance, with the Manuals and System Standards.

2. Franchisee agrees not to transmit or cause any other party to transmit consumer advertisements or solicitations by e-mail or other Digital Media without Franchisor's prior written consent as to: (a) the content of such advertisements or solicitations; and (b) Franchisee's plan for transmitting such advertisements. In addition to any other provision of this Agreement, Franchisee agrees that it will be solely responsible for complying with any laws pertaining to sending e-mails, including but not limited to the Controlling the Assault of Non-Solicited Pornography and Proprietary Marketing Act of 2003 (known as the CAN-SPAM Act of 2003).

3. Franchisee must promptly discontinue any advertising or promotion using Social Media, whether or not previously agreed to by Franchisor, upon notice from Franchisor that it reasonably considers that such use of Social Media does not conform to the System Standards. Upon the expiration or termination of this Agreement, Franchisee will assign ownership (to the extent Franchisor does not already own them) of all domain names, account names, handles, and user names used by Franchisee in its business under this Agreement and Franchisee will take all such actions as Franchisor reasonably requires to disassociate Franchisee from any such names and Social Media pages.

Discussion:

With the increased importance of online activities in franchise networks, including marketing, promotion, and product/service distribution, as well as the advent of social media, provisions governing the presence and conduct of the franchisees online are now seen as standard in franchise agreements in most every industry. With the exception of some large, cross-border master license/master franchise arrangements, most franchise agreements include significant restrictions on the franchisees' online presence. For example, the franchisees are typically not permitted to establish or operate their own website; the franchisors will, instead, maintain a website for the system and may dedicate pages for individual franchised units. The franchisors may use advertising fund monies, or, in some cases, charge an additional "digital marketing" fee to the franchisees in order to support the franchisor's online activities, including development and maintenance of the system website. The franchisees may also be prohibited from transmitting advertisement and other promotional material electronically, including by e-mail, without the franchisor's approval.

However, some franchisors tend to be more liberal when it comes to the franchisees' social media presence, permitting (and sometimes encouraging) the franchisees to be active on social media, so long as those activities are in compliance with the franchisor's social media policies and other standards and protocols. If the franchisors grant the franchisees independent use and management of the franchisees' social media, then minimally, the franchisors should require that the franchisor be granted administrator access to the site and that all social media posts comply with the franchisor's system standards. Administrator access gives the social media site operator authority to communicate with the franchisor and gives the franchisor the ability to manage the site (or even take down the site) if the franchisees are not complying with system standards.[185]

XVIII. Reservation Systems

A. Electronic Systems

1. Reservation System

Subject to Section XX, Franchisor will make the Reservation System available to the Hotel. Franchisee will cause the Hotel to participate in the Reservation System in accordance with the Standards and this Agreement. Franchisor is not required to make the Reservation System available to the Hotel for any reservations occurring after the expiration or termination of this Agreement.

2. Honoring Reservations

Franchisee will provide its prices and rates for use in the Reservation System in accordance with the Standards. Franchisee will: (i) honor any prices, rates or discounts that appear in the Reservation System or elsewhere; (ii) honor all reservations made through the Reservation System or that are confirmed; and (iii) not charge any Hotel guest a rate higher than the rate specified for the Hotel guest's reservation in the Reservation System or, if not made through the Reservation System, in the reservation confirmation. Franchisee will also honor all pricing and terms for any other product or service offered in connection with the Hotel.

3. Electronic Systems Provided under License

As a condition to using the Electronic Systems, including the Reservation System, Franchisee will execute the Electronic Systems License Agreement. The Electronic Systems that are proprietary to Franchisor or third-party vendors, as applicable, will remain their sole property. Franchisee will treat the Electronic Systems as confidential at all times. The Electronic Systems may be modified, replaced or become obsolete, and new Electronic Systems may be created to meet the needs of the System and changes in technology. If Franchisor determines that it is necessary to amend or replace the Electronic Systems License Agreement because of such events, Franchisee will execute the then-current form of, or an amendment to, the Electronic Systems License Agreement.

4. Access to Information

Franchisor may access the Electronic Systems to obtain marketing, sales and guest information and Franchisee will take all actions reasonably necessary to provide such access. Franchisor and its Affiliates may use any data related to the Hotel,

185. *See* Chapter 5 for additional discussion relating to social media.

Franchisee and its Affiliates obtained through the Electronic Systems, including Guest Profile Data.

5. Interim Remedies

If (i) Franchisee fails to comply with any provision of this Agreement after receipt of written notice of noncompliance and such failure to comply continues beyond the time period specified in such notice; or (ii) any event or circumstance occurs that would give Franchisor a right to terminate this Agreement under Section XX (each, a "Noncompliance Event"), Franchisor may, in addition to any other remedies, suspend the Hotel from the Reservation System while such Noncompliance Event remains uncured. Once the Noncompliance Event is cured, Franchisor will promptly reconnect the Hotel to the Reservation System.

Discussion:

Customer reservations are a key element of franchised businesses in certain industries, most notably the hotel/lodging business and the car rental business, both of which are now heavily franchised. These businesses invest millions of dollars into developing, maintaining, and refining their reservations systems, and it would not be an overstatement to say that these reservations systems are one of the most critical aspects, and, indeed, a core driver, of these businesses. Therefore, strong provisions related to the franchisees' participation in the reservation system in these systems are necessary components of the franchise agreement.

Fundamentally, the franchisees must be required to participate in the reservation system (as it exists at the time that the franchise agreement is signed and as it may evolve in the future) at all times during the term, including honoring reservations made through the reservation system at the rates at which the reservation was made (the franchisee determines and provides the rates to the franchisor for input into the reservation system). Subject to its right to suspend the franchisees from the reservation system as discussed in the following, the franchisor will also generally have a corresponding obligation to provide a reservation system to franchisees through which reservations at the franchised unit may be made during the term of the franchise agreement.

Specific protocols and procedures with which franchisees must comply in connection with their participation in the reservation system are generally set forth in the franchisor's standards and manuals. Additionally, many franchisors require franchisees to sign separate "participation" or "license" agreements addressing more technical aspects of the reservation and related systems.

The franchisees are generally required to pay a reservation fee to the franchisor in addition to royalties and other amounts payable under the franchise agreement. Reservation fees come in different forms, including a flat amount per reservation (which may vary depending on the channel, e.g., online versus voice, through which the reservation is made), a percentage of the rate that the customer pays to the franchisee, or broader "services fee" covering reservation services as well as other services.

Typically, the franchise agreement will provide that the reservation fee must be paid, but, unlike the royalty or other amounts payable under the franchise agreement, the specific amount of the reservation fee is generally not set forth in the franchise agreement. Instead, details of the manner in which the reservation fee is then currently determined are included in the franchisor's FDD. This is primarily because most franchisors view reservation fees primarily as a cost-recovery mechanism, and costs to operate a reservation system can change over the term of a franchise agreement. This can be an issue in negotiations of the franchise agreement, but, given the need for consistency in the manner in which they charge for reservation services across the system, the franchisors will rarely provide any caps or assurances on the amount of reservation fees a franchisee will be required to pay; the franchisees generally gain comfort from the fact that the franchisors will not "single out" one or a group of the franchisees and generally charge a consistent rate across the entire system.

Consistent with the treatment of customer data in other franchise systems, the franchisors in franchise systems that rely heavily on reservations systems take the position that they own the customer/guest data obtained through the reservation system. The ownership of this data takes on enhanced importance for the franchisors in these types of systems given the significant amount (and sensitivity) of information they obtain from customers through the reservation process. Information, including guest preference data, is extremely valuable to these types of franchisors, so they are generally not willing to negotiate any changes to these provisions.

Access to the franchisor's robust reservation system is one of the primary reasons many franchisees in these industries choose to become the franchisees of a particular system, especially given the continued consolidation in the hotel and car rental businesses. Simply put, reservation systems drive business to the franchisee's unit. The franchisors, therefore, can use access to the reservation system as leverage to induce a noncompliant franchisee to become compliant and include provisions in their franchise agreements that give the franchisor the right to suspend noncompliant franchisees from the reservation system as an alternative remedy to termination.

5

Operating Manual, Advertising, Trademarks, and Other Intellectual Property

Corby Anderson and Rebekah Prince

XIX. Operating Manual and Confidentiality

A. Compliance with and Ownership of Manual

Franchisee must conduct the Franchised Business strictly in accordance with all of the provisions set out in the Manual as amended from time to time.

Franchisee hereby acknowledges that the contents of the Manual are on loan to Franchisee and must at all times remain in the custody of Franchisee.

Franchisor may from time to time revise the contents of the Manual. All such additions, deletions or modifications shall be effective five (5) business days after Franchisor has given notice to Franchisee in accordance with this Agreement or, at Franchisor's option, once Franchisor has provided Franchisee with an electronic copy of the revisions to the Manual, unless five (5) business days is too short a period and not commercially reasonable, in which case Franchisee shall have a commercially reasonable period of time to modify its operations to adopt the change. In the event of a dispute about the contents of the Manual, the master copies maintained by Franchisor at the principal offices will control.

Franchisor shall furnish to Franchisee at no additional charge an electronic copy of the Manual at or before the time of the Training Program. The Manual shall at all times remain the sole, confidential property of Franchisor. Upon the expiration or termination of this Agreement for any reason whatsoever, Franchisee shall immediately return the Manual to Franchisor and shall retain no copy or reproduction. Except as specifically permitted by Franchisor, at no time may Franchisee, or its employees or agents, make, or cause to be made, any copies or reproductions of all or any portion of the Manual or disclose the terms thereof to any other person except employees and agents of Franchisee when required in the operation of the Franchised Business by means of electronic communication. The Manual may not be forwarded to anyone and no electronic copy provided to anyone except that Franchisee may share it with members of Franchisee's management to enable them to perform their duties to Franchisee as long as the persons with whom it is shared are informed that the Manual is considered Franchisor's confidential information and agree to keep its contents confidential.

Discussion:

While the franchise agreement lays out the franchisee's legal obligations, the manual lays out the guidelines for running the business. The manual is at the heart of an effectively run system. It contains key information about how to operate the business and protect the goodwill of the brand.[186] The manual provides the franchised business's mission statement, vision, and values.[187] Furthermore, the manual sets out the products that can or cannot be sold, suppliers from whom the franchisee can purchase products, marketing approaches and strategies, performance standards, and compliance guidelines.[188]

Most franchisors include a clause in the franchise agreement that requires the franchisee to comply with all provisions of the manual. Of course, some franchisors choose to characterize their manual, or portions of it, as suggestions rather than strict obligations. In these cases, the clause should be drafted accordingly. This has become more important as drafters consider the implications of the joint employer standard, as detailed in Chapter 4. Whether the manual requires strict compliance or suggests guidelines will depend on the particular subject matter and, most importantly, the nature of the franchised business. If a specific product, method, or service is integral to the brand of the franchise, such as a recipe or unique fitness method, the uniformity necessary to deliver the same experience to customers across locations will require strict compliance. In contrast, requiring a POS system

---

186. Sherman, *supra* note 71, at 107.

187. Franchise Specialists, *Operations Manual*, https://www.franchisespecialists.com/articles/333-operation-manuals.

188. LegalVision, *The Franchisor's Guide: Franchise Operations Manual*, https://legalvision.com.au/franchisors-guide-franchise-operations-manual/.

that has certain basic features can serve as a guideline that the franchisee can then use to make a purchase based on his or her operating needs and budget. Striking the proper balance may prevent legal liability and foster a better relationship with the franchisee by allowing flexibility when it does not impact the franchise system's brand.

Perhaps the most important part of the previously mentioned clause is how the term "manual" is defined in the agreement. The manual may be a traditional operations manual or it may also include other things, such as a proprietary style guide, directives, descriptions of the system, and any amendments, supplements, derivative works, and replacements, whether embodied in electronic or other media, the franchisor's website, the intranet, or the like. It is important for the franchisor to craft a comprehensive definition of what is included in the manual so that the definition, whether within the clause or in a defined terms section, fully informs the franchisee of all sources of requirements it must comply with. If the definition is incomplete, then the franchisee's obligations as set out in the manual will not accurately and fully represent the franchisor's intentions.

It is important for a franchisee to understand the rights he or she is buying in a franchise relationship. Franchisees sometimes assume they are buying perpetual rights to use the system, trademarks, and manual, which would be akin to ownership rights in those items. However, as mentioned earlier in this chapter, the franchise relationship merely confers a temporary right to use the franchisor's system, trademarks, and manual to conduct business.[189] These rights expire at the end of the franchise term (subject to any renewal provisions that may exist). This can be difficult to understand for the franchisees, who may think that paying a franchise fee and monthly royalties confers ownership rights in the content of the manual. Including language that describes the return of the information upon expiration, termination, or transfer helps to communicate that the right to use the information in the manual is temporary and must be treated as such.

(i) Franchisor's Right to Change the Manual

The franchisor should make clear that it reserves exclusive rights to change the manual. Otherwise, a franchisee may make a number of incorrect assumptions, namely, that the manual is static, that changes are open to negotiation, or that the franchisee may make its own changes to the manual. Such changes might undercut or conflict with the efforts and intentions of the franchisor and hurt the goodwill and success of the brand by sending conflicting messages to customers.[190]

By reserving exclusive rights to change the manual and requiring the franchisees to comply with all such changes, a franchisor can preserve its ability to adapt the system to changing conditions over time. For example, the flexibility to update the manual permits a franchisor of a bakery system to expand its menu from cookies and cakes to other trending bakery items. A franchisor that failed to include this

189. SHERMAN, *supra* note 71, at 110–11.
190. Hurwitz & Schnell, *supra* note 36.

reservation of rights might have to wait to execute such new menu concepts until the next round of franchise disclosure documents (FDDs) and franchise agreements are distributed and signed. For existing franchisees, it would actually require the franchisor to wait until the expiration of their existing terms. A system is a dynamic entity, and the franchise agreement must be drafted with the understanding that changes will need to occur to keep the system healthy and competitively relevant. Particularly with a new and growing business, revisions will be necessary as the franchisor responds to changes in processes, customers' needs, and demands dictated by the market and competition. Failing to include language to reserve rights to change the manual will make it difficult, if not impossible, to effectively run a franchise system. A franchisor must be able to adapt and ensure that its franchisees adapt at the same rate to protect the goodwill of the brand by providing consistency and eliminating confusion for customers across outlets. Because changes to the manual can affect not only how the franchisee operates its business, but how the customer experiences the business, it is important for franchisees to understand that changes to the manual can occur, and that they must comply not only with the current manual, but with any future updates or revisions. If changes will occur frequently, a statement about where to find the most accurate and up-to-date information and which information controls can help a franchisee meet its obligations to stay current and in compliance with the manual's requirements. Franchisees looking to curtail the extent to which a change in the manual can impact the system may negotiate a clause such as the one below.

> Franchisor agrees that although such modifications to the Manual may be material in that they may have an effect on the operation of the Franchised Business, they may not conflict with or materially alter the terms of this Agreement.

The franchisor should consider including additional language stating the timeframe the franchisee has to comply with changes to the manual. The timeframe may differ depending on the modification, such as a protocol change that could be implemented in a matter of days or a product or equipment change that may require more time to implement. The franchisees may also request a limit to the number of changes that can be made to the manual within a certain timeframe. The franchisor can anticipate this by setting reasonable guidelines for the frequency of updates, not only to foster a good relationship with the franchisees but to build a consistent, identifiable brand for customers. A costly modification is likely to receive pushback from the franchisees as well. Accordingly, a cap on expenditures or the frequency of equipment upgrades, and so on, may be included in the agreement (or included in the manual and referenced in the agreement). The franchisor should consider the feasibility of certain changes in different markets, balancing the strength and consistency of the system against a fair relationship with the franchisees. In general, the franchise agreement should give the potential franchisee a good sense of what the expectations are for running the business and what kind of obligations those expectations place on the franchisee. A more detailed discussion relating to modernization requirements (and related caps and timeframes) is included in Chapter 4.

Courts will generally enforce changes to the operating manual as long as they are reasonable and do not fundamentally change the rights and obligations of the parties under the franchise agreement. Courts generally uphold system changes when they are backed by clear and explicit language in the franchise agreement regarding the right of the franchisor to make changes.[191] The franchisors should provide a reasonable amount of time to incorporate those changes. For instance, implementing a new point of sale software may take longer than adding a new food item to the menu. Relying on a "reasonable" timeframe will help ensure that the provision is upheld if ever challenged.

(ii) How Manual Is Maintained and Accessed

The franchisee must have access to a current and complete manual to comply with the franchisor's requirements for operating the franchised business. Both the form in which the manual is issued and the method used to provide updates affect how franchisees can ensure that they have access to a current and complete manual. Franchisors have increasingly turned to issuing manuals electronically, as, for example, on an intranet site. In that case, updating and maintaining the manual should be relatively easy for the franchisor, and accessing the manual should be relatively easy for the franchisee. By contrast, when manuals are made available in "hard copy," with each franchisee taking custody of its own copy, the franchisee bears a greater burden for ensuring that it maintains, and can access, a current and complete manual. When hard copies of the manual are issued, a franchise agreement typically specifies that the franchisor, in its sole discretion, may periodically furnish updates to the manual, in various formats (via letter, e-mail, bulletin, videotape, audio tape, and the like), and the franchisee is responsible for maintaining the updates and complying with them.

B. Nondisclosure and Confidentiality

> Franchisee acknowledges that it has had no part in the creation or development of nor does it have any property or other rights or claims of any kind in or to any element of the System, the Trademarks or any matters dealt with in the Manual. Franchisee also acknowledges that all disclosures made to Franchisee relating to the System, including, without limitation, the specifications, standards, procedures and the entire contents of the Manual, are communicated to Franchisee solely on a confidential basis and as trade secrets, in which Franchisor has a substantial investment and a legitimate right to protect against unlawful disclosure. Accordingly, Franchisee agrees to maintain the confidentiality of all such information during the term of this Agreement and at any time thereafter and may not disclose any portions of the Manual or any information whatsoever with respect to Franchisee's or Franchisor's business affairs or the System, other than as may be required to enable Franchisee

191. *See* Bores v. Domino's Pizza LLC, 530 F.3d 671 (8th Cir. 2008); Nat'l Franchisee Ass'n v. Burger King Corp., 715 F. Supp. 2d 1232 (S.D. Fla. 2010).

to conduct its business. Franchisee further agrees not to use any such information in any other business or in any manner not specifically approved in advance in writing by Franchisor.

Discussion:

The confidentiality clause is one of the most important clauses in the franchise agreement, because it protects the proprietary information that makes the franchised business's products and services unique. A new product variation, an innovative service feature, or a special ingredient can distinguish a franchisor from its competitors. Whether it is a simple recipe or a complex methodology, franchisors must be diligent to keep their system information confidential and prevent their franchisees from disclosing this confidential information or using it for any purpose beyond the franchised business. The manual is meant to be used; thus, a franchisor cannot guard its manual so closely that it makes the manual available only upon request.[192] Likewise, many systems have proprietary information that goes beyond the manuals themselves. For example, a bakery franchise cannot guard its recipes so closely that it prevents franchisees from accessing the very product they are licensing from the franchisor. Accordingly, a franchisor must draft a nondisclosure and confidentiality clause that is clear and enforceable, and that adequately protects the system's confidential information and trade secrets, both during the term of the franchise agreement and after termination, expiration or transfer.

Some franchisees may mistakenly believe that only information they consider uniquely proprietary should be treated as confidential. They may not realize that many aspects of how the business is run, such as marketing and operating strategies, are also confidential. Therefore, the clause should specify what is to be protected, listing all items and information that are to be treated as confidential, including the manual. If confidential information is defined earlier in the agreement—for example, in a definitions section—the clause can use a defined term rather than a list. The goal is to be as broad and inclusive as possible to adequately protect the franchised business.

Because the confidentiality clause is intended to protect the system's confidential information from competitors, the franchise agreement should require not only the franchisee, but anyone who has a certain level of ownership in the franchisee and those who will attend training and run the business to sign a nondisclosure and confidentiality agreement as well. A statement that these individuals will be required to sign a separate nondisclosure and confidentiality agreement, such as the sample below, can be added to the end of this section.

We may require that you obtain an executed nondisclosure and confidentiality agreement in a form satisfactory to us from any persons owning a minority interest in you, your Designated Manager and other key employees.

---

192. Proimos v. Fair Automotive Repair Inc. 808 F.2d 1273 (7th Cir. 1987).

From a practical standpoint, the franchisor may need to include a carve-out for passive investors who sign the franchise agreement or guaranty but will not be actively involved in running the franchised business. While these passive investors will still have access to confidential material, it may be unreasonable to expect them to comply with the provision, which arguably may not apply to them. Franchisors may draft their franchise agreements aggressively but should understand that this will likely be a point of contention for passive investors.

Franchise agreements are written with the assumption that even though franchisees may provide innovations to the system, that does not make them co-creators of the system. Franchisors emphasize their control and ownership in the system throughout the franchise agreement. For example, franchise agreements typically prohibit or require prior written consent for changing trade dress, suppliers, software programs, or any other substantial aspect of the system. Franchisors should draft this language clearly to avoid confusion and conflict. A sample clause might read as follows:

> You acknowledge that you do not own any rights in the Trademarks or the System. You agree that you will not hold yourself out to the public as owning any such rights, and that you will never contest the validity of, or our rights in, any Trademarks or the System. You acknowledge and agree that all goodwill and ownership rights arising out of your use of the System and the Trademarks accrue solely to us. You acknowledge and agree that now and hereafter you shall assert no claim to any goodwill by virtue of the licensed use of the System and the Trademarks, and that you will not dispute or impugn the validity of any of the Trademarks or our rights thereto.

Even if a franchisee's input has influenced a change in the manual as the franchised business grows, the franchisee does not own or have any rights to any part of the system, trademarks, or manual. Franchise agreements should make this point clear. A sample clause follows:

> Franchisee agrees and acknowledges that if Franchisee develops any component of the System that Franchisor permits or adopts for use in the Franchised Business, such component will belong to Franchisor and Franchisee shall have no right or interest in such component, other than the right to use it as long as the agreement is in effect and as long as Franchisor retains such item as part of the System.

This language further emphasizes that the franchisee has only a license to use the system and therefore must keep system information confidential and must return it and cease to use it when the franchise is transferred or the franchise agreement expires or is terminated.

If the core of the franchised business involves providing services, such as accounting and tax preparation services or cleaning services, it may be unreasonable to prohibit a franchisee from using system information in another business, especially if the franchisee practiced in the area before becoming a franchisee. Franchisees who have practiced in the field of expertise of the franchise prior to signing their agreements may not agree to refrain from using all system information in another business.

Furthermore, courts are unlikely to enforce non-competes against these individuals due to the public's interest in receiving those services and the protection of those individuals' ability to make a living. In *Duffner v. Alberty*, the court struck down a non-compete agreement in which a doctor was prohibited from practicing medicine within 30 miles of a particular city, citing the public's right to have access to doctors.[193] In *Atlanta Bread Co. Int'l v. Lupton-Smith*, the court struck down a non-compete agreement that prohibited an individual from engaging in the bakery/deli business in any capacity because it was an unreasonable restraint on the individual's ability to make a living.[194]

Courts typically take a common law reasonableness approach to non-competes, so keeping their restrictions limited as to time and territory will help ensure that they will be upheld and enforced. The franchisor should be able to show that the time and territory restrictions are no broader than is necessary to protect a legitimate business interest. If a franchisee enters a service-based franchise system with preexisting knowledge and skills, a fair balance would be to provide that during the term of the agreement, the franchisee may not engage in any competitive business, and after the term of the agreement, the now-former franchisee may not compete in his or her former territory or in or near the territories of current franchisees. Many courts find this approach a reasonable way to protect the interests of both the franchisor and other existing franchisees, without causing excessive hardship on the former franchisee. A more detailed discussion of non-compete provisions follows in Chapter 6.

XX. Advertising

A. Advertising Funds

> Recognizing the value of uniform advertising and promotion to the goodwill and public image of the System, Franchisee agrees that Franchisor may maintain and administer a general advertising fund or funds (the "Fund") for such national, regional, local and other advertising programs as Franchisor, in its sole discretion, may deem necessary or appropriate. The Fund is not a trust or escrow account, and Franchisor has no fiduciary obligation to Franchisee, or to any Franchisees, with respect to the Fund. Franchisor has the absolute right to direct the creative concepts, materials, endorsements and media used in the advertising programs, as well as the placement and allocation of the programs.

---

193. Duffner v. Alberty, 718 S.W.2d 111, 114 (Ark. Ct. App. 1986); *cf.* Cleveland Hair Clinic, Inc. v. Puig, 986 F. Supp. 1227 (N.D. Ill. 1996).

194. Atlanta Bread Co. Int'l v. Lupton-Smith, 292 Ga. App. 14, 663 S.E.2d 743 (2008), *aff'd*, 285 Ga. 587, 679 S.E.2d 722 (2009).

Franchisee must contribute to the Fund in each year an amount equal to XX% of the Gross Sales for such year. Any amounts required to be paid to the Fund must be paid together with the royalty fees and must be based on Gross Sales for the preceding week.

Any delinquent payments of advertising fees and royalties received will be allocated between the Fund and Franchisor according to the respective percentages of advertising fees and royalties owed. Any costs incurred in collecting such delinquent payments (including, without limitation, reasonable attorney fees) will be allocated between the Fund and Franchisor in proportion to the respective percentages of advertising fees and royalties owed, but in no event may the collection costs allocated to the Fund exceed the delinquent advertising fees contributed to the Fund.

The Fund will be used and expended for media costs, commissions, market research costs, creative costs and production costs, including, without limitation, the costs of creating promotions and artwork, printing costs and other costs relating to advertising and promotional programs undertaken by Franchisor. Franchisor reserves the right to place and develop such advertisements and promotions and to market on behalf of the System, either directly or through an advertising agency retained or formed for such purpose or through co-operative advertising groups composed of Franchisees designated by Franchisor.

The Fund will be accounted for separately from the other funds of Franchisor. The Fund may not be used to defray any of Franchisor's general operating expenses, except for any reasonable salaries, administrative costs and overhead (calculated on a fully allocated basis) that Franchisor may incur in activities reasonably related to the administration or direction of the Fund and its advertising programs (including, without limitation, conducting market research, managing programs supported by the Fund, and retaining outside agencies).

An unaudited statement of the operations of the Fund will be prepared annually and will be made available to Franchisee upon written request to Franchisor. The Fund will pay the cost of preparing such statement. If Franchisor is required by law to commission an audit of the Fund, then the costs of such an audit will be paid from the Fund.

Any sums remaining in the Fund at the end of a fiscal year must carry over in the Fund to the next fiscal year.

Franchisee acknowledges and agrees that the Fund is intended to maximize general public recognition and patronage of businesses for the benefit of all outlets and Franchisees in the System, and that Franchisor undertakes no obligation in administering the Fund to ensure that any particular Franchisee benefits directly or pro-rata from the placement or conduct of such advertising and promotion.

The Fund may not be used for any initiative intended solely to market the sale of franchises. Franchisee acknowledges and agrees, however, that certain activities supported by the Fund, including, without limitation, maintenance of the website, public relations activities, and community involvement activities, may include information about franchising opportunities.

Discussion:

Advertising fund clauses are extremely common in franchise agreements.[195] The idea behind advertising funds is relatively simple: a franchisor can arguably conduct more effective advertising once it has pooled the smaller amounts received from its franchisees.[196] Even if a franchisor is not staffed appropriately at the outset of the franchise relationship to handle the formation and management of an advertising fund, the franchise agreement should provide for the franchisor's ability to form and administer a fund in the future. The pooling of funds allows the franchisor to invest in more expensive, and presumably more valuable, advertising on a larger scale.[197] These funds can be managed by the franchisor, by an advertising agency, or, in certain circumstances in mature franchise systems, by a franchisee association.[198] Franchisees often support these funds because the funds can increase exposure and sales at their franchised businesses.

Conflicts may arise when the franchisees feel they are not getting enough return for their contributions to the fund. Because it is often difficult for the franchisees to measure the local impact of a nationwide or larger-scale advertising campaign, they may believe and claim that these advertising funds were used improperly.[199] Franchisors may be able to temper such criticisms by giving the franchisees the ability to influence advertising decisions, including how advertising revenue is spent, through a franchise advisory council.[200]

From a drafting perspective, this clause should address the structure of the program, permissible uses of advertising funds, the advertising approval process, and how the funds received from each franchise will be accounted for and used.[201] Advertising funds can be raised by charging each franchisee a percentage of gross sales or a flat fee. Some franchisees may prefer a flat fee because it is predictable. And the franchisees with higher gross sales, paying a percentage of those sales for advertising, may believe their contributions are giving a "free ride" to the franchisees with lower gross sales. For the franchisor, charging a flat fee will guarantee a certain amount of money for the advertising fund.[202] But if the franchisees' gross sales are increasing, the franchisor is likely to collect more money for advertising if it charges a percentage of gross sales. With increasing sales, the franchisor can scale up the advertising program correspondingly.

In terms of drafting, it is especially important to consider points of contention that may arise between the franchisor and the franchisees over the advertising fund. Transparency in the advertising provisions regarding issues where conflicts of interest can arise between the franchisor and the franchisees can help eliminate, or

195. Blair & Lafontaine, *supra* note 54, at 55.

196. *Id.*

197. ABA, Fundamentals of Franchising—Canada 121 (Peter Snell & Larry Weinberg, eds., 2004).

198. Sherman, *supra* note 71, at 109.

199. Carden & Klarfeld, *supra* note 110, at 12.

200. Dillon, Vines, & Tegt, *supra* note 56, at 12 and n.47.

201. Asbill, Barkoff, & Selden, *supra* note 4, at 34; *see also* Chernow, Olson, & Prince, *supra* note 53, at 22–23.

202. Shane, *supra* note 26, at 97.

at least blunt, some of these points of contention. For example, where funds may be used to cover administrative costs associated with advertising, the franchisor should expressly disclose that fact. The franchisor should define what "administrative expenses" are, either directly or by example, and should consider including a cap on the amount of advertising funds that may be used to defray administrative expenses. Franchisees may also require an upfront commitment from the franchisor that company-owned and -operated units will pay advertising fees and benefit from the advertising fund on the same basis as other franchised units, such as in the sample below.

> Contributions to the Fund, and benefits from the Fund, for any units owned or operated by Franchisor or its affiliates will be the same as for franchised units owned and operated by franchisees.

In addition, the franchisor should make clear that advertising funds collected from the franchisees will not be used for any initiative intended solely to promote the sale of franchises. When royalties and advertising fees are paid together, and the franchisor collects delinquent payments, the franchisor should state whether those delinquent payments will be allocated to both royalties and advertising funds, and, if so, how. Finally, the franchisor can promote transparency by including an obligation to report to the franchisees on the activities of the advertising fund. The sample provision requires that the franchisor provide an annual unaudited statement of the fund's operations and make that statement available to the franchisees upon request. In some jurisdictions, a franchisor must disclose in its FDD whether it provides such an annual accounting to the franchisees. The franchisor also may commission an annual audit of the advertising fund, which may be required by law in some circumstances, and may share that information with the franchisees.

The advertising provision should state that the franchisor will administer the fund in its sole discretion and that there is no guarantee that individual units will benefit from the advertising. This provision should also make clear that the franchisor owes no fiduciary duty to the franchisees with respect to any advertising fees collected from them or administered on their behalf. Such language disclaiming any fiduciary duty on the part of the franchisor has become virtually universal in franchise agreements since the seminal decision in *Broussard v. Meineke Discount Muffler Shops*.[203] In that case, the district court upheld a jury's finding that franchisor Meineke had a fiduciary duty to administer the franchise system's advertising fund and breached that duty.[204] On appeal, however, the Fourth Circuit held that the district court erred in finding that a fiduciary duty exists between franchisors and their franchisees generally, and in the advertising fund context particularly.[205]

203. Broussard v. Meineke Discount Muffler Shops, 155 F.3d 331 (4th Cir. 1998).

204. *Broussard*, 958 F. Supp. 1087 (W.D.N.C. 1997).

205. *Broussard*, 155 F.3d at 343–44. *See also* Barry M. Heller & Robert Zarco, *Fundamentals 201: The 7 Most Significant Franchise Cases of All Time*, ABA 37th Annual Forum on Franchising W-1, at 8–12 & n.34 (2014).

Drafters should be aware of alternatives to advertising funds. For instance, the idea of a fund could be abandoned altogether in favor of adding advertising fees to the royalty payments (or other fees). In this situation, the franchisee could advocate to draft requirements on how those fees are to be spent (to ensure that the fees are spent on advertising).[206]

B. Local Advertising

Franchisee must use best efforts to promote and advertise the Franchised Business and participate in any local marketing and promotional programs that Franchisor establishes from time to time. In addition to the Advertising Fee, Franchisee is required to spend XX% of Gross Sales on approved local marketing and promotion. Upon Franchisor's request, Franchisee must provide itemization and proof of local marketing and an accounting of the money it has spent on approved local marketing. If Franchisee fails to make the required expenditure, Franchisor has the right to collect and contribute any deficiency to the Fund.

Franchisee has the right to conduct such advertising and promotions of the Franchised Business as Franchisee in its reasonable discretion desires, provided that:

1. Franchisee must advertise and promote only in a manner that will reflect favorably on Franchisor, Franchisee, the products and services and the good name, goodwill and reputation thereof;
2. Franchisee must submit all proposed advertising and promotions to Franchisor for its approval, which approval may not be unreasonably withheld or unduly delayed. Franchisee may not use any advertising or promotions until Franchisor has given its written approval of such advertising or promotions;
3. Franchisee must prominently display, at its expense, in and on the Premises, signs of such nature, form, color, number, location, size and content as Franchisor may direct or approve in writing from time to time. Such signs must be purchased from Franchisor or, at Franchisor's option, from suppliers approved by Franchisor; and
4. Franchisee hereby acknowledges that all rights, including, without limitation, all intellectual property rights, in all advertising and promotional material prepared by or on behalf of Franchisor are and will at all times remain the property of Franchisor.

Discussion:

There are several reasons why a franchisor might give franchisees the responsibility of advertising locally (and require them to do so). The franchisor might not be located in the area of the franchised business and might not have the resources to research that area's market and develop an appropriate advertising strategy to meet its needs. Franchisors who recognize this limitation will allow the franchisees to make at least some advertising decisions for their local area's market. In some systems, the franchisor may want to give the franchisees more leeway to choose their

206. Carden & Klarfeld, *supra* note 110.

own methods for promoting their businesses, at least in part to get buy-in from the franchisees on the importance of advertising initiatives. In smaller systems, local advertising handled by franchisees can be a stopgap measure to get the franchisee used to spending a percentage of their gross sales on advertising before the franchisor is able to implement a national advertising fund.

To limit conflicts between advertising efforts across regions, ensure brand consistency and minimize risks of liability, franchisors often will require that all advertising plans be approved. If the franchisor does this, it will be better able to ensure that a consistent message is being sent to customers across various regions.

Despite the desire for consistency, franchisors sometimes accommodate a franchisee's desire to offer and advertise specialized products. But once a franchisor and franchisee start down this road, it may be difficult to turn back. This difficulty is illustrated in a local advertising dispute between KFC Corp. and one of its multi-unit franchisees who saw a lucrative market for offering Halal chicken (prepared according to Islamic laws and customs), along with KFC's standard menu items, in franchises located in predominantly Muslim communities.[207] For nearly 15 years, KFC approved the franchisee's offering and advertising of Halal chicken, helped him find Halal-certified processors and distributors and allowed him to display annual certifications from a local Islamic society. This model proved so successful that the franchisee opened additional locations in 2010 and 2012 based on their proximity to Muslim communities. In 2016, however, KFC demanded that the franchisee stop marketing chicken as Halal and remove Halal-related signage from his stores. KFC attributed its decision to a policy it introduced in 2009 prohibiting franchisees from making religious dietary claims. The franchisee sued KFC for breach of contract, promissory estoppel, and declaratory and injunctive relief, but the court dismissed each of these claims. Regardless of past practices, the franchise agreement unambiguously allowed KFC to bar the franchisee from advertising his product as Halal and imposed no "specialized, overarching reasonableness requirement"[208] on the franchisor's decisions about advertising, the court concluded. It also rejected the franchisee's argument that he could make "truthful disclosures" about obtaining products from Halal-certified suppliers, because those statements constitute advertising, which falls under the franchisor's "complete control," according to the franchise agreement.[209] This decision should alert franchisees to the perils of relying on leeway in local advertising unless that leeway is expressly permitted in their franchise agreements or in addenda to the agreements. In terms of drafting, the franchisor should retain ownership of the intellectual property used in advertising, including copyrights and trademark rights. Some franchisors will also draft clauses that specifically outline what kind of local advertising media can or should be used.[210] From a franchisee's perspective, there should be a clear understanding of what advertising freedoms exist, if any.

---

207. Lokhandwala v. KFC Corp., Case No. 17-cv-5394, 2018 WL 509959 (N.D. Ill. Jan. 23, 2018).

208. *Id.* at *6.

209. *Id.* at *4.

210. Mathews, DeBolt & Percival, *supra* note 25, at 185.

Some franchisors require local advertising, while others merely grant the franchisee permission to conduct local advertising. There is a fundamental difference between these two options, and it is critical that the franchisee understand this clause in its franchise agreement. If the franchisor requires the franchisee to advertise locally, the franchisee should consider proposing a clause that allows for a lower sum to be spent in the first year. If the franchisor must pre-approve all local advertising efforts, then the franchisee should consider negotiating a limit on the time period for the approval process. For example, the franchisor may provide that if its written approval of a franchisee's submission is not received within a certain number of business days after receipt, then approval is deemed denied, unless the franchisee then renews its written request for approval and receives no response from the franchisor within a particular time period after receipt, in which case the franchisor's approval is deemed granted. Such a provision typically is followed by the franchisor's reservation of the right to require the franchisee to discontinue use of any particular advertising material at the franchisor's sole discretion.

Finally, it can be difficult to draw distinctions regarding which changes to a franchisee's premises—such as changes in signage—count toward meeting required local advertising expenditures versus making necessary improvements. Whether in the franchise agreement itself or in the operations manual, the franchisor should consider clarifying the changes that count as local advertising expenditures.

C. Social Media Advertising

Franchisee may not promote the Franchised Business or use the Trademarks in any manner on any social media site existing now or in the future (including, without limitation, on blogs, Facebook, LinkedIn, Twitter, Instagram, Flickr, Tumblr, Pinterest, Google+, Vine and Snap Chat) or on file-, audio- or video-sharing sites, without Franchisor's prior written consent. Franchisor has final authority over all social media marketing, and Franchisee must comply with Franchisor's brand standards regarding use of social media in the operation of the Franchised Business. Franchisee may not post communications about the Franchised Business or the Franchise System that would disclose the System's confidential or proprietary information, violate any relevant laws, regulations or guidelines or violate the terms of use imposed by the social media site. Franchisee may not post communications about the Franchised Business or the Franchise System on any social media site that is not authorized by Franchisor for use by Franchisee. Franchisee must ensure that policies it adopts for its employees' social media use are consistent with the requirements for social media advertising set forth herein.

Franchisor is under no obligation to provide Franchisee with access to branded social media pages or other social media assets. Any social media pages or other social media assets that Franchisor, in its sole discretion, chooses to make available to Franchisee will be provided only on condition that Franchisee updates them regularly. Any such social media pages or other social media assets maintained by Franchisee shall be deemed "advertising" and shall be subject to all terms of this

Section XX.X. Franchisor has the right, but not the obligation, to conduct social media campaigns on behalf of all, or any subset of, Franchisees via local social media.

Discussion:
The degree of control franchisors should exert over the system's social media presence and the degree of freedom franchisees should have in asserting a social media presence are questions being played out in franchise systems of every type and size.[211] Some franchisors prohibit franchisees' use of social media in connection with their franchised businesses. Other franchisors give franchisees free reign to use social media. As a middle ground, franchisors may encourage franchisees to maintain an active social media presence but allow them to post only content developed or pre-approved by the franchisor that is customized to their location. Drafters should consider a number of factors in determining the appropriate level of control for a particular franchise system, including, for example, the culture of the system; the targeted customers for the system's products or services, and how those customers make purchasing decisions; and the level of oversight and support that the franchisor can provide to franchisees using social media.

For social media marketing and advertising to work effectively, the franchisor and the franchisees must ensure that their social media efforts are coordinated with other promotional efforts and are consistent with the system's brand. Many provisions of the franchise agreement can be relevant to social media, including not only advertising but also control, use, and ownership of the trademarks and copyrighted material; protection of confidentiality and privacy; and control, use, and ownership of social media assets at and after termination. All sections of the franchise agreement that touch on social media should be evaluated together to ensure that their terms are consistent, not contradictory.

Requirements and guidelines for use of social media must be flexible enough to adapt to the dynamic environment of constantly changing laws, regulations, guidelines[212] and technologies that affect this field. This may be an argument for keeping the governance of social media use, to the extent possible, in the operations manual, where changes are easier to make, instead of in the franchise agreement.[213] Franchisors must also be careful not to exert more control than is necessary over use of social media, to avoid the risk of vicarious liability.[214] Finally, in addition to the risk

211. See generally Bruno Floriani, Ama Romaine, & Clay A. Tillack, *Your Ad Here: The Perils and Rewards of Advertising in Social Media*, ABA 38th Annual Forum on Franchising, W-24 (2015); Corby C. Anderson & Carol Anne Been, *Protecting the Franchise Brand in the Age of Social Media*, ABA 33rd Annual Forum on Franchising, W-16 (2010).

212. *See, e.g.*, Fed. Trade Comm'n, *Guides Concerning the Use of Endorsements and Testimonials in Advertising*, 16 C.F.R. § 255.0–255.5.

213. See generally Amy Cheng, Craig Dietz, & David W. Oppenheim, *Operating Manuals: The Devil Is in the Details*, ABA 31st Annual Forum on Franchising, W6 (2008).

214. *See, e.g.*, Doctor's Associates, Inc. v. QIP Holder LLC, No. CIV.A306CV1710VLB, 2010 WL 669870 (D. Conn. Feb. 19, 2010) (denying motion for summary judgment, court held it could not determine whether franchisor Quiznos was actively responsible for user-generated videos in "meat, no meat" advertising contest that made disparaging representations about Subway).

of violating traditional advertising laws, regulations and guidelines, what franchisors, franchisees, and employees post on social media can risk violating privacy, publicity and free speech rights, as well as labor laws.[215]

D. Grand Opening Advertising

Franchisee must conduct certain advertising and public relations activities in connection with the opening of the Franchised Business. Franchisor requires Franchisee to spend, in addition to the required local advertising contribution described above, $XX for such opening activities, which must be spent some time within XX days prior and XX days following the opening of the Franchised Business, unless otherwise approved in writing by Franchisor. In addition, Franchisee must perform opening advertising and promotions as required by this paragraph any time Franchisee (i) relocates the Franchised Business or (ii) reopens the Franchised Business after having it closed for XX days or more. Upon Franchisor's request, Franchisee must provide Franchisor with proof of these expenditures. Franchisor has the right, but not the obligation, to collect and administer these funds on Franchisee's behalf.

Discussion:
The grand opening is a critical moment for any business. It sets the stage for future business and sends a message to potential customers about the value the business will bring. Given its importance, many franchisors require their franchisees to spend a certain amount of money on the grand opening. The franchisor can either include a separate clause for the advertising to be spent on the grand opening or designate a certain amount of the other required advertising expenditures that must go toward this event.

E. Advertising Cooperatives

Franchisor has the right to designate local or regional advertising markets, and, if designated, Franchisee must participate in and contribute to the cooperative advertising and marketing programs in Franchisee's designated advertising market. If established, Franchisee must contribute a minimum of XX% of Gross Sales to the local cooperative, which satisfies the local marketing requirement described in subparagraph B. If, however, the cooperative votes to spend a percentage greater than that per location, Franchisee must contribute such amount. Each Franchised Business, including those operated by Franchisor or its parent or affiliates, within a designated local advertising area is a member of the local advertising cooperative, and each such Franchised Business has one vote on all matters requiring a vote.

---

215. *See, e.g.*, MikLin Enters, Inc. d/b/a Jimmy John's v. National Labor Relations Board, No. 14-3009, Slip. Op. (8th Cir. July 3, 2017) (upholding NLRB's ruling that MikLin supervisors violated National Labor Relations Act by making Facebook posts encouraging employees to harass and disparage an employee for being a union supporter, thereby causing the employees to fear they would incur similar treatment if they supported the union).

Each advertising cooperative will be required to adopt governing bylaws that meet Franchisor's approval. Franchisor will provide each advertising cooperative with a sample form of bylaws, containing certain terms and conditions that Franchisor requires. The bylaws cannot modify the voting structure set forth in this paragraph. Franchisee will be required to contribute to the cooperative the percentage designated by a majority vote of the cooperative's members. Franchisor reserves the right to administer the advertising cooperative's funds and require payment from its members via electronic funds transfer. The contribution amount designated by the cooperative must be based on a percentage of Gross Sales and per Franchised Business, and must be at least $XX. The members of each cooperative and their elected officers will be responsible for the administration of the advertising cooperative. Each advertising cooperative must engage the services of a professional advertising agency or media buyer that has expertise in the industry and the particular market, and that is approved by Franchisor. All promotional and advertising materials, creative execution and media schedules must be approved by Franchisor in writing prior to their implementation.

Each advertising cooperative will be required to prepare annual financial statements, which must be made available to all members of the cooperative and to Franchisor upon request. Upon Franchisor's request, each advertising cooperative must submit its meeting minutes to Franchisor. Franchisor has the right to require advertising cooperatives to be formed, changed, dissolved or merged.

Discussion:

An advertising cooperative is formed when franchised businesses in the same general region combine advertising efforts and funds. The idea behind advertising cooperatives is that franchisees can do more effective and potentially less expensive advertising when they pool their resources. An advertising cooperative is not suitable for every system; it usually requires a critical mass to be effective, and it usually works best in more densely populated areas.[216]

It is important for the franchisor to set out detailed rights and obligations in this area in the franchise agreement. Sometimes the franchisor will give the franchisees the right to establish an advertising cooperative. Sometimes the franchisor will require them to do so. Further, the franchisor may decide to operate exclusively under advertising cooperatives, an advertising fund, or both. Even if the franchisor sees no need to draft for the possibility of an advertising cooperative, it might decide to include a provision for one so that the option is available in the future.

The sample clause adds a level of formality to the operation and rules surrounding the advertising cooperative by requiring that the franchisee members adopt and abide by certain bylaws. This level of formality is not universal, but it is certainly recommended. Also note that the franchisee agrees in advance to abide

---

216. Stephen Spinelli, Jr., Robert M. Rosenberg, & Sue Birley, Franchising: Pathway to Wealth Creation 97 (2004).

by the majority's views on whether the financial contribution to the cooperative will increase. This is key, although again not universal, as otherwise the franchisee would later need to consent to any increase.

Cooperatives can be useful, but they are not without challenges. For example, a cooperative is typically operated by the franchisees within a region, and if those franchisees do not get along, that may prevent the cooperative from functioning smoothly and effectively. Other problems may occur when the franchisees fail to make required payments to the cooperative. What rights or obligations does the franchisor have to collect such unpaid amounts? And will the franchisor be called upon to guarantee the payment of advertising placements by the franchisees in the cooperative? If the cooperative purchases an advertisement that lists the names and addresses of its members and one or more of those members do not make their required payments, may the remaining members delete the listings of those who do not pay? If so, will the deleted franchisees have a claim against the franchisor for failure to provide advertising as required by the franchise agreement? Careful drafting is needed to anticipate and address questions such as these.

XXI. Trademark Licensing and Other Intellectual Property

A. Trademark Ownership

Neither this Agreement nor the operation of the Franchised Business in any way gives Franchisee any interest in the Trademarks other than the right to use the Trademarks solely in connection with the Franchised Business, solely in accordance with the terms and conditions of this Agreement and solely during the term of this Agreement. Franchisee may not use the Trademarks in any manner calculated to represent that it is the owner of the Trademarks. Neither during the term of this Agreement nor after a Transfer or the expiration or termination of this Agreement may Franchisee contest the validity or enforceability of the Trademarks, attempt any registration of the Trademarks or take any action that would dilute the value of the goodwill attaching to the Trademarks. All goodwill associated with the Trademarks will inure exclusively to the benefit of Franchisor.

Without in any way restricting or limiting the terms above, Franchisee covenants and agrees as follows:

1. Upon any request by Franchisor, Franchisee will execute such applications or agreements or such other instruments in such form and with such parties as Franchisor in its sole discretion specifies, protecting the interests and rights of Franchisor in the Trademarks, or complying with any applicable regulations or legislation related to trade names, trademarks, trade dress or other similar subjects;
2. Franchisee will not use the Trademarks or any variations thereof as any part of its corporate, firm or business name or for any other purposes, except in accordance with the terms and conditions of this agreement or as may otherwise be specifically authorized in advance in writing by Franchisor; and

3. Upon a Transfer, or the expiration or termination of this agreement for any reason, Franchisee shall immediately cease all uses of the Trademarks (including any colorable imitations thereof) for any purposes whatsoever, and shall not promote itself as a person or entity that currently conducts or previously conducted business under the Trademarks.

Discussion:
Trademarks are the cornerstone of every franchise relationship[217] and the franchisor's most valued asset. Between the parties, the franchise agreement is the most appropriate place for a franchisor to protect this asset.[218] Thus, the franchisor should explicitly state that the franchisee may not contest ownership of the trademarks under any circumstances.[219]

This section emphasizes that the right to use the trademarks exists only "during the term of the franchise agreement" and that the franchisee must cease all uses of the trademarks upon a transfer or termination or expiration of the franchise agreement. These provisions anticipate and respond to "the most common situation prompting trademark enforcement actions in the franchise context," the holdover franchisee.[220] When a franchisor terminates a franchise agreement, some franchisees disregard or contest the termination and continue to operate the franchised business using the franchisor's trademarks. These holdover franchisees typically argue that they were wrongfully terminated.[221] Thus, they contend, they are still valid franchisees and are still entitled to use the franchisor's trademarks. In these instances, including the language "during the term of the franchise agreement" may not budge stubborn franchisees. In fact, the right to use a franchisor's trademark ends at the termination of the franchise agreement, even without such a direct statement.[222] Even so, from a practical standpoint, it is in the franchisor's best interest to make this limitation clear to all franchisees to set up proper expectations for the franchise relationship.

The franchisor should state that any goodwill that inures in the trademarks remains the sole and exclusive property of the franchisor.[223] In fact, almost all franchise agreements assert the franchisor's ownership of the goodwill.[224] This claim can be difficult to enforce if a franchisor expands its franchise system to other countries, where the delineation between goodwill ownership is more difficult to assert.[225]

217. Asbill, Barkoff & Selden, *supra* note 4, at 37.

218. Duffin & Watson, *supra* note 14, at 132.

219. Asbill, Barkoff, & Selden, *supra* note 4, at 37–38.

220. Christopher P. Bussert & Linda K. Stevens, *Trademark Law Fundamentals and Related Franchising Issues*, *in* FUNDAMENTALS OF FRANCHISING 34 (4th ed., ABA, 2015).

221. *See, e.g.*, Wyndham Hotels and Resorts, LLC v. North Star Mt. Olive, LLC, No. 10-cv-2583, 2013 U.S. Dist. LEXIS 44468 (D.N.J. Mar. 28, 2013); Dunkin Donuts Franchise Rest. LLC v. ABM Donuts, Inc., No. CA 11-cv-270 S, 2011 WL 6026129 (D.R.I. Oct. 4, 2011).

222. *See, e.g.*, United States Jaycees v. Phila. Jaycees, 639 F.2d 134, 209 U.S.P.Q. (BNA) 457 (3d Cir. 1981).

223. Asbill, Barkoff, & Selden, *supra* note 4, at 37–38.

224. *See* Robert W. Emerson, *Franchise Contract Clauses and the Franchisor's Duty of Care Toward Its Franchisees*, 72 N. L. REV. 905, 974 (1994).

225. Robert W. Emerson, *Franchise Goodwill: Take a Sad Song and Make It Better*, 46 U. MICH. J.L. REFORM 349, n.27 (2013), *available at* http://repository.law.umich.edu/mjlr/vol46/iss2/1 (describing how French courts have decided goodwill ownership disputes between franchisors and franchisees).

The franchise agreement often identifies the franchisor's then-current principal trademarks (for example, in an appendix to the agreement),[226] but should also make clear that the franchisor has the right to modify its trademarks from time to time.

Consistency in the use of trademarks is essential for maintaining the value of the system's brand. In view of the importance of this consistency, the franchisor must restrict the franchisee's use of its trademarks. The agreement also should specify how the trademarks may be used by the franchisee. Franchisors may prohibit certain uses of the trademarks or may include a more restrictive statement that the trademarks may not be used in any manner not expressly set forth in the agreement.[227]

B. Notice of Independent Ownership and Operation and Identification of Franchised Business

> Franchisee may use the Trademarks on various materials, such as business cards, stationery and checks, provided that Franchisee: (i) accurately depicts the Trademarks on the materials as Franchisor prescribes; (ii) includes a statement on the materials indicating that the business is independently owned and operated by Franchisee; (iii) does not use the Trademarks in connection with any other trademarks, service marks or trade names without Franchisor's prior written approval; and (iv) makes available to Franchisor, upon Franchisor's request, a copy of any materials depicting the Trademarks. Franchisee must post a prominent sign in the Franchised Business identifying Franchisee as a Franchisee in a format that Franchisor deems acceptable, including an acknowledgment that Franchisee independently owns and operates the Franchised Business, and that the Trademark is owned by Franchisor and licensed to Franchisee. All of Franchisee's internal and external signs must comply with Franchisor's guidelines, requirements and practices, as they are modified from time to time.

Discussion:
To help customers know the party they are doing business with and to limit the franchisor's risk of vicarious liability, franchise agreements often require franchisees to display notices that identify the franchisee and make clear that the franchised business is independently owned and operated by the franchisee. Franchisors should ensure that this notice is prominently placed and visible to the franchisee's customers.[228] The franchisor should also require the franchisee to disclose that it is an independent contractor on all documentation that the franchisee provides to third parties (including, without limitation, contracts and business cards).[229]

---

226. Asbill, Barkoff, & Selden, *supra* note 4, at 37–38.
227. *Id.*
228. Perkins, Yatchak, & Hadfield, *supra* note 18, at 174.
229. *Id.*

For instance, plaintiffs injured at a franchised business sometimes bring vicarious liability claims, arguing that the franchisee was the franchisor's apparent agent at the time of the incident that resulted in the injury. Under the doctrine of apparent agency, a principal may be held vicariously liable in tort for injury caused by the negligent acts of its apparent agent if the alleged principal has represented, or permitted it to be represented, that the party dealing directly with the plaintiff is its agent, and if the plaintiff relies on this representation in dealing with the agent.[230] (See also Chapter 10, Section XXIX.C., Independent Contractor.)

C. Infringement of Trademarks

Franchisee must notify Franchisor in writing upon discovering any claim of infringement or unfair competition or other challenge to Franchisee's right to use the Trademarks, or upon discovering any use of or claims to the Trademarks by anyone other than Franchisor or its licensed Franchisees. Such notification must be given promptly, and in no event longer than XX calendar days after discovery by Franchisee. Franchisee may not communicate with anyone except Franchisor and counsel in connection with any such infringement, challenge or claim, except pursuant to judicial process. Franchisor shall have the absolute right to determine whether it takes any action in connection with any such infringement, challenge or claim, and the sole right to control any litigation or other proceeding arising out of any infringement, challenge or claim relating to the Trademarks. Franchisee must sign any instruments and documents, render any assistance, and perform any acts that Franchisor or its attorneys deem necessary or advisable to protect and maintain Franchisor's interest in any litigation or proceeding related to the Trademarks or otherwise to protect and maintain Franchisor's interest in the Trademarks.

Franchisor agrees to indemnify Franchisee against and to reimburse Franchisee for all damages for which Franchisee is held liable in any proceeding arising out of the use of any of the Trademarks in compliance with this agreement, and for all costs reasonably incurred by Franchisee in the defense of any such claim brought against it or in any such proceeding in which it is named as a party.

Discussion:

Great care should be taken when drafting clauses concerning the infringement of trademarks, given the importance of the trademarks to the franchisor. As demonstrated in the sample clause, it is important for the franchisor to maintain control over the handling of any litigation or threatened litigation with respect to trademark infringements, to provide adequate protection for the trademarks.[231] This clause

230. Restatement (Second) of Agency §§ 27, 267 (1958) (One who represents that another is his servant or other agent and thereby causes a third person justifiably to rely upon the care or skill of such apparent agent is subject to liability to the third person for harm caused by the lack of care or skill of the one appearing to be a servant or other agent as if he were such).

231. Duffin & Watson, *supra* note 14, at 132.

requires the franchisee to notify the franchisor of trademark infringement in two separate circumstances, both of which are important: first, if a third party claims infringement by the franchisee, and second, if the franchisee becomes aware of a third party that appears to be using the trademarks without permission. The franchisor should specify how quickly the franchisee is expected to notify the franchisor of infringement of the trademarks. Notification should be given as quickly as possible, so that the franchisor can issue a cease and desist demand and, if warranted, seek injunctive or other appropriate relief without delay.

The second paragraph of the sample clause is the franchisor's indemnity of the franchisee if a third party sues the franchisee for infringement for using the trademarks as permitted by the franchise agreement. Such a provision is seen most often when a franchisor is new and its trademarks are not yet well established and perhaps not yet even registered.

D. Additions and Modifications of Trademarks

> Franchisor has the absolute right in its sole discretion to adopt new Trademarks for use with the System and to modify or discontinue the use of any of the existing Trademarks, without liability to Franchisee. Such additions or modifications may be made for any reason Franchisor deems necessary or advisable, including, without limitation, the rejection of any pending application for registration of a Trademark, the cancellation or revocation of any registration of a Trademark, the discovery of superior rights held by any third party in a Trademark, the change or addition of products or services offered through the System in connection with a Trademark, or the need to refresh the System's brand. Upon reasonable written notice from Franchisor, Franchisee, at its expense, will make all changes or modifications to the Trademarks specified by Franchisor.

Discussion:

As with the clauses regarding system and manual changes, most franchise agreements give exclusive rights to the franchisor to modify or discontinue any of its trademarks or add new trademarks. This allows franchisors to maintain flexibility to react to infringement challenges and adapt to changes in the system and in the market. Some agreements delineate which party must pay the costs associated with re-branding when changes in the trademarks occur.[232] Although the sample provision allocates this cost to the franchisee, a franchisor can expect pushback on this requirement, particularly when the change results from a third party challenge to the trademarks.

The business purpose behind this clause is to allow the franchisor to make any necessary changes to the system to remain competitive in the marketplace.[233] It is in the best interests of the franchisee to allow for such changes, because the franchisee

232. Asbill, Barkoff, & Selden, *supra* note 4, at 38.

233. Hurwitz & Schnell, *supra* note 36, at 44–45.

presumably will benefit from the business judgment of the franchisor in this regard. That being said, there have been some noteworthy situations where franchisees did not accept the wholesale change of the system name and litigation ensued.[234]

E. Copyrights

> Franchisee acknowledges that Franchisor owns the worldwide copyrights and other intellectual property rights to all components of the System that are original works of authorship subject to copyright, including, without limitation, marketing materials, website text, artwork, photographs, musical compositions, sound recordings, audiovisual works, computer software, and architectural designs, (collectively, the "Copyrighted Materials"). Franchisee acknowledges and agrees that it may not make translations, copies, adaptations of or modifications to the Copyrighted Materials without the prior written consent of Franchisor.
>
> Neither this agreement nor the operation of the Franchised Business in any way gives Franchisee any interest in the Copyrighted Materials other than the right to use the Copyrighted Materials solely in connection with the Franchised Business, solely in accordance with the terms and conditions of this agreement and solely during the term of this agreement.
>
> Franchisee acknowledges that Franchisor will own the copyrights and all other rights to translations, modifications and adaptations of or to the Copyrighted Materials made by Franchisee from time to time. Franchisee hereby assigns to Franchisor its copyrights and economic rights and waives any moral rights and similar rights with respect to the translated, modified or adapted Copyrighted Materials, and agrees to execute any and all instruments and documents, render such assistance and perform such acts and things as may, in the opinion of Franchisor, be necessary or advisable in furtherance of such assignment and waiver. Franchisee will require the same assignment, waiver and covenant in favor of Franchisor by Franchisee's Officers and employees and by any independent contractors or other third parties who translate, modify or adapt the Copyrighted Materials.

Discussion:

From print, broadcast, and digital marketing materials to architectural designs to computer software code and much more, copyrighted materials are a valuable asset for the franchisor. Between the parties, the franchise agreement is the most appropriate place for a franchisor to protect this asset. Thus, the franchisor should explicitly state that the franchisee may not claim ownership of, or contest the franchisor's ownership of, the system's copyrighted materials.

This section emphasizes that the right to use the copyrighted materials exists only during the term of the franchise agreement and that franchisee must cease all uses of the copyrighted materials upon a transfer or termination or expiration of the

234. *See, e.g.*, Independent Ass'n of Mailbox Ctr. Owners, Inc. v. Sup. Ct. of San Diego Cnty., 133 Cal. App. 4th 396 (Cal. Ct. App. 2005).

franchise agreement. This section also anticipates the common situation in which a franchisee adapts franchisor's copyrighted materials, and it makes clear that franchisor owns all copyrights in such adaptations.

F. Patents

Discussion:

[Patent language added if appropriate]

If franchisor owns a patent or patents in any process, machine, manufactured article, or chemical composition, or any improvement to any of these, and intends to grant a license to franchisees to use this patented matter, it will need to draft an agreement to protect its rights. Such protection is usually provided for in a separate license agreement, rather than in the franchise agreement, although where the franchise system depends on the franchisee's use of the patented invention, it is typical to see references to the patented invention included in the scope of definitions of the "system" and in other references to the franchisee's right to use the invention and limitations on the right to use it, throughout the agreement.

6

Accounting, Records, Reports, Audits, and Inspections; Insurance; Restrictive Covenants

Himanshu Patel and Brian B. Schnell

XXII. Accounting, Records, Reports, Audits, and Inspections

A. Bookkeeping, Accounting, and Records

Franchisee shall establish and continuously use an inventory, ordering, bookkeeping, accounting and record-keeping system conforming to the requirements Franchisor prescribes from time to time, including, without limitation, invoices, cash receipts, inventory records, purchase orders, payroll records, check stubs, bank deposit receipts, sales tax records and returns, cash disbursement journals and general ledgers together with such other equipment, records and documents as Franchisor may from time to time require. Franchisor's requirements may include computerized point-of-sale (POS), inventory, ordering, bookkeeping and accounting systems Franchisor establishes from time to time. In the event that Franchisor requires the establishment of, or specifies changes to, the computerized POS, inventory, ordering, bookkeeping, accounting or record keeping systems for its franchisees, Franchisee agrees to purchase or lease all necessary computer hardware and software, and to utilize such systems and pay all fees charged by Franchisor or others for the use and maintenance of such systems. Franchisee and all personnel employed by Franchisee shall record, at the time of sale all receipts from sales or other transactions, whether for cash or credit, on POS systems, cash registers or other equipment, software and any related technology or systems, which may only be available from a single source designated by Franchisor. No requirement that Franchisor prescribes under this Section, including without limitation any employee related information, is intended to exercise control over Franchisee's day-to-day operation of the Franchised Business or to assume any responsibility for Franchisee's obligations under this Agreement.

Discussion:

(i) Mandating a Uniform and Transparent System

The primary reason franchisors insist that the franchisees use a uniform accounting, record-keeping, and/or reporting system is to ensure the reliability and accuracy of the revenues that the franchisees generate from their franchised businesses. Many franchisors utilize a point-of-sale (POS) system that typically serves as a key component of the cash register system for the business. Ideally, the POS system then is integrated with other technology components to generate records and reports at both the individual franchisee's unit level as well as systemwide.

Record keeping and reporting are crucial for the integrity of the franchise system, as a franchisor's failure to enforce the requirement on a uniform basis can lead to certain franchisees underreporting as well as the franchisor failing to fully understand the fundamental unit level performance of the franchise system. When drafting this provision, the contract drafter must understand fully the importance of enabling the franchisor to unequivocally establish, maintain, and enforce the record-keeping and reporting requirements. This is not a provision that should include references to recommendations, suggestions, or alternatives, but rather frame the language using terms like requires, prescribes, mandates, or other similar terms that reflect the franchisor's absolute right to impose these standards.

Any uniform system is a helpful tool for franchisors receiving royalty fees, brand fund fees, and other fees based on gross revenues, as they can collect, review, confirm, analyze, and utilize the fee and revenue information with more confidence both on a unit level and systemwide basis. A uniform and transparent system also makes it more difficult in the unfortunate circumstances where a franchisee underreports sales or operates the business with two sets of books.

With the increasing availability of more customized and sophisticated technology capable of multiple functions that exceed the typical revenue reporting and other transaction-focused data, many franchisors are mandating a specific POS system that is used in all brand locations (corporate and the franchisee owned). These POS systems are highly functional and can generate valuable information that focus on unit level economics, important brand metrics and customer data and other key performance indicators that are relevant to the specific business and industry. Some franchisors go beyond the customized POS system and mandate a proprietary system that must be purchased from the franchisor, an affiliate of the franchisor, or a single approved outside vendor. If so, the franchise agreement (and franchise disclosure document, FDD) should properly disclose this single source requirement and how the franchisor or affiliate may derive revenue from those required purchases. The sample provision addresses this single-sourcing point.

In addition to the historical reasons for these uniform systems and requirements (these reasons still hold true today), prudent franchisors focus on the key benefits that franchisees can realize from a more robust POS system, including (1) clearer understanding and ability to focus on the unit level economics of the business and all operational components that impact unit level profitability, and (2) better access to education and training opportunities that the franchisee can choose to utilize so its employees are better prepared to deliver on the brand promise to customers.

(ii) Modification to the POS System

It also is crucial for the contract drafter to understand and recognize that the technology in these areas is constantly changing, so the language in the franchise agreement must enable the franchisor to require changes and upgrades as necessary. For example, the sample provision permits the franchisor to require specific changes to the POS system or bookkeeping, accounting, or record-keeping systems and requires the franchisee to pay for those changes, including fees associated with those changes. Technology-related upgrades or changes like mandating a new POS system can cause significant franchisee frustration and potential system conflict.[235] Domino's faced this challenge when it announced that all franchisees must purchase and install the PULSE system by June 30, 2008. In *Bores v. Domino's Pizza, LLC,* several franchisees claimed that the language in their franchise agreements did not permit Domino's to mandate the PULSE system, but rather allowed the franchisees to take the PULSE specifications and purchase the POS computer

---

235. Franchisees often object that POS systems (customized or generic) are not adequately tested prior to a required rollout, do not work properly, and any attempts at troubleshooting are ineffective, will not deliver what each franchisee deems is important to their business or individual circumstances, or simply cost too much based on performance.

The dispute between Wendy's International (Wendy's) and Davco Restaurants (Davco), one of Wendy's largest multi-unit franchisees back in the early 2000s, illustrates how a franchisor mandated POS upgrade can create conflict in a franchise system. The dispute related to Wendy's decision to require franchisees to undertake a significant remodel program that included an upgrade to the POS system. When Davco refused to comply with the franchisor mandates, Wendy's sued Davco to terminate the relationship. Davco's resistance was similar to the position that a franchisee often takes when they question their franchisor's upgrade decisions, with the refusal to comply based on the franchisee's cost to implement the upgrade without any corresponding return on the investment. The Wendy's/Davco dispute was settled in mid-year 2017 when it was announced that Wendy's purchased 140 restaurants from Davco and sold them to NPC International, another large multi-unit Wendy's and Pizza Hut franchisee. As part of the deal, NPC agreed to remodel 90 of the 140 acquired restaurants over a number of years and also agreed to build new units. *See* Beth Ewen, *NPC In, DavCo Out as Wendy's Puts to Rest 3-Year Dispute*, Franchise Times, June 6, 2017.

hardware and software meeting those specifications from any source.[236] In reversing the district court's decision that the contract language only allowed Domino's to specify component parts and technology rather than the specific PULSE system available only from a single source, the court of appeals focused on dictionary definitions of "specification" and "any" in concluding that specifications permitted Domino's to specify a computer system with comparable capabilities or the PULSE system and that "any source" includes "one, some, every or all."[237] The dispute in *Bores* underscores the importance of the single-sourcing language that is included in the last sentence of the preceding sample provision.

The challenge with POS systems is that technology improvements are constantly occurring, so franchisors must balance the desire to upgrade the technology with the challenges that any technology upgrade presents. Those challenges often include franchisees resisting change that often is more frequent than they believe is necessary, the additional costs that can be attendant to technology upgrades, the temporary business disruption that often is created with technology change, and the education and training that is required with implementing and utilizing new technology. In light of those challenges, a franchisor is well served to continuously emphasize how the franchisor requirements regarding POS systems and other bookkeeping, accounting, and record-keeping requirements enhance a franchisee's ability to better understand unit level performance and enable the franchisee to make decisions on how they can improve their unit level profitability.

One final point for franchisors to consider when drafting record-keeping and reporting provisions is to recognize the potential joint employment related issues (discussed in greater detail in Chapter 4) that can arise if the franchisor exercises or exerts too much control over the franchisee's day-to-day operation of the franchisee's business. Drafters should expressly state that these requirements are not intended, and, in fact, do not exert that type of control over the day-to-day operation of the business, including wage and hour, hiring and discharging employees, or any other employment-related matters.[238] To that end, franchisors should, if pos-

236. *See* Bores v. Domino's Pizza, LLC, 530 F.3d 671 (8th Cir. 2008) (The key franchise agreement language in dispute was section 8.2 of the franchise agreement, which stated, in part, "We will provide you with the specifications for computer hardware and software. You may purchase items meeting our specifications from any source.").

237. *Id.* Although the court of appeals noted that the *Bores* lawsuit involved nothing more than different interpretations of an unambiguous contract, the parties engaged in very expensive and contentious litigation, all of which underscores that the drafter of a franchise agreement must carefully consider each word or phrase used, especially with critical contract provisions.

238. *See, e.g.*, Gessele v. Jack in the Box, Inc., 2016 U.S. Dist. LEXIS 172061 (D. Or. Dec. 13, 2016) (franchisor was not joint employer where it provided franchisees with optional scheduling software); Ochoa v. McDonald's Corp., 2015 U.S. Dist. LEXIS 129539 (N.D. Cal. Sept. 24, 2015) ("simply providing the ISP software is not enough to convert McDonald's into an employer"); Vann v. Massage Envy Franchising LLC, 2015 U.S. Dist. LEXIS 1002 (S.D. Cal. Jan. 5, 2015) (finding franchisor not joint employer even though the franchise agreement required franchisees to "obtain the Computer System, software licenses, maintenance and support services, and other services related to the Computer System from the suppliers we specify); McFarland v. Breads of the World, LLC, 2011 U.S. Dist. LEXIS 20703 (S.D. Ohio Feb. 1, 2011) (holding that franchisor was not a joint employer where it had access to the point of sale cash register records required to pay royalties and franchise fees); Reese v. Coastal Restoration & Cleaning Servs., 2010 U.S. Dist. LEXIS 132858, at 11–12 (S.D. Miss. Dec. 15, 2010) (holding that the franchisor was not a joint employer where the franchise agreement required the franchisee to obtain the computer

sible, disclaim any potential for or actual access to information regarding employee scheduling and compensation levels or structure. A final best practice that reinforces this point is for a franchisor to clearly articulate, in its writings and actions, the role of any POS/computer system and how the franchisee will use the POS/computer system in the operation of its business.

B. Reports and Financial Information

Franchisee shall furnish to Franchisor such reports as Franchisor may require from time to time. Without limiting the generality of the foregoing, Franchisee shall furnish to Franchisor in the form from time to time prescribed by Franchisor (which will include Franchisor prescribed chart of accounts) and together with such detail and breakdown and copies of supporting records as Franchisor may from time to time require:

1. by the [e.g., Tuesday] of each week a report of the Gross Sales for the preceding week [(Monday to Sunday)], signed and verified by Franchisee;
2. within XX days after the end of each month, a balance sheet and profit and loss statement for the Franchised Business for the months;
3. within XX days after the end of each fiscal year of the Franchised Business, financial statements for the Franchised Business, including a balance sheet, profit and loss statement, a change in cash position statement and a statement of retained earnings for such period, which statements shall be prepared by an independent certified public accountant, and signed and verified by Franchisee; and
4. within XX days of the due date, a true copy of all tax returns, schedules and reports filed by Franchisee for income, corporate, sales tax, employer health tax, or workers compensation purposes.

Discussion:

Reporting requirements are a contract provision that can be overlooked when drafting the franchise agreement. The drafter should understand the franchisor's business, the industry in which the franchisor and the franchisees operate, and the franchisor's approach to what type of reports will be useful to the franchisor, the franchisees, and the franchise system overall. Consideration should be given to what reports are important on a weekly, monthly, quarterly, or annual basis and whether any of the reports should be prepared by a professional that the franchisee engages for those services. For example, although a franchisor generally does not require a franchisee to have the franchisee's annual financial statements audited by an outside accountant, the franchisor might require the franchisee to have that outside accountant prepare the annual statements (as indicated in the preceding sample

hardware and software as the franchisor required). Contra Ocampo v. 455 Hospitality LLC, 2016 U.S. Dist. LEXIS 125928 (S.D.N.Y. Sept. 14, 2016) (denying franchisor's motion to dismiss joint employment claim where franchisor required a particular computer system to track revenue and operations); Cano v. DPNY, Inc., 287 F.R.D. 251, 257, 260 (S.D.N.Y. 2012).

provision). The benefit of that type of approach is that the franchisee does not need to incur the costs of a full audit of the annual statements, but they still are prepared by the outside professional rather than a franchisee preparing those statements on their own, which may result in errors or inaccuracies.

Franchisors should emphasize that their record-keeping and reporting requirements, including the submission of financial statements, are all tools for (1) confirming that the franchisee is properly recording and reporting financial information and then paying the appropriate amount of fees based on gross sales or any other related payment obligation, (2) each franchisee to truly understand how its business is doing financially and how the franchisee compares with other franchisees in the system (in healthy franchise systems, the franchisees embrace competition with their fellow franchisees on unit level performance metrics), (3) the franchisor's field consultant and the franchisee to determine how to measure and improve performance at the unit profitability level, and (4) how the franchisor will measure its overall effectiveness in supporting franchisees.

As noted in the last part of the sample provision, a franchisee's reporting obligations also should include a franchisees' tax reporting obligations as a way to confirm that the franchisee is reporting the same or consistent information to the franchisor and the appropriate tax authorities. The tax reporting requirement also allows the franchisor to monitor the franchisees' obligations to comply with all applicable laws.

With the enhanced capabilities of technology that allow improved access and visibility to the actual numbers of each franchisee's business and a more robust focus on unit level economics, including a franchisee's bottom line profitability, more franchisors are enforcing these reporting provisions. With required reporting, a franchisor can use the more detailed expense information available to it to prepare more robust financial performance representations that they can include in Item 19 of its FDD. Franchisors who are looking to bring business savvy franchise candidates into their systems realize that those candidates are going to expect more comprehensive financial performance information than average unit gross sales information. Those candidates often are looking for gross or net profit information at the unit level, specifically from franchised units rather than just corporate or affiliate-owned units. One of the ways to ensure that a franchisor has that information available for consideration and analysis is to require that the franchisees report that information to the franchisor on a regular basis. Another key component to the reporting requirement and any subsequent analysis for any Item 19 disclosures is that the franchisor requires all the franchisees to use the franchisor's prescribed chart of accounts (as noted in the lead-in part of the sample provision).

Franchisors also can rely on these reporting requirements to catch rogue franchisees who are underreporting and should be terminated. In *Dunkin' Donuts v. Strategic Venture Group, Inc.*, the court concluded that the franchisor had good cause and properly terminated the franchisee's franchise agreements for the franchisee's bookkeeping irregularities and violations of the tax laws in breach of the franchisee's obligation to comply with all applicable laws, noting Dunkin Donut's thorough investigation that begin in 2005 and resulted in a notice of termination in April 2007. Specifically, the court referenced the information the franchisor gathered in interviews, discussions, meetings, and detailed loss prevention report prior to issuing the proper termination notice in accordance with the franchise agreement and the New Jersey Franchise Practices Act.[239]

The final point of emphasis is that prudent franchisors take advantage of the enhanced record-keeping and reporting opportunities to aggregate unit information on an individual, region or group, or systemwide basis to allow each franchisee more visibility into key financial and brand information to measure its performance with other franchisees and units in the system, all of which should foster more franchisee engagement with one another and the brand.

C. Inspection and Audit of Books and Records

> Franchisor shall have the right, during normal business hours and without prior notice to Franchisee, to inspect or audit, or cause to be inspected or audited the financial books, records, bookkeeping and accounting records, documents or other materials in respect of the Franchised Business, including the right, without limitation, to have a person on the Premises to check, verify and tabulate Gross Sales, and/or to examine and make copies of all accounting and business records and procedures.
>
> In the event that any such audit or inspection shall disclose an understatement of Gross Sales, royalty or other material financial information related to the Franchised Business, Franchisee shall pay to Franchisor, within XX days after receipt by Franchisee of the inspection or audit report, the royalty and other sums due on account of such understatement. Further, if such audit or inspection is made necessary by the failure of Franchisee to furnish reports, financial statements or any other documentation as herein required, or if it is determined by any such audit or inspection that Franchisee's records and procedures were insufficient to permit a proper determination of Gross Sales for any year or part thereof to be made, or that Gross Sales, royalty or other material financial information for the period in question were understated by XX% or more of the Gross Sales actually received, or that Franchisee was not complying with each of the provisions of Section XX, Franchisee shall immediately take such steps as may be necessary to remedy such default in accordance with any Franchisor requirement and Franchisee shall promptly pay to Franchisor all costs incurred in connection with such audit or inspection, including, without limitation,

239. Dunkin' Donuts Franchised Restaurants LLC v. Strategic Venture Grp, Inc., Civ. Action No. 07-1923 SRC, 2007 WL 2332190 (D.N.J. Aug. 13, 2007). In making its determination, the judge noted that the one of the franchisee's principals had the education, background, and experience to possess a level of sophistication that made him aware of the violations. Other judges at times will look beyond the language of the franchise agreement and take into account statutory considerations when a franchisee's failure to comply with its tax obligations may result in termination of a franchise. *See, e.g.*, Chevron, U.S.A., Inc. v. Mebatah, 148 F. Supp. 2d (2009) (franchisor was enjoined from terminating a franchisee under the federal Petroleum Marketing Practices Act of 1979, as the court determined that the franchisee's failure to report his state sales tax was not a term fundamental to the franchise relationship nor did the term have real importance or great consequence to the relationship, despite the franchisor's statements that the franchisee's actions resulted in the franchisor's inability to trust the franchisee).

charges of an accountant and the travel expenses, room, board and compensation of employees of Franchisor or its designee who performed the audit or inspection. In the event any audit or inspection reveals any understatement of XX% or more as stated above, Franchisor has the right as it deems necessary to conduct further audits or inspections for up to two years thereafter, at Franchisee's expense for all costs and expenses of the subsequent audit or inspection. Franchisee acknowledges and agrees that if a subsequent audit or inspection reveals any understatement of XX% or more, in addition to any other available remedies, Franchisor will have the right to terminate this Agreement without any opportunity to cures in accordance with Section XX of this Agreement.

If Franchisee's records and procedures were insufficient to permit a proper determination of Gross Sales, Franchisor shall have the right to deliver to Franchisee an estimate, made by Franchisor, of Gross Sales for the period under consideration and Franchisee shall immediately pay to Franchisor any amount shown thereby to be owing on account of the royalty fees and other sums due on account of any understatement. Any such estimate shall be final and binding upon Franchisee.

Discussion:

Inspections fall into two categories: (1) books and records in order to evaluate the integrity of franchisee reporting, and (2) evaluation of the franchisee's premises and its adherence to the system standards in the operation of the franchised business. Each category is important to the viability and sustainability of the franchise relationship, the franchise business model, and the ability for the franchisees to deliver consistently on the customer experience.

The franchisor's right to audit in most instances should dissuade any franchisee from not playing by the rules when it comes to accurate record keeping and reporting in accordance with the franchisor's prescribed formats and methodologies. If the threat of an audit is not enough of a deterrent, then the franchisor should exercise its audit rights and inspect the franchisee's books and records. If a franchisor does not have the right or available resources on its team, then it can engage a third party representative, preferably someone who has the capabilities and experience to effectively conduct the audit and issue its findings.

The stakes often are high when the franchisees fail either a financial audit or operational evaluation, with termination of the franchise as a consequence frequently included in franchise agreements, such as outlined in Chapter 8. Typically, the franchisees assert that financial audits are punitive in nature and nothing more than a subterfuge to the franchisor wanting to terminate the franchisee and take over the franchisee's business or market. Franchisees also often claim that they do not have all the financial information available for the audit or that their bookkeeper failed to properly maintain the required records, neither of which is a legitimate reason for not complying with an audit request, especially with the current record-keeping technology that most franchisors use.

With those franchisee perspectives in mind, the contract drafter should clearly state what information the franchisor has the right to inspect or audit and when and where the franchisor can conduct the inspection or audit. The sample provision describes the information that the franchisor can inspect or audit and that the inspection or audit will take place during normal business hours at the franchisee's business premises. Other options can include before or after normal business hours or off-site, although those modifications can make it more difficult to get all required information in an efficient manner.

The language in the audit provision should clearly state (1) what happens if an audit reveals underreporting (the sample language states that the franchisee must pay any amount due to any understatement immediately), (2) what aspects of the audit might lead to immediate termination (the sample language states that underreporting of the specified percentage or more gives the franchisor the right to terminate immediately), and (3) when the franchisee will be required to pay for the costs incurred by the franchisor or its designee in conducting the audit (the sample language requires the franchisee to pay the audit costs in the instances of a certain level of underreporting and for all subsequent audits that the franchisor chooses to conduct within the following two-year period).

One point that franchise candidates will raise from time to time is that they do not want to be subject to termination if any underreporting or understatement is not intentional or due to an error by their bookkeeper or some employee or some other similar reason. The franchisor will take that point into consideration as part of its decision on where to establish the underreporting percentage variance that results in the franchisee paying for the audit or termination. Other factors that the franchisor will consider in establishing that percentage include the average revenue of the franchised business (for example, a 3 percent underreporting percentage for a franchise system with an average unit volume of $400,000 might be reasonable, while 2 percent or something less might be reasonable for a franchise system with an average unit volume of $1 million or more). While each system selects its own figure, it is very rare for franchisors to use a number lower than 2 percent or higher than 5 percent in this provision.

The franchisors should proactively design their financial audit process with the understanding that franchisees often file lawsuits in challenging either a franchisor's right to audit or the audit results with allegations that the audit was secretive, inappropriate, or with the intent to constructively terminate without good cause.[240]

Although a franchisor should reserve the right to conduct an audit without notice in those instances where it feels the franchisee is intentionally underreporting or doing business off the books, in most instances the franchisor should conduct the audit/financial inspection in accordance with a prescribed protocol, including a request for all necessary financial documents and records, tax returns, and other related items that allow the franchisor to cross-check information. In many of those instances, a subsequent audit is necessary to ensure the franchisee has taken the

240. *See* Sandhu v. 7-Eleven, Inc., 45. F. Supp. 3d. 426 (2014) (court refused to grant the plaintiff franchisee's motion for injunctive relief to enjoin the alleged constructive termination, noting that despite plaintiff's allegations that the audit was part of a nationwide scheme to improperly intimidate and terminate franchisees, not one scintilla of objective evidence demonstrated that the audit was either inaccurate or conducted outside the scope of the franchise agreement and the plaintiff franchisee declined to allow a subsequent audit).

appropriate steps to correct the situation and is on the right track. On the other hand, as noted in the sample provision, if a subsequent audit reveals that the franchisee continues to underreport, then the drafter should clearly provide that the franchisor has the right to terminate the franchise agreement without any opportunity to cure.

The final point worth noting in the sample provision is the franchisor's right to estimate gross sales and any amounts owed based on those estimated amounts if the information that the franchisee has provided is insufficient to conduct an audit. In such an instance, the franchisor will typically be able to estimate a franchisee's gross sales based on other aspects of the franchisee's business like inventory purchases or certain cost percentages and how they compare to other franchised businesses. While certain franchisees may object to this type of provision, the explanation that addresses that objection is that the franchisee is in complete control as to whether the provision is triggered, as all it needs to do is make sure it is complying with the record-keeping procedures and that the required information is available for any audit or inspection. From the franchisor's perspective, this can be an important tool to help it address situations in which the franchisee has not maintained accounting records or has commingled revenue from more than one business.

D. Right to Inspect Franchised Business and Premises

Franchisor and/or its representatives shall have the right at all times, without notice to Franchisee, to inspect the Premises and the furnishings, equipment and fixtures thereon, the products, to take inventory of such products, and otherwise to examine the manner in which Franchisee is conducting its business; in the event of any such inspection, Franchisee and its staff shall co-operate fully. Franchisor or its authorized representative has the right to enter your Restaurant at all reasonable times during the business day for the purpose of making periodic evaluations and to ascertain if the provisions of this Agreement are being observed, to inspect and evaluate your building, land and equipment, and to test, sample, inspect and evaluate Franchisee's supplies, ingredients and products, as well as the storage, preparation and formulation and the conditions of sanitation and cleanliness in the storage, production, handling and serving. Franchisor or its representative also has the right to interview Franchisee, its employees and subcontractors, marketing contacts and customers pertaining to matters of compliance with this Agreement and the System and to photograph, videotape or audiotape any such interviews and/or observation/inspection of the operation of the Restaurant with or without Franchisee's knowledge and without prior notice to Franchisee. Franchisee hereby consents to Franchisor's use of any such audio or video recording for training, marketing or any other purpose. Any evaluation or inspection Franchisor conducts is integral to Franchisor's right to monitor and protect its Trademarks and is not intended to exercise control over Franchisee's day-to-day operation of the Restaurant or to assume any responsibility for Franchisee's obligations under this Agreement.

Any failure of an inspection is a default under the Agreement. Further, if Franchisor determines that any condition in the Restaurant presents a threat to customers or public health or safety, Franchisor may take whatever measures Franchisor deems necessary, including requiring Franchisee to immediately close the Restaurant until the situation is remedied to Franchisor's satisfaction.

Discussion:

A franchisor's evaluation or inspection of a franchisee's business premises and operations should focus on the key elements like system standards, brand standards, any preparation and delivery of the authorized products and services, and the overall customer or guest experience provided by the franchisee and its team. Any evaluation or inspection of a franchisee's business premises or operations will include to some degree subjective determinations by the person conducting the evaluation or inspection. While that subjectivity may not relate to points like whether a franchisee is using approved products or properly cooking food products or whether employees are wearing approved uniforms, subjectivity does enter the equation with items like whether a franchisee's customer service standards meet the franchisor requirement or whether certain fixtures need replacing now or next year or any of other subjective requirements that could result in a franchisee failing the evaluation or inspection.

Recognizing the subjective nature of certain key parts of any evaluation or inspection, the franchise agreement language on franchisor's right to conduct the evaluation or inspection must be unequivocal on what can be inspected and evaluated, when it can be inspected and evaluated, and the manner in which it can be inspected and evaluated.

Lawsuits involving inspection or evaluation disputes often turn on the written communications related to the inspection or evaluation. Franchisors must educate and train their field support teams and any audit personnel on the critical importance of smart writing and creating accurate exhibits. In *McDonald Corporation v. Robertson*, the court of appeals concluded that the district court had properly terminated the Robertson's franchise and enjoined the franchisee from continuing to run a McDonald's restaurant, based on the franchise agreement language that required the franchisee to operate the restaurant in accordance with quality, safety, and cleanliness (QSC) standards prescribed by the franchise agreement and by McDonald's business and policy manuals and based on a record that established a detailed record regarding multiple QSC audits and franchisee's multiple failures to comply with food safety checklists and procedures.[241]

One other key point that should be called out in this section is the need to address any joint employer-related risks by clearly stating that any evaluation or inspection is integral to a franchisor's right to monitor and protect its brand and trademarks and is not intended to exercise control over a franchisee's day-to-day operation of the business, as is stated in the last sentence of the sample provision.

241. *See* McDonald's Corp. v. Robertson, 147 F.3d 1301 (11th Cir. 1998) (The court of appeals was not persuaded by the franchisee's claims that they were operating the restaurant in the same manner and according to the same high standards for food, safety, and service that they had for the past 26 years.).

XXIII. Insurance

Franchisee must purchase and maintain in full force and effect, at Franchisee's expense and from a company Franchisor accepts, insurance that insures both Franchisee and Franchisor, and any other persons Franchisor designates by name. The insurance policy or policies must be written in accordance with the standards and specifications (including minimum coverage amounts) set forth in writing by Franchisor from time to time, and, at a minimum, must include the following (except as different coverages and policy limits may be specified for all franchisees from time to time in writing): (i) "special" causes of loss coverage forms (sometimes called "All Risk Coverage" or "All Peril Coverage") on the Franchised Business, Franchised Business improvements and all furniture, fixtures, equipment, supplies and other property used in the operation of the Franchised Business, for full repair and replacement value, except that an appropriate deductible clause is permitted; (ii) business interruption insurance covering a minimum of [e.g. 12] months loss of income, including coverage for Franchisor's Royalty Fees (for example, in the event of a fire or destruction of the Premises, the insurance must cover Franchisor's average royalty payments (based on the previous [12-month] timeframe, or if a shorter timeframe, the total operating timeframe for the Franchised Business) during the rebuilding process); (iii) comprehensive general liability insurance including product liability insurance and contractual liability insurance; (iv) workers' compensation insurance covering all of Franchisee's employees; (v) motor vehicle insurance; (vi) umbrella liability insurance which also includes employers liability; (vii) "Per Location" aggregate limits when multiple franchise locations are insured under one comprehensive general liability and umbrella liability policy(cies); (viii) naming Franchisor and any other Franchisor designated affiliates as additional insured parties on all liability policies required by this subparagraph; (ix) severability of interests and/or separation of insured's provisions must be included in the liability policies and all policies must be primary and non-contributing with any insurance policy carried by Franchisor; and (x) any other such insurance coverages or amounts as required by law or other agreement related to the Franchised Business.

The insurance coverages referenced in (iii), (iv), (v), (vi), and (vii) must commence as of the date Franchisee signs this agreement. The insurance coverages referenced in (i) and (ii) of this subparagraph must commence as of the date construction begins at the Franchised Business. Franchisee must deliver to Franchisor at commencement and annually or at Franchisor's request a proper certificate evidencing the existence of such insurance coverage and Franchisee's compliance with the provisions of this subparagraph. The insurance certificate must show Franchisor's status as an additional insured and provide that Franchisor will be given XX days' prior written notice of a material change in or termination or cancellation of the policy. Franchisor also may request copies of all policies. Franchisor may from time to time modify the required minimum limits and require additional insurance coverages, by providing written notice to Franchisee, as conditions require, to reflect changes in relevant circumstances, industry standards, experiences in the franchise system, standards of liability and higher damage awards. If Franchisee does not procure and maintain the required insurance coverage required by this Agreement, Franchisor has the right, but not the obligation, to procure insurance coverage and to charge the costs to Franchisee, together with a reasonable fee for the expenses Franchisor incurs in doing so. Franchisee must pay these amounts to Franchisor immediately upon written notice. Franchisor also reserves the right to designate an insurance agency or broker that Franchisee must use for in order to comply with Franchisee insurance obligations.

Franchisee acknowledges that these minimum insurance requirements do not constitute advice or a representation by Franchisor that such coverages are necessary or adequate to protect Franchisee from losses in connection with the Franchised Business. Nothing in this Agreement restricts Franchisee from obtaining insurance with higher policy limits and/or additional coverage.

Discussion:

Insurance provisions in a franchise agreement are crucial to protect the brand and the trademarks and the overall value of the network, which includes the investments franchisees have made in their businesses. Insurance provisions also properly serve as a risk allocation measure. In order to protect those assets and investments properly, a franchisor must require that the franchisees carry the right types of insurance with adequate levels of coverage. As a result, many franchise agreements contain detailed provisions relating to insurance like the preceding sample included.

The trap that a drafter can encounter is to assume that the insurance language in the franchise agreement is standard boilerplate language, rather than detailed discussions with the appropriate members of the franchisor's management team and experienced insurance brokers familiar with franchising and the industry in which the franchisor operates in order to determine for that particular franchise agreement what are the appropriate types and levels of coverage.[242] For example, a restaurant brand that serves alcohol will want to include liquor liability-type coverages, and a business that includes use of a vehicle will need to have sufficient vehicle coverage.

The language in the sample provision also includes details on additional insureds and the right to modify insurance requirements, including different types of coverage. Franchisees can suffer catastrophic losses if they do not have proper insurance coverage, which can result in harm to the franchise system and brand.

New franchisees who have not previously owned and operated small businesses often fail to appreciate the importance of adequate insurance coverage. They claim that the requirements are cumbersome, time consuming, and premiums often are too expensive. Whether it is a new franchisee who does not understand the importance of having appropriate insurance coverage or a franchisee who lets its insurance coverage lapse for failure to pay premiums or any other reason, the franchisor

---

242. *See, e.g.*, Estate of Anderson v. Denny's Inc., 987 F. Supp. 2d 1113, 1124 (D. N.M. 2013) (franchise agreement required franchisee to obtain various forms of comprehensive general liability insurance, including (1) obtain and maintain insurance of at least $1 million, combined single limit, and (2) include franchisor as an additional insured on such policies; to defend, indemnify, and hold harmless franchisor against any and all loss, costs, expenses (including attorneys' fees), damages and liabilities, however caused, resulting directly or indirectly from or pertaining to the use, condition, or operation of the restaurant).

simply cannot allow a franchisee to operate without the proper insurance in place. Those types of situations are why the franchisor must include language that (1) requires the franchisee to provide proof of insurance coverage prior to opening and on an annual basis, and (2) allows the franchisor to obtain coverage on behalf of that the franchisee and charge the costs back to the franchisee.

Drafting the insurance provisions also requires the drafter to review and understand the franchisee's indemnification obligations.[243] For a detailed discussion related to indemnification, please see Chapter 10.

The franchisors must prioritize franchisee education and training on insurance-related matters and a review of the insurance requirements under the franchise agreement. As noted in the sample provision, a franchisor also should strongly consider including language in this provision that gives the franchisor the right to designate an insurance agency/broker as a preferred vendor. This agency will play a key role in helping the franchisees understand the business and business model as well as the risks and risk profiles that exist in the operation of the business. Its personnel will understand the specific industry in which the franchisees operate as well as the technical understanding of the insurance industry. They will educate the franchisees on the importance of maintaining adequate insurance coverage and timely and properly filing claims and related documents and also will be on top of any new insurance products that might be available in the marketplace.

XXIV. Restrictive Covenants and Trade Secrets

A. Competition during Term of Agreement

> Franchisee and the Guarantor (in consideration of Franchisor entering into this Agreement), jointly and severally, covenant and agree that, beginning on the Commencement Date, and during the Initial Term and any renewal period thereof, each of Franchisee, any stockholder of Franchisee if Franchisee is a corporation, any member if Franchisee is a limited liability company, any partner of Franchisee if Franchisee is a partnership, the Guarantor, and any of their respective spouses and children, shall not either individually or in partnership or jointly or in conjunction with any person, firm, association, syndicate or corporation, as principal, agent, stockholder or in any

243. *See, e.g.*, Marriott Intern., Inc. v. Amco Ins. Co., No. 2:09-CV-04205, 2010 WL 2195566, at *3 (W.D. Mo. 2010) (Franchise agreement provided that franchisee's indemnity of franchisor would survive if the franchise agreement were terminated, and that the franchisee maintain comprehensive liability insurance naming franchisor and its employees as unrestricted uninsured. The insurance policy was for Apr. 2007–Apr. 2008; however, the franchise agreement ended in Nov. 2007. Five days after the termination of the franchise agreement, a franchisee employee was raped and killed while working and her estate sued. The court held that the insurance policy agreement only included franchisor and an additional insured due to its franchise agreement with franchisee, only for as long as the franchise agreement lasted. The franchise agreement ended five days before the incident, so franchisor lost its additional insured protection at that time.); *see also* Bassett v. Burger King Corp. 2010 WL 4259682, at *1 (Mich. Ct. App. Oct. 28, 2010) (franchise agreement clarified that the obligation to indemnify and defend franchisor is separate and distinct from the franchisee's obligation to maintain insurance).

manner whatsoever, carry on or be engaged in or be concerned with or interested in or advise, lend money to, guaranty the debts or obligations of or permit their names or any part thereof to be used or employed *in any business operating or franchising a [type of business should be specifically described here] business of any kind (***"Competing Business"***).*

Discussion:

Franchise agreements typically include in-term non-compete covenants, which restrict competition during the term of the franchise agreement. These provisions routinely ban competition within a certain mileage radius of the franchised location and sometimes within the territory of other franchisees or company-owned stores as well. No matter how well drafted, if such restrictive covenants are not enforceable, they are of little value to the franchisor.[244] Because restrictive covenants restrain trade and freedom of enterprise, courts typically subject them to strict or close scrutiny. Depending on the jurisdiction, covenants not to compete may be subject to state contract law, franchise statutes, and more generally applicable statutes that cover franchising as well as other enterprises.[245]

In-term noncompetition covenants are important to the franchisors for a variety of reasons. These restrictions protect the franchised trademarks, promote loyalty from the franchisees, and help to prevent the threat of customer loss.[246] In-term noncompetes are critical to the franchisors because unlike the employment context, where employees typically owe their employers a duty not to compete elsewhere while employed, the franchisees are independent contractors of a franchisor and, without an in-term covenant not to compete, otherwise may not be restricted under the law from competing, even during the term of the franchise agreement.[247]

(i) Judicial Scrutiny

Most courts scrutinize in-term (as well as post-term) noncompetition covenants using a four-part test. The covenant must be (1) ancillary to the main purpose of an otherwise lawful contract;[248] (2) necessary to protect the enjoyment of legitimate benefits of the contract;[249] (3) reasonable and not impose an undue hardship on the

244. Peter J. Klarfeld, *Introduction* to COVENANTS AGAINST COMPETITION IN FRANCHISE AGREEMENTS xv (Peter J. Klarfeld, ed., 2d ed. 2003).

245. For a helpful discussion of the legal background, judicial treatment, and enforcement of non-compete covenants in franchise agreements, see Michelle L. Evans, *Enforceability of Covenant Not to Compete*, American Jurisprudence Proof of Facts 3d (June 2016).

246. Asbill, Barkoff, & Selden, *supra* note 4, at 46.

247. Klarfeld, *supra* note 244, at xvii.

248. *See, e.g.*, Scott v. Snelling and Snelling, Inc., 732 F. Supp. 1034 (N.D. Cal. 1990).

249. *See, e.g.*, Boulanger v. Dunkin' Donuts Inc., 442 Mass. 635, 815 N.E.2d 572, 578 (2004) (finding that protection of trade secrets, confidential information, and good will are legitimate business interests but restraint of ordinary competition is not a legitimate interest); Tutor Time Learning Centers, LLC v. Larzak, Inc., 2007 WL 2025214 (N.D. Ind. 2007) (finding the good will established between a childcare center and its customers/parents is a legitimate business interest).

franchisee;[250] and (4) not injurious the public or against public policy.[251] Such inquiries are very fact-specific and depend on the particular franchise at issue.[252] If a covenant not to compete has an unreasonable term, many courts rewrite the contract and correct the offending term (so-called blue pencil states).[253] On the other hand, some courts will declare the entire covenant invalid if any part of it is unreasonable or against public policy.[254]

Courts have traditionally allowed in-term non-competes to be broader in scope than post-term non-competes, to protect a franchisor's legitimate expectation that a franchisee's efforts, focus, and use of know-how is directed solely to the franchised business during the term of the franchise agreement.[255] In some jurisdictions, however, courts apply the same strict scrutiny to in-term covenants as post-term covenants, despite the realities of the franchise relationship. Notably, in the 2009 Georgia case *Atlanta Bread Co. Int'l, Inc. v. Lupton-Smith*,[256] the Georgia Supreme Court refused to enforce, and invalidated as a matter of law, an in-term non-compete

250. Certified Restoration Dry Cleaning Network, L.L.C. v. Tenke Corp., 511 F.3d 535, 546 (6th Cir. 2007) ("In evaluating a non-competition clause for reasonableness, Michigan courts generally examine the clause's duration, geographic scope, and the type of employment prohibited."); Comedy Club, Inc. v. Improv West Associates, 553 F.3d 1277, 1289–93 (9th Cir. 2009), *cert. denied*, 130 S. Ct. 145, 175 L. Ed. 2d 36 (2009) (finding an in-term covenant unreasonable when it restrained the franchisee from participating in a similar business anywhere in the contiguous 48 states for a period of over 14 years).

251. Although this factor is less often litigated than its counterparts, some courts have considered injury to the public when determining whether to invalidate the restrictive covenant. *See* Interstate Automatic Transmissions v. W.H. McAlpine Co., Inc., No. C 80-320,1981 WL 2193 (N.D. Ohio June 17, 1983) (stating a covenant not to compete would be injurious to the public if there are an inadequate amount of transmission repair shops in the Toledo market, but ultimately finding no public injury). However, many states have a strong public policy in favor of freedom of contract that presents an often insurmountable hurdle when arguing that a covenant should not be enforced based on public policy. *See, e.g.*, Colonial Properties Realty Ltd. P'ship v. Lowder Const. Co., Inc, 567 S.E.2d 389, 393 (Ga. Ct. App. 2002) (noting that Georgia has a strong public policy in favor of freedom of contract); Oliver v. Quynn, 303 P.3d 1119, 1128 (Wyo. 2013) ("We do not lightly interfere with the freedom of contract between parties." (internal quotation omitted)).

252. For example, the fourth factor sometimes turns on the effect the restriction has on the public's ability to access the specific goods and services offered by the franchise. *See Interstate Automatic Transmissions*, 1981 WL 2193, at *2.

253. Hometask Handyman Services, Inc. v. Cooper, No. C07-1282RSL, 2007 WL 3228459 (W.D. Wash. Oct. 30, 2007) (revising covenant not to compete to include a 25-mile radius restriction on competition rather than an unreasonable 100-mile restriction); *but see* Gandolfo's Deli Boys, LLC v. Holman, 490 F. Supp. 2d 1353, 1357 (N.D. Ga. 2007) ("Georgia law considers franchise agreements to be analogous to employment contracts, and covenants in such agreements receive strict scrutiny and are not blue-penciled.") (decided prior to codification of O.C.G.A. 13-8-50-59 as set forth in note 257, *infra.*).

254. Bendinger v. Marshalltown Trowell Co., 338 Ark. 410 (1999) (overly broad non-compete covenant cannot be modified to render it reasonable even if the contract at issue contains a severability clause); Watson v. Waffle House, Inc., 253 Ga. 671 (1985) (pursuant to law at the time, overbroad restrictive covenants in franchise agreements are strictly construed against franchisor and deemed void); CAE Vanguard, Inc. v. Newman, 246 Neb. 334 (1994) (covenant must be enforced as written or not at all).

255. *See, e.g.*, McDonald's Systems, Inc. v. Sandy's Inc., 195 N.E.2d 22 (Ill. Ct. App. 1963) (drawing distinction, under Illinois law, between in-term and post-term non-compete covenants); *see also* Gray & Murray, *Covenants Not to Compete and Nonsignatories: Enjoining Unfair Conspiracies*, 25 FRANCHISE L.J. 107 (2006 WL 1681841).

256. Atlanta Bread Co. Int'l, Inc. v. Lupton-Smith, 679 S.E.2d 722 (Ga. 2009); *see also* Early v. MiMedx Group, Inc., 768 S.E.2d 823 (Ga. App. 2015) (citing *Atlanta Bread Co.* with approval and finding that an in-term restrictive covenant that requires an employee "to devote her full working time" to the employer constituted an illegal and unenforceable restraint of trade).

in a franchise agreement on the basis that it did not meet the strict requirements typically applied to post-term non-competes with respect particularly to territory and nature of the business. Because Georgia applied a nonseverability rule, the court also invalidated the franchisor's more narrow post-term non-compete. This case is somewhat of an anomaly particular to Georgia law at that time and the facts, but the result starkly demonstrates the impact local law may have on non-competes, including the in-term covenants that most franchisors view as critical.[257]

(ii) Protection of Confidential Information and Goodwill

Well-drafted restrictive covenants can be a very useful tool for franchisors seeking to protect their business interests from former or current franchisees who generally have liberal access to the franchisor's proprietary information. This information often includes employee training manuals, advertising information, and useful policies and procedures that lead to the effective operation of the business. To many franchisors, this type of information can be an invaluable asset that allows for the quick set up and easy operation of many new franchised locations. Protecting this proprietary information is understandably seen as necessary to ensuring the preservation of the franchisor's trademarks, trade secrets, goodwill, and brand identity.[258]

A critical function of a post-term non-compete to a franchisor is protection of its goodwill.[259] Goodwill is the value a business has over and above its assets attributable to the willingness of its customers to continue to patronize the business, as well as its ability to draw new customers to the business in the future.[260] In a franchise context, goodwill consists of the ability of a franchisor to draw and continue customer relations by reason of a franchisee's use of its "system," that is,

257. Following this case, the Georgia legislature took steps to change state law on this issue through legislative action, by passing HB 173 (codified at O.C.G.A. 13-8-50-59). Georgia's citizens approved the constitutional amendment in the general election of 2010. For a case interpreting restrictive covenants under the new law, *see* PointeNorth Insurance Group v. Zander, 2011 U.S. Dist. LEXIS 113413 (N.D. Ga. Sept. 30, 2011) (covenant purported to prohibit a former employee from soliciting or accepting business from clients. Such a covenant would have been completely unenforceable under Georgia's old non-compete law. Under the new law, however, court enjoined employee from soliciting any of employer's customers with whom she had contact during her employment).

258. *See, e.g.*, The Maids Int'l, Inc. v. Maids on Call, LLC, 8:17CV208, 2017 WL 4277146, at *7 (D. Neb. Sept. 25, 2017) (holding that "a business has an interest in protecting its goodwill, customer lists, know-how, trade secrets, trademarks, and the integrity of its franchise system."); Get In Shape Franchise, Inc. v. TFL Fishers, LLC, 167 F. Supp. 3d 173, 199 (D. Mass. 2016) (noting that "the protection of trade secrets, other confidential information, and the good will the employer has acquired through dealings with his customers constitute legitimate business interests" for the purposes of determining the validity of a non-competition agreement); Rocky Mountain Chocolate Factory, Inc. v. SDMS, Inc., 06-CV-01212-WYD-BNB, 2006 WL 8251823, at *5 (D. Colo. Dec. 8, 2006) ("National protection of trademarks is necessary in order to secure to the owner the goodwill of his business and to protect the ability of consumers to distinguish among competing producers.").

259. For a major franchisor with several locations in a given marketplace, the service mark or name is often the most significant element of the franchisor's goodwill. McDonald's restaurants, for example, are so ubiquitous that the McDonald's mark alone is a major draw to the chain of restaurants. For many smaller systems, however, the method of doing business contributes more to goodwill than the mark.

260. DNB Fitness, LLC v. Anytime Fitness, LLC, 11-CV-4892, 2012 WL 1952662, at *2 (N.D. Ill. May 30, 2012) ("Goodwill has been defined as the favor won from the public and the probability that customers will continue their patronage.").

the combination of its mark and method of doing business.[261] The franchisee obviously contributes to the development of goodwill during the franchise relationship when it uses the franchisor's system, but the franchisee never owns the goodwill.[262] This is true because the essential tools for developing the goodwill—the mark and method of doing business—belong to the franchisor.[263]

(iii) Trade Secrets

In addition to customer goodwill, trade secrets can be one of the franchisor's most valuable assets that deserves protection. Most states have adopted, in some form, the Uniform Trade Secret Act (UTSA).[264] Notably, 48 states and the District of Columbia have adopted their trade secret laws from the UTSA.[265] The two states that have not—Massachusetts and New York—rely on common law principles for the protection of trade secrets.[266] The UTSA defines a trade secret as:

> information, including a formula, pattern, compilation, program, device, method, technique, or process, that:
>
> (i) derives independent economic value, actual or potential, from not being generally known to, and not being readily ascertainable by proper means by, other persons who can obtain economic value from its disclosure or use, and
>
> (ii) is the subject of efforts that are reasonable under the circumstances to maintain its secrecy.[267]

---

261. *See id.*

262. LaGuardia Associates v. Holiday Hosp. Franchising, Inc., 92 F. Supp. 2d 119, 125 (E.D.N.Y. 2000) ("By authorizing the franchisee to use its trademarks and to sell its products or services, the franchisor is essentially lending its national goodwill to the franchisee.").

263. *See id.*

264. *See* UTSA § 1 (Unif. Law Comm'n 1985).

265. *See* Ala. Code. § 8-27-1 *et seq.*; Alaska Stat. § 45.50.910 *et seq.*; Ariz. Rev. Stat. § 44-401 *et seq.*; Ark. Code Ann. § 4-75-601 *et seq.*; Cal. Civ. Code § 3426 *et seq.*; Colo. Rev. Stat. § 7-74-101; Conn. Gen. Stat. § 35-50 *et seq.*; Del. Code Ann. tit. 6, § 2001 *et seq.*; D.C. Code § 48-501 *et seq.*; Fla. Stat. Ann. § 688.001 *et seq.*; Ga. Code Ann. § 10-1-760 *et seq.*; Haw. Rev. Stat. § 482B-1 *et seq.*; Idaho Code Ann. § 48-801 *et seq.*; 765 Ill. Comp. Stat. Ann. 1065/1-9 *et seq.*; Ind. Code. Ann. § 24-2-3-1 *et seq.*; Iowa Code Ann.§ 550.1 *et seq.* Kan. Stat. Ann. § 60-3320 *et seq.*; Ky. Rev. Stat. Ann. § 365.880 *et seq.*; La. Rev. Stat. Ann. § 51:1431 *et seq.*; Me. Rev. Stat. Ann. tit. 10, § 1541 *et seq.*; Md. Code Ann., Com. Law § 11-1201 *et seq.*; Mich. Comp. Laws Ann. § 445.1901–.1910; Minn. Stat Ann. § 325C.01 *et seq.*; Miss. Code Ann. § 75-26-1 *et seq.*; Mo. Rev. Stat. § 417.450–.467; Mont. Code Ann. § 30-14-401 *et seq.*; Neb. Rev. Stat. § 87-501 *et seq.*; Nev. Rev. Stat. § 600A.010 *et seq.*; N.H. Rev. Stat. Ann. § 350-B:1 *et seq.*; N.J. Stat. Ann. § 56:15-1 *et seq.*; N.M. Stat. Ann. § 57-3A-1 *et seq.*; N.C. Gen. Stat. § 66-152 *et seq.*; N.D. Cent. Code § 47-25.1-01 *et seq.*; R.C. § 1333.61 *et seq.*; Okla. Stat. Ann. tit. 78, § 85 *et seq.*; Or. Rev. Stat. § 646.461 *et seq.*; 12 Pa. Cons. Stat. § 5392 *et seq.*; R.I. Gen. Laws § 6-41-1 *et seq.*; S.C. Code Ann. § 39-8-1 *et seq.*; S.D. Codified Laws § 37-29-1 *et seq.*; Tenn. Code Ann. § 47-25-1701 *et seq.*; Tex. Civ. Prac. & Rem. Code Ann. § 134A.001 *et seq.*; Utah Code Ann. § 13-24-1 *et seq.*; Vt. Stat. Ann. tit. 9, § 4601 *et seq.*; Va. Code Ann. § 59.1-336 *et seq.*; Wash. Rev. Code Ann. § 19.108.010 *et seq.*; W. Va. Code R. § 47-22-1 *et seq.*; Wis. Stat. Ann. § 134.90; Wyo. Stat. Ann. § 40-24-101 *et seq.*

266. *See* Mass. Gen. Laws ch. 266, §§ 30(4), 60A; Ashland Mgmt. Inc. v. Janien, 82 N.Y.2d 395, 406 (1993) (applying the definition of "trade secret" from Restatement of Torts § 757 cmt. b).

267. UTSA § 1(4); *see also* Australian Gold, Inc. v. Hatfield, 436 F.3d 1228, 1244–45 (10th Cir. 2006) (citing the identical language of the Oklahoma Uniform Trade Secret Act); Sheffield Metals Cleveland, LLC. v. Kevwitch, 1:17 CV 1120, 2018 WL 1290990, at *6 (N.D. Ohio Mar. 13, 2018) (Ohio Uniform Trade Secret Act); Elenza, Inc. v. Alcon Labs. Holding Corp., 183 A.3d 717, 721 (Del. 2018) (Delaware Uniform Trade Secret Act).

Therefore, the two main considerations when determining whether something qualifies as a trade secret are economic value and secrecy. The information must not be generally known to, or readily ascertainable by proper means by, members of the public—including the franchisor's competitors. "Proper means" includes independent invention, reverse engineering, observation in public use, and information from published literature.[268] "Improper means," on the other hand, includes "theft, bribery, misrepresentation, breach or inducement of a breach of duty to maintain secrecy, or espionage through electronic or other means."[269]

Misappropriation of trade secrets is prohibited under both federal and state law.[270] A trade secret can be misappropriated in a number of ways. The most common of these occurs when the trade secret is (1) acquired by improper means[271] or (2) disclosed or used by a person who, at the time of disclosure or use, knew or had reason to know that the trade secret had been acquired under circumstances giving rise to a duty to maintain its secrecy or limit its use.[272]

Even if a franchisor takes care to protect its trade secrets, from time to time, misappropriations can still occur. This often takes the form of a current or former franchisee opening and/or operating a competing business that offers many of the same or similar products and/or services as those provided by the franchise. There are many different types of trade secrets that can be implicated in a franchise transaction that this common situation may cause to arise. Courts analyzing trade secret laws have found, in certain circumstances, the following types of information to be

---

268. UTSA § 1 cmt; *see also* N. Highland Inc. v. Jefferson Mach. & Tool Inc., 377 Wis. 2d 496, 557 (Wis. 2017) ("After all, any individual piece of 'information' satisfies the definition of 'trade secret' only if it also meets the independent economic value and secrecy requirements. . . ."); Crosby v. Koenig, LACV 38232, 2001 WL 34780402, at *2 (Iowa Dist. Oct. 31, 2001) ("Both elements of economic value and secrecy must [be] proved.").

269. UTSA § 1(1); Yager v. Vignieri, 16CV9367(DLC), 2017 WL 4574487, at *3 (S.D.N.Y. Oct. 12, 2017) (citing the Defend Trade Secrets Act, 18 U.S.C. § 1839(6)).

270. *See, e.g.*, CaremarkPCS Health, LLC v. New Hampshire Dep't of Admin. Services, 167 N.H. 583 (2015) (analyzing under UTSA); Pfizer Inc. v. Oregon Dept. of Justice ex rel. Kroger, 294 P.3d 496 (Or. Ct. App. 2012) (same); BlueEarth Biofuels, LLC v. Hawaiian Elec. Co., 780 F. Supp. 2d 1061 (D. Haw. 2011) (analyzing under Hawai'i Uniform Trade Secrets Act); BP Chemicals, Ltd. v. Baloun, 183 F. Supp. 2d 1158 (E.D. Mo. 2000) (analyzing under Missouri Uniform Trade Secrets Act); Share Corp. v. Momar Inc., 2010 WL 933897 (E.D. Wis. 2010) (analyzing under Wisconsin Uniform Trade Secrets Act).

271. *See* UTSA § 1(1) ("'Improper means' includes theft, bribery, misrepresentation, breach or inducement of a breach of a duty to maintain secrecy, or espionage through electronic or other means.").

272. *See* UTSA § 1(2), which defines "misappropriation as:

> (i) acquisition of a trade secret of another by a person who knows or has reason to know that the trade secret was acquired by improper means; or
>
> (ii) disclosure or use of a trade secret of another without express or implied consent by a person who
>
> > (A) used improper means to acquire knowledge of the trade secret; or
> >
> > (B) at the time of disclosure or use, knew or had reason to know that his knowledge of the trade secret was
> >
> > > (I) derived from or through a person who had utilized improper means to acquire it;
> > >
> > > (II) acquired under circumstances giving rise to a duty to maintain its secrecy or limit its use; or
> > >
> > > (III) derived from or through a person who owed a duty to the person seeking relief to maintain its secrecy or limit its use; or
> >
> > (C) before a material change of his [or her] position, knew or had reason to know that it was a trade secret and that knowledge of it had been acquired by accident or mistake."

protected: (1) business systems, formats, or methods;[273] (2) franchise manuals;[274] (3) business plans and strategic information;[275] (4) product information, recipes, and formulas;[276] (5) customer and supplier information;[277] (6) new product development plans;[278] and (6) proprietary computer software and technology.[279] While each of these types of information can amount to a trade secret entitled to protection, there is no general rule. Whether a particular piece of information amounts to a trade secret is a fact-specific inquiry and can depend on a number of factors, including the law in the relevant jurisdiction and the relative weight given to the evidence

273. *See, e.g.*, Uhlig LLC v. Shirley, 2012 WL 2923242, at *5 (D. S.C. July 17, 2012) (noting that a "compilation trade secret" is a collection of information that "work[s] together to embody a definite methodology, process, technique, or strategy."); Tan-Line Studios v. Bradley, 1986 WL 3764, at *7 (D. Pa. Mar. 25, 1986) (noting that plaintiff had meticulously developed a cohesive and defined strategy for the development, marketing, and operation of an indoor tanning studio such that the plaintiff's "entire methodology for conducting a tanning studio constitutes a trade secret. Therefore, plaintiff need not identify with specificity those individual aspects of [plaintiff's] business about which [defendant] appropriated information.").

274. *See, e.g.*, Gold Messenger, Inc. v. McGuay, 937 P.2d 907, 911 (Colo. Ct. App. 1997) (franchisor's manual contained trade secret information and had value as a trade secret); Total Car Franchising v. Wilhovsky, 2002 WL 34727053, at *14 (D.N.J. Mar. 28, 2002) (granting injunctive relief because "Plaintiff provided for confidentiality by informing franchisees that the processes outlined in the Manual constituted trade secrets and by developing a policy to protect such trade secrets and/or other confidential information"); SmokEnders, Inc. v. Smoke No More, Inc., 1974 WL 20234, at *3 (S.D. Fla. 1974) (the court found that the plaintiff's franchise manual had been "vital to the commercial success" of the plaintiff and was "valuable property").

275. *In re* Integrated Health Services, Inc., 281 B.R. 231, 237–38 (Bankr. D. Del. 2002) (business plan that mapped out employer's analysis of how it could enter market of supplying nurses to nursing homes, and that contained results of employer's research into viability of such a venture, qualified as "trade secret" entitled to protection); Verizon Comm. Inc. v. Pizzirani, 462 F. Supp. 2d 648, 659 (E.D. Pa. 2006) (citing PepsiCo, Inc. v. Redmond, 54 F.3d 1262, 1270 (7th Cir. 1995) (holding that, although not the typical case, strategic information regarding price, distribution, and marketing can fall within the realm of trade secret protection)).

276. *See, e.g.*, Synthes, Inc. v. Emerge Med., Inc., 25 F. Supp. 3d 617, 709 (E.D. Pa. 2014) (design drawings containing product information including "critical features" were entitled to trade secret protection); Mike's Train House, Inc. v. Lionel, L.L.C., 472 F.3d 398, 410 (6th Cir. 2006) ("[T]he design drawings here are properly considered trade secrets even though they contain a mixture of secret information (e.g., dimensions, tolerances, and data-reference points) and non-secret information."); Magistro v. J. Lou, Inc., 270 Neb. 438, 443 (2005) (finding that pizza recipes were trade secrets entitled to protection); Interbake Foods, L.L.C. v. Tomasiello, 461 F. Supp. 2d 943, 966 (N.D. Iowa 2006) (recipes and manufacturing processes with respect to ice cream sandwiches constituted trade secrets); ProLine Products, L.L.C. v. McBride, 324 P.3d 430, 432 (Okla. Civ. App. 2014) (formula for cold-patch asphalt was a trade secret).

277. *See, e.g.*, Philips Elecs. N. Am. Corp. v. Hope, 631 F. Supp. 2d 705, 721 (M.D. N.C. 2009) (finding that a select market data analysis based on special knowledge of specific customer needs and preferences contained in "[c]ustomer pricing lists, cost information, confidential customer lists, and pricing and bidding formulas may constitute trade secrets"); Guang Dong Light Headgear Factory Co., Ltd. v. ACI Int'l, Inc., 2008 WL 53665, at *15–16 (D. Kan. Jan. 2, 2008) (finding plaintiff's identification of trade secrets as collective information used to manage a specific customer relationship, including "price quote requests, sample requests, pricing, specification information, actual samples that had been submitted, purchase orders, sales orders, specifications, and shipments" was sufficiently identified to overcome summary judgment in suit against former employee who misappropriated a customer prospect after forming his own company).

278. *See, e.g.*, Estee Lauder Co. Inc. v. Batra, 430 F. Supp. 2d 158, 176 (S.D.N.Y. 2006) (finding trade secrets where employee was knowledgeable about marketing plans and "confidential products currently under development and product innovations scheduled for the coming years" and possessed "confidential information about the stage of development of products in the pipeline").

279. *See e.g.*, Misys Intern. Banking Sys., Inc. v. TwoFour Sys., LLC, No. 650101/2004,2004 WL 3058144, at *4 (N.Y. Sup. Ct. Nov. 23, 2004) (finding trade secrets where employee had knowledge of pricing and the "functional design" of the employer's proprietary software product).

supporting the trade secret claim.[280] Alternatively, and in order to most effectively protect this valuable information, franchisors may wish to specifically define what information may constitute a "trade secret" within the text of the franchise agreement so as to leave no doubt in the eyes of the court whether such information is entitled to protection.[281] However, in order to successfully eliminate the uncertainty a fact-specific inquiry could produce, franchisors must ensure that the agreement clearly defines the information as a "trade secret."[282]

(iv) Application of Non-Compete

Finally, covenants not to compete may focus not only on the franchisee and guarantors but also on family members of the franchisee. These clauses depend on the particulars of the franchise situation; if the family members are more heavily involved in the franchised business then care should be given to the drafting of such clauses to be appropriately inclusive. Essentially, the franchisor should restrict competition by anyone who is significantly involved in the daily running of the franchised business, to the extent enforceable under applicable law. Franchisors and franchisees alike should be aware of implications that different wording of in-term non-compete provisions may have on their respective rights and obligations. Franchisors must take care to ensure that the in-term restrictive covenant is narrowly tailored to accomplish the goal of developing a successful franchise location with its franchisee, and not seek to unduly burden a franchisee's rights. At the same time, the franchisees must be aware of the nature of the covenant(s) they are agreeing to in order to avoid unnecessary, and likely costly, future litigation regarding their rights to work in other enterprises during the term of their franchise agreement.

B. Competition after Transfer, Expiration, or Termination of Agreement

> In the event of a Transfer, or the expiration or termination of this agreement for any reason whatsoever, Franchisee and the Guarantor (in consideration of Franchisor entering into this agreement) jointly and severally covenant and agree that each of Franchisee, any stockholder of Franchisee if Franchisee is a corporation, any member if Franchisee is a limited liability company, any partner of Franchisee if Franchisee is

---

280. *See, e.g.*, Thermodyn Corp. v. 3M Co., 593 F. Supp. 2d 972, 986 (N.D. Ohio 2008) ("The determination of whether information constitutes a trade secret is a highly fact-specific inquiry."); Bimbo Bakeries USA, Inc. v. Botticella, 613 F.3d 102, 113 (3d Cir. 2010) (same); Commonwealth Dep't of Pub. Welfare v. Eiseman, 85 A.3d 1117, 1126 (Pa. Commw. Ct. 2014) (same); Woo v. Fireman's Fund Ins. Co., 154 P.3d 236, 239 (Wash. Ct. App. 2007) (same).

281. *See, e.g.*, Port-a-Pour, Inc. v. Peak Innovations, Inc., 49 F. Supp. 3d 841, 850 (D. Colo. 2014) (noting that the agreement specifically defined the term "trade secret"); McGowan & Co., Inc. v. Bogan, 93 F. Supp. 3d 624, 646 (S.D. Tex. 2015) (same); *but see* Rogerscasey Inc. v. Nankof, 02 CIV. 2599 (JSR), 2002 WL 726655, at *1 (S.D.N.Y. Apr. 23, 2002), *aff'd*, 50 Fed. Appx. 461 (2d Cir. 2002) ("While the agreement broadly defines 'Trade Secrets,' that definition is cabined by California law. . . .").

282. *Cf.* Agency Solutions.Com, LLC v. TriZetto Group, Inc., 819 F. Supp. 2d 1001, 1015 (E.D. Cal. 2011) ("At the outset, the court notes that although the agreement defines 'Confidential Information,' it does not do so in a way that enlarges or modifies the definition of Trade Secret or Confidential Information beyond their traditional legal boundaries.").

a partnership, the Guarantor, and any of their respective spouses and children, shall not, at any time during the period of XX years from the date of such Transfer, expiration or termination, either individually or in partnership or jointly or in conjunction with any person or persons, firm, association, syndicate, company or syndication as principal, agent, stockholder or in any other manner whatsoever carry on, be engaged in or be concerned with or interested in or advise, lend money to, guaranty the debts or obligations of or permit its name or any part thereof to be used or employed in any Competing Business, or franchising Competing Businesses, at the Franchised Business, within the Territory, or within XX miles of the perimeter of the Territory. This XX-year period shall be tolled during any period of noncompliance and extend thereafter.

Discussion:
In addition to in-term non-compete covenants, franchise agreements include a post-term covenant that restricts competition following the termination or expiration of the agreement. Post-term non-compete covenants are equally, if not more, important to the franchisors than in-term covenants because they allow the franchisor to continue to protect its valuable assets—such as its brand, trademarks, trade secrets, and goodwill—even after the franchise relationship has ended.[283]

(i) Judicial Scrutiny

From a structural standpoint, most jurisdictions require that post-term covenants be reasonable in temporal and geographic reach, line-of-business, or other scope (such as the type of activities restricted or particular market segment or customers that are off limits), and necessary to protect a franchisor's legitimate business interest.[284] Post-term noncompetition covenants are generally subject to the same four-part test articulated previously.[285] Further, it is important to note that post-termination covenants against competition often are subject to more strict judicial scrutiny than in-term covenants given their restraint on trade following the end of the contractual relationship and their potential impact on a former franchisee's ability to earn a livelihood. As

283. For a more complete discussion on trade secret protection, *see* discussion, Section XXIV.A.(iii), in this chapter.

284. *See, e.g.*, 7-Eleven, Inc. v. Kapoor Bros. Inc., 977 F. Supp. 2d 1211 (M.D. Fla. 2013) (applying Florida law and finding that a restrictive covenant prohibiting franchisee from continuing to operate convenience stores located at the same premises for one year after termination was warranted); AAMCO Transmissions, Inc. v. Romano, 42 F. Supp. 3d 700 (E.D. Pa. 2014) (applying Pennsylvania law and finding that a ten-mile radius of the former franchised location was reasonable); *but see* Outdoor Lighting Perspectives Franchising, Inc. v. Harders, 747 S.E.2d 256 (N.C. Ct. App. 2013) (finding that a restrictive covenant prohibiting the former franchisee from having involvement in *any* competing business was not reasonably necessary to protect the franchisor's legitimate business interests); Unlimited Opportunity, Inc. v. Waadah, 290 Neb. 629, 861 N.W.2d 437 (2015) (Covenant which prohibited a franchisee from operating a competing business in any other territory in which a franchise of franchisor operated for one year, was not reasonable in both space and time because franchisor operated on a multistate and international basis.).

285. *See, e.g.*, Certified Restoration Dry Cleaning Network, L.L.C., 511 F.3d at 546; Quizno's Corp. v. Kampendahl, 2002 WL 1012997 (N.D. Ill. 2002) (two-year, five-mile radius from original location restriction valid); ServiceMaster Residential/Commercial Services, L.P. v. Westchester Cleaning Services, Inc., No. 01 Civ. 2229 (JSM), 2001 WL 396520 (S.D.N.Y. 2001) (one-year, single county restriction valid).

described in the following, post-term non-competes therefore must be reasonable in geographic, temporal, and line-of-business scope, and necessary to protect a franchisor's legitimate business interest to pass muster in most jurisdictions.

Even with the need for a franchisor to protect vital business information—such as trade secrets—, historically, post-term restrictive covenants have been looked down upon by some courts because they necessarily require restrictions on free trade.[286] With respect to both in-term and post-term covenants, enforceability, judicial approaches, and the permissible parameters of the covenants vary by jurisdiction, sometimes widely.[287] As mentioned previously, some states permit courts to "blue pencil" an overly broad covenant and enforce a reworked scope that is, in the court's view, more reasonable.[288] Elsewhere, the law prohibits courts from blue penciling, which may render a covenant, even if just slightly too broad, void in its entirety.[289]

In one recent case, for example, the Supreme Court of Nebraska reiterated its rejection of the blue pencil rule.[290] In this case, the franchisor, Unlimited Opportunity, Inc.—also known as Jani-King—was in the business of offering for sale franchises of its professional janitorial and maintenance services. Under this particular business model, the franchisor actually solicited and negotiated with customers, and allowed the franchisee in that given area to perform the cleaning services. The defendant/franchisee, Waadah, signed a franchise agreement that contained the following non-compete provision:

> Franchisee . . . agrees that, during the term of this Agreement and for a continuous uninterrupted period of (2) years thereafter . . . commencing upon expiration or termination of this Agreement, . . . Franchisee . . . shall not . . . (d) Own, maintain, operate, engage in or have any interest in any business (hereinafter referred to as "Competing Business") which is the same as or similar to the business franchised under the terms of this Agreement, which Competing Business operates, solicits business, or is intended to operate or solicit business: (i) within the Territory of this Agreement; and (ii) for a period of one (1) year commencing upon expiration or termination of this Agreement (regardless of the cause for termination), in any other territory in which a Jani-King franchise operates.[291]

The franchise agreement was ultimately terminated. After termination of the agreement, the franchisee diverted a number of Jani-King's customers to his new, competing business, and Jani-King sued its former franchisee for damages relating

286. *See* United States v. Am. Tobacco Co., 221 U.S. 106, 180 (1911) (noting the "fundamental right of freedom to trade").

287. For a helpful survey of the law of covenants not to compete as they relate to franchising, *see* Michelle L. Evans, *Enforceability of Covenant Not to Compete*, American Jurisprudence Proof of Facts 3d (June 2016).

288. *See e.g.*, Aamco Transmissions, Inc. v. Romano, CV 13-5747, 2016 WL 792498, at *7 (E.D. Pa. Mar. 1, 2016), *vacated*, CV 13-5747, 2016 WL 7374544 (E.D. Pa. June 27, 2016).

289. *See, e.g.*, Gray & Murray, *supra* note 255, at 16–17, and materials cited therein.

290. Unlimited Opportunity, Inc. v. Waadah, 290 Neb. 629, 861 N.W.2d 437, 439 (2015).

291. *Id.*

to the breach of the noncompetition agreement. Upon reviewing the franchise agreement, the trial court found that the restrictive covenants contained within the agreement were overly broad because Jani-King operated on a nationwide basis. Therefore, the court found that requiring its franchisees to refrain from operating a similar business "in any other territory in which a Jani-King franchise operates" effectively precluded the franchisee from operating a similar business anywhere in the country. The Nebraska Supreme Court affirmed, reiterating that the language of the noncompetition provision, for all intents and purposes, provided no territorial limitation, making it unreasonable.[292] Thus is the danger some franchisors face when not being mindful of the practical implications of their restrictive covenants in states that do not allow blue penciling.

(ii) Scope

Given the differences in state law, it is critical that franchisors do their homework to determine their actual protectable interest and, once determined, narrowly tailor the non-compete covenants to protect that interest. In doing so, the drafters must consider how courts in the jurisdiction whose law the franchisor has chosen to apply to the franchise agreement approach covenants not to compete, as well as the laws in the states where the franchisees are likely to be located. Most franchisors either are or hope to be national, which means that a franchisor may have to draft its standard non-compete covenant with an eye toward the majority approach, and then handle particular jurisdictional differences (to the extent they may significantly impact enforceability or approval by regulators)[293] either through state- or franchisee-specific addenda.[294]

Franchisors also must consider their franchisee target market when drafting or negotiating non-compete provisions. As the business model of franchising becomes more widely used, and competition for savvy, well-capitalized franchisees heats up, this may be an area where a franchisor needs to be more flexible and understand that "competitive business" should be narrowly defined. For instance, it is not realistic for a food franchisor to expect a publicly traded company or even a large multi-unit operator not to have *any* interest in another restaurant concept (without defining what type of restaurant truly is competitive with the franchised business). Being too broad in the non-compete provision may foreclose opportunities to

292. Unlimited Opportunity, Inc. v. Waadah, 290 Neb. 629, 861 N.W.2d 437, 439 (2015); *Contra McCart v. H&R Block, Inc.*, 470 N.E.2d 756 (Ind. App. 3d 1984) (holding that a non-signatory to an H&R Block franchise agreement, the husband of the franchisee, could be enjoined from competing with Block after the termination).

293. Notably, some states, such as California, completely prohibit post-termination noncompetition covenants as void against public policy. *See, e.g.*, Sonoma Tires, Inc. v. Big O Tires, LLC, C 11-0818 RS, 2013 Westlaw 12173748, at *7 (N.D. Cal. Jan. 22, 2013), *order clarified*, C 11-0818 RS, 2013 Westlaw 12174138 (N.D. Cal. Apr. 19, 2013) ("The franchise agreement's post-termination covenant not to compete is void and unenforceable as against California's strong public policy promoting competition embodied in Section 16600.").

294. For example, franchisor may wish to add language stating that if the franchise agreement contains a provision that is inconsistent with the laws of a particular state, the law of the particular state will control.

attract a certain level or type of franchisee.[295] In general, when drafting a post-term restrictive covenant, the franchisors should first determine the ultimate goal of the covenant, and then choose geographic, temporal, and other scope restrictions that are narrowly tailored to serve that goal.[296] The more narrowly drafted a restrictive covenant is, the more likely it is that the provision will be enforceable.

Another related interest of a franchisor that is protected by the post-term non-compete is its desire to refranchise—or sell the former franchisee's area to a new franchisee.[297] By refranchising the area, the franchisor capitalizes on the goodwill that has been created by the former franchisee's use of the franchise system.[298] If, however, the former franchisee is allowed to continue to compete, it will be extremely difficult, if not virtually impossible, for the franchisor to refranchise the area within the foreseeable future.[299] One way that a franchisor may effectively protect this invaluable asset is by including a provision in the franchise agreement that allows the franchisor to assume the lease to the franchise property or otherwise allows the franchisor a right of first refusal in any potential sale of the franchise.[300] Such provisions may allow the franchisor to maintain a hold of the customer goodwill developed at the franchise location without the need for a court determination of the enforceability of a post-term restrictive covenant.[301]

---

295. For example, a pizza franchise may have one or more of the following type restrictions: (1) no competition within the system niche (e.g., pizza restaurants); (2) no involvement in any business that provides the same or similar goods or services (e.g., restaurants that serve pizza or other flatbread items; Italian restaurants); and (3) no involvement with any restaurant that serves any item from the franchisor's menu. The non-compete clause may also have geographic and time-based restrictions such as: (1) no competition within a radius of former territory (Nebraska case is a great illustration); (2) no competition within a radius of other franchisee territories; (3) no passive ownership (either at all or except for small interests in public companies); and (4) no competition for a period of time (e.g., two years).

296. Whether a particular provision is ultimately deemed appropriate is a fact-intensive analysis. *Compare* Ledo Pizza Sys., Inc. v. Singh, 983 F. Supp. 2d 632, 642 (D. Md. 2013) (finding reasonable a post-term restrictive covenant that "prohibits operation of a dine in or carry-out restaurant within ten miles of [former franchisee territory]" for two years) *with* Golden Krust Patties, Inc. v. Bullock, 957 F. Supp. 2d 186, 199 (E.D.N.Y. 2013) (finding a two-year, ten-mile restriction overbroad given that New York residents "will not travel ten—or even five miles—to a fast food establishment").

297. *See, e.g.*, Smallbizpros, Inc. v. Court, 414 F. Supp. 2d 1245, 1251 (M.D. Ga. 2006) (noting that a franchisor's ability to "re-franchise" is essential to maintain customer goodwill and the integrity of the franchise system, which would be significantly impaired if the post-term restrictive covenant was not enforced); HomeTask Handyman Servs., Inc. v. Cooper, No. C07–1282RSL, 2007 WL 3228459, at *3 (W.D. Wash. Oct. 30, 2007) ("Allowing [defendant] to exploit the company's good will and her former customer base would place HomeTask at a distinct disadvantage in attempting to re-franchise the area or otherwise recapture the market.").

298. *Smallbizpros, Inc.*, 414 F. Supp. 2d at 1251.

299. *Id.*

300. *See, e.g.*, Get In Shape Franchise, Inc. v. TFL Fishers, LLC, 167 F. Supp. 3d 173, 201 (D. Mass. 2016) (the franchise agreement at issues granted the franchisor "the right to purchase any or all inventory, equipment, supplies, signs, advertising materials, and items bearing Franchisor's Names and Marks, at fair market value, and to assume the lease for the [franchise] location").

301. Such provisions could prove especially effective in states such as California, where post-term restrictive covenants are void as a matter of law.

For many franchisors, a post-term non-compete is literally the glue that holds the system together.[302] If a former franchisee is allowed to conduct business as usual (except now it can no longer use the franchisor's name), it will likely continue to maintain the same customer relationships it had as a franchisee. This is true because it is not the name itself that has become the essence of the business, but it is the relationship between the customer and the former franchisee developed using the franchise system that creates goodwill.[303]

302. Depending on various factors, however, a larger or more unique franchise may be able to limit the restrictions contained within its franchise agreements based upon several factors, such as the strength of its marks, the proprietary nature of its products or ingredients, or the prevalence of strong loyalty/incentive programs. For example, a former McDonald's franchise location will probably not continue to pull in the same amount of customers once it de-identifies as a McDonald's. Similarly, if a particular product relies heavily on proprietary ingredients that can only be purchased by franchisees, the former franchisee may be unable to create a product of the same taste/quality as the franchise without heavy noncompetition restrictions.

303. *See e.g., Smallbizpros, Inc.*, 414 F. Supp. 2d at 1251; *HomeTask Handyman Servs., Inc.*, 2007 WL 3228459, at *3.

7

Transfer, Assignment, Death, or Incapacity of the Franchisee

Andra Terrell and Trish Treadwell

XXV. Transfer

Prospective franchisees often see the terms of franchise agreements as onerous. The agreements may be long-term, governing franchise relationships that may last not only decades but generations. The transfer provision—almost universally present—provides at least one exit strategy for a franchisee looking to end its franchise relationship or to know that a viable exit strategy exists. This planned exit can be an important term in any standard franchise agreement and a healthy part of any franchise system. A transfer provision is integral to balancing the franchisor's desire to pick and choose its franchisees and protect the particular franchised business and the franchise system in general juxtaposed against the franchisee's need or desire to change ownership of the franchised business because of changed relationships or circumstances, problems with the operation or profitability of the franchised business, or the desire of the franchisee or one or more of its owners to capitalize on the value of the franchised business.[304]

From the franchisee's perspective, a transfer of ownership presents a way to cash out on a successful business investment prior to the expiration of the term, or to cut its losses if the franchised business operations and profits did not meet expectations. A transfer gives the franchisee the ability to recoup the value of its business as a going concern and the flexibility to time its exit for a variety of reasons, such as industry or market shifts, as well as personal reasons such as retirement, divorce, or incapacity.

From the franchisor's perspective, a transfer is one way to assist a struggling franchisee to exit the system without going through a taxing default and termination process, to bring a franchisee's financial accounts current, to mandate an upgrade to then-current standards for the location, or to get a better operator in place to improve the franchise operations and results. It is a good sign of a healthy system if there is demand to purchase existing franchises.[305] On balance, all parties benefit from protection of the right to transfer the franchise.

This chapter presents sample transfer provisions from both a franchisor and franchisee perspective. As discussed next, various state laws impact the rights and restrictions associated with a franchisee's ability to transfer or assign a franchise agreement, but the franchise agreement provides the controlling language in most states. In a typical franchise agreement, the franchisor has an unrestricted right to transfer, but the franchisee must comply with a specific process, restrictions, and transferee criteria.

A. Definition of a Transfer

> For purposes of this Franchise Agreement, "Transfer" shall mean to sell, assign, transfer, convey, gift, encumber, mortgage, grant a security interest in, or otherwise dispose of or encumber all or any of the Franchisee's interest hereunder or any assets of the Franchised Business, including the lease for the Premises (except to another Principal). Transfer includes any such sale, assignment, transfer, conveyance, gift, encumbrance, or other disposal that occurs by operation of law. Transfer shall also include any transfer of this Franchise Agreement and the rights and obligations hereunder to a corporation or other business entity that is completely or majority owned and controlled by Franchisee.

Discussion:
The definition of transfer in the sample provision is purposefully broad in order to cover various methods of dividing ownership or interest in the franchise among individuals or business entities to protect the franchisor's control over what individual

304. Phyllis A. Truby & David A. Beyer, *Fundamentals 201: Transfers and Assignments in Franchising,* ABA 37th Annual Forum on Franchising 26 (2014).

305. Carden & Klarfeld, *supra* note 110, at 37.

or business has the right to operate using the franchisor's trademark and operating system.

If the franchisee is selling, assigning, transferring, or conveying ownership of the franchise, as part of the transfer process the franchisor should review the transfer agreement or other documentation and to identify the transferee and any monetary payment or other consideration given to the franchisee in exchange for an ownership interest. The franchisor should also consider ensuring that it has the opportunity to consider whether the transfer is in the best interest of the system, and, if not, what remedies the franchisor may have to prevent the proposed transfer. The franchisor may have a right of first refusal (a topic discussed later in this chapter). Alternatively, the franchisor may have other restrictions on the transfer that make a proposed transfer unworkable.

(i) Foreclosure and Subordination

Inclusion of encumbrances, mortgages, and security interests in the definition of a transfer enables the franchisor to prevent parties that lend funds to the franchisee from becoming owners-in-fact of the franchise and from foreclosing on the franchise if the franchisee's debt is not paid. Franchisors that want to enforce rigorous selection of franchisees should be especially cautious of foreclosure risks and prepare for this issue in the drafting of transfer language. If a franchisee encumbers some or all of its franchise interest, those ownership rights could land in the hands of a reseller or simply go to the highest bidder without regard to a new owner's competitive interests, abilities, or qualifications to operate a franchised business.

A transfer restriction that disallows security interests is likely to be waived, deleted, or otherwise ignored because franchisees need the ability to obtain financing, which generally requires some form of security interest or provision of business-related collateral. Franchisors of systems heavily reliant upon outside financing should expect franchisees to request exceptions to this provision through subordination or intercreditor agreements. Such agreements can be drafted, however, to permit lenders to take a first-position security interest in a specific asset, such as designated inventory or equipment, but not in the franchise itself. An example of such subordination language is presented next:

> All rights and interests of Franchisor under the Agreement are hereby expressly subordinated and made secondary and inferior to the liens, security interests, and assignments created or existing by virtue of the Loan Documents, including without limitation those certain Security Agreements and/or Deeds of Trust (hereinafter called the "Security Instrument") executed or to be executed by Borrower for the benefit of Lender covering and securing the Loan and all other notes given in substitution therefor or in renewal, increase, extension or rearrangement thereof, in whole or in part, and all indebtedness incurred or arising pursuant to the provisions of the Security Instrument. Notwithstanding the foregoing, Lender shall not have any security interest in or to the franchise rights or trademark license granted in the Franchise Agreement.

(ii) Amount of Interest Transferred

The sample clause also includes the phrase "any or all" as a threshold for the amount of interest a franchisee can transfer without obtaining the franchisor's approval. By making this threshold broad, the franchisor can control, through subsequent restriction and exception provisions, the ability of the franchisee to transfer any percentage of ownership, no matter how small, to individuals, shareholders, members, or other business entities, subject to applicable state law. By doing so, the franchisor can ensure that it knows—and, more importantly, approves of—everyone with an ownership interest in the franchise.

Franchisees, on the other hand, will likely object to such broad language, especially a franchisee with multiple owners that may wish to transfer small percentages of ownership for a variety of reasons, such as to raise additional capital. Franchisees may also object to this broad provision because of its impact on succession planning and the desire to continue the franchise in the case of death or incapacity. Finally, an unintended consequence of no small concern is that the franchisor must prepare itself to monitor and handle transfer requests from the franchisee in all these situations, which can become a cumbersome process.

In addition to tempering the restrictions on transfers and possibly limiting the need for approval to transfers by and to only certain "critical individuals" (a concept discussed later in this chapter), the franchisor should consider only regulating franchisee transfers that meet a certain percentage of the controlling interest. Next is an example of how a franchisor can modify the definition of transfer presented in the sample clause to permit what the franchisor defines as de minimus transfers of interest:

> For purposes of this Franchise Agreement, "Transfer" shall mean to sell, assign, transfer, convey, gift, encumber, mortgage, grant a security interest in, or otherwise dispose of or encumber more than XX% of Franchisee's interest hereunder or a controlling interest of the franchise granted herein or in any assets of the Franchised Business, including the lease for the Premises (except to another Principal) but specifically excluding equipment, inventory, the Agreement or the trademark license contained in the Agreement. Transfer includes any such sale, assignment, transfer, conveyance, gift, encumbrance, or other disposal that occurs by operation of law.

Even with a modified definition of a transfer, franchisees will seek to maximize their transfer options. Accordingly, a franchisee may seek alternative arrangements that do not have the look or feel of a traditional sale or transfer and could be overlooked by a franchisor. In some systems, franchisees may take advantage of provisions like the preceding language to execute a series of 10 percent transfers in an effort to execute an "under the radar" transfer. The prohibition in this provision against the franchisee transferring a "controlling interest" is critical to prevent the franchisee from executing the type of transfer the franchisor wishes to prohibit.

Other methods of transferring ownership without an actual sale could include gifting or conveying ownership rights through a will. Some of these transfer variations are addressed later in this chapter.

B. Transfer by Franchisee

1. Contract for Personal Services

> The franchise granted under this agreement is personal to the Franchisee and is a contract for the personal services of Franchisee. The Franchisor, in entering into this agreement, relied on information Franchisee provided related to Franchisee's business skills, business acumen and experience, personal character, education, credit rating, and financial resources (individually, if Franchisee is a natural person; or in reliance on such qualifications of the owners, members, partners, or stockholders of Franchisee, if Franchisee is a legal entity).

Discussion:

In the absence of language restricting assignability, contracts are generally assignable.[306] A contract for personal services, however, cannot be unilaterally transferred or assigned because it depends on the specific skill, judgment, experience, or other qualifications of the party contracting to provide the services.[307] This provision is important for a franchisor to be able to maintain control over the assignability or transferability of the franchise agreement after having made the very personal decision to select and approve a franchisee based on his or its financial strength, personal interest and character, and specific business experience and aptitude.[308] A franchisor may use the "personal services contract" language offensively to prevent a transfer by withholding consent.[309] In *Burger King Corp. v. H & H Restaurants, LLC*, for example, Burger King enforced its refusal to consent to a transfer because a proposed transferee did not "demonstrate to Burger King's satisfaction that it met the financial, character, managerial, ownership, or other criteria."[310]

Moreover, incorporating personal services language is critical if the franchisee must have a specific license to operate, such as a trade, professional, or service industry.[311] Loss of the licensed individual means the franchise cannot operate. The following provision, as a condition of the franchisor's consent to transfer, supports the franchisor's position that the franchise agreement is a personal services contract as well as one that requires specialized qualifications:

> Franchisor shall not unreasonably withhold its consent to transfer provided Transferee demonstrates of adequate business standards and character, financial capabilities

306. *See* 29 Williston on Contracts § 74:22 (4th ed. 2017).

307. *See In re* Terry, 245 B.R. 422, 428 (Bankr. N.D. Ga. 2000), citing Yellow Cab of Cleveland, Inc. v. Greater Cleveland Reg'l Transit Auth., 595 N.E.2d 508, 511 (Ohio Ct. App. 1991).

308. *But see* Section XXVI.B.2 *infra* regarding transfer pursuant to bankruptcy.

309. *See, e.g.*, Enfield Equip. Co., Inc. v. John Deere Co., 64 F. Supp. 2d 483, 485–86 (D. Md. 1999).

310. Burger King Corp. v. H & H Restaurants, LLC, No. 99-2855, 2001 U.S. Dist. LEXIS 24038, 2001 WL 1850888 (S.D. Fla. Nov. 30, 2001).

311. Trade industries requiring licensure may include painting, plumbing, or electrical. Painting, for example, requires licensure in Michigan, including completion of 60 hours of courses. Jarrett Skorup, Why Does Michigan License Painters? Mackinac Center for Public Policy Blog (June 23, 2017, 3:00 PM), https://www.mackinac.org/why-does-michigan-license-painters. Professional industries such as medical, dentistry, or accounting, and service industries such as real estate and home healthcare all require specialized licensure.

> and resources, skills and experience, including any licensure or certification required by law to operate the franchise as required in this franchise agreement.

(i) Critical Individuals

Another way to ensure retention of the licensed individual in the previous example is for the drafter to include clauses in the transfer provision that require the franchisee to designate a "critical individual" and to restrict the ability of that critical individual to transfer ownership or otherwise lessen his or her involvement in the franchise. Many franchise agreements accomplish this by requiring the franchisor and franchisee to identify and agree upon an operator with primary responsibility for carrying out the duties and obligations of the franchisee and restricting that critical individual from involvement in other businesses. The identification of this critical individual often impacts many parts of the franchise agreement, with that person being required to attend certain training, sign certain acknowledgments, and agree to be personally involved in the franchised business, as discussed in other chapters. Additionally, the franchisor may want to stipulate that the critical individual must own a certain amount of the franchisee's business entity. An example of this type of designation is presented next:

> If Assignee is a business entity, Assignee shall appoint an individual as its "Designated Operator," which is defined as the contact person with authority to act in all matters for the Assignee and who has primarily responsibility for operating the franchise granted hereunder. The Designated Operator shall own at least XX% of the Assignee unless Franchisor provides its written consent otherwise.

Due to the importance of the critical individual, drafters may want to require the franchisee to give adequate prior notice of the critical individual's departure to provide adequate time to source, vet, and train a replacement in the same rigorous manner as when the franchisor initially qualified the franchisee. These conditions will help ensure a qualified primary operator of the franchise.

(ii) Personal Services versus Adherence to Standards

On the other hand, a franchisee may also rely on the concept of personal services to avoid specific enforcement of the franchise agreement.[312] Drafters should familiarize themselves with the tension between asserting that the agreement is based on personal services versus adherence to brand requirements.

In *Husain v. McDonald's Corp.*, a multi-unit franchisee purchased additional units through a transfer from another franchisee.[313] As part of the transfer, McDon-

312. 5A Corbin on Contracts § 1204, at 398 (1964) (obligations to render personal service or employ another in personal service cannot be specifically enforced). *See, e.g.*, Husain v. McDonald's Corp., 205 Cal. App. 4th 860, 868, 140 Cal. Rptr. 3d 370, 376 (2012).

313. 205 Cal. App. 4th 860, 862, 140 Cal. Rptr. 3d 370, 371–72 (2012).

ald's agreed to offer a new 20-year franchise term for three transferred units that had remaining terms of less than ten years. McDonald's denied ever receiving an acceptance of the extension offers and later revoked the offers. Prior to the expiration of the transferred unit franchise agreements at issue, the franchisee sought to enjoin McDonald's from terminating the franchise agreements; McDonald's cross-complained for an injunction requiring the franchisee to surrender the restaurant.[314]

McDonald's argued its franchise agreements were contracts for personal services and not subject to the remedy of specific enforcement by either party in the event of a breach, relying on language in the franchise agreements about operators maintaining a "close personal working relationship" with McDonald's.[315] The court disagreed, finding that the franchisee needed little skill, specialized knowledge, or judgment to operate a McDonald's franchise that was characterized by a strict system with comprehensive operational controls, standards, and specifications. The court cited the following language from the "form license agreement":

> The foundation of the McDonald's System and the essence of this License is adherence by Licensee to standards and policies of Licensor providing for the uniform operation of all McDonald's restaurants . . . including, but not limited to, serving only designated food and beverage products; the use of only prescribed equipment and building layout and designs; strict adherence to designated food and beverage specifications and to Licensor's prescribed standards of Quality, Service and Cleanliness.[316]

The court found this language regarding the strict adherence to prescribed standards was the real "essence" of the franchise agreement, not a "close personal working relationship" or any use of discretion or independent judgment by franchisees.[317] As a result, the court upheld the preliminary injunction requiring McDonald's to permit the franchisee to continue operating during the pendency of the litigation.

To avoid this result, it is important that drafters balance the importance of adherence to system standards against a franchisee's exercise of the skill, experience, discretion, and judgment that may justify defending the franchise agreement as a personal services contract. The franchisor should consider identifying in the franchise agreement what aspects of the franchised business may require the

314. *Id.* at 866, 140 Cal. Rptr. 3d at 374.

315. *Id.* at 867, 140 Cal. Rptr. 3d at 376.

316. *Id.* at 869, 140 Cal. Rptr. 3d at 377.

317. The court also noted that McDonald's statements about its "very robust market" for resales and how easily the franchisee could have sold its franchises also countered the argument that the franchise agreements were personal services contracts because McDonald's made it sound as though anyone could meet the obligations of the contracts. *Id.* at 871, 140 Cal. Rptr. 3d at 378–79 ("it can hardly be said no performance save that of [the franchisee] could meet the obligations of the contract").

The court contrasted McDonald's franchise agreement language with the language in a management services agreement between a multi-unit Embassy Suites franchisee and the franchisor. *Id.* at 867–68, 140 Cal. Rptr. 3d at 376 (citing Woolley v. Embassy Suites, Inc., 227 Cal. App. 3d 1520, 1525, 278 Cal. Rptr. 719, 721 (Ct. App. 1991)). The court distinguished *Woolley* because the management agreement was "distinctly personal and non-delegable," called for "a series of complex and delicate business decisions," and required "mutual cooperation and trust." *Id.*

franchisee's discretion and judgment and consider excluding language that contrasts with that concept.[318]

2. No Transfer without Prior Written Consent

Because this is a contract for Franchisee's personal services, Franchisee shall not Transfer all or any of the Franchisee's interest hereunder or in any assets of the Franchised Business, including the lease for the Premises (except to another Principal or pursuant to the terms and conditions set forth in this Agreement), nor shall the Franchisee issue any further shares in the Franchisee's capital (except to the Principals) or admit new owners, partners, or members without in each case obtaining the prior written consent of the Franchisor, which consent shall not be unreasonably withheld; provided, however, that prior to any proposed Transfer, Franchisor has the unfettered right to require that any or all of the conditions listed in this section be met.

Discussion:

This language provides the heart of the transfer provision,[319] but it is also rife with some of the greatest areas of concern: What does it mean that consent shall not be unreasonably withheld? What impact does the implied covenant of good faith and fair dealing have on a franchisor's withholding of consent?

(i) Franchisor-Friendly Language

The preceding sample language uses the limiter that the franchisor will not "unreasonably withhold" consent. For several non-relationship jurisdictions,[320] such lim-

---

318. The franchise agreement at issue in *Husain* expired on Dec. 31, 2009. Although McDonald's ultimately prevailed and terminated the litigated franchise agreements, it spent almost five years litigating whether the franchise agreements were personal services contracts. *See* Husain v. McDonald's Corp., No. A136623, 2013 WL 6636836, Cal. App. 1 Dist., Dec. 17, 2013, *unpublished/noncitable* (Dec 17, 2013), *rehearing denied* (Jan 08, 2014) (affirming order granting sanctions against franchisee resulting in termination of case).

319. *See* Williston, *supra* 306, at § 74:22 ("Contract provisions prohibiting the assignment of rights under the contract will ordinarily be upheld, depending on the particular facts and circumstances."); 3 McCarthy on Trademarks and Unfair Competition § 18:43 (5th ed. 2017) ("A trademark licensee cannot sub-license the mark without express permission from the licensor. Without specific authorization from the trademark owner, the licensee's right to use the licensed mark is personal and cannot be sold or assigned to another. The reason is that because the trademark owner has a duty to control the quality of goods and services sold under the mark, it must have the right to pass on the abilities of new potential licensees.").

320. Nineteen states have "franchise relationship laws," which are laws governing termination or nonrenewal of a franchise agreement: *See* Ark. Code Ann. § 4-72-201 to -210 (Michie 1991); Cal. Corp. Code §§ 31,000–31,516 (West 1977 & Supp. 1994); Cal. Bus. & Prof. Code § 20000 *et seq.* (West 1987 & Supp. 1995); Conn. Gen. Stat. § 42-133E (1992); Del. Code Ann. tit. 6, § 2551 (1975 & Supp. 1992); Haw. Rev. Stat. § 482E-6 (1993); Illinois Franchise Disclosure Act of 1987, 1987 Ill. Laws, P.A. 85-551, Ill. Ann. Stat., ch. 121 1/2, PP 1701-1744 (Smith-Hurd Supp. 1995); Ind. Code § 23-2-2.5-1 to -51 (Burns 1989 & Supp. 1994); Iowa Code Ann. § 523H.1-.17 (West Supp. 1995); Mich. Comp. Laws Ann. § 445.1501–.1546 (West 1989 & Supp. 1992); Minn. Stat. Ann. § 80C.01–.30 (West 1986 & Supp. 1994); Miss. Code Ann. § 75-24-53 (1993); Mo. Code Ann. § 407.410.1 (1993); Neb. Rev. Stat. §§ 87-401 to -410 (1987 & Supp. 1992); N.J. Stat. Ann. § 56:10-1 to -15 (West 1989 & Supp. 1993); S.D. Codified Laws § 37-5A-1 to -87 (1986 & Supp. 1992); Tenn. Code Ann. § 47-25-1501 to -1511 (Supp. 1992); Va. Code Ann. § 13.1-557 to -574 (Michie 1994); Wash. Rev. Code § 19.110.010–.940 (1993); Wis. Stat. Ann. § 135.01–.07 (West 1989 & Supp. 1995). The District of Columbia, Puerto Rico, and the Virgin Islands also have substantive franchise legislation: D.C. Code Ann. § 29-1201 to -1208 (Supp. 1994); P.R. Laws Ann. tit. 10, § 278–278d (1978 & Supp. 1989); V.I. Code Ann. tit. 12A, § 132

ited language is a complete concession to the franchisee. A franchisor could elect to use stronger language to maintain stricter control over transfers and the selection of transferees. For example:

> Franchisor's prior written consent is a necessary condition precedent to the sale, assignment, delegation, transfer, conveyance, gift, pledge, mortgage, encumbrance, or hypothecation of any direct, indirect, or beneficial interest of a franchised business, of this agreement, or in any interest or rights granted under this agreement. Except as specifically provided in this Agreement, Franchisor has the absolute and unfettered right to withhold its consent to a transfer of any interest. Franchisor may withhold consent to transfer, to the extent allowed by law, with or without cause, for no reason or any reason not deemed unlawful. In addition, Franchisor also has the sole and unfettered right to require any or all of the following conditions precedent to its consent to a transfer.

A number of courts have enforced the franchisor's authority to refuse to approve transfers if the franchise agreement specifies that the franchisor may withhold consent.

In *Larese v. Creamland Dairies, Inc.*, the U.S. Court of Appeals for the Tenth Circuit found that the franchise agreement contained merely an expression of the franchisor's need to consent, and thus implied that it could not do so unreasonably.[321] The court explained:

> [T]he franchisee has invested time and money into the franchise and, in doing so, has created benefits for the franchisor. We do not find it an excessive infringement of the franchisor's rights to require that the franchisor act reasonably when the franchisee has decided that it wants out of the relationship. The franchisee should not be forced to choose between losing its investment or remaining in the relationship unwillingly when it has provided a reasonable alternative franchisee.[322]

But the court went on to provide an important caveat to this holding, stating:

> We do not hold that a provision which expressly grants to the franchisor an absolute right to refuse to consent is unenforceable when such an agreement was freely negotiated. . . . Rather, *Franchisor must bargain for a provision expressly granting the right to withhold consent unreasonably*, to insure that the franchisee is put on notice. Since, in this case, the contracts stated only that consent must be obtained, Creamland did not have the right to withhold consent unreasonably.[323]

(1982). Robert W. Emerson, *Franchise Terminations: Legal Rights and Practical Effects When Franchisees Claim the Franchisor Discriminates*, 35 AM. BUS. L.J. 559, n.68. The concept of relationship states is discussed elsewhere in this book, including in Chapter 8.

321. 767 F.2d 716, 717–18 (10th Cir. 1985).

322. *Id.* at 717–18.

323. *Id.* at 718.

Over ten years later, the U.S. Court of Appeals for the Eighth Circuit sharply disagreed with the holding in *Larese* and provided full discretion to the supplier that retained the right to approve any assignment of a dealer contract.[324] The court in *Taylor Equipment* held that the contract term contained no limitation on the right to choose an assigned dealer, and thus the right to withhold consent was absolute and unrestricted by a court's or jury's after-the-fact determination of "reasonableness" or "good faith." The court did consider the line of cases that require that the party withholding consent to a transfer not be dishonest—even if unreasonable—regarding the basis for withholding consent.[325] It held that such dishonesty only extended to "an intent to take 'opportunistic advantage'" of the need to sell, as opposed to inconsistent, unreasonable, or untrue bases for withholding consent.[326] To avoid the entire question of dishonesty, the parties should strive for honesty in fact in all communications and keep the issue out of the hands of a judge or jury.

If parties do impose upon themselves a reasonableness standard not required by statute (and without additional clarity of the standard), there is a risk that one party could perceive the standard as an objective measure of reasonableness, but the other party could interpret the term as permitting some subjectivity. This ambiguity may lead to a fact-finder determining whether the agreement may be assigned instead of the parties. Accordingly, when drafting, the parties should state the standard and all pertinent conditions clearly and consistently.[327]

(ii) Impact of State Relationship Laws

Unsurprisingly, franchise agreements that grant a franchisor the power to refuse a transfer without "good cause" are less popular among franchisees who consider that there may come a time when they need or want to transfer the franchised business, which they have built through substantial effort and investment.

---

324. Taylor Equip., Inc. v. John Deere Co., 98 F.3d 1028, 1032–34 (8th Cir. 1996); *see* also Enfield Equip. Co. v. John Deere Co., 217 F.3d 838 (4th Cir. 2000) (finding Maryland's highest court would agree that the implied covenant applies to all contracts but only to protect the reasonable expectations of the parties and not to override an express right to limit a distributor from assigning its agreement without prior written consent if included as part of that contract without limitation); C. Pappas Co. v. E. & J. Gallo Winery, 610 F. Supp. 662, 667 (E.D. Cal. 1985), *aff'd sub nom.* 801 F.2d 399 (9th Cir. 1986) (upholding winery's right to limit transfer of distribution rights where agreement was expressly not assignable and finding no violation of the obligations of good faith and fair dealing). These decisions construe the right to withhold consent as an unlimited right, without any additional language. On the other hand, in *Larese*, the court said that the parties could have an unlimited right to refuse a transfer, but that unlimited right needed to be stated expressly. *Larese*, 767 F.2d at 718.

325. *Id.* at 1033–34 (citing Original Great Amer. Chocolate Chip Cookie Co. v. River Valley Cookies, Ltd., 970 F.2d 273, 280 (7th Cir. 1992) ("Contract law imposes a duty, not to 'be reasonable,' but to avoid taking advantage of gaps in a contract in order to exploit the vulnerabilities that arise when contractual performance is sequential rather than simultaneous.")).

326. *Id.* at 1034.

327. *See, e.g.*, Richter v. Dairy Queen of S. Arizona, Inc., 131 Ariz. 595, 596, 643 P.2d 508, 509 (Ariz. Ct. App. 1982). The court held, in *Richter*, that the first half of the transfer provision allowed an assignment upon the reasonable consent of the franchisor (an objective standard), but the second half of the provision language gave the company the right to use its judgment to determine whether the assignee was qualified (subjective standard). Ultimately, the court held that both parties had argued that the franchisor had to act reasonably (using an objective standard) and that the franchisor had not argued in the trial court that it had a subjective right to determine an assignee's qualifications.

In many jurisdictions, the state legislature has resolved this issue in a manner more favorable to franchisees. Currently, Arkansas,[328] California,[329] Hawaii,[330] Iowa,[331] Michigan,[332] Minnesota,[333] Nebraska,[334] and New Jersey[335] have laws that either specify conditions for a franchisee transfer or restrict a franchisor from withholding consent if the franchisee meets certain conditions and the proposed transferee meets the requisite qualifications.[336] Then, the fight shifts to whether the franchisor properly or reasonably determined that the franchisee or prospective transferee met the conditions.

As a practical matter, a drafter working with a franchisor that will operate in any of these states should consider methods to ensure that transfers are not refused in violation of applicable state law. It is advisable for the franchisor to establish either a uniform transfer policy for the system that complies with these states' requirements, or draft clear addenda for the affected states and ensure that these addenda are maintained with the applicable franchise agreements.

(iii) Special Industry Laws

In addition to these state laws that are generally applicable to franchised business transfers, specific industry statutes (e.g., alcohol distributors, car and equipment dealers, and gas stations) may have laws that protect transfers and limit a franchisor's ability to restrict transfers.[337] The careful drafter will always check whether industry-specific statutes may apply to transfer requirements for the franchisor.

---

328. Ark. Code Ann. § 4-72-205 (2017) (requiring franchisee to give written notice of a proposed transfer and requiring franchisor to respond, within 60 days, either with an acceptance or a recitation of the material reasons for disapproval; failure to respond within 60 days is deemed approval).

329. Cal. Bus. & Prof. Code § 20027 (2017).

330. Haw. Rev. Stat. § 482E-6(2)(I) (2017) (similar to Arkansas, but franchisors must respond within 30 days and disapproval must be for good cause).

331. Iowa Code Ann. § 523H.5(1) (2017) ("If the proposed transferee does not meet the reasonable current qualifications of the franchisor, the franchisor may refuse to permit the transfer, provided that the refusal of the franchisor to consent to the transfer is not arbitrary or capricious.").

332. Mich. Comp. Laws Ann. § 445.1527(g) (2017) (permits withholding consent when transferee (1) fails to meet the franchisor's reasonable qualifications or standards; (2) is a competitor of the franchisor; (3) refuses to agree in writing to comply with lawful obligations; or (4) fails to cure any default in the existing franchise agreement).

333. Minn. Stat. § 80C.14 (subdiv. 5) (2017) (franchisor may withhold consent where proposed transferee fails to meet qualifications and standards generally required of franchisees).

334. Neb. Rev. Stat. § 87-405 (2017) (similar to Arkansas).

335. N.J. Stat. Ann. § 56:10-6 (2017) (similar to Arkansas).

336. *See* Claudia K. Levitas & Allan P. Hillman, *Hot Topics on Transfer and Assignment*, ABA 28th Annual Forum on Franchising W-16, at 14–15 (2005) (reviewing state franchise relationship statutes dealing with transfer); Philip F. Zeidman, Legal Aspects of Selling and Buying § 9:55 (3d ed. Sept. 2017).

337. Although most of these state laws still require a franchisee, dealer, or distributor to obtain prior consent to transfer its rights, such consent typically cannot be withheld unreasonably or is guided by a specific process for approval. *See* Ala. Code § 28-9-5(3) (transfer of distributorship rights requires notice of intent to transfer and prior approval); Tex. Bus. & Com. Code Ann. § 57.153 (2017) (permitting termination of distribution rights if prior approval for transfer not obtained). *But see* Iowa Code Ann. § 322A.12 (2017) (mandating acceptance of a motor vehicle franchisee's transfer of the dealership, unless franchiser can demonstrate that the transfer would be substantially detrimental to distribution or the franchisee is unable to obtain appropriate license).

In *Texas Ujoints, LLC v. Dana Holding Corp.*,[338] the U.S. District Court for the Eastern District of Wisconsin vacated its prior grant of summary judgment to a distributor-transferee, and granted summary judgment to the manufacturer. The court held that, although no agreement between the manufacturer and original distributor, between the manufacturer and any subsequent distributor, or any agreement between the original and subsequent distributors required the manufacturer's prior consent to an assignment, Texas law (Texas Fair Practices of Equipment Manufacturers, Distributors, Wholesalers, and Dealers Act) permitted a supplier to terminate an agreement with good cause, which included a distributor or dealer selling its dealership or distribution rights without the supplier's consent. It was undisputed that the original distributor had transferred its purported distribution rights to the subsequent distributor.

(iv) Small Business Administration

In addition to state law, the Small Business Administration (SBA) and other lenders object to restrictions on the franchisee's ability to transfer. The SBA's 7(a) program, in particular, is frequently used by franchisees to obtain funding. The SBA recognizes that, to protect their brand and operating system, franchisors legitimately wish to review and approve assignees in a transfer. The SBA will not approve a loan, however, to a franchisee if the franchise agreement contains an unfettered right to decline a transfer as shown in the sample language discussed previously. In fact, the SBA requires that the franchisor's review and approval of a franchise transfer shall "not be unreasonably withheld or delayed."[339] To accomplish this, the SBA requires franchisors and franchisees obtaining an SBA-guaranteed loan to sign a franchise agreement addendum that includes the following language regarding transfer:

> **CHANGE OF OWNERSHIP**
>
> If Franchisee is proposing to transfer a partial interest in Franchisee, and Franchisor has an option to purchase or a right of first refusal with respect to that partial interest, Franchisor may exercise such option or right only if the proposed transferee is not a current owner or family member of a current owner of Franchisee. If the Franchisor's consent is required for any transfer (full or partial), Franchisor will not unreasonably withhold such consent. In the event of an approved transfer of the franchise interest or any portion thereof, the transferor will not be liable for the actions of the transferee franchisee.[340]

While a few franchise systems can operate without relying on SBA funding, the vast majority of franchise systems regularly rely on SBA loans. Consequently, drafters should familiarize themselves with this and other SBA requirements and consider whether to structure agreements so that they conform with language that will be required.

338. No. 13-CV-1008, 2015 WL 9295394, at *4 (E.D. Wis. Dec. 21, 2015), *aff'd*, 844 F.3d 617 (7th Cir. 2016).
339. Small Business Administration SOP 50 10 5 (I), Jan. 1, 2017.
340. SBA Form 2462 (02-2017).

(v) Additional Laws

In determining whether a transfer is preventable or not, it is important to look at related areas of law in addition to franchise or industry-specific laws. For example, in *Lucy v. Amoco Oil Co.*,[341] Amoco leased commercial property to a franchisee as part of the franchise relationship. Although Amoco was able to dismiss the counts for wrongful termination of the franchise agreement and for violation of the Petroleum Marketing Practices Act, the widow and daughters of the deceased franchisee were able to state age and gender discrimination claims in violation of Michigan's Elliott-Larsen Act,[342] which prohibits discrimination in real estate transactions. Amoco argued that the real substance of the parties' relationship and of the transaction at issue was the franchise relationship and the termination of the same. The U.S. District Court for the Eastern District of Michigan found, however, that Amoco elected to link its franchise agreement with the real estate lease—as opposed to divesting itself of its holdings to a separate entity. Accordingly, Amoco could not argue that it was not subject to Elliott-Larsen.[343]

Bankruptcy provides another body of law that can create issues and lead to transfer missteps if the parties are not wary.[344] A franchisee that declares bankruptcy may seek to assume and assign its franchise agreement. Bankruptcy law favors such an assignment because it increases the value of the debtor's estate. It is so favored that, under Section 365(f)(1) of the Bankruptcy Code, expressly unassignable agreements may be deemed assignable, unless "*applicable law* excuses a party . . . from accepting performance from or rendering performance."[345] "Applicable law" under section 365(c) can refer to trademark law, state contract common law (e.g., common law governing personal services contracts), or industry-specific statutes.[346] There is, however, a split among jurisdictions regarding how to interpret the language of section 365(c)—some jurisdictions analyze the debtor's ability to assume the contract, others analyze if the debtor actually seeks to assume the contract.[347] Further, courts are split whether a trademark license, which is the foundation of

341. Lucy v. Amoco Oil Co., 582 F. Supp. 1168, 1172 (E.D. Mich. 1984); *see also* Shree Krishna, LLC v. Broadmoor Inv. Corp., No. W2011-00514-COA-R3CV, 2012 WL 312254, at *13 (Tenn. Ct. App. Feb. 1, 2012) (affirming trial court's ruling that landlord unreasonably refused to consent to assignment of lease based on desire to get more favorable lease terms when the lease agreement permitted an assignment of the original terms and consent could not be unreasonably withheld).

342. Mich. Comp. Laws Ann. § 37.2502 (West).

343. *Lucy*, 582 F. Supp. at 1172.

344. Jason Binford, *Assigning a Franchise Agreement over the Franchisor's Objection: Bankruptcy May Make It Possible*, 32 Franchise L.J. 71 (Fall 2012).

345. 11 U.S.C. §§ 365(c), (f)(1) (2017) (emphasis added).

346. *See In re* XMH Corp., 647 F.3d 690, 695 (7th Cir. 2011) ("The term 'applicable law' means any law applicable to a contract, other than bankruptcy law.") (citing additional cases). Some courts have interpreted section 365(c) narrowly to exclude only personal services contracts from assignment. *See In re* Taylor Mfg., Inc., 6 B.R. 370, 372 (Bankr. N.D. Ga. 1980). The language of the statute, however, could be interpreted more broadly as in *XMH Corp. See also In re* James Cable Partners, L.P., 27 F.3d 534, 538 n.9 (11th Cir. 1994); Binford, *supra* note 344, at 77.

347. "Hypothetical" jurisdictions analyze the debtor's ability to assume the contract even if the debtor only wishes to assume the contract. "Actual" jurisdictions analyze whether the contract can be assigned only if the debtor actually wishes to assign, not assume, the contract. *See Binford, supra* note 344, at 74.

a franchise agreement, is assumable or assignable in bankruptcy.[348] Similar arguments were used to object to assignment of copyrights and patents in bankruptcy cases.[349] Thus, depending on the jurisdiction, the debtor may not be able to assign the franchise agreement if the franchisor objects.

Franchise laws are not the only laws that can affect a franchisee's right to transfer or a franchisor's right to deny transfer. In *Uninsured Employers Fund v. Crowder*, individual franchisees neglected to formally transfer their franchised business and franchise agreement to the corporate entity formed to operate the franchised business.[350] Subsequently, the business's workers' compensation insurance lapsed and an injured employee brought suit against the individual franchisees, the franchisor, and the franchised business entity that employed him. Despite the lack of any written or franchisor-approved transfer from the individual franchisees to the franchisee entity, the court found the individuals were not the employers.[351]

3. Notice of Intent to Transfer by Franchisee

> Any proposed Transfer by the Franchisee shall be initiated by the Franchisee providing the Franchisor with not less than XX days' notice prior to the proposed Transfer date of the Franchisee's intention to Transfer this agreement. Any actual, attempted, or purported Transfer or Encumbering (including whether by operation of law or otherwise) without the Franchisor's prior written consent shall constitute a breach of this agreement and shall be null and void. The Franchisee agrees to initiate the Transfer process by advising the Franchisor of the intent to Transfer its Franchised Business by sale or otherwise and requesting procedural/administrative instructions.

Discussion:

Notice of an intent to transfer is a way to ensure the franchisor is alerted to the transfer, but also to ensure, as previously discussed in this chapter, that the franchisor has adequate time to source, vet, and train a replacement in the same rigorous manner as when the franchisor initially qualified the franchisee. Additionally, if the franchisor has a right of first refusal, the notice may trigger the franchisor's time period to consider whether to exercise its right of first refusal.

Drafters should keep in mind that good procedures for handling notices of intent to transfer are key to an effective and efficient transfer process. Checklists can be helpful, whether the checklist is included in the franchise agreement or in

348. Courts cite the Lanham Act of 1946 to rule that trademark licenses are not assignable over the licensor's objection. *Binford, supra* note 344, at 74–75 (discussing *In re* N.C.P. Marketing Group, Inc., 337 B.R. 230 (D. Nev. 2005), *aff'd* by 279 F. App'x 561 (9th Cir. 2008), in which the court ruled goodwill and trademarks are assignable and the licensor has the ability to control the "identity of licensees").

349. *Id.* (discussing Miller v. Glenn Miller Prods., 318 F. Supp. 2d 923, 933 (C.D. Cal. 2004), in which the court used "well established" copyright and patent law to support its ruling that a trademark was not assignable in a bankruptcy).

350. Uninsured Employer's Fund v. Crowder, Bus. Franchise Guide (CCH) ¶ 15,794, 2016 WL 2605624 (Ky. May 5, 2016).

351. *See id.*

response to receipt of notice of an intent to transfer. Of course, the checklist must be consistent with the franchise agreement language, but it could help crystalize a series of notices, agreements, and approvals tied to short deadlines.

The amount of notice a franchisor requires prior to an intended transfer varies between systems. Notice that is too close in time to the intended transfer invariably leads to problems with the franchisor's ability to vet the proposed transferee, so the franchisor should build in enough time to review the proposed transaction and prepare its own documentation to approve the transfer.

The sample provision includes language that voids any attempt to transfer or encumber the interest in the franchised business. This is critical language, particularly in systems with less sophisticated franchisees. Despite clear prohibitions in the franchise agreement, some franchisees do transfer the franchised business and notify the franchisor after the transaction has purportedly closed.

4. Transfer by Franchisee to an Entity Franchisee Completely Owns and Controls

Notwithstanding the provisions of this Section, Franchisee may, subject to the following terms and conditions in this subsection, transfer this Franchise Agreement and the rights and obligations hereunder to a corporation or other business entity that is completely owned and controlled by Franchisee, including any and all issued and outstanding shares:

(a) Franchisee must provide organizing documents that (i) show transferee entity is newly organized; (ii) define the transferee entity's sole purpose as confined exclusively to acting as franchisee under this Franchise Agreement; (iii) confirm that the initial Franchisee remains the sole owner of the stock, interest, or membership of any transferee entity; and (iv) disclose the names, addresses, and contact information for all officers, directors, or other principals of the transferee entity;

(b) Franchisee remains personally liable in all respects under this Franchise Agreement.

(c) Franchisee continues to devote its best efforts to the day-to-day operation and development of the Franchised Business;

(d) Franchisee and transferee entity must execute a document to which Franchisor is a party, in such form as shall be approved by Franchisor, and in which it agrees to be a party to and be bound by all of the provisions of this Franchise Agreement; and

(e) Franchisee is the sole owner of the stock, partnership interest, or membership of the entity and has complete authority to act for the entity.

Discussion:

Franchisors generally do not make exceptions to their strict control over transfers, except as mandated under state relationship laws. However, a transfer by a natural person franchisee to a business entity completely owned and controlled by that natural person is an exception that franchisors generally make.

Franchisees seek such transfers for many reasons, for example: (1) tax benefits, (2) business reorganization, (3) business expansions, and/or (4) changes in key personnel. Many franchisees begin the process of purchasing a franchise without having organized a business entity. These internal transfers are not "sales" requiring disclosure under the FTC Act.[352] In some states, transfer from a natural person to an entity that person completely owns and controls is completely exempt from the definition of a transfer.[353] They are so common that a franchisor may want to avoid the rigor of a formal consent to transfer process or assessment of a transfer fee, but instead treat these types of transfers separately from other bona fide transfers where the individuals operating the franchise change. Although the formalities may be relaxed, documenting these internal transfers remains important to ensure the critical individual discussed previously in this chapter continues its role under the new entity. The designated franchisee is the person liable in the event of a default or other issue resulting in litigation, and it is necessary to identify the correct party in the event of any litigation. Moreover, multi-unit franchisees or franchisees with development agreements often have separate entities for each unit, and it is important to establish a clean line of succession and liability. The preceding sample provision shows language that is typical in a franchise agreement that permits this type of transfer.

(i) Newly Organized Entity

A franchisor does not want a franchisee entity that is already in existence and potentially saddled with prior, undisclosed financial obligations or duties regarding a different business. Thus, many franchisors will include language as found in subpart (a) in the preceding to limit the transferee entity to only a newly created business that is exclusively purposed as a franchisee under this particular franchise agreement.

(ii) Continuing Liability

To the extent that a franchisor and franchisee fail to maintain clean or accurate records of these internal transfers, most franchisors include language in the franchise agreement generally or in the transfer provision (see subpart (b) in the preceding) to establish that the original franchisee, whether a natural person or a business, remains fully liable under the franchise agreement, regardless of any transfer. A franchisee should look for such holdover liability provisions and determine if they can be negotiated away if, for example, the individual owner has signed a personal guaranty. These internal transfers do not cushion an individual owner from liability with respect to obligations to the franchisor. The benefits are to the franchisee's own operations and to its relationships and potential liabilities with customers or other third parties.

352. 16 C.F.R. § 436.8(6) (2016) (listing exemptions from FTC Rule disclosure requirements).

353. Truby & Beyer, *supra* note 304, at 9–11 (identifying Iowa's statutory, enumerated events that do not constitute a transfer requiring franchisor's consent (*see* Iowa Code § 523H.5 (2017))).

The preceding sample provision requires the franchisee to remain liable for the obligations under the franchise agreement after transfer. This method helps the franchisor ensure who it can depend on to fulfill all the requirements of the franchise. Further, the franchisor knows that by requiring the selling franchisee to provide a personal guarantee, that franchisee will have "skin in the game" and thus ensure the purchasing franchisee is a viable, reliable franchise candidate. It will come as no surprise to the experienced practitioner that the selling franchisee may object to continuing to be personally liable for another individual or entity it doesn't control. The selling franchisee may ask for elimination of the provision, but as an alternative, the franchisor can limit the guarantee to a specific timeframe, certain obligations, or cap liability at a certain amount. An example of this alternative language is presented in the following:

> Limited Guaranty of Assignor and Guarantors. Guarantors and Assignor agree to jointly, severally, irrevocably and unconditionally guaranty the payment and performance of the Obligations by Assignee/Owner; provided, however, that the guaranty by Guarantors and Assignor of the Obligations of Assignee/Owner shall terminate one year from the date of this Consent, if and only if Assignee/Owner pays when due all financial obligations to Franchisor under the Franchise Agreement (as defined herein) between the date of this Consent and such termination date. In addition, and notwithstanding anything else in this Agreement to the contrary, the Guarantors' and Assignor's liability under the Guaranty shall be limited to Assignee/Owner's past due royalty obligations under the Franchise Agreement only, and shall be limited to no greater than [insert amount] with respect thereto.

5. Transfer by Franchisee to Entity in Which Franchisee Has a Controlling Interest

> Notwithstanding the provisions of this section, Franchisee may, subject to the following terms and conditions in this subsection, transfer this Franchise Agreement and the rights and obligations hereunder to a corporation or other business entity in which Franchisee maintains a controlling interest, meaning a majority ownership or interest or the percentage interest or ownership required under the transferee entity's operating documents to establish control:
>
> (a) Franchisee must provide organizing documents that (i) show transferee entity is newly organized; (ii) define the transferee entity's sole purpose as confined exclusively to acting as franchisee under this Franchise Agreement; (iii) disclose the names, addresses, and contact information for all owners, officers, directors, partners, members, or other principals of the transferee entity; (iv) identify the percentage interest for each party identified in subpart (a)(iii); and (v) provide personal background and financial information regarding all owners of the transferee entity;
>
> (b) Franchisee remains personally liable in all respects under this Franchise Agreement;

(c) Franchisee continues to devote its best efforts to the day-to-day operation and development of the Franchised Business; and

(d) Franchisee and transferee entity must execute a document to which Franchisor is a party, in such form as shall be approved by Franchisor, and in which transferee entity agrees to be a party to and be bound by all of the provisions of this Franchise Agreement.

Discussion:

Closely related to a transfer to a solely owned entity is a transfer to an entity in which the franchisee has a controlling interest. Like transfers in the first category, these transfers are also likely to be permitted in the terms of the franchise agreement or be easily negotiated. Critically, entities in which the transferor franchisee only has a "controlling interest" instead of sole ownership present some risk because it means that there are other, noncontrolling owners who can impact the franchise operations. Franchisees may wish to restructure ownership of the franchise by transferring to another entity it controls for a variety of reasons, such as to provide interest to other family members or even to add partners for financial or operational reasons. In this scenario, the franchisor may want to require additional personal or financial information regarding any business partners, shareholders, or members, and even family members. A franchisor will have to determine, however, whether to draft a transfer provision that permits the transfer to move forward subject to receipt of that additional information, or whether the franchisor wants to reserve the right to disapprove of a proposed transfer based on its review of the additional information.

If the franchisee having controlling interest retains its controlling interest post-transfer, or if the critical individual discussed earlier in this chapter remains part of the franchise, the franchisor may wish to relax its formalities regarding transfers by not requiring as rigorous a vetting process or by charging a transfer fee. Although the franchisor may relax the formalities, the franchisor should include requirements that it receive copies of the franchisee entity's articles of incorporation or organization, bylaws, any distribution of shares, and a comprehensive list of directors and officers. A franchisor should also require that the transferee entity's formation documents incorporate any of the franchisor's restrictions on transfer. For example:

(a) The total number of [shareholders/owners/members] of the [corporation or other business entity] shall not exceed [insert number] individuals or [insert number] corporations.

(b) The [corporation or other business entity] shall neither encumber nor assign nor permit the transfer of any [shares/ownership interest] in the [corporation or other business entity] without Franchisor's prior written consent.

(c) The transfer of any [stock/ownership interest] is subject to the terms and conditions of a Franchise Agreement with Franchisor.

Franchisors should also be aware that a franchisee's shareholders, members, or owners may not be individuals but instead business entities. In that scenario, the franchisor may want to limit the number of business entities comprising the franchisee in order to ensure which entity is truly liable for the franchisee. As an alternative, the franchisor can request a personal guarantee from one of the shareholders, members, or owners, or request a corporate guarantee if one of the business entities satisfies the franchisor's needs.

C. Conditions of Transfer

It may seem counterintuitive to focus any significant amount of energy on stipulating the conditions of a transfer when drafting a franchise agreement that a franchisor anticipates will be an enduring agreement that forms the basis of a long-term relationship with franchisees. Yet, transfers are very common in the franchise industry, and a franchisor must be prepared to protect its system and goodwill just as the franchisee must prepare to protect its substantial investment and at least know how to seek and obtain transfer approval. Most commonly, a franchisor will want to specify conditions that closely mirror the qualifications a new franchisee would have to meet, including requiring that any physical facilities, equipment, and computer systems meet then-current standards.

The sample clause in the following is provided in two sections with discussion after each portion. It provides for a relatively complete list of common conditions of transfer. In addition to setting forth these conditions of transfer, state statutory and common law will determine (in addition to the franchise agreement language) whether a franchisor reasonably approved or withheld approval for a transfer. This latter issue is what creates much of the litigation surrounding franchise transfers, although there is little that can be done to draft one's way out of a determination of what is reasonable and what is not.

1. Commonly Included Conditions of Transfer

(a) In considering the request for a Transfer, the Franchisor may consider, among other things, the financial history and qualifications, credit standing, franchise and other business experience, education, and ability to operate the Franchised Business, and of the proposed transferee and its owners, partners, members, managers, principal stockholders, directors, and officers, as appropriate. In addition, the Franchisor shall be entitled to require as a condition precedent to the granting of its consent that:

(b) the proposed transferee providing, to the satisfaction of the Franchisor, a business plan indicating that the proposed transferee possesses the required level of business experience and acumen necessary to operate the Franchised Business and other evidence that the proposed transferee has the qualifications, apparent ability, and credit standing to operate the Franchised Business;

(c) the proposed transferee or an affiliate of the proposed transferee is not a competitor of the Franchisor;

(d) the Franchisor is provided with a copy of the final agreement of purchase and sale between the Franchisee and the proposed transferee and all documents referred to therein as relied upon by the parties;

(e) the proposed transferee shall have entered into a written assignment of the Franchise Agreement in a form prescribed or approved by the Franchisor or, at the option of the Franchisor, shall have executed a new Franchise Agreement in the form then being used by the Franchisor, which may provide for a higher royalty and for greater expenditures for advertising and promotion than are provided hereunder, and shall have executed such other documents and agreements as may be requested by the Franchisor in connection with the Transfer;

(f) the proposed transferee providing guarantees from anyone whom the Franchisor may request, guaranteeing the proposed transferee's performance of its obligations under the agreements to be entered into;

(g) the proposed transferee completing, to the satisfaction of the Franchisor, such training in the operations of the Franchised Business, at the proposed transferee's or the Franchisee's sole expense, as the Franchisor may require;

(h) the Franchisee paying to the Franchisor, any fees and/or expenses which may be incurred by the Franchisor in dealing with the Franchisee's said application for approval and the Franchisor's then existing Transfer fee, which Transfer fee shall not exceed XX% of the Franchisor's then existing initial franchise fee charged to new Franchisees;

Discussion:

Each of the subparts in the preceding sample provision of transfer conditions are commonly included conditions that tend to ensure that any transferee is, at a minimum, meeting the requirements and qualifications of a new franchisee. These conditions are often the ones embedded in state franchise statutes governing a franchisee's request for approval and a franchisor's reasonableness in granting or withholding consent.[354]

Subparts (a) through (g) of this sample provision are relatively straightforward conditions that tend to leave little room for a franchisor's subjective standards.[355] Objective standards provide clarity for both parties, but also take away some of the "wiggle" room if the franchisor would prefer not to support the transfer. Language like that expressed in subpart (b) can suffer from a lack of specificity if the franchisor is, for example, unclear about to whom or by what date the final purchase and

---

354. *See supra* note 320; *see, e.g.*, Ark. Code Ann. § 4-72-205(c) ("No transfer . . . shall be valid unless the transferee agrees in writing to comply with all of the requirements of the franchise then in effect."); Cal. Bus. & Prof. Code § 20029(a) (requiring provision of copies of all documents related to sale and transfer).

355. *See* Devayatan, LLC v. Travelodge Hotels, Inc., No. 614CV561ORL41TBS, 2016 WL 3477205, at *6–8 (M.D. Fla. June 27, 2016) (transferee agreed to make renovations and upgrades to hotel property, which resulted in significant higher costs than it anticipated, but court held franchisor had not misrepresented the scope of work; in connection with termination of transferee's franchise agreement, however, the court denied franchisor's summary judgment motion regarding whether it violated the covenant of good faith and fair dealing for terminating based on less material issues).

sale agreement should be delivered. A franchisor may benefit from such ambiguity because it can be used as a simple, objective standard by which to withhold consent. Thus, a franchisee or prospective transferee should be certain to get specific answers in writing for any objectively measurable criteria like dates and the transmission of documents.

(i) Requirement to Sign a New Franchise Agreement

Subpart (e) makes a taxing demand by requiring that any transferee take over the old business but be expected to pay newer, higher royalties and ad fees and possibly take on other newer obligations. This provision may make it more difficult for a struggling franchisee to sell an existing franchise because a prospective transferee may not view the purchase favorably if it sees a business suffering and is then asked to invest even more into a system that could not save the outgoing franchisee. Also, if the transfer is to an existing franchisee, it may refuse to purchase the franchise if the terms would be less favorable than its terms under other franchise agreements. In other scenarios, the transferee may benefit substantially from receiving the full term granted under a new franchise agreement rather than whatever amount of time remains under the transferor's existing franchise agreement.

If a franchisor requires a transferee to sign a new franchise agreement instead of taking an assignment of the existing franchise agreement, state franchise registration/disclosure laws and the FTC Rule designate the transfer as a "sale" of the franchise.[356] Franchisors may want the transferee to sign a new franchise agreement for a variety of reasons, such as updating the terms and conditions of old franchise agreements that the franchisor may have changed significantly over time (e.g., royalties and ad fees, arbitration clauses, minimum or maximum renewal terms, or development agreement procedures). This requirement will also help the franchisor to have all its franchisees on similar versions of franchise agreements. If the franchisor wants the transferee to sign a new franchise agreement, the franchisor will need to provide disclosures to the transferee in accordance with state franchise registration/disclosure laws and the FTC Rule. Because franchisors are often interested in having these transfers go to existing franchisees, they are often willing to negotiate these conditions of transfer, especially if it would mean that a high-performing multi-unit franchisee obtains an additional unit and is able to keep all of its franchise agreements with consistent terms.

(ii) Personal Guaranties

Often, a franchisor learns that the true economic engine behind a franchisee is the spouse or a parent or a child—someone who was never identified in the application process. As a result, inadequate protection of the business is likely even with a personal guarantee from the individual who signed the franchise agreement. A transfer gives a franchisor the opportunity to go back and ensure proper protection

356. FTC Rule, 16 C.F.R. § 436.1(t).

by the transferee owners, the spouse, and to determine whether other persons need to provide guarantees as well (see subpart (f)). In addition, a franchisor can keep the outgoing franchisee as a personal guarantor. The requirement for personal guarantees will depend upon whether the transfer is a "sale" of a franchise as mentioned previously. If it is a sale, the terms must be consistent with the franchise disclosure document (FDD). For example, if the system's FDD states that all persons with a more than 20 percent ownership interest must sign a guarantee, a franchisor cannot require all owners with a 10 percent ownership interest to sign a guarantee simply because it is a transfer.

(iii) Transfer Fees

Transfer fees as set forth in subpart (h) are typical in franchise systems to reimburse franchisors for the effort involved in dealing with the process of vetting, approving, and documenting a transfer within the system. Like all other fees discussed in this book, there is no single standard for the amount of such fees and they can vary widely from modest flat fees to significant percentages of the then-current initial franchise fee. Franchisors must consider the anticipated level of difficulty in dealing with all the parts of the transfer process in determining how to set this fee.

In addition, a franchisor should verify whether state relationship laws impose any limits on the transfer fees charged to a franchisee or transferee. Washington's statute governing the relations between franchisor and franchisee, for example, permits transfer fees only to the extent they compensate the franchisor for directly incurred transfer expenses.[357]

(iv) Attempts to Bind the Transferor to Further Liability

Beyond only the language of the guarantee, a franchisor may want to make it explicit that its approval of the transfer does not constitute a waiver of claims against the franchisee. In other words, even if the transfer receives approval, the original franchisee is still liable under its franchise agreement (both in cases where there is an assignment of the agreement as well as in those where there is a termination of the original agreement). The franchisor may want the selling franchisee to be liable for the new franchisee's actions and ability to meet its obligations under the franchise agreement. This "continuing guarantee" may look similar to the clause shown in the following:

> The Franchisee shall continue to be liable for the transferee's compliance with the terms and conditions of the Franchise Agreement for a period of [insert time frame] after transfer.

357. WASH. REV. CODE ANN. § 19.100.180 (West) and Wash. Regs., Restrictions on Transfer of Franchises, BUS. FRAN. GUIDE (CCH) ¶ 5470.76.

The continuing guarantee in the preceding makes the selling franchisee have "skin in the game," that is, an interest in providing the franchisor with a well-qualified franchisee that does not have a substantial risk of default of the franchise agreement.

Franchisors must keep in mind, however, that the SBA frowns upon these continuing guarantees and considers them evidence of excessive control. In fact, a franchisor may even have to sign the SBA addendum mentioned previously, which prevents the franchisor from holding the selling franchisee liable for the actions of the transferee.

(v) Transferee Meeting Standards

Subpart (g) harkens back to the idea that franchise agreements are personal services contracts and that a franchisor should be able to have some subjective control over its franchise relationship partners. Some state laws may preclude the subpart (g) language relying on the franchisor's "satisfaction."[358] A franchisor, if permitted under state law, may also consider explicitly recognizing as a condition to transfer its right and ability to consider the transferee's character and reputation and that of its owners, partners, members, managers, principal stockholders, directors, and officers, as appropriate.

1. Commonly Included Conditions of Transfer (continued)

(i) the Franchisee and the proposed transferee agree to perform all maintenance and upgrades required to bring the Franchised Business up to the Franchisor's then-current standards for a Franchised Business, including upgrading any computer hardware and software as the Franchisor may require;

(j) as of the date of the Franchisee's request for consent and as of the effective date of Transfer there shall be no default in the performance or observance of any of the Franchisee's obligations under this Agreement or any other agreement between the Franchisee and the Franchisor or any affiliate or supplier thereof, and if the Franchisee intends to transfer its rights of possession of the Premises, that the Franchisee have obtained the consent of all necessary parties to the assignment of any licenses, and the lease or sublease, to the proposed transferee;

(k) as of the date of the Franchisee's request for consent and as of the effective date of Transfer, the Franchisee shall have settled all outstanding accounts with the Franchisor, its affiliates, and all other trade creditors of the Franchised Business up to the date of closing of the proposed Transfer;

(l) the Franchisee shall have delivered to the Franchisor, in a form satisfactory to the Franchisor, a complete release of the Franchisor, its directors and officers, and their affiliates and the directors and officers thereof from all obligations of any such persons under this Franchise Agreement; and

358. *See, e.g.*, HAW. REV. STAT. § 482E-6(2)(I) (prohibiting the refusal of a transfer except where there is good cause).

(m) the purchase price to be paid to the Franchisee by the proposed transferee, or if applicable, the proposed encumbrance and associated debt, is reasonable under the circumstances considering, among other things, the debt and interest charges being acquired or already in existence, royalty and marketing fees, and costs for any required system upgrades.

Discussion:

(i) Franchisee Defaults and Noncompliance

Subparts (i) and (j) impose an obligation on the franchisee, or sometimes the proposed transferee, to upgrade the franchised business and ensure that there is no current default. Franchisors favor this language to prevent franchisees from passing a problematic location on to a new operator without fixing the defaults, and to avoid having transferees start their operations in the system with a business that is already out of compliance. However, drafters should keep in mind that this type of language may pose timing issues because transfers are often occurring when a franchisee is in default or close to it.[359] For that reason, it may be necessary to clarify whether the franchisee may attempt a transfer if in operational or financial default. Some franchisees may want to attempt to press for a tolling agreement or hold on the termination process to permit a franchisor time to evaluate and approve a proposed transfer.

Typically, the franchisor will prevail in a dispute over whether it must approve a transfer that does not meet its reasonable standards as articulated in the franchise agreement. For example, in *H.B. Automotive Group, Inc. v. Kia Motors America*,[360] the U.S. District Court for the Southern District of New York found that Kia was entirely within its right to refuse to consent to the proposed transfer of the Bronx Kia franchise when the transfer did not occur within the allotted time, the termination notice had already been given, and the prospective transferee had not completed its application and, as a current franchisee, had below-standard customer scores.[361]

The sample provision in subparts (i) and (j) requires there to be no default of any financial or operational matters at the time of the request for consent to transfer. This language is deliberate. Requiring the transferor to be free from defaults can avoid having the parties expend significant time, money, and energy to close on a

359. *See, e.g.*, Epps Chevrolet Co. v. Nissan N. Am., Inc., 99 F. Supp. 3d 692, 699 (E.D. Ky. 2015) (granting dealer's motion to dismiss because obligation to evaluate a proposed transfer within the statutory 60-day period ceased when dealer terminated the franchise agreement); Kumon N. Am., Inc. v. Timban, No. CIV. 13-4809 RBK/KMW, 2014 WL 2812122, at *2 (D.N.J. June 23, 2014) (dismissing breach of contract and violation of New Jersey Franchise Practices Act counterclaims against franchisor after it stayed termination for several weeks but ultimately did not agree to transfer or to give franchisee additional opportunities to identify a buyer). *But see* Powerhouse Motorsports Grp., Inc. v. Yamaha Motor Corp., 221 Cal. App. 4th 867, 881, 164 Cal. Rptr. 3d 811, 823 (2013), as modified on denial of reh'g (Dec. 24, 2013) (finding dealer unreasonably withheld consent to sale of franchise agreement, despite prior receipt of notice of termination). *See also* Levitas & Hillman, *supra* note 336, at 5 (discussing cases regarding timing of notice of termination as opposed to notice of request to transfer).

360. Bus. Franchise Guide (CCH) ¶ 15,813, 2016 WL 4446333 (S.D.N.Y. Aug. 22, 2016).

361. *Id.* at *5.

transfer only to face last-minute issues that might disrupt the entire transfer or cause further delay due to the transferor's failure to cure a default.[362] While the franchisor can be assured that a struggling franchisee is likely to ask for flexibility in this term, if a franchisor is looking for a way to withhold consent to a particular prospective transferee, an agreement to such a proposed deferral of any cure until the closing of the transfer is easily denied and is likely to be upheld under the sample language.

On the other hand, the franchisor can also have the prospective transferee agree to effectuate the cure of the financial or other defaults if it is confident the prospective transferee can do so. In that case, the franchisor could modify subpart (j) with the language shown in the following:

> [A]s of the date of Franchisee's request for consent and as of the effective date of Transfer, Franchisee agrees and acknowledges it has committed the defaults listed in Schedule A (the "Defaults"), and Franchisor agrees to provide its consent to the Transfer provided that Transferee cures the Defaults by doing or causing to be done the actions listed in Schedule B no later than XX days after the Effective Date of the transfer. Transferee agrees and acknowledges that if it fails to cure as required, Franchisor shall have the right to immediately terminate the Agreement.

(ii) Release

Subpart (l) requires a release of the franchisor, which, again, is a common provision, although some state laws may require that any releases are mutual or limited in scope. A franchisor may need to be prepared to limit a release at least to only those claims arising out of the operation of the specific franchised business subject to the transfer. Further, the franchisor may also wish to make the release effective only upon completion of certain conditions, such as payment of royalties due prior to the effective date of the transfer.

(iii) Oversight of Business Purchase Price

Subpart (m) may appear intrusive on the part of a franchisor, and it is a less common provision. The goal is to ensure the transferee is not setting itself up for imminent failure by overpaying for the purchase price of the transferred franchised business and still have to make real estate lease payments, future royalty and marketing fees, and all other required business expenses. Control over this condition gives the franchisor the ability to coordinate a renegotiation on the sale price or offer discounts or

---

362. It is important to think of any possible outstanding accounts for which the franchisee could be liable or create liability; many are not always obvious. For example, in Jeff Schmitt Chevrolet, Ltd. v. Ohio Dep't of Job & Family Servs., No. 14AP-917, 2015 WL 4545120, 2015-Ohio-3010, ¶ 1 (Ohio Ct. App. July 28, 2015), the plaintiff purchased the assets of a General Motors franchise, but it did not purchase the GM franchise license, which was non-transferable. Ohio law said that a business is a successor-in-interest by operation of law if there is a transfer of all property integral of the operation of the trade or business. Without specifically determining whether the GM license was "integral," plaintiff was deemed a successor for purposes of calculating its unemployment compensation contributions.

incentives.[363] It also gives the franchisor final authority over the value of transferred franchises to prevent franchisees from lowering the market value by selling them for less than market—arguably in competition with the franchisor. A franchisee is likely to balk at this exercise of control even if it is part of the franchise agreement. It will argue that if it is able to sell its franchise at a higher price, then that should show that the market price for the business should be higher. If the sale is for less than the franchisor expected, that is also a market indicator. This provision is certainly one that a franchisee should review carefully and determine whether to negotiate. At the same time, transferee failure is not uncommon as a result of overpaying for a business, and some franchisors choose to include a provision like this rather than watch transferee franchisees struggle.

(iv) A Word about Unauthorized Transfers

Many agreements expressly provide consequences for an unauthorized transfer. This can be important in any dispute; a franchisor wants any unauthorized transfer to be void, and any attempted or actual unauthorized transfer to be a default or grounds for termination, respectively. The franchisor should give thought to those consequences and put them into the franchise agreement. Consequences may be tricky if the unapproved transferee can satisfy the conditions of transfer, making it difficult for the franchisor to argue that its consent to transfer is not unreasonably withheld. Depending on drafter preference, sometimes this alternative remedy or course of action is included in the transfer provision language and sometimes it is placed elsewhere in the agreement, such as with a remedies or penalties section. The authors recommend placing it outside of the transfer provision because otherwise it waters down what should be a requirement for franchisor approval and the stated, hefty consequences for an unauthorized transfer. Faced with an unauthorized transfer that cannot be unwound, however, it would be wise to have an alternative remedy or a valuation for that violation. Potential language to address such a situation might look like this:

> Alternative Transfer Fee. If Franchisee or any Owner attempts or completes a transfer in violation of this Agreement, Franchisor, instead of terminating this Agreement based on the breach, has the right, upon notice to the transferor and any Guarantor, to collect a transfer fee from any of them equal to XX.

Any such remedy should be very system-specific and case-specific. The preceding clause could set the penalty at a multiple of the transfer fee otherwise owed, at a flat rate, at a percentage of the initial franchise fee, or some other calculation. Overall, a franchisor has to determine which conditions of transfer align with the system's personality and culture, financial requirements, and marketability.

---

363. In Zuckerman v. McDonald's Corp., 35 F. Supp. 2d 135, 138 (D. Mass 1999), the U.S. District Court for the District of Massachusetts found that McDonald's did not act arbitrarily in requiring that the sale price for plaintiffs' five franchises be lowered by the amount needed for reinvestment in the stores. The transfer provision of the franchise agreement included specified criteria on which the franchisor was to evaluate a proposed transfer, and the court found that those criteria related to McDonald's concerns about the continued viability of the franchise. *Id.*

2. Refusal to Consent Not Unreasonable; Consent Not a Release of Franchisee

The refusal of the Franchisor to consent to the proposed Transfer based upon the noncompliance with any of the foregoing conditions shall not be deemed to be an unreasonable withholding of such consent. The Franchisor's consent to a Transfer shall not operate to release the Franchisee from any liability under this Franchise Agreement.

Discussion:

A franchisor would lose control of its system if it did not maintain the right to approve of its franchisees. Accordingly, if a proposed transfer violates the conditions of transfer, a franchisor's refusal to consent is rarely found unreasonable, arbitrary, or unenforceable. Even where a franchisor (assuming consistent with state relationship laws) grants itself the sole discretion to consent to a transfer based on subjective measures of competency and experience, courts are likely to enforce that right if provided in the franchise agreement.[364] Unless knowingly bolstered by applicable state law (or lack thereof) and binding precedent, however, franchisors may want to protect themselves as much as possible by making these consent-to-transfer decisions with at least some objective criteria in mind if not expressly identified in the franchise agreement. They want the final decision based on a legitimate business decision that will be defensible in court. Hence, the sample language provided in the preceding incorporates the reasonableness requirement.[365] Although the reference to the conditions of transfer provides some criteria for whether the decision was reasonable, the language and conditions are all subject to interpretation by a court, and courts will place the greatest weight on whether the decision to withhold consent related to the transferee's ability to successfully take over the franchise.[366]

D. Right of First Refusal

Without in any way derogating from the Franchisor's right to reject a proposed Transfer in accordance with this agreement, if at any time or times during the Initial Term, or any renewal of this agreement, the Franchisee obtains a bona fide offer (the "Offer") to acquire the whole or any part of its interest in the Franchised Business, which the Franchisee wishes to accept, the Franchisee shall promptly give written notice thereof to the Franchisor together with a true copy of the Offer. Upon receipt of

364. John E. Berg, Marisa D. Faunce, & Jose Padilla, *Greying of a Franchise System: How to Deal with an Aging Franchisee Population*, in IFA 50th Annual Legal Symposium, at 2–5 (2017), citing Perez v. McDonald's Corp., 60 F. Supp. 2d 1030, 1035 (E.D. Cal. 1998) (finding consent not arbitrarily withheld because, among other things, applicants failure to complete training was a legitimate business concern); Burger King Corp. v. H & H Restaurants, LLC, No. 99-2855, 2001 U.S. Dist. LEXIS 24038, 2001 WL 1850888, at 5 (S.D. Fla. Nov. 30, 2001) (permitting franchisor's decision because franchise agreement provided for it to be made in franchisor's "sole judgment"); Walner v. Baskin Robbins Ice Cream Co., 514 F. Supp. 1028, 1029 (N.D. Tex. 1981) (allowing transfer disapproval for any reason without regard to good faith or proper motives if permitted under contract).

365. Terrence M. Dunn, *Franchisor's Control Over the Transfer of a Franchise*, 27 Franchise L.J. 233, 234–35 (2008) (identifying various "reasonable" grounds courts have cited for disapproving a proposed transfer).

366. *Id.* at 235.

such notice and Offer, the Franchisor shall have the option of purchasing the property forming the subject matter thereof upon the same terms and conditions as those set out in the Offer except that:

1. there shall be deducted from the purchase price the amount of any commissions, fee or transfer fee that would otherwise have been payable to the Franchisor, any broker, agent or other intermediary in connection with the Transfer;
2. the Franchisor shall have the right to substitute cash for any other form of consideration specified in the Offer and to pay in full the entire purchase price at the time of closing.

The Franchisor may exercise its option at any time within XX days after receipt of the said notice by giving written notice to the Franchisee. If the Franchisor declines to exercise such option and if such Transfer is approved by the Franchisor in accordance with this agreement, the Franchisee shall be at liberty to complete the Transfer to such third party transferee in accordance with the Offer, provided that, notwithstanding the terms of the Offer, such transaction must be completed within XX days of the date on which the Franchisor notifies the Franchisee of its approval of such transaction. If the transaction is not completed within XX days, the foregoing provisions of this right of first refusal shall apply again in respect of the proposed Transfer and so on from time to time;

Discussion:

In the attempt to protect the franchised business from ending up in the "wrong" hands, from the franchisor's perspective, many franchisors will insist on a right of first refusal. This right allows the franchisor to prevent any transfer that is of concern by giving the franchisor the opportunity to purchase the franchised business first. Frankly, a franchisor with a strategic initiative to reconsolidate and have more corporate stores may use a right of first refusal to acquire certain franchises for itself as well. This clause should include details on when the franchisor wants notice of a proposed transfer, with copies of proposed agreements. The franchisor also should provide for its right to ask for additional information, as well as the right to negotiate with the potential transferee. Lastly, the franchisor should state a period of time reserved for a full review of the offer.[367]

Evaluating whether to exercise a right of first refusal can be difficult. Franchisors should consider whether they will evaluate all the terms of the offer, or just parts of the offer. For example, the sale price may look good, but what if the franchisor doesn't want the inventory included in the deal? A clause requiring the franchisor to accept the deal as presented would require the franchisor to take the inventory. In that case, the franchisor may want a right of first offer instead of a right of first refusal, which would enable the franchisor to submit its own offer at terms and conditions it prefers. A right of first offer clause should be similar to that presented in the following:

367. *Id.* at 50–51.

> If the franchisee wishes to sell the franchised business, the franchisee must first present the franchisor with a written "Notice of Intent to Sell", specifying, at a minimum, what will be sold, the minimum sale price and proposed closing date. Franchisor shall have a period of XX days to respond with its written offer, or franchisee may pursue offers from other qualified candidates.

The franchisor should also consider whether it might purchase the franchisee's stock if it sells all or part of its stock in the franchised business. If not, the franchisor may want to include a clause stating that it will only exercise its right of first refusal to purchase the assets of all or substantially all of the franchised business.

Finally, franchisees that own several businesses may sell those assets in a massive asset purchase agreement to defeat a franchisor's right of first refusal. Two possible workarounds for this situation are (1) to require that a franchisee separate the sale of the franchise business into a separate asset purchase agreement, or (2) to require that the franchisee clearly delineate the sale price of the franchise business and the associated assets in the asset purchase agreement.

Franchisors should keep in mind that exercising a right of first refusal in a bankruptcy case may not be achievable. Some courts have ruled a franchisor exercising such a right has a chilling effect on the debtor's ability to reorganize or for the bankruptcy estate to recover maximum value.[368] Other courts have ruled the right of first refusal was a part of the original negotiation of the franchise agreement that the court should not destroy.[369] Accordingly, applicable law and venue may impact a franchisor's ability to exercise its right of first refusal in bankruptcy.

E. Transfer or Assignment by the Franchisor

> The Franchisor shall have the right to transfer this agreement to any person or legal entity without prior notice to, or consent of the Franchisee. Specifically, and without limitation of the foregoing, the Franchisee agrees that the Franchisor may sell its assets, its interest in the Trademarks or the System to a third party; may offer its securities privately or publicly; may merge, acquire other entities or be acquired by another entity directly or indirectly; may undertake a refinancing, recapitalization, leveraged buyout or other economic or financial restructuring; and with regard to any or all of the above sales, assignments and dispositions, the Franchisee expressly and specifically waives any claims, demands, or damages against the Franchisor arising from or related to the transfer and from any and all future liability under any of the terms, covenants, or conditions, express or implied, contained in this agreement, which have been assigned. In the event of a transfer or assignment of this agreement

368. *In re* Adelphia Communications Corp., 359 B.R. 65 (Bankr. S.D.N.Y. 2007). In *Adelphia*, the bankruptcy court ruled that enforcement of the franchisor's right of first refusal would "be destructive with respect to maximizing value and have a chilling effect on bankruptcy actions." Similarly, in *In re* Chicago Investments, 470 B.R. 32 (Bankr. D. Mass. 2012), the court ruled enforcement of the right of first refusal would chill the possibility of debtors receiving higher offers.

369. *In re* IT Group, 302 B.R. 483 (D. Del. 2003) (finding right of first refusal was not "ipso facto" unenforceable and failure to enforce that right would be usurping a property right).

by the Franchisor, the Franchisor shall be freed and relieved of any and all liability under this agreement. The Franchisee agrees to look solely to the assignee for performance of the Franchisor's obligations hereunder that have been assigned. Nothing contained in this agreement shall require the Franchisor to continue any business operating under the System or to offer any services or products, whether or not bearing the Trademarks, to the Franchisee if the Franchisor assigns its rights in this agreement in accordance with the provisions of this subparagraph.

Discussion:

A franchisor may want to transfer its business to an affiliate or sell to a third party (e.g., a private equity investor). Thus, it is important for a franchisor explicitly to reserve the right to do so in the franchise agreement. Otherwise, a franchisor might be obliged to seek consent from each franchisee to assign each and every franchise agreement. The preceding sample clause expressly provides the franchisor the right to transfer and assign the system and agreement and relieves the franchisor of all obligations under the agreement at the time of the transfer.

In negotiating this section, some prospective franchisees may wish to insist that any new franchisor possess certain qualifications. A franchisee will want assurances that the system will remain in appropriate and competent hands, well-funded, and with a strategic plan consistent with what the prior franchisor expressed when the franchisee came on board. Established franchisors, however, are unlikely to negotiate conditions on their transfer right. Instead, franchisors typically insist on an unrestricted right to assign the system and agreement.[370] From a franchisor's perspective, clauses that put conditions on a franchisor's transfer right limit their flexibility and invite claims by disgruntled franchisees.[371]

As with franchisee-initiated transfers, some industry statutes govern and restrict the rights of franchisors to transfer their interests in certain gas station properties.[372] In *RWG Ventures, Inc. v. Sunoco*, the plaintiff-franchisees brought claims against Sunoco under the 2014 amendment to the Virginia Petroleum Products Franchise Act, or the Right of First Refusal Amendment, which prohibits gas station franchi-

370. For the types of claims that may arise over franchisor transfers, particularly transfers to a competing franchisor, *see generally* Kirk W. Reilly, L. Seth Stadfeld, & Phillip L. Wharton, *Litigation After Acquisition of a Competing Franchise System*, ABA 29th Annual Forum on Franchising W-6, at 12–13 (2006). As the authors note, "[t]he best claim available to a franchisee would be that the transfer of its franchise agreement to the acquiring entity breached express contract terms. Normally this claim is not available, however, because most modern franchise agreements contain language allowing the franchisor to assign the contract without franchisee consent." Foreclosing franchisee claims is, of course, one of a franchisor's goals when drafting such a clause.

371. Such claims typically involve fact issues about whether the conditions have been met, which means not only the expense of discovery, but also that claims may survive dispositive motion practice. *See, e.g.*, A.J. Temple Marble & Tile, Inc. v. Marble Care, Inc., 618 N.Y.S.2d 155 (N.Y. Sup. Ct. 1994) (denying summary judgment to the defendant upon the plaintiff/franchisee's argument that the transferee lacked sufficient experience, where the franchise agreement permitted franchisor transfer only when "(1) the assignee shall, at the time of assignment, be financially responsible and economically capable of performing the obligations of the Franchisor hereunder, and (2) the assignee shall expressly assume and agree to perform such obligations.").

372. *See, e.g.*, RWG Ventures, Inc. v. Sunoco, Inc. (R & M), No. 1:15CV0662 (AJT/MSN), 2015 WL 9281276, at *1 (E.D. Va. Nov. 20, 2015).

sors from transferring interests in the property without first making sale offers to the dealers in the area.[373] There, the U.S. District Court for the Eastern District of Virginia determined that Sunoco was a franchisor but that it did not make a transfer as intended under the law (because it made only what amounted to an internal transfer from one entity to an affiliated entity) and that the amendment was not in effect at the time of the transaction at issue.[374] Outside of mandates from industry-specific laws, a franchisor typically does not create and would not agree to limits on its transfer rights.[375]

Finally, because an assignment of rights and obligations under a contract does not release the assignor of continuing liability, a franchisor is likely to include language in its right to transfer provision to release itself from future or continuing liability if the assignee fails to perform the assumed obligations. This provision should expressly state that the franchisor is discharged from any and all liability and that the franchisor's assignee is substituted as the sole obligor. As with a franchisor's general right to transfer, it is unlikely that this provision would be on the negotiating table.

XXVI. Death or Permanent Incapacity

Upon the death or permanent incapacity of the Franchisee or a controlling owner of the Franchisee, if such person has at the date of such death or permanent incapacity a spouse or any adult children surviving, the following shall apply:

A. if the surviving spouse and/or adult child desire and are, in the reasonable opinion of the Franchisor, capable of carrying on the Franchised Business, the said spouse and/or adult child shall have the right to continue to operate the Franchised Business provided that they shall directly covenant and agree with the Franchisor to be bound by the terms and conditions of this agreement and any other agreements made between the Franchisor and the Franchisee;

B. if the surviving spouse and/or an adult child do not desire or are not, in the reasonable opinion of the Franchisor, capable of carrying on the Franchised Business, or cannot devote their full time and attention to the Franchised Business or if the Franchisee does not have a spouse or adult child surviving, the Franchisor shall have the right, such right to be exercised by

373. Va. Code Ann. § 59.1–21.15:2.

374. *Sunoco*, 2015 WL 9281276, at *5–6.

375. Although not directly related to the drafting of the franchise agreement and transfer provision, it is notable that franchisors electing to exercise their right of assignment in a corporate reorganization should be prepared to update their franchise disclosure documents in accordance with state franchise registration/disclosure laws and the FTC Rule. *See* Corbin on Contracts, *supra* note 312, § 866 at n.31; *see also* Prime Northgate Plaza, L.P. v. Lifecare Acquisition Corp., 985 F. Supp. 815, 818 (N.D. Ill. 1997); Boswell v. Lyon, 401 N.E.2d 735, 744 (Ind. App. 1980). For additional information regarding potential concerns with the impact on the disclosure documents, *see* Alan R. Greenfield, Theresa Leets, & Karen B. Satterlee, *Franchise Disclosure Challenges for Large, Sophisticated or Multi-Brand Franchise Companies*, ABA 37th Annual Forum on Franchising 5 (2014).

the Franchisor giving written notice to the Franchisee or to the Franchisee's estate within XX days of the date of the Franchisee's death or death of the controlling owner of the Franchisee or the date upon which the Franchisee's or controlling owner's permanent incapacity arises, to purchase all or any part of the assets of the Franchisee used in the operation of the Franchised Business for a purchase price equal to the "asset value" of the Franchisee's assets less all proper business liabilities assumed by the Franchisor as of the date the said purchase is completed. To satisfy the aforesaid purchase price, the Franchisor shall pay the difference between the "asset value" and the amount of the liabilities assumed by it, on the date of the completion of the purchase by way of cash or certified check.

The Franchisee or any controlling owner shall be deemed to have a "permanent incapacity" if the usual participation of the Franchisee or any controlling owner in the Franchised Business is significantly curtailed for a cumulative period of XX days in any XX month period during the term of this agreement, including renewals, due to physical and/or intellectual incapacity as determined by a medical provider or as evidenced by the appointment of a guardian, custodian, or trustee.

Discussion:

Most franchise agreements include provisions concerning how a franchisor may respond upon the death or incapacity of a franchisee, often including that a franchisor may step in to operate the franchised business on an interim basis or to designate a manager until the parties can reach a final resolution. If the franchise is not sold or otherwise transferred within a reasonable period, a franchisor may grant itself the power to terminate the franchise. A franchisor's approach on this language in the agreement should depend on the nature of the franchise system, the prevalence of individual (nonbusiness entity) franchisees, and whether the general structure of the franchised businesses involves general managers or other key personnel who can operate the franchise in the absence of the franchisee or controlling owner.

Another factor that determines how a franchisor responds to the death or incapacity of a franchisee is whether the franchisor has permitted, encouraged, or even required franchisees to use succession-planning trusts, which would allow the franchised business to avoid becoming mired in an individual franchisee's probate issues.[376] With less formality, a franchisor could require that a franchisee always have an established operational succession plan in place that has the franchisor's approval.

It is common for the franchisor to allow the family, heirs, or estate of a deceased franchisee to continue the operations of the franchised business immediately after death, even if not thereafter. In fact, some state laws may specifically require the franchisor to allow a surviving spouse, heirs, or estate of a deceased franchisee to

376. Berg, Faunce, & Padilla, *supra* note 364, at 2–5.

operate the franchise for a "reasonable" time after the franchisee's death.[377] Most often, relatives still must satisfy the franchisor's requirements (i.e., financial, character, and competency requirements). If the family or heirs do not satisfy such requirements, the franchisor typically requires the sale of the franchised business to someone who successfully meets those requirements.[378] Of course, the business reason behind this clause is that the franchisor wants to ensure that suitable, well-capitalized franchisees are running its franchises. As noted, state statutes in some jurisdictions may override the contract terms in this area.

In these clauses, it is crucial to include a definition of incapacity to avoid as much conflict as possible. For example, if a franchisee or controlling owner with critical responsibility for the operation of the franchised business is unexpectedly and severely injured in an accident, co-owners and family may want the franchisor to consider only the time when the franchisee is unconscious as the incapacitation period. From the franchisor's perspective, if this critical person is not back at work within the period designated as establishing a permanent incapacity, then the transfer process may be initiated even if the individual is conscious and able to give some limited operating instructions. Drafters include such a section to avoid ambiguity surrounding what (or what length of time) constitutes incapacitation for purposes of the agreement and its implications. Again, state law may override the contractual terms with respect to a franchisee's death or incapacity.[379]

Although many agreements have provisions dealing with death and incapacity and, as noted, it is common to permit a sale to or by family or heirs, there is not a universal approach to what happens if there are no heirs or family capable of stepping in, or if those individuals cannot sell within a reasonably short period of time. In that situation, some franchisors insist on the right to purchase as if the franchise agreement were being terminated, meaning a purchase for a depreciated book value, with little or no amount for going concern value. In other situations, the franchisor is obliged to pay what may approach fair market value. So, in the sample clause, the important but missing feature is the definition of "asset value." However, franchisors should be aware that the SBA does not permit a predetermined asset

---

377. *See, e.g.*, Cal. Bus. & Prof. Code § 20027(a); Ind. Code Ann. § 23-2-2.7-2(3).

378. Carden & Klarfeld, *supra* note 110, at 39.

379. *See, e.g.*, Ind. Code Ann. § 23-2-2.7-2(3) (violation of act to deny "the surviving spouse, heirs, or estate of a deceased franchisee the opportunity to participate in the ownership of the franchise under a valid franchise agreement for a reasonable time after the death of the franchisee, provided that the surviving spouse, heirs, or estate maintains all standards and obligations of the franchise"); *see also* Ind. Code Ann. § 23-2-2.5-51 (West 2017) ("Any designated family member of a deceased service station franchisee may succeed to the ownership of the existing agreement if all of the following conditions are met: (1) The designated family member gives the service station franchisor written notice of the intention to succeed to the service station agreement within thirty (30) days of the service station franchisee's death; (2) The designated family member agrees to be bound by all terms and conditions of the existing owner's franchise agreement; (3) There is no good cause for the service station franchisor to refuse to honor the succession.").

value, but rather, will require the asset value be determined by an appraiser chosen by both parties at the relevant time as shown in the following clause:

FORCED SALE OF ASSETS

If Franchisor has the option to purchase the business personal assets upon default or termination of the Franchise Agreement and the parties are unable to agree on the value of the assets, the value will be determined by an appraiser chosen by both parties. If the Franchisee owns the real estate where the franchise location is operating, Franchisee will not be required to sell the real estate upon default or termination, but Franchisee may be required to lease the real estate for the remainder of the franchise term (excluding additional renewals) for fair market value.[380]

This method of valuation is more time-consuming and expensive than assigning a predetermined value, but is a cost attributable to the need to allow franchisees access to SBA-guaranteed loans.

380. SBA Form 2462, *op. cit.*

8

Termination and Default

Bethany L. Appleby and Iris Figueroa Rosario

XXVII. Termination and Default

A. Events of Default and Right of Termination

The possibility of termination is one of the most effective motivators of franchisee compliance, and the power to terminate is one of the most important ways that the franchisor controls its system.[381] The default and termination section is an integral part of a franchise agreement, and therefore franchisors should take care in drafting it. Franchisors will rely on the section's events of termination and notice and cure provisions (subject to any statutory requirements) when issuing a default notice if a default occurs. Franchisors should therefore be clear, specific, and concise when listing the bases for default in the franchise agreement.[382] Although the franchisor will likely want to include a "catchall" provision for termination for material breach of the agreement not otherwise listed, explicitly listing grounds for termination can reduce disputes about whether a particular breach is egregious enough to justify termination.

381. Blair & Lafontaine, *supra* note 54, at 55.

382. Joseph J. Fittante, Jr. & Meredith Bauer, *Defaults and Terminations: An Unfortunate Reality of a Challenging Economy*, 28 FRANCHISE L.J. 214, 216 (Spring 2009) (*Practice Pointers: Drafting Notices of Defaults and Termination*).

Because termination severs the business relationship, usually with finality, and because the parties usually bear post-termination obligations (both outlined by the contract and by relevant statutes),[383] parties should be clear on exactly what events will provide grounds for termination and what cure period, if any, is required. The franchisor should ensure that its default and termination section provides adequate notice to the franchisee concerning the potential grounds for default. A court may view unfavorably a termination not well grounded in a franchise agreement.[384]

Regardless of the care the franchisor takes in crafting and following its default and termination provisions, franchisors and franchisees should be aware that state statutes may override them. Some states impose their own, non-waivable protections that may include mandatory notice and cure periods far longer than those set forth in the franchise agreement.[385] In addition, some states require state-specific addenda to franchise agreements or franchise disclosure documents (FDDs) that can affect the parties' rights and obligations.[386] These requirements generally override the contractual terms, to the extent inconsistent with the statute, and they vary by jurisdiction. Even conscientious franchise contract administrators can get tripped up on the competing requirements of state statutes and contract terms. In addition, franchisors may inadvertently provide protections by including a contractual choice of law provision choosing the law of a state with protections greater than those available in the franchisee's own jurisdiction.[387]

State franchise relationship statutes also often require franchisors to have statutorily defined "good cause" for termination, and what constitutes "good cause" varies by jurisdiction.[388] Certain states define good cause to mean a franchisee's failure

---

383. *Id.*

384. Courts will dismiss breach of contract claims if not founded in the agreement. *See, e.g.*, Fabbro v. DRX Urgent Care, LLC, 616 Fed. Appx. 485, 487 (3d Cir. 2015) ("[P]laintiffs' breach of contract claims fail because, as the District Court correctly observed, 'Plaintiffs have failed to cite to a single provision of the Franchise Agreement that has been breached.'"). In that case, the franchisee alleged that the franchisor had underestimated start-up costs and the franchisee's capital investment, but failed to articulate how these failings amounted to a breach of the agreement since it could not point to any section of the agreement in support of its claim. *See also* Century 21 Real Estate LLC v. All Professional Realty, Inc., 889 F.2d 1198, 1123 (E.D. Cal. 2012) ("Once again, All Professional fails to cite the provision of the franchise agreement it is relying on for this claim [the franchisor's alleged failure to provide the "tools and systems"].").

385. *See, e.g.*, CAL. BUS. & PROF CODE § 20020 (requiring a minimum 60-day notice and cure period), N.J. STAT. ANN. § 56:10-5 (requiring 60-day notice period for most termination grounds). Many other states also have notice and cure periods that franchisors may find onerous. *See, e.g.*, FRANCHISE DESK BOOK, SELECTED STATE LAWS, COMMENTARY AND ANNOTATIONS (W. Michael Garner, ed., 2d ed. 2012).

386. *See* Beata Krakus, Halima M. Majdid, & Diana V. Vilmenay, *My Addenda Say What? A Review of State Mandated FDD and Franchise Agreement Addenda*, ABA 39th Annual Forum on Franchising (Nov. 2016).

387. *See* discussion of choice of law provisions, *infra* at Chapter 9, Section XXVIII.C.; *see also* Dep't of Motor Vehicles v. Mercedes-Benz of North Am., Inc., 408 So. 2d 627, 629 (Fla. Dist. Ct. App. 1981) (disregarding Mercedes-Benz's argument that the New Jersey Franchise Practices Act applied only to franchises located in New Jersey and applying the New Jersey choice of law clause in the parties' agreement in finding that the franchisor had consented to the transfer of the Florida franchise in failing to timely respond under the act.). To minimize this risk, the franchisor may want to carve out state franchise protections in the franchise agreement's choice of law clause, depending on the potential extraterritorial application of the chosen law.

388. Fittante, Jr. & Bauer, *supra* note 382, at 214.

to comply substantially with the franchise agreement's requirements.[389] States often require the franchisees' noncompliance to be "material" before permitting termination even if the franchise agreement does not explicitly require it.[390] Other states' franchise statutes apply a standard of "unjust" termination or require "reasonable cause" or "just cause."[391] It is also important for the franchisors and the franchisees not only to read the words of a particular relationship statute's permissible grounds for termination, but also how courts have interpreted the statute's language in particular cases.[392] Because there are many (and sometimes changing) state franchise relationship laws that can override contractual termination provisions, franchisors should ensure that their franchise agreements contain provisions that allow courts to sever or "blue pencil" unenforceable provisions and should also consult the relevant franchise relationship laws before terminating a franchise agreement. Franchisors should also perform a choice-of-law analysis, mindful of any statutory provisions that prohibit contractual waiver of certain protections.

Further, some state statutes provide for a "wind up" period in which the franchisor and the franchisees are required to take certain actions before they can completely end their relationship. For instance, some state statutes require that the termination or the cancellation of a franchise cannot take effect until 60 days after receipt of a notice of termination.[393] The rationale behind this period is to allow for an orderly end to the relationship.[394] Other statutes go even further and require that

389. *See, e.g.*, Michigan Franchise Investment Law, Mich. Comp. Laws Ann. § 445.1527 ("Good cause shall include the failure of the franchisee to comply with any lawful provision of the franchise agreement and to cure such failure after being given written notice thereof and a reasonable opportunity, which in no event need be more than 30 days, to cure such failure."); Washington Franchise Investment Protection Act, Wash. Rev. Code § 19.100.180 (similar wording); N.J. Stat. Ann. § 56:10-5 (Good cause is defined as "limited to failure by the franchisee to substantially comply with those requirements imposed upon him by the franchise.").

390. *See, e.g.*, Dunkin' Donuts Inc. v. Priya Enterp., Inc., 89 F. Supp. 2d 319, 323 (E.D.N.Y. 2000) (finding as a matter of law that franchisee's failure to comply with quality control requirement in franchise agreement amounted to a material default); General Motors Corp. v. New A.C. Chevrolet, Inc., 263 F.3d 296, 318 (3d Cir. 2001) (discussing good cause grounds for termination under the New Jersey Franchise Practices Act in terms of a material breach); *see also* Genevieve A. Beck & Ellen R. Lokker, *The Materiality Requirement for Franchise Terminations*, ABA 29th Annual Forum on Franchising (2006).

391. *See* Del. Code Ann. tit. 6, § 2552 ("Termination of a franchise by a franchisor shall be deemed to be 'unjust,' or to have been made 'unjustly,' if such termination is without good cause or in bad faith."); Virginia Retail Franchises Act, Va. Code Ann. § 13.1-564 ("It shall be unlawful for a franchisor to cancel a franchise without *reasonable cause* or to use undue influence to induce a franchisee to surrender any right given to him by any provision contained in the franchise.") (emphasis added).

392. For example, the Connecticut Franchise Act, Conn. Gen. Stat. § 42-133e, requires good cause for termination. Courts have held that "good cause [under the Connecticut Franchise Act] is not limited to providing contractual breaches of the franchise agreement, but may be based on a franchisor's legitimate business reasons." Petereit v. S.B. Thomas, Inc., 63 F.3d 1169, 1184 (2d Cir. 1995).

393. *See, e.g.*, Cal. Bus. & Prof. Code § 20020 (California's Franchise Relations Act, which requires "notice at least 60 days in advance of the termination"); N.J. Rev. Stat. § 56:10-5 (New Jersey's Franchise Practices Act requiring "at least sixty days in advance of such termination . . .").

394. *See, e.g.*, Sawyer v. BP Oil, Inc., 619 F. Supp. 1268, 1272 (D.D.C. 1985) (finding that "[i]n giving the franchise a 90 day notice period, the PMPA [Petroleum Marketing Practices Act] grants to the franchisee time to preserve the franchise or to wind up his affairs.") (citing California Petroleum Dist. v. Chevron U.S.A., Inc., 589 F. Supp. 282, 285 (E.D.N.Y.1984)).

the franchisor purchase the franchisee's inventory and equipment upon a termination of a franchise.[395] Franchisors therefore should take care that they are complying with the state statutes that by law vary the terms of their contracts, and franchisees should look beyond their contract's terms for possible additional franchisor obligations. Given the high stakes of termination for the franchisees and the complex interplay between contract and state franchise laws, it is not surprising that default and termination disputes comprise much of the litigation in franchising.

As discussed previously, default provisions vary in each franchise system and are enforced differently in each state. It is therefore critical for franchisors to ensure that their franchise agreements contain default and termination provisions that are enforceable in every state where they conduct business. Franchisee compliance with the franchise agreement terms is essential to maintaining a healthy franchise system. Enforced and enforceable compliance standards also benefit the franchisee community, because good operations throughout the system can enhance the value of the brand and boost sales at franchised locations. With respect to drafting, national franchisors typically manage the variation among the state law requirements through state-specific addenda, crafted in a manner acceptable to state regulators that amend the standard contract provision where necessary.[396] Many franchisors include the state-specific addenda as exhibits to their base FDD given to prospective franchisees regardless of location. This procedure can help ensure that prospective franchisees have been properly disclosed with the information and reduce the administrative burden of making sure that the appropriate state-specific addendum is provided.

As further discussed below, defaults that are grounds for termination are frequently separated into three categories: (1) those that are viewed as incurable and provide grounds for immediate termination, usually without a notice requirement;[397] (2) those that provide grounds for termination immediately upon notice; and (3) those that require notice and an opportunity to cure before termination actually occurs.

The sample clauses in the following give a good introduction to the types of categories of defaults typically found in a franchise agreement. The types of default will vary, however, from each franchise system, depending on the type of franchise system—for example, whether it is a food franchisor or child care franchisor and

395. California Franchise Relations Act, CAL. BUS. & PROF. CODE § 20022(a), states: "Except as provided in this section, upon a lawful termination or nonrenewal of a franchisee, the franchisor shall purchase from the franchisee, at the value of price paid, minus depreciation, all inventory, supplies, equipment, fixtures, and furnishings purchased or paid for under the terms of the franchise agreement or any ancillary or collateral agreement by the franchisee to the franchisor or its approved suppliers and sources, that are, at the time of the notice of termination or nonrenewal, in the possession of the franchisee or used by the franchisee in the franchise business. The franchisor shall have the right to receive clear title to and possession of all items purchased from the franchisee under this section."

396. Regulator-imposed requirements can sometimes give rise to ambiguities that can complicate litigation. *See, e.g.*, Laxmi Investments, LLC v. Golf, USA, 193 F.3d 1095 (9th Cir. 1999); *but see* Bradley v. Harris Research, Inc., 275 F.3d 884, 898 (9th Cir. 2001) (explaining Laxmi's limited application).

397. For a discussion of incurable defaults, *see* Jason J. Stover, *No Cure, No Problem: State Franchise Laws and Termination for Incurable Defaults*, 23 FRANCHISE L.J. 217 (Spring 2004).

whether the system is established or fairly new. In the latter case, it is possible that the default provisions may not be as onerous given the franchisor's interest in trying to attract candidates to its business.

1. Automatic Termination

Automatic Termination: Franchisee will be in default of this Agreement, and the Agreement will automatically terminate without notice to Franchisee:

(a) if Franchisee becomes insolvent or makes a general assignment for the benefit of creditors;
(b) if Franchisee files a petition in bankruptcy or a petition is filed against Franchisee and not opposed by Franchisee;
(c) if Franchisee is adjudicated bankrupt or insolvent;
(d) if a receiver or other custodian (permanent or temporary) of Franchisee's assets or property, or any part thereof, is appointed by any court of competent jurisdiction;
(e) if proceedings for a composition with creditors under the applicable law of any jurisdiction is instituted by or against Franchisee;
(f) if a final judgment remains unsatisfied or of record for thirty days or longer (unless a supersedeas bond is filed or other steps are taken to stay effectively the enforcement of such judgment in the relevant jurisdiction);
(g) if Franchisee is dissolved;
(h) if execution is levied against Franchisee's property or business;
(i) if suit to foreclose any lien or mortgage against the premises or equipment of any Franchised Business is instituted against Franchisee and not dismissed within thirty days; or
(j) if the real or personal property of any Franchised Business is sold after levy by any sheriff, marshal, constable or equivalent governmental authority.

Discussion:

The preceding sample clause pertains to those breaches that provide the franchisor with "automatic" grounds for terminating a franchise agreement. That is, the ability to terminate without the requirement of providing any prior notice of termination.

A few of the provisions in the prceding sample clauses deal with the franchisee's insolvency or bankruptcy petition, and these types of clauses are commonly referred to as ipso facto clauses. Courts have generally held that insolvency or the imminent threat of insolvency constitutes good cause to terminate under the franchise agreement.[398] Even state franchise statutes specifically mention the "bankruptcy or insolvency of the franchisee" as a "good" basis for termination.[399] However, these types

398. Open Pantry Food Marts of Wisconsin v. Five, Inc., Bus. Franchise Guide (CCH) ¶ 8113 (Wis. Cir. Ct. 1984) (the franchisee's insolvency was good grounds to terminate under the Wisconsin Fair Dealer Act); Pat's King of Steaks, Inc. v. Pat's Int'l, LTD, 1986 U.S. Dist. LEXIS 23715 (E.D. Pa. June 25, 1986) (terminating the franchise agreement based upon the franchisee's insolvency and failure to pay taxes).

399. *See, e.g.*, Minn. Stat. § 80C.14(3)(b) (defining good cause for termination to include "bankruptcy or insolvency of the franchisee"); Miss. Code Ann. § 75-24-53 (same); Mo. Rev. Stat. § 407.405 (same).

of clauses are generally unenforceable under federal bankruptcy law.[400] And, certain state franchise regulators, such as Maryland, require that a franchisor state in its FDD that this type of clause is unenforceable under federal bankruptcy law. Despite federal bankruptcy laws, franchisors continue to include these ipso facto clauses in their agreements. The preceding sample has some modifying language that is more "franchisee friendly" than some in that termination is not automatic if a foreclosure proceeding is dismissed within 30 days or if the franchisee opposes a creditor's bankruptcy petition. A franchisee's lawyer may want to attempt push back if a proposed agreement does not contain similar protective language.

2. Termination upon Notice without Opportunity to Cure

Franchisee will be in default and Franchisor may, at its option, terminate this Agreement and all rights granted by it without affording Franchisee any opportunity to cure the default (effective immediately upon receipt of written notice by Franchisee), upon the occurrence of any of the following events:

(a) if Franchisee fails to complete construction of the Franchised Business and to open for business within one hundred eighty (180) days of execution of this Agreement. Franchisor may, but is not required to, extend this period to address unforeseen construction delays, not within the control of Franchisee;

(b) if Franchisee at any time ceases to operate the Franchised Business or otherwise abandons the Franchised Business by failing to operate the Franchised Business for more than three consecutive days without written permission from Franchisor, or loses the right to possession of the premises of the Franchised Business, or otherwise forfeits the right to do or transact business in the jurisdiction where the Franchised Business is located. Provided, however, that if, through no fault of Franchisee, the Premises are damaged or destroyed by an event not within the control of Franchisee such that repairs or reconstruction cannot be completed within one hundred eighty (180) days thereafter, then Franchisee shall have thirty (30) days after such event in which to apply for Franchisor's approval to relocate and/or reconstruct the Premises, which approval shall not be unreasonably withheld, but may be conditioned upon the payment of an agreed minimum royalty to Franchisor during the period in which the Franchised Business is not in operation;

(c) if Franchisee is convicted of a felony involving moral turpitude, or any other crime that Franchisor believes is reasonably likely to have an adverse effect

400. *See* 11 U.S.C. § 365(e)(1) ("Notwithstanding a provision in an executory contract or unexpired lease, or in applicable law, an executory contract or unexpired lease of the debtor may not be terminated or modified, and any right or obligation under such contract or lease may not be terminated or modified, at any time after the commencement of the case solely because of a provision in such contract or lease that is conditioned on—(A) the insolvency or financial condition of the debtor at any time before the closing of the case; (B) the commencement of a case under this title; or (C) the appointment of or taking possession by a trustee in a case under this title or a custodian before such commencement."). *See also* 11 U.S.C. § 541(c), which provides that a contract is a property of the estate, regardless of any ipso facto provision that conditions termination based on insolvency or bankruptcy.

on the System, the Trademarks, the goodwill associated therewith, or Franchisor's interest therein;

(d) if a threat or danger to public health or safety results from the construction, maintenance, or operation of the Franchised Business or from the material violation of any health and safety laws, rules, or regulations which poses a significant public health and safety concern, or if the Franchised Business is closed as a result of a failed inspection by the health department and in such event Franchisor determines, in its sole discretion, that critical violations of applicable health codes are the result of repeated or material failure by Franchisee to comply with the requirements of the Agreement or the health department. Notwithstanding anything in this Agreement to the contrary, Franchisor shall have the right, in lieu of exercising any right of termination, to require that the Franchised Business be closed to the public and/or remain closed until the applicable food, health, or safety matters are cured;

(e) if Franchisee, or any partner, shareholder, or member of the Franchisee purports to transfer any rights or obligations under this Agreement or any interest in Franchisee to any third party without Franchisor's prior written consent contrary to the transfer provisions of this Agreement;

(f) if Franchisee fails to comply with the in-term non-competition covenants in this Agreement or fails to obtain execution of the covenants required from the owners of Franchisee;

(g) if, contrary to the terms of this Agreement, Franchisee discloses or divulges the contents of the Manual or any other confidential information provided to Franchisee by Franchisor;

(h) if an approved transfer is not effected as required by this Agreement, following the death or mental incapacity of a person as described therein;

(i) if Franchisee knowingly maintains false books or records, or submits any false reports to Franchisor (including, but not limited to, information provided as part of Franchisee's application for his franchise), or underreports gross sales;

(j) if Franchisee or any individual, group, association, limited or general partnership, corporation or other business entity which directly or indirectly controls, is controlled by, or is under common control with Franchisee; or which directly or indirectly owns, controls, or holds power to vote ten percent (10%) or more of the outstanding voting securities of Franchisee; or which has in common with Franchisee one or more partners, officers, directors, trustees, branch managers, or other persons occupying similar status or performing similar functions ("Affiliate") commits any act of default under any other Franchise Agreement, Development Agreement (except for failure to meet the development schedule thereunder), lease or sublease, asset purchase agreement, promissory note, or any other agreement entered into by Franchisee or an affiliate of the Franchisee, and Franchisor or any affiliate or predecessor of, or successor to, Franchisor, if Franchisee fails to cure that default within the cure period applicable to the breach of that other agreement.

(k) if Franchisee materially defaults more than three times in any twelve (12) month period, whether or not cured after notice;
(l) if Franchisee uses any of the Trademarks in any unauthorized manner; or
(m) if Franchisee engages in any conduct or practice that is fraudulent, unfair, unethical, or a deceptive practice.

Discussion:
Franchisees should also be aware that some breaches of a clearly drafted franchise agreement provision could be grounds for termination upon notice without the opportunity to cure.[401] Courts have recognized that certain defaults are inherently "incurable," such as repeated financial defaults, underreporting, misbranding of product, selling outside of the permitted territory, and remaining closed for business for an impermissible period of time.[402] In addition, a franchisee's fraudulent conduct that impacts the franchise or the brand is also grounds for immediate termination.[403] An example can include a franchisee's or its principal's conviction of a crime. In such cases, courts typically take the position that this type of conduct is not curable.[404]

Franchisors need to understand the logic behind incurable defaults as opposed to those that merit exercise of discretion or time to cure, which is discussed in the next section. From a business perspective, franchisors generally will want franchisees to be confident that they can conduct their businesses without fearing precipitous or unreasonable termination and should consider providing cure periods to the extent consistent with the franchisor's business goals as well as the contractual requirements.

If the franchisee receives a termination notice that provides for a notice period but no opportunity to cure, the franchisee should consider working with the franchisor to determine whether an immediate sale of the franchise would be permitted. If the defaulting franchisee will be out of the system and replaced by a new one

401. *See, e.g.*, The Original Great Am. Chocolate Chip Cookie Co., Inc. v. River Valley Cookies, Ltd., 970 F.2d 273 (7th Cir. 1992) (franchisee's repeated late payment of invoices, bounced checks, underreporting sales, and other breaches justifies termination of franchise agreement without opportunity to cure); Wisser Co. v. Mobil Oil Corp., 730 F.2d 54, 59 (2d Cir. 1984) (misbranding of gasoline requires no advance notice or opportunity to cure prior to termination). As the Second Circuit stated, "the proposition that a franchisee always has the right to cure a default is obviously wrong." *Id.*

402. For a discussion of incurable defaults, see Chad J. Doellinger, *Incurable Breaches: A Fresh Look at an Old Problem*, 32 FRANCHISE L.J. 3 (Winter 2013).

403. *See, e.g.*, Lippo v. Mobil Oil Corp., 776 F.2d 706, 724 (7th Cir. 1985) (Posner, J., dissenting) (Judge Posner discussing in the context of the sale of unapproved gasoline products how this type of fraudulent behavior cannot be undue: "'Lippo could no more cure his breach in selling misbranded gasoline simply by ceasing to sell it than the singer could cure her default by showing up the next night.").

404. *Id.; see also, e.g.*, Dunkin' Donuts Inc. v. Martinez, No. 01-3589-Civ., 2003 WL 685875, at *9 (S.D. Fla. 2003) ("As a general proposition, a franchisee's violation of the law [for tax fraud] may justify termination of its franchise agreement on the principle that the 'good faith belief of the franchisor that the franchisee is untrustworthy or engages in fraudulent practices undermines the entire franchise relationship.'") (citing Humboldt Oil Co. v. Exxon Co., 695 F.2d 386, 389 (9th Cir. 1982), *cert. denied*, 485 U.S. 1021 (1988)); Dunkin' Donuts, Inc. v. Taseski, 47 F. Supp. 2d 867, 877 (E.D. Mich. 1999) (enforcing Dunkin's termination of franchise agreement under the obey all laws provision when franchisees underreported sales, underpaid their obligations, and falsified financial records).

who has not engaged in the prohibited conduct, the franchisor may prefer that to a potential protracted legal battle with the terminated franchisee or the possibility of a temporarily "dark" location.

The previously-noted sample provisions are fairly typical and generally contained in franchise agreements. These include the "three strikes" rule, which gives a franchisor the right to terminate if a franchisee receives three defaults or more in the preceding 12-month period. In addition, many franchise agreements give the franchisor the right to terminate a network of affiliated entities. The preceding sample cross-default provision is fairly open-ended, but generally many franchisors tie the underlying "default" that is the basis for terminating under the cross-default provision to something very serious, such as fraudulent conduct by the franchisee that affects the relationship between the parties or the franchisee's violation of a material law.

In addition, section 2.b in the preceding sample clause gives the franchisor the right to terminate if the franchisee ceases to operate the franchised business for a period of "three consecutive days." However, the provision also includes a "franchisee-friendly" carve-out in the event the franchisee is unable to operate the business due to no fault of its own, including in the event of a natural disaster (e.g., hurricane) or other contingency completely out of the franchisee's control. An example of the latter type of situation may include a highway construction that effectively forces the franchise business to close either temporarily or permanently.

3. Termination with Opportunity to Cure

> Franchisor may also terminate for any default of Franchisee's obligations under this Agreement. Except as outlined above, upon any default by Franchisee that is capable of being cured, Franchisor may terminate this agreement only by giving written Notice of Termination stating the nature of such default to Franchisee at least ten days prior to the effective date of termination if the default is for failure to pay royalties, contribute to the Fund (including cooperative contributions, if any are due and/or any other financial obligations owed to Franchisor by Franchisee), and thirty (30) days, prior to the effective date of termination for any other default; provided, however, that Franchisee may avoid termination by curing such default to Franchisor's satisfaction within the ten (10) day or thirty (30) day period, as applicable. If any such default is not cured within the specified time, this Agreement shall terminate without further notice to Franchisee effective immediately upon the expiration of the ten (10) day or thirty (30) day period, as applicable, or such longer period as applicable law may require.

Discussion:

Finally, the third category of default is those that require the franchisor to provide franchisee notice and an opportunity to cure. The previously-noted provision is fairly typical of provisions contained in a franchise agreement. These include providing a franchisee in financial default a period in which to bring its account current. In addition, franchisors typically provide a franchisee with an opportunity to cure standard defaults for health, safety, and sanitation violations or some other violation of the franchisor's system standards. For example, some food franchisors further categorize these types of defaults into "emergency" defaults that give the franchisor the right to close a restaurant immediately in order to rectify a health violation or require a franchisee to cure the problem within 24 to 48 hours. The type of default that is "curable" depends on the franchise system, and a franchisor should therefore tailor its default and termination provisions to the needs of its system.

B. Liquidated Damages

> Upon Franchisor's termination of this Agreement in accordance with its terms, Franchisee shall pay to Franchisor within 30 days of the date of the termination, as liquidated damages for the premature termination of this Agreement and not as a penalty, an amount equal to XX times the continuing royalty fees payable to Franchisor in respect to the last 12 months of the Franchised Business' active operations or the entire period the Franchised Business has been open for business, whichever is the shorter period. Franchisee acknowledges and agrees that such liquidated damages are a reasonable approximation of the damages Franchisor will incur resulting from the premature termination of the Franchise Agreement as a result of breach by Franchisee, are appropriate because actual damages incurred by Franchisor will be difficult or impossible to ascertain, are not a penalty, and shall not affect Franchisor's right to, and are not in lieu of, any other payment or remedy, damages or relief to Franchisor.

Discussion:
Franchisors frequently, although not universally, include liquidated damage clauses in their franchise agreements. The Restatement (Second) of Contracts, section 356(1), which many states have adopted, allows a contracting party to recoup liquidated damages. It states:

> Damages for breach by either party may be liquidated in the agreement but only at an amount that is reasonable in the light of the anticipated or actual loss caused by the breach and the difficulties of proof of loss. A term fixing unreasonably large liquidated damages is unenforceable on grounds of public policy as a penalty.[405]

Liquidated damage clauses provide a contractually agreed upon formula for calculating the franchisor's damages resulting from the termination of the franchise agreement before the end of its natural term due to the franchisee's breach. Franchisors that choose to include such a clause have recognized that it is difficult to calculate the attendant loss of having lost a location plus the time involved in having to replace the franchisee's revenue and possible harm to the brand's goodwill. For these franchisors, including the clause makes sense, since it allows both parties to understand what it will cost in the event there is a premature termination of the franchise agreement, without the expense and complexity of calculating and proving the precise damages incurred. The provision's purpose therefore is to save the

405. Restatement (Second) of Contracts, § 356(1).

expense of litigation in having to prove up damages at a later date.[406] Absent such a clause, a franchisor may face challenges in proving its actual damages resulting from premature termination, as well as protracted discovery and fact disputes with the terminated franchisee over this category of damages.[407] The franchisee, of course, would prefer to pay nothing at all after termination, but at least a liquidated damages provision can reduce uncertainty and the cost of litigation.

As noted previously, drafters should be aware that liquidated damages cannot be used as a form of penalty and therefore must not be disproportionate to the franchisor's harm. As one court has noted, if damages are easily calculable, then the liquidated damages clause is a penalty and not a remedy.[408] In particular, and broadly speaking, a court may enforce a liquidated damage clause if it is established that the parties intended liquidated damages not as a penalty but as a reasonable approximation of damages to compensate the franchisor for harm resulting from the franchise agreement's premature termination due to the franchisee's breach; that the liquidated damages amount set at the time of contract was a reasonable estimate of actual damages that the franchisor would incur; and that actual damages were difficult to ascertain.[409] A court will generally take into account these factors in assessing if the clause is a true approximation of a party's damages or a penalty.[410]

The preceding provision provides for a liquidated damages clause expressed as a multiple of the continuing royalties payable to the franchisor for the preceding 12-month period. Courts will weigh the previously-noted factors in assessing if this is a reasonable calculation of a franchisor's damages. Liquidated damages are calculated differently depending on the franchise system. What constitutes reasonable compensation for one system will differ for another. While certain franchise systems will attempt to calculate loss of royalties, other systems, such as hotel franchisors (which typically use liquidated damages in their contracts) will try to account for the loss of room revenue that they would have generated had there not been a breach of the parties' contract. Even within those systems that base their liquidated damages clause on loss of royalties, the clause will vary depending on the length of time it takes a system to sell and establish a new unit. So, for example, if a franchisor knows that it can typically sell a territory within 12 months and it will take

406. *Id.* Restatement (Second) of Contracts, § 356 cmt a.

407. *See, e.g.*, Meineke Car Care Centers, Inc. v. RLB Holdings, LLC, No. 3:08cv240-RJC, 2009 WL 2461953, at *6 (W.D.N.C. Aug. 10, 2009) (rejecting franchisor's request for lost profit damages because the franchisee's two shops were not profitable and one of the stores was operating at a loss for certain years); No. 3:06-cv-180-W, 2007 WL 1100841, at *2 (W.D.N.C. Apr. 12, 2007) (denying claim for lost profits because the franchise was not generating any profits and the franchisor had failed to show "that such [alleged] profits would have been realized except for the breach of the contract.").

408. Lake River Corp. v. Carborundum Co., 769 F.2d 1284, 1289–90 (7th Cir. 1985) (applying Illinois law and stating "[i]f damages would be easy to determine then [at the time of contracting], or if the estimate greatly exceeds a reasonable upper estimate of what the damages are likely to be, it is a penalty.").

409. Deborah S. Coldwell, Altresha Q. Burchett-Williams, & Melissa L. Celeste, *Liquidated Damages*, 29 Franchise L.J. 211 (Spring 2010) (surveying United States jurisdictions).

410. *See, e.g.*, Choice Hotels Int'l, Inc. v. Smith Hotel Props., LLC, No. 5:09-CV-00285-80, 2011 U.S. Dist. LEXIS 48928 (E.D.N.C. May 6, 2011) (finding that the liquidated damages provision was not an unenforceable penalty; rather, it was a reasonable attempt to put Choice Hotels in the position it would have been absent the breach, and was not grossly excessive).

less than six months to open the unit, then perhaps the drafter should take that into account in determining the multiple of continuing royalties in the previously noted provision so that the provision does not appear more of a penalty than a remedy.

Franchise parties also should keep in mind that the enforceability of a liquidated damages clause depends on the state jurisdiction. In some states, such as Minnesota and North Dakota, liquidated damages provisions are not enforceable.[411] Other states, such as Utah, will not enforce a liquidated damages provision if it is unconscionable.[412] Franchisors should therefore be aware of applicable state laws, and court decisions interpreting them, before proceeding to enforce liquidated damage clauses.[413]

For its part, a franchisee should understand that, because liquidated damages in certain states are presumptively valid, it should pay particular attention to this clause in the franchise agreement. To the extent it can, the franchisee should seek to cap the damages up front before it enters into any franchise agreement with a franchisor. The savvy drafter will also keep in mind that some prospective franchisees will view a particularly high liquidated damages calculation as an indication that the franchisor may be unreasonable in many aspects of its operations. Rather than negotiate a cap, those franchisees may simply opt to join a different system.

C. Termination by the Franchisee

> Franchisee may terminate this Agreement as a result of Franchisor's breach of a material provision of this Agreement provided that: (i) Franchisee provides Franchisor with written notice of the breach that identifies the grounds for the breach; and (ii) Franchisor fails to cure the breach within thirty (30) days after Franchisor's receipt of the written notice. If Franchisor fails to cure the breach, the termination will be effective sixty (60) days after Franchisor's receipt of Franchisee's written notice of breach. Franchisee's termination of this Agreement under this subparagraph will not release or modify Franchisee's post-termination obligations set out in this Agreement.

---

411. *See* Minn. R. 2860.4400; Minn. Stat. § 80C.01-22; Nolan v. HairColorXpress Int'l, LLC, Bus. Franchise Guide (CCH) ¶ 13,049 (D. Minn. Mar. 8, 2005); Holiday Hospitality Franchising, Inc. v. H-5, Inc., Bus. Franchise Guide (CCH) ¶ 12,216 (D. Minn. Mar. 26, 2001); Securities Commissioner Policy Regarding Conduct That Is Unfair, Unjust, or Inequitable to North Dakota Franchisees, Bus. Franchise Guide (CCH) ¶ 5,340.05; N.D. Cent. Code § 51-19-09 (authorizing the commissioner to deny the effectiveness of any registration if the commissioner finds that the offer, sale, or purchase of the franchise would constitute misrepresentation or deceit to purchases, or that the offeror is engaging in fraudulent or deceptive practices in connection with the offer). The North Dakota Securities Commissioner considers a liquidated damages clause to be unfair, unjust, or inequitable to North Dakota franchisees.

412. *See* Cantamar, L.L.C. v. Champagne, 2006 UT App. 321,142 P.3d 140, n.6 (Utah Ct. App. 2006).

413. The 2010 *Franchise Law Journal* article *Liquidated Damages*, authored by Coldwell, Burchett-Williams, & Celeste, *supra* note 409, is extremely helpful in determining the state-by-state views and procedures on the enforceability of liquidated damages. Not only does the article offer an expanded discussion of this topic, the article provides an appendix providing a 50-state survey of the various tests for enforceability used by each state. *Id.*

Discussion:
Most franchise agreements provide few, if any, explicit termination rights to the franchisee, and even fewer franchisees ever formally terminate their franchise agreements. Nonetheless, basic contract law generally allows parties to terminate their contractual obligations for the other party's material breach.[414] Failing franchisees often close down or abandon their franchises, and then may sue their franchisors for breach and damages (or franchisors may sue for closing or abandoning the business). However, as in the preceding sample clause, the franchisee sometimes is granted the explicit right to terminate if the franchisor fails to cure a breach. The sample clause is relatively favorable for the franchisee. In more restrictive agreements, the franchisor will often restrict the franchisee's ability to terminate to "material breaches." Typically, a franchisee with the right to terminate also will be restricted from doing so if the franchisee itself is in breach of the agreement in any way. The franchisor also will often require reasonable notice and a period of time to cure.[415] In addition to a termination right exercisable upon cause and after notice and an opportunity to cure, some franchise agreements may give the franchisee a "without cause" termination right exercisable during a particular time period and upon certain conditions. It should also be noted that the "good cause" and other franchise relationship statutes should not limit a franchisee's, as opposed to the franchisor's, ability to terminate, giving the parties wide latitude to provide for termination at the franchisee's option.

Note, though, that even if the franchisee exercises a right to terminate (whether for cause or not), it must comply with any contractual post-termination obligations it would have had if the franchisor had terminated the franchise agreement or the agreement had expired. Those obligations typically involve, as detailed in the following section, the requirement that the franchisee give up use of the system and trademarks and perform other post-termination obligations, including complying with any enforceable post-termination non-compete provisions. Although this is a logical end result of any franchise agreement's termination, it usually gives a non-defaulting franchisee little comfort. Even if the franchisee believes that the franchisor is in default, rather than declare a default and terminate the agreement, the franchisee often will sue for damages and continue to perform under the terms of the franchise agreement. The termination, along with the enforcement of post-termination covenants, comes with too much of a downside for the franchisee. The franchisee might therefore consider negotiating with the franchisor that certain post-termination obligations will not apply upon a franchisor's breach and the franchisee's resulting termination of the franchise agreement.

---

414. *See, e.g.*, Restatement (Second) of Contracts § 242 (discussing circumstances significant in determining when remaining duties are discharged).

415. Asbill, Barkoff, & Selden, *supra* note 4, at 52–53.

D. Franchisee Obligations on Termination

Upon the expiration or termination of this Agreement for any reason whatsoever, the following shall apply:

1. Franchisee shall, immediately upon Franchisor's request (in order that Franchisor may protect the Trademarks and Franchisor's other franchisees), permit Franchisor or its representatives to enter the Premises and, at Franchisor's option, to cure any default by Franchisee, to operate the Franchised Business for Franchisor's account or to secure Franchisee's complete and timely compliance with the other post-termination obligations set forth in this Agreement;
2. Franchisee shall pay to Franchisor, within XX days after the effective date of termination or expiration, all royalties, advertising fees and other charges then due and unpaid by Franchisee including, but not limited to Franchisor's costs and expenses in re-entering the Premises and in completing the acts specified in this Agreement;
3. Franchisee shall immediately discontinue the operation of the Franchised Business, use of the System and the use of the Trademarks and other proprietary rights licensed under this Agreement, and similar names and marks, or any other designations or marks associating Franchisee with Franchisor or the System. Franchisee shall cease displaying and using all signs, stationery, letterhead, packaging, forms, containers, Manuals, bulletins, instruction sheets, printed matter, advertising and other physical objects used from time to time in connection with the System or containing or bearing any of the Trademarks or other names, marks or designations, and shall not thereafter operate or do business under any name or in any manner or that might tend to give the general public the impression that it is associated with Franchisor or the System or that it is operating a business similar to a [particular type of] business or that it previously conducted its business under the Trademarks;
4. if Franchisee retains possession of the Premises, Franchisee shall promptly and, at its expense, make such modifications to the interior and/or exterior decor of the Premises as Franchisor shall require to remove all identification as a [particular type of] business;
5. Franchisee shall promptly execute such documents or take such actions as may be necessary to abandon Franchisee's use of any assumed name containing any of the Trademarks adopted by Franchisee and to remove (in respect of the next publication), at Franchisor's request, Franchisee's listing as a [particular type of] business from the yellow pages, all other telephone directories and all other trade or business directories and to assign to Franchisor or any other party designated by Franchisor all of Franchisee's telephone numbers and listings in connection with the Franchised Business; and within XX days after the effective date of expiration or termination, Franchisee shall return to Franchisor all items making up the Manual, all other confidential material provided to Franchisee by Franchisor and all other materials required to be returned in accordance with this Agreement or the Manual.

Discussion:

The sample clause provides a fairly typical list of the actions that the franchisee is required to take upon a franchise agreement's expiration or termination, regardless of the method or means of termination and regardless of whether the franchisor or franchisee terminates the agreement. Some franchise systems vary the requirements in other ways, for instance, requiring that the franchisee assign to the franchisor the premises' telephone number and submit its files and customer lists to the franchisor.[416] For certain franchisors, such as tax franchisors, the franchise agreement makes clear that this information is proprietary and that the customer lists and files belong to the franchisor. The franchise agreement further prohibits the franchisee from using this proprietary information after termination. Franchisees therefore should carefully review these provisions before termination and take their obligations into account when planning any post-termination business activities. Franchisees should also review any post-termination non-compete obligations that may be elsewhere in their agreements and determine whether those are enforceable under applicable law and should also be aware of any other obligations that may survive termination, including other confidentiality, indemnification, or dispute resolution forum obligations.[417]

A post-termination clause is intended to provide for an orderly transition of the franchise and is very important in that regard. Upon the agreement's termination or expiration, the franchisee should be required to discontinue all use of any trademarks, remove any and all visual identification of the trademarks and return the manual and any other confidential information.[418] Often, the timeframes for doing so are quite short, sometimes only a few days. In addition, the franchisor usually requires the return or destruction of any item previously associated with the trademarks. This might include the return of any confidential manual or, as stated previously, any telephone numbers used or an assignment of the lease for the former franchise premises. It may also prohibit the former franchisee from indicating in any way its former affiliation with the franchisor.[419]

The clause also protects the franchisor's proprietary system. The preceding sample clause makes plain that the authorization to use the trademarks, system, and goodwill ends upon termination or expiration of the agreement. The clause is also meant to protect against any harm to the system's goodwill by the former franchisee's continued use or display of the trademarks or retention of the franchisor's

416. Little Caesar Enterprises, Inc. v. Little Caesar's VA, Inc., BUS. FRANCHISE GUIDE (CCH) ¶ 14,199 (E.D. Va. 2009) (granting the franchisor's request for an injunction and requiring the franchisee to comply with the post-termination obligations, including ceasing to use the same telephone number of the business it formerly franchised). *See also* Brenco Enterprises, Inc. v. Takeout Taxi Franchising Sys., Inc., No. 177164, 2003 Va. Cir. LEXIS 86, at *19 (Va. Cir. Ct. May 23, 2003) (ordering the franchisee to return the telephone numbers, directory listings, and customer databases they had used in their franchise businesses since those were the franchisor's property rights pursuant to the parties' franchise agreements).

417. *See generally* Chapter 8 Section G *infra.*

418. Carden & Klarfeld, *supra* note 110, at 4.

419. *Id.*

valuable confidential and proprietary material. It is crucial where possible that leases allow the franchisor to access the premises to remove signage and otherwise de-identify, generally at the former franchisee's expense. This will help eliminate confusion and roadblocks erected by uncooperative landlords to whom rent may be owed.

Further, if a former franchisee fails to de-identify the former location, the post-termination obligations give the franchisor an additional contract claim against the franchisee in addition to its statutory recourse under trademark, trade secret, and other laws. Franchisees should be aware that a franchisor can and often will move for an injunction to enforce the post-termination obligations, including ensuring that the franchisee properly de-identifies and does not breach any applicable enforceable covenant not to compete.[420]

E. Franchisor's Right to Repurchase

> Upon the expiration or termination of this Agreement for any reason whatsoever, save and except in the event of a purchase, Franchisor shall have the right, but not the obligation, such right to be exercised by notice in writing delivered to Franchisee within XX days of the date of expiration or termination of this Agreement for any reason whatsoever, to purchase from Franchisee all or any portion of the inventory located on the Premises or otherwise held by Franchisee for the purposes of sale or distribution at the Premises, and/or all or any part of the fixtures, equipment, furniture or other assets located on, in or at the Premises or otherwise used in connection with the Franchised Business.

Discussion:

In addition to requiring the franchisee to return or destroy all trademarked or proprietary items, the franchisor may want to reserve the right to repurchase some or all of the assets used in the franchised business, including unique, system specific inventory, fixtures, or equipment.

The rationale behind this clause is to recapture items of value upon the relationship's end, either to use by another franchisee or company-owned location or sell them elsewhere or to prohibit the former franchisee from doing so. If the franchisor does not recapture these items, then the former franchisee may be able to sell them, risking damage to the franchisor's goodwill or making it difficult for the franchisor or a new franchisee to operate at the former franchisee's location. In states such as California in which it is difficult or impossible to prohibit a former franchisee from competing against the franchisor immediately after the end of the agreement, this

420. *See, e.g.*, Little Caesar Enterprises, Inc. v. Little Caesar's VA, Inc., BUS. FRANCHISE GUIDE (CCH) ¶ 14,199 (E.D. Va. 2009) (granting the franchisor's request for an injunction and requiring the franchisee to comply with the post-termination obligations, including ceasing to use the same telephone number of the business it formerly franchised).

clause can allow the franchisor to recapture equipment and inventory and make it more costly for a franchisee to form a competitive business.

The amount of time that the franchisor will want to reserve for its decision about whether or not to repurchase business assets varies slightly, but is often about one month. Franchisors should ensure that they have reserved enough time to make this business decision, but they should also consider that franchisees in many business concepts will immediately begin to sell and/or move equipment, furniture, fixtures, inventory, and other items, so as a practical matter a franchisor that wants to repurchase the business assets may need to move relatively quickly in some scenarios.

It is helpful to include in the agreement a mechanism for determining the buy-back price. Many franchisors include the right to repurchase items at the depreciated book value so that they do not have to pay any additional amounts for the goodwill. A franchise agreement may include a dispute mechanism in the event the parties cannot come to an agreement on the repurchase value of the inventory or equipment. These may require that the parties hire an independent appraiser (or appraisers) to assess the state of the inventory. A typical provision will require the parties to agree to one or two "mediators" that will independently assess the evidence and the state of inventory and equipment, and provide a reasonable appraisal that both parties must accept.

In some jurisdictions, state franchise statutes alter the requirements of the agreement and require the franchisors to repurchase certain franchisee equipment or inventory upon termination in specific circumstances.[421] States that have these provisions include California,[422] Connecticut,[423] and Hawaii.[424] Additionally, Hawaii

---

421. For a chart of particular state statutory requirements and a helpful discussion of return and repurchase issues, as of 2008, *see* Clay A. Tillack & Mark E. Ashton, *Who Takes What: The Parties' Rights to Franchise Materials at the Relationship's End*, 28 Franchise L.J. 88 (Fall 2008). *See also* Gary R. Batenhorst, *Breaking Up Is Hard to Do: Challenges and Opportunities in Franchisor Buyback Rights and Obligations*, 30 Franchise L.J. 97 (Fall 2010).

422. Cal. Bus. & Prof. Code § 20035 ("In the event a franchisor terminates or fails to renew a franchisee, in violation of this chapter, the franchisee shall be entitled to receive from the franchisor the fair market value of the franchised business and franchise assets and any other damages caused by the violation of this chapter."). The parties should be aware that the requirement to repurchase inventory or equipment in California also applies in the event of any lawful termination if the franchisor takes over the former franchisee's lease. It does not apply if the franchisee is permitted to retain the premises where it operated the franchise. *See, e.g.*, Cal. Bus. & Prof. Code § 20022.

423. Conn. Gen. Stat. § 42-133f(c) ("Upon termination of any franchise the franchisee shall be allowed fair and reasonable compensation by the franchisor for the franchisee's inventory, supplies, equipment and furnishings purchased by the franchisee from the franchisor or its approved sources under the terms of the franchise or any ancillary or collateral agreement; provided no compensation shall be allowed for personalized items which have no value to the franchisor.").

424. Haw. Rev. Stat. § 482E-6(3) ("Upon termination or refusal to renew the franchise the franchisee shall be compensated for the fair market value, at the time of the termination or expiration of the franchise, of the franchisee's inventory, supplies, equipment and furnishings purchased from the franchisor or a supplier designated by the franchisor; provided that personalized materials which have no value to the franchisor need not be compensated for. If the franchisor refuses to renew a franchise for the purpose of converting the franchisee's business to one owned and operated by the franchisor, the franchisor, in addition to the remedies provided in this paragraph, shall compensate the franchisee for the loss of goodwill. The franchisor may deduct from such compensation reasonable costs

and other states require franchisors to compensate the franchisee for the goodwill generated at the location upon the occurrence of termination or nonrenewal.[425]

F. Additional Remedies

> Franchisee expressly consents and agrees that, in addition to any other remedies Franchisor may have, at law or under this Agreement, nothing in this agreement shall bar Franchisor's right to obtain injunctive relief against threatened conduct that will cause it loss or harm, under the usual equity rules, including the applicable rules for obtaining restraining orders and preliminary injunctions.

Discussion:

Drafters typically include a clause describing additional remedies so that the franchisor can obtain injunctive relief in the event of default, prior to or without having to resort to termination. The franchisor typically drafts this section so that it preserves its right to alternative means for recourse in the event of default.[426] Some franchise agreements require the parties to mediate their dispute before either can proceed with any litigation proceeding, including arbitration.[427] These pre-dispute provisions typically mandate as a prerequisite before filing any lawsuit that the parties negotiate their dispute or submit it to nonbinding mediation.[428] A typical provision could provide:

> "Except as otherwise provided below, the parties must first meet to mediate their dispute with a National Franchise Mediation Program and in accordance with this body's then-current rules. Notwithstanding the above, this section shall not bar either party from obtaining injunctive relief against threatened conduct that will cause it loss or damages."

---

incurred in removing, transporting and disposing of the franchisee's inventory, supplies, equipment, and furnishings pursuant to this requirement, and may offset from such compensation any moneys due the franchisor.").

425. *See id.*; *see also* WASH. REV. CODE § 19.100.180(2)(i) ("Refuse to renew a franchise without fairly compensating the franchisee for the fair market value, at the time of expiration of the franchise, of the franchisee's inventory, supplies, equipment, and furnishings purchased from the franchisor, and good will, exclusive of personalized materials which have no value to the franchisor, and inventory, supplies, equipment, and furnishings not reasonably required in the conduct of the franchise business: PROVIDED, That compensation need not be made to a franchisee for good will if (i) the franchisee has been given one year's notice of nonrenewal and (ii) the franchisor agrees in writing not to enforce any covenant which restrains the franchisee from competing with the franchisor: PROVIDED FURTHER, That a franchisor may offset against amounts owed to a franchisee under this subsection any amounts owed by such franchisee to the franchisor.").

426. *See, e.g.*, Barbara A. Bagdon & Mary M. Kellerman, *When Will Courts Issue Preliminary Injunctions to Enforce Restrictive Covenants in Franchise Agreements?* 28 FRANCHISE L.J. 141 (Winter 2009); Deborah S. Coldwell & Kay Lynn Brumbaugh, *Proving Entitlement to Preliminary Injunctions Against Franchisees*, 18 FRANCHISE L.J. 87 (Winter 1999).

427. *See also* Elizabeth M. Weldon & Patrick W. Kelly, *Prelitigation Dispute Resolution Clauses: Getting the Benefit of Your Bargain*, 31 FRANCHISE L.J. 1 (Summer 2011); *see also* discussion in Chapter 9, Section XXVIII.A.

428. *Id.* The enforcement of these provisions depends on the jurisdiction. Courts will often allow a party to file suit even with a pre-dispute provision. *Id.* (discussing case law on this subject).

The carve-out is important in those situations where a party needs to seek immediate injunctive relief. Without this carve-out language, a party may not be able to seek this relief in court.

G. Survival of Covenants

> Notwithstanding the expiration or termination of this Agreement for any reason whatsoever, all covenants and agreements to be performed and/or observed by Franchisee and/or the Guarantor under this Agreement or which by their nature survive the expiration or termination of this Agreement hereof shall survive any such expiration or termination.

Discussion:
In almost every franchise agreement, the parties intend that at least some rights and obligations survive the termination or expiration of the agreement. It is crucial for the franchisor to address the survival of certain franchise agreement terms to avoid an argument that all rights and obligations end when the contract does. Drafters may include a general clause such as the preceding sample or, for the removal of doubt, a clause that specifically identifies, by contract section, which rights and obligations survive termination or expiration. Common examples include dispute resolution requirements, such as the obligation to arbitrate or litigate in a particular forum, confidentiality and indemnification obligations, obligations regarding intellectual property, and the requirement not to compete, when enforceable. As the U.S. Supreme Court has explained, under the common law,

> contractual obligations will cease, in the ordinary course, upon termination of the [contract]. Exceptions are determined by contract interpretation. . . . [S]tructural provisions relating to remedies and dispute resolution—for example, an arbitration provision—may in some cases survive in order to enforce duties arising under the contract.[429]

Because exceptions are determined by contract interpretation, the more clearly drafted the survival terms, the better.[430]

429. Litton Financial Printing Div., a Div. of Litton Business Systems, Inc. v. N.L.R.B., 501 U.S. 190, 207–08, 111 S. Ct. 2215 (1991). In *Litton*, the Court further explained that a post-expiration claim "arises under the contract" only if "it involves facts and occurrences that arose before expiration, where an action taken after expiration infringes a right that accrued or vested under the agreement, or where, under normal principles of contract interpretation, the disputed contractual right survives expiration of the remainder of the agreement." *Id.*

430. Notwithstanding the standard nature of survival clauses, disputes that concern them do still arise in the franchise context. For example, *see* Meineke Car Care Centers, Inc. v. RLB Holdings, LLC, No. 3:08cv240-RJC, 2009 WL 2461953 (W.D.N.C. Aug. 10, 2009) (holding, when deciding a summary judgment motion on franchisor's claim for prospective damages, that royalty and advertising fund fee contract provisions did not survive termination under the franchise agreement's terms and therefore any future obligation with respect to them ended upon termination); Doctor's Associates, Inc. v. Thomas, 898 So.2d 159 (Fla. Dist. Ct. App. 2005) (rejecting former franchisee's argument that arbitration requirement ceased upon termination of the franchise agreement; arbitration clause did not exclude its application to post-termination disputes and therefore survived); Johnson v. Polaris Sales, Inc., 257 F. Supp. 2d 300, 309–10 (D. Me. 2003) (considering survivability of arbitration clause by examination of survival clause in dealer agreement and common law); Carvel Corp. v. Eisenberg, 692 F. Supp. 182, 183–85 (S.D.N.Y. 1988)

From a drafting perspective, survival clauses also serve the purpose of alerting franchisees that they have obligations that survive termination or expiration of the franchise agreement, and franchisees should take surviving provisions into account in planning their future business activities. To lessen any ambiguity, franchise agreements will typically state which covenants and contractual provisions survive. These include the post-termination covenant against competition, which a franchise agreement will clearly specify that it survives for a certain number of months or years after the agreement's expiration or termination.

(contractual interpretation of survival clause to determine whether restrictive covenant survived contract expiration as well as termination).

9

Dispute Resolution

Marisa Faunce and Michael D. Joblove

XXVIII. Dispute Resolution and Litigation

A. Mediation

Before any party may bring an action in court or against the other, or commence an arbitration proceeding (except as noted below), the Parties must first meet to mediate the dispute. A complaining party must submit all claims to mediation within XX days after providing notice of the claim to the other party. The mediation shall take place in the city in which Franchisor's headquarters are located at the time of the commencement of the mediation. Each party shall identify an officer with decision-making authority who shall attend the mediation. Any such mediation will be non-binding and conducted by the American Arbitration Association in accordance with its then current rules for mediation of commercial disputes. The parties shall equally share the costs of the mediation.

Notwithstanding the foregoing, the Parties agree that the following claims will not be subject to mediation: (1) any action for declaratory or equitable relief, including, without limitation, actions seeking preliminary or permanent injunctive relief, specific performance, other relief in the nature of equity to enjoin any harm or threat of harm to such party's tangible or intangible property, brought at any time, including, without limitation, prior to or during the pendency of any mediation or arbitration proceedings initiated under this Agreement, and (2) any action in ejectment or for possession of any interest in real or personal property.

Franchisee acknowledges and agrees that Franchisor may, through the Manuals, or otherwise in writing, designate: (1) another administrative entity, in lieu of the American Arbitration Association, to administer any mediation required to be brought under this Section XX.X, and (2) different procedures or rules for any such mediation.

Discussion:

As the use of alternative dispute resolution techniques evolve, it is becoming increasingly important for drafters to consider including mediation or arbitration clauses in their franchise agreements.[431] Mediation is a dispute resolution method where a neutral trained mediator attempts to bring the parties to a settlement of their dispute, usually through a structured process. The franchisors and the franchisees alike may desire a mandatory mediation clause in the hope that it will help foster the resolution of disputes before those disputes result in arbitration demands or lawsuits. Further, a pre-suit settlement will avoid the franchisor's obligation to disclose the dispute in Item 3 of their franchise disclosure document (FDD), which may be required in the event of a lawsuit, and the concomitant ten-year disclosure requirement if a post-litigation lawsuit is settled with a payment or other material consideration provided by the franchisor.[432] Besides the primary purpose of avoiding litigation, the franchisors and the franchisees also may be interested in a mandatory mediation clause to the extent that it may provide them with advance notice that a claim is brewing. The franchisors also may benefit to the extent that the clause acts to slow or stop the franchisee claims by providing a pre-suit hurdle that must be cleared.[433] Courts have regularly stayed or dismissed suits filed prior to the parties complying with contractual pre-suit mediation requirements.[434] As a practical business matter, a mandatory pre-suit mediation clause may foster early resolution of a dispute. The party invoking mediation will be signaling its readiness to sue

431. Asbill, Barkoff, & Selden, *supra* note 4, at 4.

432. 16 C.F.R. § 436.5 (2007).

433. *See* Edward Wood Dunham, *Enforcing Contract Terms Designed to Manage Franchisor Risk*, 19 Franchise L.J. 91, 92 (Winter 2000) (discussing two federal dealership opinions in which the auto manufacturer won summary judgment "because the dealer had ignored mandatory mediation procedures and the contractual deadlines for mediation had passed").

434. Portland, LLC v. DeVito Builders, Inc., 317 F.3d 41 (1st Cir. 2003) (party could not invoke agreement's arbitration clause where party failed to comply with contract's pre-suit mediation requirement before attempting to enforce the arbitration provision); Tattoo Art, Inc. v. Tat Intern., LLC, 711 F. Supp. 2d 645, 651 (E.D. Va. 2010) ("the Court begins with the proposition that failure to mediate a dispute pursuant to a contract that makes mediation a condition precedent to filing a lawsuit warrants dismissal"); 3-J Hospitality v. Big Time Design, Inc., No. 09-61077, 2009 WL 3586830, at *2 (S.D. Fla. Oct. 27, 2009) (parties failure to proceed with requisite pre-suit mediation precluded enforcement of arbitration under the contract); USA Flea Mkt., LLC v. EVMC Real Estate Consultants, Inc., No. 06-0431, 2007 WL 470501, at *3 (M.D. Fla. Feb. 13, 2007) (granting summary judgment due to plaintiff's failure to satisfy pre-suit mediation requirement); Mortimer v. First Mount Vernon Indus. Loan Ass'n, No. 03-1051, 2003 WL 23305155, at *3 (D. Md. May 19, 2003) (dismissing complaint for plaintiff's failure to comply with pre-litigation mediation requirement).

and force the parties to seriously resolve the dispute or risk time, cost, and money battling out the dispute in court. The disadvantage to early mediation is in the lack of information available. Neither party will have had the benefit of discovery that would be available in a lawsuit. As a result, both parties will feel strongest in their positions. Outside counsel, in particular, will not be educated as to information in the possession of the opposing party which may undercut what his or her client is telling the attorney about the facts of the case. Due to the lack of information, the parties may feel less at risk, and less willing to compromise at an early mediation.

Franchise agreement mediation clauses typically include terms setting forth the circumstances in which mediation must or may be used and where the mediation will take place. Agreements also may include specific detail about pre-mediation steps, who is required to attend, who pays the costs, how the mediation should be documented, and over what period the mediation occurs.[435] In addition, mediation clauses often include requirements for the qualifications and selection of the mediator.[436] Some or all of these types of details can be important to sort out in the franchise agreement, particularly because once a dispute has arisen, the parties may not be able to agree on much of anything. It is worth noting that the preceding sample provision explicitly provides that the location of the mediation will be the "city in which Franchisor's headquarters are located at the time of the commencement of the mediation," rather than a specific city, to provide the franchisor with flexibility in case the franchisor relocates its headquarters.[437] Alternatively, the parties may negotiate a mutually convenient, neutral location or, depending on the jurisdiction, agree that mediation take place in the franchisee's home city or state, so as not to impose overly burdensome conditions on the franchisee. In negotiating the mediation clause, the franchisee may request that any pre-suit mediation occur in its jurisdiction. The franchisor will have the greater resources to incur such a cost, and its agreement to do so will evince a commitment to attempt a workout of any dispute without resorting to litigation. Additionally, the franchisee may want to attempt to narrow the franchisor's exceptions to any pre-suit mediation requirement to injunction claims to protect trademarks and enforce noncompetition provisions, to matters involving public health and safety, and to eviction actions.

---

435. Asbill, Barkoff, & Selden, *supra* note 4, at 64.

436. *Id.* at 63.

437. *Practice Pointer: Franchisor Considerations*, 27 FRANCHISE L.J. 120 (Fall 2007). Floating forum selection clauses that account for the possibility that a franchisor's headquarters may change over time are generally enforceable as long as they can be determined by immutable facts and do not leave the required forum to the whim of the franchisor. *Compare* Bovis Home, Inc. v. Chmielewski, 827 So. 2d 1038, 1039 (Fla. Dist. Ct. App. 2012) (clause calling for venue in the district where the party's principal place of business is located was unambiguous and enforceable), *and* Lyon Fin. Serv., Inc. v. Will H. Hall & Son Builders, Inc., 2005 WL 503371, at *4 (D. Minn. Mar. 4, 2005) (although state of forum may change, it does not give the lessor the freedom to choose its forum; it must sue in its home state), *with* Central Ohio Graphics v. Alco Capital Resource, Inc., 221 Ga. App. 434, 472 S.E.2d 2 (1996) (venue clause permitting suit at one party's choice in any district with jurisdiction unenforceable for failing to constitute a meeting of the minds as to what would constitute a proper forum), *and* Lopez v. United Capital Fund, LLC, 88 So.3d 421 (Fla. Dist. Ct. App. 2012) (clause permitting seller to sue in county of its choice unenforceable).

B. Arbitration

Except as qualified below, any dispute between Franchisee and Franchisor or any of their respective affiliates, officers, directors, employees, agents (including area representatives) or owners arising under, out of, in connection with or in relation to this Agreement, the Parties' relationship, or Franchisee's Franchised Business must be submitted to binding arbitration under the authority of the Federal Arbitration Act without reference to any state arbitration statutes and must be determined by arbitration administered by the American Arbitration Association pursuant to its then-current commercial arbitration rules and procedures. The arbitration shall take place in the city where Franchisor's headquarters are located at the time of the commencement of the arbitration action. The arbitration shall be heard by one (1) arbitrator who has at least XX years of experience in franchise law. The arbitrator must follow the law and not disregard the terms of this Agreement.

Any arbitration must be on an individual basis and the Parties and the arbitrator will have no authority or power to proceed with any claim as a class action or otherwise to join or consolidate any claim with any other claim or any other proceeding involving third parties. In the event a court determines that this limitation on joinder of or class action certification of claims is unenforceable, then this entire commitment to arbitrate will become null and void and the Parties must submit all claims to the jurisdiction of the courts.

A judgment may be entered upon the arbitration award by any state or federal court in the state where Franchisor maintains its headquarters or the state where Franchisee's Franchised Business is located. The decision of the arbitrator will be final and binding on all parties to the dispute; however, the arbitrator may not under any circumstances: (1) stay the effectiveness of any award pending termination of this Agreement; (2) assess punitive or exemplary damages; or (3) make any award which extends, modifies or suspends any lawful term of this Agreement or any reasonable standard of business performance set by Franchisor.

Notwithstanding the foregoing, the Parties agree that the following claims will not be subject to arbitration: (1) any action for declaratory or equitable relief, including, without limitation, seeking preliminary or permanent injunctive relief, specific performance, other relief in the nature of equity to enjoin any harm or threat of harm to such party's tangible or intangible property, brought at any time, including, without limitation, prior to or during the pendency of any arbitration proceedings initiated hereunder, and (2) any action in ejectment or for possession of any interest in real or personal property.

Discussion:

Arbitration clauses have become increasingly complex in recent years and are important for drafters to consider carefully.[438] In contemplating whether an arbitration clause is desired, the franchisor typically will balance, among other factors,

438. Asbill, Barkoff, & Selden, *supra* note 4, at 63.

whether the benefits of avoiding juries[439] and avoiding the precedential effect of rulings outweigh the cost of losing the right of appeal in all but the most limited circumstances.[440] Arbitrations typically do not provide a mechanism for a motion for summary judgment, an effective tool to enforcing integration clauses standard in most franchise contracts and in enforcing unambiguous contract language. Another disadvantage is the inability to conduct depositions of third parties. Arbitrators lack the authority to compel nonparty witnesses to appear at depositions,[441] and there is a split of authority regarding the arbitrators' power to compel nonparties to produce documents prior to a hearing.[442] And, because one of the very limited bases for challenging an arbitration award is the arbitrators' exclusion of evidence, most arbitrators err heavily on permitting the introduction of extensive evidence, including evidence a court would typically exclude.[443] As a practical matter, therefore, arbitration often is not a faster or more cost effective dispute resolution mechanism than a judicial forum, particularly given typical arbitration rules and standards (and arbitrator preferences) with respect to full, unfettered discovery and loose evidentiary standards.[444] For these and other reasons, some franchisors and their counsel have begun to disfavor arbitration clauses, although others continue to favor arbitration clauses and it is not uncommon for franchise agreements to include them.[445] One important remaining benefit is the general enforceability of class action and collective waivers in arbitration clauses.[446]

---

439. This benefit of arbitration is diminished by the enforceability of pre-suit jury trial waivers in most states. Pre-suit jury trial waivers are not enforceable in California and Georgia. *See, e.g.,* Rincon EV Realty v. CP III Rincon Towers, 8 Cal. App. 5th 1, 213 Cal. Rptr. 3d 410 (Ct. App. 2017) (choice of New York law in agreement unenforceable as to question of whether agreement's jury waiver provisions were enforceable; pre-dispute jury trial waiver unenforceable under California law); Bank South, N.A. v. Howard, 264 Ga. 339, 444 S.E.2d 799 (1994) (pre-litigation contractual waiver of right to jury trial not enforceable).

440. *See.* Carden & Klarfeld, *supra* note 110, at 5.

441. *See* COMSAT Corp. v. Nat'l Sci. Found., 190 F.3d 269, 275 (4th Cir. 1999) (Nowhere does the FAA grant an arbitrator the authority to order non-parties to appear at depositions.); *see also* Matria Healthcare, LLC v. Duthie, 584 F. Supp. 2d 1078, 1080 (N.D. Ill. 2008) (Congress did not empower arbitrators to subpoena nonparty witnesses to appear at deposition.).

442. *Compare* Sec. Life Ins. Co. of Am. v. Duncanson & Holt (*In re* Sec. Life Ins. Co. of Am.), 228 F.3d 865, 870–71 (8th Cir. 2000) (holding that implicit in the power "to subpoena relevant documents for production at a hearing is the power to order the production of relevant documents for review by a party prior to the [arbitration] hearing"); Am. Fed. of Television & Radio Artists, AFL-CIO v. WJBK-TV (New World Commc'ns of Detroit, Inc.), 164 F.3d 1004, 1007 (6th Cir. 1999) (authorizing subpoenas to a nonparty for pre-hearing arbitration documents), *with* Life Receivables Tr. v. Syndicate 102 at Lloyd's of London, 549 F.3d 210 (2d Cir. 2008) (no document subpoenas permitted), *and* Hay Grp., Inc. v. EBS Acquisition Corp., 360 F.3d 404, 413–14 (3d Cir. 2004) (holding that a pre-hearing subpoena for documents was unenforceable).

443. The very limited grounds listed by which a court can vacate an arbitration award under the Federal Arbitration Act are set out at 9 U.S.C. §§ 10 and 11. These include "refusing to hear evidence pertinent and material to the controversy." *Id.* at § 10(a)(3). A court must confirm an award under the Federal Arbitration Act unless it is vacated, modified, or corrected as prescribed by sections 10 and 11 of the act. Hall St. Assocs. L.L.C. v. Mattel, Inc., 552 U.S. 576, 582 (2008).

444. For a discussion of effective judicial forum selection clauses, see the discussion in this chapter at Section XXVIII.D.

445. *See* Julianne Lusthaus, Mary Leslie Smith, & Quentin R. Wittrock, *Is Franchising Abandoning Arbitration? Current Trends in Arbitrating Franchise Disputes*, ABA 32nd Annual Forum on Franchising 4–5 and 10–12 (2009).

446. American Exp. Co. v. Italian Colors Restaurant, 570 U.S. 228 (2013); AT&T Mobility LLC v. Concepcion, 563 U.S. 333 (2011).

The preceding clause is an example of a relatively detailed arbitration provision. Generally, arbitration clauses should state what types of disputes will be subject to arbitration; what arbitration service will administer the arbitration;[447] what rules (or deviations from the rules) will apply, including with respect to pre-hearing, evidentiary, and discovery issues; how many arbitrators will decide the dispute; where the arbitration hearing will be held; who bears the arbitration expenses; and the extent of the arbitrator's power. An important element in any such clause is a carve-out for obtaining interim injunctive relief. The carve-out will permit the parties to seek emergency injunctive relief from a court, without the delay that may be attendant to awaiting the appointment of arbitrators to hear the issues, and will allow for prompt relief in the event of trademark infringement or where food safety issues may be of concern.[448]

Other issues that may be covered in an arbitration clause include such things as minimum arbitrator qualifications, and pre-hearing and hearing procedures.[449] Because both the arbitrator's and arbitration administrator's authority flows from, and is bounded by, the parties' contractual agreement to arbitrate, sophisticated franchisors may wish to include a quite detailed arbitration provision to ensure that they know exactly what kind of arbitration proceeding will take place. In that regard, the clause may limit the amount of discovery based on the amount in controversy. For example, the agreement may provide that discovery in disputes under a specific amount in controversy shall be limited to document exchanges, or to a minimal number of depositions.[450] In the absence of contractual specifics, the arbitrators generally have broad discretion in determining the scope of discovery.[451] Of course, governing law—and courts' case-by-case analysis under that law—may override certain arbitration provisions, no matter what the contract provides.[452] However, the ability to override an arbitration clause is strictly limited to defenses

---

447. The provision provides that the American Arbitration Association will administer the arbitration. There are numerous other associations that administer arbitrations, and the authors do not recommend any association over any others.

448. *See* Am. Exp. Fin. Advisors, Inc. v. Makarewicz, 122 F.3d 936, 940 (11th Cir. 1997) (reversing lower court ruling that arbitrator should decide the question and upholding court's power to award interim relief pursuant to plain language of arbitration provision); Apartment Inv. & Mgmt. Co. v. Flamingo/South Beach 1 Condo. Ass'n, Inc., 84 So. 3d 1090 (Fla. Dist. Ct. App. 2012) (claim for equitable injunctive relief was properly brought in court where arbitration provision contained an exception for a party to seek injunctive relief in a court of competent jurisdiction).

449. Asbill, Barkoff, & Selden, *supra* note 4, at 64–66.

450. Courts will enforce any contractual stipulations regarding discovery, given the policy of enforcing arbitration agreements by their terms. *See* Volt Info. Sci. v. Bd. of Trustees of Leland Stanford Jr. Univ., 489 U.S. 468, 474 (1989) (explaining that the Federal Arbitration Act was "designed to overrule the judiciary's longstanding refusal to enforce agreements to arbitrate . . . and place such agreements upon the same footing as other contracts") (external citations omitted).

451. *See* American Arbitration Association, *Rules: Commercial Arbitration Rules and Mediation Procedures (including Procedures for Large, Complex Commercial Disputes)* R-21 (October 1, 2013), https://www.adr.org/sites/default/files/commercial_rules.pdf.

452. As just one example, an arbitration clause must be balanced enough, including with respect to the place of hearing, that it is not deemed unconscionable. *See, e.g.*, Nagrampa v. MailCoups, Inc., 469 F.3d 1257, 1289–90 (9th Cir. 2006) (*en banc*).

generally available to the enforcement of any contract clause such as fraud, duress, or unconscionability.[453]

Enforcement of an arbitration award depends upon a court's entry of a final judgment based upon the award. A motion to confirm the award and enter judgment may be made to a court designated by the parties in their contract or, if none is specified, to the U.S. district court in which the award was made.[454] A court must confirm the award absent very limited circumstances such as fraud or corruption by the arbitrators, the refusal to hear evidence material to the dispute, or where the arbitrators exceeded the powers provided to them under the parties' contract.[455]

C. Governing Law

> This Agreement, the Franchise, all rights and duties of the Parties arising from or relating to this Agreement and all claims arising from the relationship between the Parties will be governed by the laws of the state of XX, provided, however, that if the covenants in Section YY of this Agreement would not be enforceable under the laws of XX, and the Franchised Business is located outside the state of XX, then such covenants shall be interpreted and construed under the laws of the state in which the Franchised Business is located. In the event of any conflict of law question, XX law will prevail, without regard to the application of XX's conflict of law rules. This subparagraph is not intended to subject this Agreement to any statute or regulation (including those that regulate the offer or sale of franchises or the franchise relationship) that would not by its own terms apply to this Agreement.

Discussion:

When a franchisor or a franchisee decides to bring a lawsuit to address claims arising out of the franchise agreement or the franchise relationship, a chief consideration is the substantive law that will apply to the dispute and how that law will impact the claims at issue. State laws governing franchise disputes vary widely, with some laws affording great protection to the franchisees and others providing a benefit to the franchisors. Since the decision as to which state's law should apply in a franchise agreement can be the difference between victory and defeat in litigation, the laws of a chosen state should be carefully evaluated to determine whether the laws would be advantageous or detrimental to potential claims.

Franchise agreements typically include a contractual "choice of law" provision similar in substance to the example preceding. Franchisors most often draft their agreements with choice of law provisions tied to their principal place of business so that they have a familiarity with the applicable law for disputes with the franchisees who are located around the country. The choice of law provision also helps

---

453. 9 U.S.C. § 2 (1947).

454. *Id.* § 9.

455. *Id.* § 10. The Federal Arbitration Act provides the exclusive means for vacating or modifying an arbitration award conducted under the act. Hall St. Assocs., L.L.C. v. Mattel, Inc., 552 U.S. 576, 585, 128 S. Ct. 1396, 1404, 170 L. Ed. 2d 254 (2008).

franchisors avoid the application of laws of their franchisees' home states that may be more protective of the franchisees.

Most courts apply the Restatement (Second) of Conflict of Laws section 187(2) to analyze the enforceability of a choice of law clause. Section 187(2) states:

> (1) The law of the state chosen by the parties to govern their contractual rights and duties will be applied if the particular issue is one which the parties could have resolved by an explicit provision in their agreement directed to that issue.
> (2) The law of the state chosen by the parties to govern their contractual rights and duties will be applied, even if the particular issue is one which the parties could not have resolved by an explicit provision in their agreement directed to that issue, unless either
> (a) the chosen state has no substantial relationship to the parties or the transaction and there is no other reasonable basis for the parties' choice, or
> (b) application of the law of the chosen state would be contrary to a fundamental policy of a state which has a materially greater interest than the chosen state in the determination of the particular issue and which, under the rule of § 188, would be the state of the applicable law in the absence of an effective choice of law by the parties.
> (3) In the absence of a contrary indication of intention, the reference is to the local law of the state of the chosen law.[456]

Having a substantial relationship to a chosen state will typically qualify as a "reasonable basis" for the parties' choice of law. For example, courts have found a reasonable basis for choosing the law of the state where (1) a party resides or maintains its principal place of business in the state; (2) the state where a party signs the agreement; (3) the state where a party will perform its obligations under the contract; or (4) the state where a party is incorporated.[457] However, one court has held that designating the choice of law of the state where contract negotiations were held did not qualify as a substantial relationship to the state.[458]

456. Restatement (Second) of Conflicts § 187 (1988 Rev.); *see also* Wingate Inns Int'l v. Swindall, No. 12-248, 2012 WL 5252247, at *6–7 (D.N.J. Oct. 22, 2012) (dismissing counterclaim under Florida Franchise Act due to a New Jersey choice of law clause); U.S. v. Kashamu, 656 F.3d 679, 684–85 (7th Cir. 2011) (declining to enforce parties' choice of law because they select a foreign law too difficult to apply); Faulkenberg v. CB Tax Franchise Sys., LP, 637 F.3d 801, 809 (7th Cir. 2011) (applying Illinois law to dispute despite Texas choice of law provision in franchise agreement because the parties cited Illinois case law in their arguments and the results would not differ from Texas law); Barker v. Golf U.S.A., Inc., 154 F.3d 788, 793 (8th Cir. 1998) (enforcing parties' choice of Missouri law in franchise agreement).

457. *See* Restatement (Second) of Conflicts § 187 cmt. f; 1-800 Got Junk? LLC v. Superior Court, 189 Cal. App. 4th 500, 513–14 (2010); Broin & Assocs., Inc. v. Genencor Int'l, Inc. 232 F.R.D. 335, 339 (D.S.D. 2005); Corface Collections N. Am. Inc. v. Newton, 430 F. App. 162, 167 (3d Cir. 2011).

458. Davis v. Siemens Med. Solutions USA, Inc., 399 F. Supp. 2d 785, 791 (W.D. Ky. 2005) (holding that New Jersey did not have a substantial relationship to the parties or the transaction between them, when the only connection to New Jersey was that contract was negotiated in a New Jersey hotel and that the individual who sent employee the contract to sign worked in New Jersey).

The laws of states and territories with franchise statutes can impact and override the parties' agreement to apply the law of a chosen state to their disputes. When drafting choice of law clauses, franchisors should carefully consider whether the chosen state's laws will result in the application of a state franchise statute that otherwise would not apply to the dispute or whether the chosen state's laws would enable the franchisor to avoid the application of a state franchise statute that may otherwise apply. For example, there are 22 states and U.S. territories that regulate aspects of the franchise relationship, including issues relating to termination and nonrenewal.[459] Many state franchise statutes, however, include anti-waiver provisions that prohibit a contractual choice of law provision from acting to avoid application of the state statute, such that those statutory provisions "trump" conflicting franchise agreement terms or common law regardless of the parties' contractual choice of law.[460] Some franchise statutes further prohibit the parties from selecting any choice of law other than the law of the state in which the franchisee and/or the franchised business is located.[461] Even if a state statute does not include a specific provision relating to choice of law, the state franchise relationship statute may still (and very often does) represent a fundamental public policy of that state, leading to application of the statute even in the face of a contrary choice of law in the franchise agreement.[462] In certain states where the franchisors are required to register their franchise disclosure documents prior to selling franchises, the franchisors may be required to adopt state-specific addenda to their FDD or franchise agreement

459. *See, e.g.*, Alaska Distributorships Law, ALASKA STAT. § 45.45.700–.790 (2014); Arkansas Franchise Practices Act, ARK. CODE ANN. § 4-72-201 to -210 (2014); California Franchise Relations Act, CAL. BUS. & PROF. CODE §§ 20000–20043 (2016); Connecticut Franchise Law, CONN. GEN. STAT. § 42-133e to -133h (1995); Delaware Franchise Security Law, DEL. CODE ANN. tit. 6, §§ 2551–2557 (2013); Hawaii Franchise Rights and Prohibition Act, HAW. REV. STAT. § 482E-6 (1978); Illinois Franchise Disclosure Act of 1987, 815 ILL. COMP. STAT. 705/18–/20 (2014); Indiana Deceptive Franchise Practices Law, IND. CODE § 23-2-2.7-1 to -7 (1987); Iowa Franchise Law, IOWA CODE § 523H.1–.17. (2007); Michigan Franchise Investment Law, MICH. COMP. LAWS § 445.1527 (1984); Minnesota Franchise Law, Unfair Practices, MINN. STAT. § 80C.14 (2015); MISS. CODE ANN. § 75-24-51 to -63 (1997); MO. REV. STAT. § 407.400–.420 (2014); Nebraska Franchise Practices Act, NEB. REV. STAT. § 87-401 to -410 (2016); New Jersey Franchise Practices Act, N.J. STAT. ANN. § 56:10-1 to -15 (2015); Rhode Island Fair Dealership Act, R.I. GEN. LAWS § 6-50-1 to -9 (2008); Utah Consumer Sales Practices Act, UTAH CODE ANN. § 13-11-1 to -23 (2014); Virginia Retail Franchising Act, VA. CODE ANN. § 13.1-564 (2014); Washington Franchise Investment Protection Act, WASH. REV. CODE §§ 19.100.180, .190 (2015); Wisconsin Fair Dealership Law, WIS. STAT. § 135.01–.14 (1999); Puerto Rico Dealers' Contracts Act, P.R. LAWS ANN. tit. 10, § 278–278e (2010); Virgin Islands Franchised Businesses Act, V.I. CODE ANN. tit. 12A, §§ 130–139 (2013).

460. *See, e.g.*, Cottman Transmission Sys., LLC v. Kershner, 492 F. Supp. 2d 461, 467–69 (E.D. Pa. 2007).

461. IND. CODE § 23-2-2.7.1(10) (1988); IOWA CODE §§ 537(A).10(3) (2011); 815 ILL. COMP. STAT. 705/41; MINN. STAT. § 80C.21 (2015); R.I. GEN. LAWS ANN. § 19-28.1-14 (2012); WASH. REV. CODE ANN. § 19.100.220(2); *see also* Wright-Moore Corp. v. Ricoh Corp. 908 F.2d 128 (7th Cir. 1990) (enforcement of choice of law provision in distributorship agreement would be contrary to Indiana's express public policy in its franchise statute's anti-waiver provisions).

462. *See* Instructional Systems, Inc. v. Computer Curriculum Corp., 130 N.J. 324, 342 (N.J. 1994) (New Jersey court holding that New Jersey Franchise Practices Act applied to dispute because of state's overriding issue in protecting its citizens despite California choice of law clause); Hengel, Inc. v. Hot 'N Now, Inc., 825 F. Supp. 1311, 1316 (N.D. Ill. 1993) (Illinois court holding Illinois franchise statute's anti-waiver clause represented fundamental public policy invalidating Michigan choice of law clause).

to address each state's statutory and regulatory policy regarding anti-waiver provisions and choice of law clauses.[463]

In drafting a choice of law provision, the key considerations are which state's law to choose and how broadly the provision is intended to apply. With respect to which law to choose, the franchisors typically select the law of the state of their headquarters, either by naming that particular state or, sometimes by using the laws of the state where the franchisor's principal place of business is located when the lawsuit is filed in case the franchisor relocates during the term of the franchise agreement. Drafters, however, should be aware that in opting for flexibility through a more open-ended provision such as this, the franchisor may be more susceptible to disputes down the road over what constitutes its "principal place of business" and, if the business location does change over the contract term, what law governed during which relevant time periods.[464] There has been significant litigation over the meaning of the phrase "principal place of business" in the analogous context of jurisdiction, with different results depending on the court (e.g., some courts focused on the level of business in the state, requiring a burdensome factual inquiry, as opposed to focusing on the physical brick and mortar location). "Headquarters" appears to have less litigation associated with the term.[465]

With respect to the breadth of the provision, drafters must consider whether they intend the choice of state law to apply solely to contract construction and interpretation or more broadly to include all aspects of the parties' relationship (including, for example, tort claims)—or something in between. State case law provides specific guidance on what particular wording works best, in various jurisdictions, to encompass which types of claims.[466] For example, if the clause is narrowly drawn and does not apply to the parties' entire relationship, some courts have found that tort claims would not be subject to the following choice of law clauses:

> [T]his Agreement shall be construed, interpreted, and enforced in accordance with the laws of the State of Maryland.[467]

---

463. Cal. Bus. & Prof. Code § 310.114.1; 815 Ill. Comp. Stat. 705/41; Md. Code Regs. 02.02.08.16; Minn. Stat. § 80C.21; R.I. Gen. Laws Ann. § 19-28.1-14; Wash. Rev. Code Ann. § 19.100.220(2); N.Y. Gen. Bus. Code § 687; N.D. Cent. Code § 51-19-09.

464. *See* Hansen v. GAB Bus. Servs., Inc., 876 P.2d 112, 113 (Colo. Ct. App. 1994) ("Here, neither party is located in New York; however, defendant was previously headquartered there for many years and conducts business nationwide. Hence, we conclude that a reasonable basis exists for applying New York law.").

465. *See, e.g.*, Hertz Corp. v. Friend, 559 U.S. 77, 92–93 (2010) (settling a split in the federal circuits adopting the "nerve center" test holding that the principal place of business "is best read as referring to the place where a corporation's officers direct, control, and coordinate the corporation's activities. It is the place that Courts of Appeals have called the corporation's 'nerve center.' And in practice it should normally be the place where the corporation maintains its headquarters—provided that the headquarters is the actual center of direction, control, and coordination, i.e., the 'nerve center,' and not simply an office where the corporation holds its board meetings (for example, attended by directors and officers who have traveled there for the occasion.").

466. *See, e.g.*, Maurice's Jewelers II, Inc. v. Pandora Jewelry, LLC, No. 16-25079, 2017 WL 3822056, at *5 (S.D. Fla. Aug. 30, 2017) (dismissing claims arising under the Florida Franchise Act based on the parties' Maryland choice of law clause).

467. Jiffy Lube International, Inc. v. Jiffy Lube of Tennessee, Inc., 848 F. Supp. 569, 575 (E.D. Pa. 1994) (holding that choice of law clause was limited to the agreement and did not extend to tort claims, which would be subject to a separate choice of law analysis).

> [This] Agreement is to be construed in accordance with the law of the State of New York without recourse to New York choice of law or conflicts of law principles.[468]

In comparison, if the clause is drafted to apply the chosen law to the relationship of the parties, then contract, tort, and statutory claims will fall under the purview of the parties' choice of law clause. For example:

> [Indiana law shall apply to] the validity, performance, interpretation, enforcement and any other aspect of our agreement or relationship.[469]

Adapting to judicial decisions, the franchisors often expressly state that the parties' choice of law does not constitute an "opt in" to the franchise regulations of that particular state, to the extent that those regulations otherwise would not apply. To avoid having a court conduct a choice of law analysis under the law of the forum, contracting parties also should state that their choice of law applies without application of the state's conflict of law principles.[470]

D. Venue and Jurisdiction

> Any cause of action, claim, suit or demand allegedly arising from or related to the terms of this Agreement or the relationship of the Parties, must be brought only in the U.S. federal district court with jurisdiction located in the county or district encompassing Franchisor's headquarters. If that court lacks jurisdiction, then the claim must be brought only in the state court with jurisdiction located in the county or district encompassing Franchisor's headquarters. Both Parties hereto irrevocably submit themselves to, and consent to, the jurisdiction of said courts. The provisions of this subparagraph shall survive the expiration or termination of this Agreement. Franchisee is aware of the business purposes and needs underlying the language of this subparagraph, and with a complete understanding thereof, agrees to be bound in the manner set forth above.

Discussion:

Franchise agreements generally include a forum selection and jurisdiction clause, and franchisors typically draft the provision both to provide for a forum in its home state and to obtain the franchisees' consent to jurisdiction in that forum. Forum selection clauses are desirable even in agreements that call for the use of arbitration as a dispute resolution mechanism to cover any claims that are not subject to the arbitration clause and to designate the court that will rule on the enforcement of an

468. Maltz v. Union Carbide Chemicals & Plastics Co., Inc., 992 F. Supp. 286, 297 (S.D.N.Y. 1998) (citing Thompson and Wallace of Memphis, Inc. v. Falconwood Corp., 100 F.3d 429, 432–33 (5th Cir. 1996) (where choice of law provisions apply to "agreement . . . and enforcement" of contract, tort causes of action are not governed by provisions).

469. Biomet, Inc. v. Smith, 238 F. Supp. 2d 1036, 1043 (2002) (holding that tort claims including defamation and tortious interference with prospective business advantage would be governed by Indiana law since they "relate to an aspect of the relationship between Smith and Biomet").

470. Simmons Foods, Inc. v. Industrial Risk Insurers, 863 F.3d 792, 797 (8th Cir. 2017) (in deciding what law applies, a federal court exercising diversity jurisdiction will apply the forum state's choice of law principles).

arbitration award. The forum selection clause and consent to jurisdiction serve different purposes from the choice of law provision; they concern where proceedings will take place, separate from which law will apply. Like choice of law provisions, however, the forum of the dispute often determines the outcome,[471] with home court advantage being of primary importance to franchisors seeking to litigate the vast majority of their cases near their headquarters where their witnesses and records are located. This home court advantage is heightened with the franchisor's ability to become familiar with the local court customs and judges as well as reduced travel and time costs for its employees.

A franchisor's ability to maintain this home court advantage became much easier in federal court in 2013 with the U.S. Supreme Court decision in *Atlantic Marine Construction Company, Inc. v. United States District Court for the Western District of Texas, et al.*[472] where the court made it clear that "when the parties' contract contains a valid forum-selection clause, that clause 'represents [their] agreement as to the most proper forum,' and should be 'given controlling weight in all but the most exceptional cases.'"[473] Prior to *Atlantic Marine*, a valid and enforceable forum selection clause was a "significant factor that figures centrally in the district court's calculus" that would be afforded "substantial" weight.[474] In reviewing a motion to transfer after *Atlantic Marine*, a federal district court "must deem the private interest factors to weigh entirely in favor of the preselected forum" noting that the parties' agreement to the forum selection clause equates to a waiver of the right to raise private interest factors such as "the right to challenge the preselected forum as inconvenient or less convenient for themselves, or their witnesses, or for their pursuit of the litigation."[475] Accordingly, drafting a valid forum selection clause should eliminate the vast majority of motions to transfer cases to an alternate forum.[476]

Several state franchise statutes constrain contractual forum selection clauses by voiding clauses that call for a judicial forum outside the franchisee's home state. In these states, the franchisors must prepare state-required addenda to their franchise agreements to conform to local law.[477] Aside from that, forum selection clauses

471. *See generally* Kerry L. Bundy & Kevin M. Kennedy, *Procedural Considerations for Filing a Franchise Complaint: Jurisdiction, Venue and Choice of Law*, ABA 27th Annual Forum on Franchising LB-3 (2004).

472. 134 S. Ct. 568, 574.

473. *Id.* (citing Stewart Org., Inc. v. Ricoh, 487 U.S. 23, 33 (1988) (Kennedy, J., concurring)).

474. *Stewart Org., Inc.*, 487 U.S. at 29.

475. *Atl. Marine*, 134 S. Ct. at 582.

476. *See id.* at 583 ("In all but the most unusual cases . . . 'the interests of justice' is served by holding parties to their bargains."); Hyatt Franchising, L.L.C. v. Shen Zhen New World I, LLC, No. 16C 8306, 2017 WL 372313, at *6 (N.D. Ill. Jan. 26, 2017) (denying motion to transfer and upholding franchise agreement's forum selection clause); Port of Subs, Inc. v. Tahoe Invs., Inc., No. 3:16-CV-00411-LRH-VPC, 2016 WL 6561560, at *3 (D. Nev. Nov. 3, 2016) (upholding forum selection clause in franchise agreements).

477. The franchise relationship statutes of California, Connecticut, Illinois, Indiana, Iowa, Louisiana, Michigan, Minnesota, North Carolina, and Rhode Island provide an avenue for franchisees to attempt to invalidate choice of forum clauses that would draw the franchisee out of its home state. CAL. BUS. & PROF. CODE § 20040.5; CONN. GEN. STAT. § 42-133(F); 815 ILL. COMP. STAT. § 705/4; IND. CODE § 23-2-2.7-1(10); IOWA CODE § 523H.3(1); LA. REV. STAT. 12 § 1042; MICH. COMP. STAT. § 445.1527(F); MINN. REV. CODE § 2860.4400(J); N.C. GEN. STAT. § 22B-3; R.I. GEN. LAWS § 19-28.1-14; *see also* Frango Grille USA, Inc. v. Pepe's Franchising Ltd., No. CV 14-2086 DSF PLAX, 2014 WL 7892164, at *1 (C.D. Cal. July 21, 2014) (holding that California law invalidated

typically are valid and enforceable, as a matter of strong public policy in favor of freedom of contract, unless "unreasonable under the circumstances."[478]

Even with the protections of *Atlantic Marine*, drafters should use caution to make forum selection clauses mandatory and not permissive.[479] A mandatory forum selection clause contains a clear directive that jurisdiction is only appropriate in the designated forum, whereas a permissive clause will "authorize jurisdiction in a designated forum" but will not "prohibit litigation elsewhere."[480] For example, a mandatory clause will use terms such as "shall," "must," and "only," and a permissive clause will use terms such as "may" and "can."[481] If a court finds a forum selection clause permissive, it will apply the pre-*Atlantic Marine* balancing of private interest and public interest factors to determine if a venue is appropriate.[482]

Importantly, drafters should be aware that a franchisee's agreement to choice of law and forum does not constitute consent to jurisdiction in that forum; the franchise agreement should include a separate and specific consent to jurisdiction. A party can contractually consent to personal jurisdiction in a forum even if personal jurisdiction would not otherwise exist.[483] From there, the choice between state and federal court depends on whether subject matter jurisdiction for federal court exists, and then both on the drafters' and parties' general views on state versus federal forums and on specific information about the courts in particular jurisdictions (such as quality of judges and jury pools, rules and procedures, litigation pace, and local or other bias).[484] Because of strict subject matter jurisdiction requirements in federal court, franchise agreements typically include language that sets the permissible forum as any court "of or sitting in" a particular state, county, or district that has subject matter jurisdiction, to include both state and federal courts.

---

the parties' choice of London, England, as the forum for a franchise agreement dispute rendering *Atlantic Marine* inapplicable); Saladworks, LLC v. Sottosanto Salads, LLC, No. CIV.A.13-3764, 2014 WL 2862241, at *3 (E.D. Pa. June 23, 2014) (upholding parties' Pennsylvania choice of forum in a franchise agreement even though the franchisee was based in California because the parties could not show that enforcement of the clause would be unreasonable). An arbitral forum is different, however. *See* Earsa Jackson & Jim Meaney, *Forum Selection Clauses after Atlantic Marine,* ABA 37th Annual Forum on Franchising 16–17 (2014).

478. *Atlantic Marine*, 134 S. Ct. at 574.

479. Waste Mgmt. of Louisiana, L.L.C. v. Jefferson Par. ex. rel. Jefferson Par. Council, 594 F. App'x 820, 821–22 (5th Cir. 2014) ("the vast majority of district courts deciding this issue have rejected *Atlantic Marine's* application to permissive forum selection clauses.").

480. *See* Excell, Inc. v. Sterling Boiler & Mech., Inc., 106 F. 3d 318, 321 (10th Cir. 1997) (forum selection clause requiring venue in the County of El Paso, Colorado, was mandatory and required the action to be maintained in state court rather than federal district court since the contract referred to a "county" rather than a "district"); *see also* Carl's Jr. Rests. LLC v. 6 Points Food Servs. Ltd., No. CV 15-9827-GHK (ASX), 2016 WL 3671116, at *3–4 (C.D. Cal. July 7, 2016) (use of a permissive forum selection clause allowed court to conduct a forum non conveniens analysis and dismiss an action brought in California in favor of a Canadian forum).

481. *See* Regal Kitchens, Inc. v. O'Connor & Taylor Condominium Constr., Inc., 894 So. 2d 288, 290 (Fla. Dist. Ct. App. 2005) (finding the following clause permissive because it did not require litigation only be held in Palm Beach County: "Any litigation concerning this contract shall be governed by the law of the State of Florida, with proper venue in Palm Beach County.").

482. *Waste Mgmt.*, 594 F. App'x at 821–22 (holding that *Atlantic Marine* does not apply to permissive forum selection clauses).

483. Ireland v. Compagnie des Banxites, 456 U.S. 694, 704–05 (1982).

484. *See* Bundy & Kennedy, *supra* note 471, at 26.

10

Other Provisions

Amy Cheng and Ann MacDonald

XXIX. General Provisions

A. No Liability

> Franchisor shall not be responsible or otherwise liable for any injury, loss, or damage suffered by any person or property directly or indirectly arising out of Franchisee's operation of the Franchised Business. Franchisor will have no liability for Franchisee's obligations to pay third parties, including any landlords and product vendors.

Discussion:

The no liability clause, in some form, is a usual feature of most franchise agreements. The franchisor has little actual control over the daily actions or omissions of the franchisee. Yet, the franchisee often incurs liability in connection with the operation of the franchised business using the franchisor's brand name. Such liability may arise with or without fault on the part of the franchisee. Therefore, the franchisor must safeguard itself from being found vicariously liable for the actions or omissions of its franchisees and for any third party claim arising out of the franchisee's operation of the franchised business. This no liability clause may also serve to protect the franchisor in the event a third party vendor seeks to make the franchisor liable for the franchisee's obligations. These theories are discussed further in the following sections.

B. Indemnification of the Franchisor

Franchisee hereby agrees, during and after the term of this Agreement, to indemnify and hold harmless Franchisor and its affiliates, and their respective owners, directors, officers, employees, agents, successors and assigns (the "Indemnified Parties") against, and to reimburse any one or more of the Indemnified Parties for, any and all liabilities, losses, suits, claims, demands, costs, fines and actions (the "Claims") of any kind or nature whatsoever directly or indirectly arising out of Franchisee's breach of this Agreement or the operation of the Franchised Business, unless (and then only to the extent that) the Claims are determined to be caused solely by Franchisor's intentional misconduct in a final, unappealable ruling issued by a court with competent jurisdiction. For the purposes of this indemnification, "claims" includes all obligations, damages (actual, consequential, or otherwise), and the cost that any Indemnified Party reasonably incurs in defending any claim against it, including, without limitation, reasonable accountants', arbitrators', attorneys' and expert witness' fees, costs of investigation and proof of facts, court costs, travel and living expenses, and other expenses of litigation, arbitration or alternative dispute resolution, regardless of whether litigation, arbitration, or alternative dispute resolution is commenced. Each Indemnified Party may defend any claim against it at Franchisee's expense and agree to settlements or take other remedial, corrective or other actions. This indemnity will continue in full force and effect subsequent to and notwithstanding the expiration or termination of this Agreement. Any Indemnified Party need not seek recovery from any insurer or other third party, or otherwise mitigate its losses and expenses, in order to maintain and recover fully a claim against Franchisee under this section. Franchisee agrees that a failure to pursue a recovery or mitigate a loss will not reduce or alter the amounts that an Indemnified Party may recover from Franchisee under this Section.

Discussion:

Indemnification clauses protect the franchisor from liability and risk related to the franchisee's operation of the franchised business or breaches of the franchise agreement. This includes protection against third party claims against the franchisor based on the franchisee's actions or omissions. Without the indemnification provisions, the franchisor could still bring a common law claim for indemnification or contribution against the franchisee in the event the franchisee breaches the franchise agreement. However, without an indemnification provision, a franchisor may not have protection from all risks associated with vicarious liability claims. From the franchisor's perspective, it is best to be as detailed as possible to make sure the franchisee bears the risk related to third party claims. Courts are more likely to enforce indemnification provisions where there is an express intent to indemnify against the indemnitee's own wrongful acts in "clear and unequivocal terms."[485] Further, courts generally take a narrow interpretation of indemnification commitments,[486] so it is important to include a detailed definition of the scope of damages to which the franchisor is entitled. The franchisor may want to also reserve the right to settle third party claims and disclaim any obligation to mitigate damages.

In a vicarious liability case, a plaintiff may claim that the liability arose from the franchisee's compliance with the franchisor's system standards.[487] Therefore, a franchisor should consider whether to require its franchisees to indemnify it for its own negligence. Some states require the word "negligence" in the indemnification clause[488] while others do not.[489] However, a franchisor should not include indemnity for the franchisor's intentional torts because courts are likely to find that

---

485. This includes indemnification provisions that expressly state the indemnification is "regardless of cause or fault or negligence." *See, e.g.*, Marquette Transp. Co. v. La. Mach. Co., 367 F.3d 398, 408 (5th Cir. 2004) ("regardless of cause" in indemnification provision was not an unenforceable exculpatory clause); *In re* Boskalis Westminster Int'l B.V., 975 F. Supp. 2d 1238, 1243–45 (S.D. Fla. 2012) ("the contract is clear under the plain language of the contract that the indemnification provisions apply regardless of cause [and] . . . [t]hough 'crude,' the [a]greement's provisions are a 'workable allocation of risk and responsibility.'") (citing cases); Banner Sign & Barricade, Inc. v. Price Constr., Inc., 94 S.W.3d 692, 697 (Tex. App. 2002) ("the express negligence doctrine is satisfied in this case by the inclusion of the following phrase in the contract's indemnification provision, 'regardless of cause or of the sole, joint, comparative or concurrent negligence or gross negligence of [defendant], its officers, agents or employees'"); Etiole Int'l, N.V. v. Miami Elevator Co., 573 So. 2d 921, 922 (Fla. Dist. Ct. App. 1990) ("In drafting the contract to say that it would be held harmless 'regardless of the cause . . . and regardless of any negligence' on its own part, [defendant] clearly expressed its intent.") (citing cases); B-F-W Constr. Co. v. Garza, 748 S.W.2d 611, 613–14 (Tex. App. 1988) ("We hold that the language 'and regardless of any cause or of any fault or negligence of contractor' meets the express negligence test because it expressly states the intent of the parties that the subcontractor would indemnify the contractor for the contractor's own negligence.").

486. Heather Carson Perkins, Sarah J. Yatchak, & Gordon M. Hadfield, *Franchisor Liability for Acts of the Franchisee*, 29 Franchise L.J. 174, 180 (Winter 2010).

487. *See, e.g.*, Hunter v. Ramada Worldwide, Inc., No. 1:04CV00062ERW, 2005 WL 1490053, at *7–8 (E.D. Mo. June 23, 2005) (plaintiff argued that the franchisor was vicariously liable for the actions of its franchisee because the franchisor had the right to control the conditions of the premises pursuant to the system standards manual); Corrales v. Days Inn Worldwide, Inc., No. 04-CV-149, 2005 WL 4655135, at *1–2 (Colo. Dist. Ct. Dec. 5, 2005) (plaintiff argued franchisor was vicariously liable because it had the right to control the operation of the franchised facility through its system standards); Bruntjen v. Bethalto Pizza, LLC, 18 N.E.3d 215, 224, 241 (Ill. App. Ct. 2014) (plaintiff sued franchisor alleging it was vicariously liable for the misconduct of an employee of its franchisee and relying on the franchisor's operational standards).

488. Perkins, Yatchak, & Hadfield, *supra* note 486, at 180 & n.104 (citing cases); *see also* Hamblin v. Lamont, 433 S.W.3d 51, 56 (Tex. App. 2013) ("Under the express negligence doctrine, 'parties seeking to indemnify the indemnitee from the consequences of its own negligence must express that intent in specific terms. Under the doctrine of express negligence, the intent of the parties must be specifically stated within the four corners of the contract.'").

489. *Id.* at 180 & n.105 (citing cases).

provision unenforceable.[490] For example, courts in the First,[491] Second,[492] Third,[493] Fourth,[494] Sixth,[495] and Seventh[496] Circuits have found that agreements to indemnify against intentional misconduct generally are void as against public policy and unenforceable.[497] Therefore, adding language that specifically carves out a franchisor's intentional misconduct may reduce the likelihood of a court concluding that the indemnification provision is void as against public policy.

Even with a robust indemnification provision, the indemnification is not valuable unless the franchisee has the wherewithal to pay its obligations. Therefore, in addition to including an indemnification clause, a franchisor should consider the financial strength of the franchisee and whether personal guarantees are necessary to protect its interest. And in connection with a personal guarantee, a franchisor may want to review financials of the individuals periodically in connection with

490. *Id.* at 180 & n.106 (citing Montgomery v. JYD Int'l, Inc., 534 So. 2d 592, 594 (Ala. 1988)).

491. *See, e.g.*, Starbrands Capital LLC v. Original MW Inc., No. 14-CV-12270-ADB, 2015 WL 5305215, at *3 (D. Mass. Sept. 11, 2015) ("Courts within this judicial district have consistently held that under Massachusetts law, a party may not indemnify or wholly exempt itself from liability for its grossly negligent or intentional conduct."); *see also* Long v. Fairbank Farms Reconstruction Corp., 824 F. Supp. 2d 197, 203 n.3 (D. Me. 2011) (applying New York law) ("'[C]ontracts intended to exculpate a party from the consequences of his own negligence,' though frowned upon and subject to close judicial scrutiny, 'are enforceable' provided that the contracts do not indemnify for intentional misconduct or gross negligence.").

492. *See, e.g.*, *In re* Residential Capital, LLC, 524 B.R. 563, 596 (Bankr. S.D.N.Y. 2015) ('"New York law does not permit a party to indemnify itself against its own intentional torts."'); *see also* Herrera v. Adams, No. CV106004615, 2011 WL 6756914, at *4 (Conn. Super. Ct. Nov. 30, 2011) ("Trial courts have not extended common-law indemnification to intentional tortious conduct[.]"); Martel v. Burkamp, No. CVH 7684, 2009 WL 2243768, at *2 (Conn. Super. Ct. July 23, 2009) ("[T]his court agrees with the majority view that there is no common law action for indemnification for intentional tortious conduct.").

493. *See, e.g.*, Spear v. Fenkell, No. CV 13-02391, 2015 WL 5582761, at *3 (E.D. Pa. Sept. 21, 2015) ("indemnification for intentional acts is against public policy, and a contract between private parties cannot change or disregard that policy").

494. *See, e.g.*, Kruis v. Allmine Paving, LLC, No. 3:13-CV-25, 2013 WL 5557484, at *5 (N.D. W. Va. Oct. 8, 2013) (holding the indemnity provision enforceable "because it does not require [defendant] to indemnify, defend, and hold harmless [plaintiff] for [plaintiff]'s . . . intentional acts").

495. *See, e.g.*, Gomba Music Inc. v. Avant, No. 14-11767, 2016 WL 1529782, at *3 (E.D. Mich. Apr. 15, 2016) ("as for indemnification under Michigan law, 'an action for indemnity can only be maintained on the basis of express contract or by a person free of negligence or fault'").

496. *See, e.g.*, Brennan v. Connors, 644 F.3d 559, 562 (7th Cir. 2011) ("[I]n Illinois, agreements to indemnify against intentional misconduct generally are void as against public policy and unenforceable."); Ruiz v. Carmeuse Lime, Inc., No. 2:10-CV-21-PRC, 2011 WL 3439221, at *3 (N.D. Ind. Aug. 4, 2011) (reasoning indemnity provisions are enforceable where they do not require the indemnification of intentional acts).

497. *But see Hamblin*, 433 S.W.3d at 57–59 (the court noted that "an indemnity provision specifically stating an intent to indemnify the indemnitee for the indemnitee's intentional torts [can] be enforceable against the indemnitor for the indemnitee's intentional acts"; however, the dissent found that "public policy should disfavor indemnity for intentional torts only in those situations where there is an intent to cause the resulting injury" and therefore "public policy does not prohibit sophisticated parties from contractually agreeing to indemnify one another for actions that may include tortious conduct, even though the contract does not so specify."); *Brennan*, 644 F.3d at 562 (noting that "Illinois law permits agreements to be construed as indemnifying a person against his own negligence (and perhaps intentional misconduct) when supported by clear and explicit language.").

the guarantee. Further, a franchisor should ensure that it is an additional insured on its franchisees' insurance policies so that insurance can provide an additional layer of protection for the franchisor. While an indemnification provision is important, without these additional considerations, an indemnification provision may not actually offer much protection.

While it is unlikely that a franchisor's form of franchise agreement will offer mutual indemnification, a sophisticated franchisee may ask for such provision. A mutual indemnification clause that mirrors the franchisee's indemnification obligations would not make sense because a franchisor would never indemnify the franchisee for liability arising out of the franchisee's operation of the business. Such a clause would cancel out the franchisee's indemnification obligations. However, some franchisors may consider indemnifying the franchisee for any liability arising out of a franchisee's use of the franchisor's trademarks, proprietary system, willful misconduct or gross negligence.

C. Independent Contractor

> The Parties hereto hereby acknowledge and agree that, except as expressly provided in this Agreement, each is an independent contractor, that no party shall be considered to be the agent, representative, master or servant of any other party hereto for any purpose whatsoever, and that no party has any authority to enter into any contract, assume any obligations or to give any warranties or representations on behalf of any other party hereto. Nothing in this Agreement shall be construed to create a relationship of employment, agency, partners, joint venturers, fiduciaries, or any other similar relationship among the Parties. Franchisee agrees to identify itself conspicuously in all dealings with customers, suppliers, public officials, personnel and others as the owner of the Franchised Business under a franchise granted by Franchisor and to place notices of independent ownership on the forms, business cards, stationery, advertising, emails, and other materials Franchisor requires from time to time. Franchisor shall have no right to hire or fire any of Franchisee's employees or independent contractors or to exercise any control over those employees or independent contractors, all of whom will be entirely under Franchisee's control and direction, and Franchisee will be responsible for their acts and omissions.

Discussion:

It is common for franchise agreements to provide that the franchisee and the franchisor are independent contractors and to disclaim the existence of any employment, agency, partnership, joint venture, or fiduciary relationship between them. The independent contractor relationship is one of the fundamental features of franchising, but this fundamental principle nevertheless has often come under scrutiny by the courts in various scenarios.

(i) Independent Contractor Issues in Claims by Third Parties

Individuals injured at franchised businesses often seek to recover damages directly from franchisors.[498] Almost invariably, these plaintiffs sue franchisors for negligence, often without regard for or knowledge of the existence of the franchise relationship. Some plaintiffs may also sue the franchisor because they believe that the franchisor is the defendant with "deep pockets." A franchise relationship alone is insufficient grounds for franchisor liability for the negligence of its franchisee, however.[499] In fact, one reason to franchise is to allocate the risk of third party liability to franchisees. Plaintiffs nevertheless claim that franchisees are the actual or apparent agents of their franchisor and that the franchisor should therefore be held vicariously liable for the franchisee's negligence,[500] and/or that the franchisor was negligent in the performance of a duty that it voluntarily assumed.[501]

Oftentimes, neither the plaintiff nor the court clearly differentiates between these different theories of liability. This has resulted in a blurring of the lines between direct and vicarious liability, and occasionally confusion about the

498. *See, e.g.*, *Hunter*, 2005 WL 1490053, at *7–8 (plaintiff argued that the franchisor was vicariously liable for the actions of its franchisee because the franchisor had the right to control the conditions of the premises pursuant to the system standards manual); *Corrales*, 2005 WL 4655135, at *1–2 (plaintiff argued franchisor was vicariously liable because it had the right to control the operation of the franchised facility through its system standards); *Bruntjen*, 18 N.E.3d at, 241 (Ill. App. Ct. 2014) (plaintiff sued franchisor alleging it was vicariously liable for the misconduct of an employee of its franchisee and relying on the franchisor's operational standards).

499. *See, e.g.*, *Hunter*, 2005 WL 1490053, at *6–8 & n.5 (franchise relationship alone was not enough to create a duty of care owed to the plaintiff); *Corrales*, 2005 WL 4655135, at *1–2 ("this license agreement, and the actions of the parties in furtherance of that agreement, establish no more than standards to safeguard the uniformity, value and integrity of the franchise system—the license agreement does not in this case amount to [the franchisor] having had a role in managing day-to-day operations of the facility that would subject [the franchisor] to liability for this plaintiff's injuries").

500. "The principal-agent relationship is an exception to the general rule that a person injured by the negligence of another must seek his remedy from the one who caused the injury. . . . [A] principal can be found vicariously liable for the torts of his agent committed within the scope of the agency or employment." *Bruntjen*, 18 N.E.3d at 239–42 (citations omitted) (affirming the ruling of the district court and holding that the franchisee was the franchisor's agent based on the franchisor's right to control many of the franchisee's daily operations); *accord* Plunkett v. Crossroads of Lynchburg, Inc., No. 6:14-CV-28, 2015 WL 82935, at *2 (W.D. Va. Jan. 7, 2015) ("courts recognize that a franchisor may be vicariously liable to a third party for personal injury upon proof that an agency relationship exists between the franchisor and franchisee"); *see, e.g.*, ZHN, LLC v. Randy Miller, LLC, No. CIV-12-1289-M, 2015 WL 1143249, at *3–4 (W.D. Okla. Mar. 13, 2015) (declining to grant summary judgment in favor of the franchisor on the issue of whether an apparent agency relationship existed between the franchisor and its franchisee).

501. In order to prove direct liability, "[courts] ask how much control [the franchisor] exercised over [the franchisee]'s daily operations to determine whether [the franchisor] assumed a duty to protect [the third party] from this practice." Lind v. Domino's Pizza LLC, 37 N.E.3d 1, 11 (Mass. App. Ct. 2015); *Plunkett*, 2015 WL 82935, at *3–4 ("cases recognize that an invitee may assert a direct claim of negligence against a franchisor, regardless of an agency relationship, where the franchisor retained control over or voluntarily undertook to recommend, inspect, etc., an instrumentality or design for the franchisee that caused the invitee's injury"); Hamrick v. Rest. Mgmt. Grp., LLC, No. 2:14-CV-02762, 2014 WL 4698489, at *5 (S.D.W. Va. Sept. 19, 2014) (denying in part franchisor defendants' motion to dismiss plaintiff's negligence claim where the plaintiff alleged that the franchisor "had control over the equipment and procedures which contributed to [plaintiff]'s injury[;] [the franchisor's] conduct created a risk of physical harm to [plaintiff]"; and "[the franchisor] owed [plaintiff] a common-law duty to exercise reasonable care").

theories. However, the key issue under direct and vicarious (actual agency) liability theories is the control exercised by a franchisor over its franchisee's operations.[502]

In analyzing such claims, courts typically examine whether a franchisor controls, or has the right to control, the day-to-day operations of its franchisee. Drafters therefore should be careful that no agency relationship can be implied from the franchise agreement. Although not dispositive of the issue,[503] franchise agreements should include provisions designating the franchisees as independent contractors, specifying that neither party is an agent, employee, servant, joint venturer, or other legal representative of the other, and that the franchisee has no power to obligate the franchisor for any purpose whatsoever.[504] In the typical franchise relationship, the franchisee remains solely responsible for hiring, firing, and training employees and for making all day-to-day decisions necessary to run the business, including safety and security measures at the franchised location.

---

502. *See* Patterson v. Domino's Pizza, LLC, 333 P.3d 723, 742–43 (Cal. 2014) ("A franchisor will be liable if it has retained or assumed the right of general control over the relevant day-to-day operations at its franchised locations"); *see also* Barrett-O'Neill v. Lalo, LLC, No. 2:14-CV-194, 2014 WL 3895679, at *3–4 (S.D. Ohio Aug. 8, 2014) ("'[t]he determinative factor in deciding whether an agency relationship exists between a franchisor and a franchisee is the degree of control the franchisor has over the operations of the franchisee's business'"); Khanimov v. McDonald's Corp., 995 N.Y.S.2d 202, 204 (N.Y. App. Div. 2014) ("In determining whether a defendant, as a franchisor, may be held vicariously liable for the acts of its franchisee, the most significant factor is the degree of control that the franchisor maintains over the daily operations of the franchisee or, more specifically, the manner of performing the very work in the course of which the accident occurred[.]"); *ZHN, LLC*, 2015 WL 1143249, at *2 ("in the context of a franchisor-franchisee relationship, when determining whether the franchisor owed a duty to the plaintiff, the Court must first look to the degree of control the franchisor maintained over the franchisee"); *Plunkett*, 2015 WL 82935, at *3 (direct liability cases "require proof that the franchisor controlled the selection of the product which caused the injury or mandated a means or method which caused the injury"); *accord* Allen v. Choice Hotels Int'l, Inc., 276 F. App'x 339, 343 n.4 (4th Cir. 2008) ("Like the vicarious liability analysis, the '[d]irect liability cases [also] look to the franchisor's actual control or retained right of control to determine the presence of a duty for purposes of evaluating whether the franchisor was itself negligent.'"); *see also* RESTATEMENT (SECOND) OF AGENCY § 220(2)(a) (1958) (a finding of vicarious liability turns on "the extent of control which, by the agreement, the master may exercise over the details of the work"); Funderburk v. Choice Hotels Int'l, Inc., No. RWT 13-CV-1078, 2014 WL 5781831, at *2 (D. Md. Nov. 5, 2014) (without evidence of defendant franchisor's control, the court granted defendant's request for dismissal).

503. *But see* Domino's Pizza, L.L.C. v. Reddy, No. 09-14-00058-CV, 2015 WL 1247349, at *2 (Tex. App. Mar. 19, 2015) ("[a] contract expressly providing that a person is an independent contractor is determinative of the relationship").

504. *Compare* Bartholomew v. Burger King Corp., 15 F. Supp. 3d 1043, 1049 (D. Haw. 2014) (even though the franchise agreement stated that "the franchisee is responsible for the day-to-day operation of his/her business," the court found that "a disclaimer of agency in a franchise agreement will not, by itself, defeat liability where the circumstances indicate that the requisite control exists"), *with* Ketterling v. Burger King Corp., 272 P.3d 527, 533 (Idaho 2012) (because "the manual indicates that the franchisee is an independent owner and operator of the restaurant who is responsible for day-to-day operation of his/her business" the court found that the franchisor could not be vicariously liable); *see also Patterson*, 333 P.3d at 725–26 (where "[n]othing contractually required or allowed the franchisor to intrude" on the franchisee's day-to-day operations, the court found the franchisor was not liable under an agency theory); Kids R Kids Int'l, Inc. v. Cope, 769 S.E.2d 616, 618 (Ga. Ct. App. 2015) (rejecting an actual agency theory of vicarious liability where the franchise agreement provided that the franchisee "will assume responsibility for the day-to-day management and operation of the [franchised] [c]enter and supervision of personnel.").

Courts look closely at franchise agreements (and associated operations manuals), because they typically impose detailed quality and operational requirements on the franchisee's operation necessary to ensure uniform customer experiences within the system.[505] Although the franchisors retain the right to conduct regular inspections to ensure compliance with system standards, where the remedy for noncompliance typically is limited to a right to terminate the franchisees from the system and collect damages for noncompliance, no agency relationship exists.[506] The "control" exercised by a franchisor to preserve system standards generally does not consist (and should not consist) of routine, daily supervision and management of the franchisee's business.[507]

Under the majority approach in the courts,

> [t]he standardized provisions commonly included in franchise agreements specifying uniform quality, marketing, and operational requirements and a right of inspection do not establish a franchisor's control or right to control the daily operations of the franchisee sufficient to give rise to vicarious liability for all purposes or as a general matter.[508]

The majority approach further holds that

> [a] franchisor may be held vicariously liable for the tortious conduct of its franchisee only if the franchisor has control or a right of control over the

505. *See generally Reddy*, 2015 WL 1247349, at *2–5.

506. *See, e.g.*, Miles v. Century 21 Real Estate LLC, No. 4:05-CV-1088 GTE, 2007 WL 92795, at *8 (E.D. Ark. Jan. 11, 2007) (holding that no actual agency relationship existed where the franchisor only retained "its right to inspect, to receive reports regarding the performance of [the franchise] and possible legal issues faced by the franchisee, and to enforce its standards through probation and termination"); Courtland v. GCEP-Surprise, LLC, No. CV-12-00349-PHX-GMS, 2013 WL 3894981, at *6 (D. Ariz. July 29, 2013) ("The fact that [the franchisor] maintained strict guidelines as to the presentation and operation of the [r]estaurant does not establish, without more, that [the franchisor] had control over the [franchised] [r]estaurant's managerial staff."); Allen v. Greenville Hotel Partners, Inc., 409 F. Supp. 2d 672, 679 (D.S.C. 2006) (where franchisor "merely maintained 'uniform service within, and public good will toward, the [franchise] system,'" the court found the franchisee was not an actual agent of the franchisor).

507. *See, e.g.*, *Patterson*, 333 P.3d at 742–43 (because the franchisor did not retain or assume control over the franchisee's day-to-day operations, the court found that no employment or agency relationship existed to support the plaintiff's claims against the franchisor for vicarious liability); *see also* Hahn v. Massage Envy Franchising, LLC, No. 12CV153 DMS BGS, 2014 WL 5100220, at *13–14 (S.D. Cal. Sept. 25, 2014) (granting in part summary judgment in favor of customers' vicarious liability theory where "[franchisor] exercised wide-reaching control over its franchisees' day-to-day operations beyond what was necessary to protect [the franchisor]'s brand and goodwill"); *Greenville Hotel Partners, Inc.*, 409 F. Supp. 2d at 679–80 (granting summary judgment in favor of franchisor, because the franchisor "did not control the [franchisee]'s daily operations").

508. *Courtland*, 2013 WL 3894981, at *6; *accord Miles*, 2007 WL 92795, at *4 ("'Retaining certain rights such as the right to enforce standards, the right to terminate the agreement for failure to meet standards, the right to inspect the premises, the right to require that franchisees undergo certain training, or the mere making of suggestions and recommendations does not amount to sufficient control.'"); *see also Plunkett*, 2015 WL 82935, at *2 ("To establish [ ] vicarious liability a plaintiff must show that the franchisor exercised control over the franchisee's operations beyond the standardization of the business identity and uniformity of the commercial service.").

daily operation of the specific aspect of the franchisee's business that is alleged to have caused the harm.[509]

In addition to vicarious liability claims, injured parties may include a claim that the franchisor is directly liable for negligence. To recover under a theory of negligence, a plaintiff must show that the franchisor owed him/her a duty, that the franchisor breached that duty, that the plaintiff suffered injury as a result of that breach, and that the franchisor's breach of that duty or negligence was the proximate cause of the injuries.[510] A duty will arise when there is a special relationship or a voluntary undertaking.[511] Because no special relationship exists between a franchisor and the customers of its franchisee, a plaintiff typically argues instead that a franchisor breached a voluntarily assumed duty.[512] A franchisor may be deemed to have voluntarily assumed a duty if it has sufficient actual control or a retained right of control over the daily operations of its franchisee.[513] The scope of liability under the voluntary assumption of duty doctrine is limited to the extent of the undertaking.[514]

509. *Ketterling*, 272 P.3d at 533; *accord Bartholomew*, 15 F. Supp. 3d at 1048 ("[F]ranchisors may be liable where they control or have the right to control day-to-day operations of the franchisee sufficient to establish an agency relationship."); *see also Plunkett*, 2015 WL 82935, at *2 ("To establish [ ] vicarious liability . . . a plaintiff must show that the franchisor exercised some control over the daily operations of the franchisee's business.").

510. *See Plunkett*, 2015 WL 82935, at *2 ("To state a cause of action for negligence . . . a plaintiff must prove the existence of a legal duty of care, a breach of that duty, and that such breach was the cause of the injury suffered."); *see also Hamrick*, 2014 WL 4698489, at *5 ("the basic elements of a negligence claim are duty, breach of that duty, causation, and damages"); *Lind*, 37 N.E.3d at 10 ("In order to succeed on a claim of negligence, a plaintiff must establish that the defendants owed him a legal duty of care.").

511. *But see Bruntjen*, 18 N.E.3d at 235 (a franchisor's "duty does not necessarily hinge on a special relationship or a voluntary undertaking, even though such relationships may help establish the foreseeability of the injury").

512. Under the voluntary undertaking theory of liability, "[o]ne who undertakes . . . to render services to another which he should recognize as necessary for the protection of a third person or his things, is subject to liability to the third person for physical harm resulting from his failure to exercise reasonable care to protect his undertaking, if (a) his failure to exercise reasonable care increases the risk of such harm, or (b) he has undertaken to perform a duty owed by the other to the third person, or (c) the harm is suffered because of reliance of the other or the third person upon the undertaking." Restatement (Second) of Torts § 324A (1965); *see also id.* § 414 ("One who entrusts work to an independent contractor, but who retains the control of any part of the work, is subject to liability for physical harm to others for whose safety the employer owes a duty to exercise reasonable care, which is caused by his failure to exercise his control with reasonable care.").

513. *See, e.g.*, *Hamrick*, 2014 WL 4698489, at *5 (where the plaintiff alleged that the defendant franchisor had "control over the equipment and procedures which contributed to [his] injury" the court found that the defendant owed plaintiff a common-law duty to exercise reasonable care); *Bruntjen*, 18 N.E.3d at 238 (citations omitted) ("[franchisor] voluntarily undertook a duty when it set a mandatory safety policy for driver's qualifications and then failed to monitor [franchisee] for compliance with its own policy"); *Plunkett*, 2015 WL 82935, at *4 (where the plaintiff alleged that the defendant franchisor "insisted upon the specific design feature of [the franchised] premises—the high-gloss floor paint—that caused [plaintiff]'s injury," the court found the plaintiff sufficiently alleged her negligence claim against the defendant); *Lind*, 37 N.E.3d at 11–12 (holding the franchisor had no legal duty to the injured third party under a theory of direct liability where the franchisor did not control the daily operations of the franchisee).

514. *Bruntjen*, 18 N.E.3d at 235 ("Where a duty of care is imposed, it is limited to the extent of the undertaking."); Braucher ex rel. Braucher v. Swagat Grp., L.L.C., 702 F. Supp. 2d 1032, 1044 (C.D. Ill. 2010) ("If a party voluntarily undertakes a duty, the duty is limited to the extent of the undertaking.").

Although courts in the past decades have analyzed the issue of whether a franchisor is a joint employer of its franchisees and concluded almost universally that no such employment relationship exists,[515] the U.S. National Labor Relations Board (NLRB) challenged this conclusion by filing a complaint against McDonald's Corp.[516] For a thorough discussion of the case history on joint employment and its standards and application to the franchise relationship, please see Chapter 4.

The potential for vicarious liability, negligence, employer and joint employer liability claims underscores the importance of including in the franchise agreement a provision that the franchisor and the franchisee are independent contractors and not agents of one another.[517] Because these clauses are not dispositive, however, it is important to remember that they will not protect a franchisor that goes "over the line" with regard to the control it exercises over the day-to-day operations of its franchisees and that franchisors should focus their control on issues that impact system standards and the brand. Unfortunately, a franchisor that is constantly worried about going "over the line" also has to respond to franchisee requests for assistance. Therefore, an overly broad "control" standard is not beneficial to either the franchisor or the franchisee and impedes the franchisor's ability to provide certain assistance requested by the franchisees.

(ii) Independent Contractor Issues in Claims by the Franchisees

Independent contractor issues also frequently arise in claims brought against a franchisor by its franchisees. In these cases, the franchisees allege that they were wrongly classified as independent contractors and allege violations of various laws applicable to employers, such as workers' compensation and wage and hour laws.[518]

For example, the Court of Appeals of Washington in *Department of Labor & Industries v. Lyons Enterprises, Inc.*,[519] held that, for purposes of Washington

---

515. *See* David J. Kaufmann, Felicia N. Soler, Breton H. Permesly, & Dale A. Cohen, *A Franchisor Is Not the Employer of Its Franchisees or Their Employees*, 34 FRANCHISE L.J. 439, 475–90 (Spring 2015); *see, e.g.*, *Patterson*, 333 P.3d at 740, 743.

516. Complaint, N.L.R.B. v. McDonald's, USA, LLC, No. 02-CA-093893 (N.Y. Nov. 29, 2012).

517. *See* Perkins, Yatchak, & Hadfield, *supra* note 486, at 179.

518. *See* Kaufmann et al., *supra* note 515, at 490–95; *see, e.g.*, Myers v. Jani-King of Phila., Inc., No. 09-1738, 2015 WL 1055700, at *1, *16 (E.D. Pa. Mar. 11, 2015) (granting the plaintiff franchisees' motion for class certification against the franchisor where they alleged that they were misclassified as independent contractors under Pennsylvania's Wage Payment and Collection Law); *see, e.g.*, Dep't of Labor & Indus. v. Lyons Enters., Inc., 347 P.3d 464, 471–74 (Wash. Ct. App. 2015) (the court held that, for purposes of Washington's workers' compensation law, the franchisor was its franchisees' employer, except for those franchisees who had subordinates of their own); Naik v. 7-Eleven, Inc., No. 13-4578 RMB/JS, 2014 WL 3844792, at *1, *9 (D.N.J. Aug. 5, 2014) (denying in part defendant franchisor's motion to dismiss for plaintiff franchisees' Fair Labor Standards Act and New Jersey Wage and Hour Law claims where franchisees alleged that they were employees of the franchisor); Jan-Pro Franchising Int'l, Inc. v. Depianti, 712 S.E.2d 648, 649–52 (Ga. Ct. App. 2011) (in reversing the decision of the superior court, the court of appeals held that the master franchisor of a commercial cleaning business was not the employer of a unit franchisee under Massachusetts law); Awuah v. Coverall N. Am., Inc., 707 F. Supp. 2d 80, 85 (D. Mass. 2010) (holding that the plaintiff franchisees were misclassified as independent contractors under Massachusetts law and granting their motion for partial summary judgment); Emp't Dep't v. Nat'l Maint. Contractors of Or., Inc., 204 P.3d 151, 152 (Or. Ct. App. 2009) (dispute over franchisee status as employees).

519. 347 P.3d 464 (Wash. Ct. App. 2015).

workers' compensation law, a commercial cleaning franchisor was its franchisees' employer, except for those franchisees who had subordinates of their own. At issue in *Lyons Enterprises, Inc.* was whether the franchisor's franchisees were "workers" within the meaning of the workers' compensation statute. To determine whether independent contractors were workers subject to the statute, the court looked to the "realities of the situation" and found that the "essence of the cleaning contracts" was that through someone's "labor," the end customer's facility was made clean.[520] The question then became whether this labor was "personal" under the statute.[521] To answer this question, the court looked to Washington Supreme Court precedent, which enumerates three types of contractors who are not covered workers: (1) those who must of necessity own or supply machinery or equipment to perform the contract; (2) those who obviously could not perform the contract without assistance; or (3) those who of necessity or choice employ others to do all or part of the work he was contracted to perform. The court reasoned that if a franchisee works alone, then he is "necessarily exerting personal labor" and a worker under law; whereas if a franchisee employs others, then he is "necessarily contributing more to the contract than his or her personal labor—it is contributing to the labor of his or her subordinates" and is, therefore, excluded from the workers' compensation statute.[522] Moreover, the court found that the franchisees' businesses were not "separate and apart" from their franchise agreements with the franchisor since they were not in the commercial cleaning business prior to their contracts, and their businesses would not survive termination of the franchise agreements because of the franchisees' covenant not to compete.[523] Based on these facts, the court ruled that franchisees who lacked subordinates were covered workers under the law, and the franchisor therefore was required to pay workers' compensation premiums for these workers.[524]

In *Depianti v. Jan-Pro Franchising Int'l, Inc.*,[525] the janitorial franchisees alleged that they were misclassified as independent contractors and were instead employees of their regional master franchisee and the franchisor.[526] The franchised concept featured a three-tiered system of franchising, in which the regional master franchisees were granted the right to sell unit franchises within their territories and enter into contracts with the franchisees in those territories.[527] The U.S. District Court for the District of Massachusetts ruled that the Georgia Court of Appeals' decision, which applied the three conditions established by Massachusetts's misclassification statute to find that (1) the janitorial franchisees were free from the franchisor's control and direction because the regional master franchisee makes its own hiring and firing decisions, holds the accounts serviced and invoices customers, and pays the janitorial franchisees; (2) the janitorial franchisees' services are

520. *Id.* at 471.
521. *Id.*
522. *Id.* at 472–73.
523. *Id.* at 473.
524. *Id.* at 469–70, 473–74.
525. 39 F. Supp. 3d 112 (D. Mass. 2014).
526. *Id.* at 116–17.
527. *Id.* at 116.

performed outside of the franchisor's usual course of business where the franchisor's usual business is establishing a trademark and cleaning system to be licensed to regional master franchisees; and (3) the janitorial franchisees operate independent businesses, barred the franchisees' claim.[528]

Where a violation of the Fair Labor Standards Act is alleged against a franchisor by its franchisees, courts have looked to six factors to determine whether the "circumstances of the whole activity" indicated an employment relationship existed.[529] These include (1) the degree of the alleged employer's right to control the manner in which the work was to be performed; (2) the alleged employee's opportunity for profit or loss depending upon his managerial skill; (3) the alleged employee's investment in equipment or material required for his task, or his employment of helpers; (4) whether the service rendered required a special skill; (5) the degree of permanence of the working relationship; and (6) whether the service rendered was an integral part of the alleged employer's business.[530] The overriding consideration is the "economic reality" of the relationship—that is, whether "the workers depend upon someone else's business for the opportunity to render service or are in business for themselves."[531]

D. Joint and Several

> If two or more individuals, limited liability companies, corporations, partnerships or other entities (or any combination of two or more thereof) shall sign or be subject to the terms and conditions of this Agreement as Franchisee or as a Guarantor, the liability of each of them under this Agreement shall be deemed to be joint and several.

Discussion:

A joint and several liability clause is a common feature in franchise agreements. For parties subject to joint and several liability, each is individually responsible for the entire obligation, whether it be a non-monetary performance requirement (such as curing a quality default or performing post-termination obligations to de-identify the former franchised location) or a monetary requirement (such as paying outstanding royalties, liquidated damages, infringement damages, or attorneys' fees and costs). The obligors, each responsible for the full amount, are left to sort out apportionment between themselves. The clause therefore allows a franchisor, as a matter of standard contract law, to pursue any or all joint and several parties as it chooses, and collect from whomever of them can satisfy any resulting judgment. This provides the franchisor with maximum flexibility to decide, upon breach, which of those parties to press for performance and/or to sue, where to sue, and how to enforce and collect, typically with an eye toward which ones are likely to provide the most leverage and liquid assets to the franchisor.

528. *Id. at* 126–27, 129.

529. *Naik*, 2014 WL 3844792, at *4.

530. *Id.*; *see also* Saleem v. Corp. Transp. Grp., Ltd., 52 F. Supp. 3d 526, 535 (S.D.N.Y. 2014).

531. *Saleem*, 52 F. Supp. 3d at 535; *see also Naik*, 2014 WL 3844792, at *4.

A franchisee with multiple owners may not want to be jointly and severally liable to the franchisor. In response to a franchisor's requirement for joint and several liability, a franchisee's owners may negotiate to enter into a contribution agreement so that if one party has to indemnify the franchisor for all of the franchisee's obligations, the other owners agree to contribute their pro rata share of the liability.

E. Waiver of Obligations

> Franchisor and Franchisee may by written instrument unilaterally waive any obligation of or restriction upon the other under this Agreement, such waiver being effective on delivery of written notice to the other or another effective date stated in the notice of waiver. No special or restrictive legend or endorsement on any check or similar item given to Franchisor will be a waiver, compromise, settlement, or accord and satisfaction. Franchisor is authorized to remove any legend or endorsement, which then will have no effect.
>
> Any waiver granted will be without prejudice to any other rights Franchisor or Franchisee has, will be subject to continuing review, and may be revoked at any time and for any reason effective on delivery of ten (10) days' prior written notice.

Discussion:
Drafters include a waiver clause so that the franchisor and the franchisee have the right to waive an obligation at some point during the term of the agreement while still reserving all of their respective rights. It is difficult to predict the future circumstances of the parties' relationship under the agreement. In practice, a party may routinely waive at least some of its obligations under the franchise agreement. Each party would probably want to retain flexibility to relieve certain obligations at any point during the term of the agreement without jeopardy to its rights under the agreement. Typically, a franchise agreement will require that any waiver be in writing and signed by an authorized employee to be effective, and include such a requirement either in this provision or elsewhere in the agreement.

F. Nonwaiver of Rights by the Franchisor

> No waiver by Franchisor of any breach by Franchisee, nor any delay or failure by Franchisor to enforce any provision of this Agreement, may be deemed to be a waiver of any other or subsequent breach or be deemed an estoppel to enforce Franchisor's rights with respect to that or any other or subsequent breach.
>
> Franchisor will not waive or impair any right, power, or option this Agreement reserves (including Franchisor's right to demand exact compliance with every term, condition, and covenant or to declare any breach to be a default and to terminate this Agreement before its term expires) because of any custom or practice at variance with this Agreement's terms; Franchisor's alleged failure, refusal, or neglect to exercise any right under this Agreement or to insist on the other's compliance with this Agreement, including any System Standard; Franchisor's waiver of or failure to exercise any right, power, or option, whether of the same, similar, or different nature,

with other Franchised Businesses; the existence of franchise agreements for other Franchised Businesses which contain provisions different from those contained in this Agreement; or Franchisor's acceptance of any payments due from Franchisee after any breach of this Agreement.

Discussion:

There are instances every day where and when a franchisee is likely not in strict compliance with the franchise agreement. Some instances of noncompliance are more serious and important than others. Regardless, the franchisor does not want to have waived its contractual rights by virtue of not having acted, or deciding not to act, on an issue. Generally, waiver occurs when a party knowingly and intentionally fails to enforce provisions of an agreement.[532] The nonwaiver provision therefore provides the franchisor with flexibility; it permits the franchisor to choose to not address certain defaults without risking its rights and without having to make every small issue a big one. In disputes, the provision helps protect the franchisor from waiver and estoppel defenses.

Courts typically enforce nonwaiver provisions. For example, even though the franchisor in *Burger King Corp. v. Kellogg* accepted late royalty payments from the franchisee, the court held that it did not waive the right to terminate, because the agreement contained a nonwaiver provision.[533] Similarly, the franchisee defendants in *Allegra Network, LLC v. AM Marketing, Inc.*,[534] argued that because the franchisor continued to deal with the franchisee after the agreement's termination, the termination itself was waived.[535] This argument was unsuccessful: the waiver provision required any waiver had to be in writing, and the court found it was enforceable.[536]

That being said, it nevertheless is common for a franchisee to counter a default by asserting that the franchisor has acquiesced in prior similar conduct by the franchisee or others. Many courts impose a tough standard for proving such a waiver. For instance, in Massachusetts, waiver requires the existence of a right, knowledge of the existence of the right, and the waiving party's actual intention to relinquish that right.[537] The waiver inquiry is focused on the conduct of the waiving party. For example, in *Dunkin' Donuts Inc. v. Gav-Stra Donuts, Inc.*,[538] a federal court in Massachusetts held that, as a matter of law, the franchisor did not waive its right to

---

532. 2 FRANCH & DISTR LAW & PRAC § 8:20.

533. Burger King Corp. v. Kellogg, BUS FRANCHISE GUIDE (CCH) ¶ 12,136 (E.D. Mich. 2001). *See also* Dunkin' Donuts Franchised Restaurants LLC v. KEV Enters., Inc., 634 F. Supp. 2d 1324 (M.D. Fla. 2009) (holding that franchisors' acceptance of late payments from franchisees did not establish waiver of right to terminate in light of franchise agreement nonwaiver provision); Ex parte Keelboat Concepts, Inc., 938 So. 2d 922 (Ala. 2002) (enforcing agreement's anti-waiver provision and holding that franchisee's failure to exercise renewal option within the six-month period stipulated by the agreement precluded renewal even if franchisor had not required strict adherence to certain terms of the agreement).

534. BUS FRANCHISE GUIDE (CCH) ¶ 12,136 (E.D. Mich. 2001).

535. *Id.*

536. *Id.*

537. Kerry L. Bundy & Scott H. Ikeda, *How Waiver, Modification, and Estoppel May Alter Franchise Relationships*, 30 FRANCHISE L.J. 3, 3 (Summer 2010).

538. 139 F. Supp. 2d 147 (D. Mass. 2001).

terminate the franchise agreement for criminal conduct even if it waited six years after learning of the conduct. The court held that, at most, there was "mere silence" by the franchisor, and absent evidence that it took affirmative steps to waive its contractual right to terminate, there was no waiver.[539] On the other hand, in some jurisdictions, waiver may be found where the party does not object to the violation or does not act on its rights for a substantial (or unreasonable) period of time.[540] In *LaGuardia Associates v. Holiday Hospitality Franchising*,[541] the U.S. District Court for the Eastern District of New York held that a franchisor waived its right to terminate a franchise agreement under New York law where it did not attempt to terminate until ten months after the franchisee's default on payment. However, temporary forbearance likely will not rise to the level of waiver.[542]

Importantly, the preceding clause stipulates that actions or inactions on the franchisor's part do not constitute waiver and also reserves the right to treat franchised businesses differently so that failure to enforce a provision against one franchisee does not preclude the franchisor from enforcing the same provision against another franchisee under different circumstances. However, the existence of a nonwaiver provision is not dispositive. In some cases, a party to a written contract may waive a provision despite the nonwaiver provision, because the nonwaiver provision itself is subject to waiver or for other reasons.[543]

G. Cross-Default

> In the event that Franchisee (or its affiliate) directly or indirectly acquires the right and franchise to operate another or other franchised businesses, any default by Franchisee (or its affiliate) in the performance or observance of any of the terms and conditions under any one agreement governing the aforesaid right and franchise shall be deemed to be an event of default under all other agreements pursuant to which Franchisee (or its affiliate) directly or indirectly owns or operates such a franchised business or businesses.

Discussion:

If a franchisee opens more than one franchised business under the franchisor's trademark and system, and defaults on one of the associated franchise agreements for those other sites, then it is common to provide that a default under one

---

539. *Id.* at 157.

540. Waiver has been found, for instance, where a franchisor did not object to the sale of non-franchise products for 25 years. Terry v. Int'l Dairy Queen, Inc., 554 F. Supp. 1088, 1095 (N.D. Ind. 1983) ("The waiver of a contractual provision may be impliedly waived by the 'knowing and willing acquiescence' of the party for whose benefit the provision was inserted.").

541. 92 F. Supp. 2d 119 (E.D.N.Y. 2000).

542. Sacred Heart Health Sys., Inc. v. Humana Military Healthcare Servs., Inc., 601 F.3d 1159, 1181 (11th Cir. 2010).

543. 13 Williston on Contracts § 39:36 (4th ed.); *see also* Ramada Franchise Sys., Inc. v. Capitol View II Ltd. P'ship Venture, 132 F. Supp. 2d 358 (D. Md. 2011) (holding that franchisee waived its overbilling claim against the franchisor because the franchisee knowingly and willingly paid higher fees, understanding that they were overcharges—express waiver was therefore unnecessary).

agreement will constitute a default under all the franchisee's agreements. From a business perspective, the franchisor wants to ensure that its franchisees are acting responsibly and according to the contractual terms of their franchise agreements, and devoting sufficient resources to all of their franchised businesses. The franchisor may be able to elicit potentially stricter compliance by having the ability to assert a cross-default and, if necessary, cross-terminations.[544] A franchisee, on the other hand, will not want any of its agreements to contain cross-default provisions. A cross-default increases the risk of a franchisee losing all of its investment.

These cross-default provisions are often one of the deal breaker points between franchisors and franchisees. If a cross-default provision exists in a secondary document such as a sublease or a software license agreement, it is unlikely that a franchisor will negotiate. A franchisor who is also the landlord will inevitably require that the sublease be terminated if the franchise agreement is terminated. However, if a franchisee is executing an area development agreement, a franchisor may consider not reserving the right to terminate the franchise agreements if the area development agreement is terminated based on failure to meet development schedule. If a franchisor terminates a franchise agreement for noncompliance with system standards, it would be concerned that such franchisee would also fail to meet system standards with respect to its other units. However, an area developer's failure to meet the development schedule may not impact a franchisee's operation of existing units. Further, a franchisee would want to ensure that investing in an area development right would not put its franchise locations at risk.

H. No Set Off by Franchisee

> Franchisee agrees that it will not, on grounds of the alleged nonperformance by Franchisor of its obligations hereunder, withhold payment of any royalty or other amounts due to Franchisor or its affiliates, whether on account of goods purchased by Franchisee or otherwise.

Discussion:

Under certain circumstances, a franchisor may owe a franchisee payments during a franchise relationship. For example, a franchisee may be entitled to a rebate from the marketing fund for a new initiative. Despite a franchisee's right to payment, a franchisor wants to ensure the franchisee makes its fee and royalty payments in full as required. Therefore, franchisors often include a clause stipulating no set off to ensure that they receive payments at all times. In other words, even if the franchisee alleges that the franchisor has breached a term of the agreement, the franchisee still will be required to pay the franchisor all fees and royalties, as the franchisee's legal

---

544. *See* Manpower Inc. v. Mason, 405 F. Supp. 2d 959, 975 (E.D. Wis. 2005) (franchisor enjoined from rescinding agreements with franchisee where the owner of the franchisee violated other agreements but not the agreements in question because there were no cross-default provisions in the other agreements and therefore those were not violated by franchisee).

remedy is to sue for damages. A franchisor may not be able to control all aspects of its rights to payment if this clause is left ambiguous or is absent.

I. Set Off by the Franchisor

> Notwithstanding anything contained in this Agreement, upon the failure of Franchisee to pay to Franchisor as and when due, any amounts of money provided for herein, Franchisor shall have the right at its election to deduct any and all such amounts remaining unpaid from any monies or credits held by Franchisor for the account of Franchisee.

Discussion:

While most franchise agreements contain a strict prohibition against the franchisee asserting a right to set off, most franchisors retain an explicit right to set off against monies they owe to the franchisee, from monies owed to them. Although the day-to-day operation of a typical franchise relationship may not involve the franchisor paying the franchisee anything, drafters should still anticipate that this scenario is likely to arise at some time over a lengthy franchise term. It can be particularly common in situations where a struggling franchisee is terminated, often for nonpayment of fees, and the franchisor either chooses to purchase its assets or is required to do so under a state relationship law.[545]

Even though a set off right may be permitted by the common law of contracts, this provision provides the franchisor with that right expressly. For example, the court in *Goldfarb v. The Robb Report, Inc.*, applied the set off rule in the absence of a set off provision in the franchise agreement.[546] The franchisee was owed $116,463.32 in unpaid sales commissions.[547] However, the franchisee also acknowledged that the franchisor was entitled to a set off of $45,000 for unpaid renewal fees.[548] The appellate court modified the franchisee's damages accordingly.[549]

Further, in *InfinaQuest, LLC v. DirectBuy, Inc.*,[550] where the franchise agreement provided the franchisor with set off rights against the franchisee, the franchisor was granted rights of set off above security rights granted to a third party. In *InfinaQuest*, the franchisee granted a security interest in its inventory to a secured party.[551] Ultimately, both the franchisor and the secured party were owed money under contracts each had with the franchisee.[552] The secured party later sued the franchisor for conversion of funds subject to the security interest, claiming that the franchisor collected money that rightfully belonged to it.[553] The court held that the

545. Some state relationship laws explicitly provide the right to offset if they require inventory repurchase. *See* CAL. BUS. & PROF. CODE § 20022(h).

546. 655 N.E.2d 211, 218 (Ohio Ct. App. 1995).

547. *Id.*

548. *Id.*

549. *Id.* at 218–20.

550. 18 F. Supp. 3d 959 (N.D. Ind. 2014).

551. *Id.* at 961–62.

552. *Id.* at 962.

553. *Id.*

secured party took its security interest in the inventory subject to a preexisting contractual right of set off.[554] The court granted summary judgment in favor of the franchisor; "the property—that is, the money—belonged to [the franchisor] and they exercised control over it pursuant to the contractual set-off rights . . . [the franchisor was] justified in [its] actions because of the contractual set-off provision."[555] This case demonstrates the power of set off provisions even as to third parties.

In sum, while common law may provide franchisors with a right to set off, including a set off provision guarantees that right.

J. Franchisee and Owner Defined

> References in this Agreement to "Franchisor" with respect to all of its rights and all of Franchisee's obligations to Franchisor under this Agreement, include any of Franchisor's affiliates with whom Franchisee deals. The term "affiliate" means any person or entity directly or indirectly owned or controlled by, under common control with, or owning or controlling Franchisee or Franchisor, as applicable. The term "control" means the power to direct or cause the direction of management and policies.
>
> References to "owner" mean any person holding a direct or indirect ownership interest (whether of record, beneficially, or otherwise) or voting rights in Franchisee (or a transferee of this Agreement and the Franchised Business or an ownership interest in you), including any person who has a direct or indirect interest in Franchisee (or a transferee), this Agreement or the Franchised Business and including any person who has any other legal or equitable interest, or the power to vest in himself or herself any legal or equitable interest, in their revenue, profits, rights, or assets.
>
> The term "person" means any natural person, corporation, limited liability company, general or limited partnership, unincorporated association, cooperative, or other legal or functional entity.

Discussion:

It is relatively common to include in the franchise agreement a provision that incorporates certain meaning into frequently used terms. These are classic "boilerplate" provisions in any commercial contract, noted more when they are omitted and a dispute arises than when they are included. However, upon analysis, any commercial or transactional lawyer should readily see the importance of deeming that singular use of a term includes the plural, and that use of the male includes any females. The preceding provision also deems the franchisor's notice to or other described action toward one of multiple franchisees or guarantors effective as if it were provided to all of them, which is a helpful provision for a franchisor. While this provision serves as additional protection for franchisors in the event a notice is not properly delivered for one of many agreements, franchisors should in practice serve notices on all applicable entities in accordance with the notice provision instead of simply relying on this provision.

554. *Id.* at 965.
555. *Id.*

K. Further Assurances

> Each of the Parties hereto hereby covenants and agrees to execute and deliver such further and other agreements, assurances, undertakings, acknowledgements or documents, cause such meetings to be held, resolutions passed and by-laws enacted, exercise their vote and influence and do and perform and cause to be done and performed any further and other acts and things as may be necessary or desirable in order to give full effect to this Agreement and every part hereof.

Discussion:
Any number of provisions in a franchise agreement may contemplate that the parties may be required to enter into some future contract, give some further consent, or execute some further document, to give effect to the intention of the first agreement. Accordingly, it is very common to include a provision that speaks to further assurances, which obligates the parties to sign those further necessary contracts, consents, forms, and so forth. Although it is not a provision that gets attention often, it is certainly noticeable if ever omitted.

This provision of the franchise agreement is invoked if one party were, for example, to intentionally fail to undertake actions necessary to fulfill its duties under the agreement, like executing a lease agreement.

A court might limit the application of a further assurances provision. As one court concluded, "[i]f a provision in an agreement does not 'contemplate' an obligation, the 'Further Assurances' clause does not allow the court to impose an obligation that may have been 'contemplated' in one or both parties' minds, but not expressed in the actual agreement."[556] In that case, because the franchise agreement was silent as to the franchisee's obligation to renew a sublease, the franchisee's refusal to renew did not violate the further assurances provision of the agreement.[557]

L. Successors and Assigns

> Subject to the restrictions on assignment herein contained, this Agreement shall be to the benefit of and be binding upon the Parties hereto and their respective heirs, executors, administrators, successors and assigns.

Discussion:
The provision regarding successor and assigns intends to make clear that the terms of the agreement are binding on the parties and anyone who in the future assumes their respective roles, either by assignment or some other succession mechanism.[558] This provision is especially critical in the event of an individual franchisee's death

556. *In re* Magna Cum Latte, Inc., No. 07-31814, 2007 WL 3231633, at *6 (Bankr. S.D. Tex. Oct. 30, 2007).

557. *Id.*

558. *See, e.g.*, H&R Block Tax Servs., Inc. v. Letha Nell Sheets, No. 06-23-DLB, 2006 U.S. Dist. LEXIS 8437 (E.D. Ky. Mar. 3, 2006) (applying Missouri successorship law and finding successor bound by assignment provision in franchise agreement).

in order to bind the successor. Of course, it is not meant to override any other provision in the agreement that specifies prior consent is needed to complete an assignment or other transfer.[559]

M. When Agreement Binding on the Franchisor

> This Agreement is not effective until signed by a corporate officer of Franchisor at Franchisor's headquarters. No field representative or salesman is authorized to execute this Agreement on behalf of Franchisor. Franchisee is advised not to incur any expense or obligation with respect to the proposed Franchised Business until Franchisee has received a fully executed copy of this Agreement from Franchisor.

Discussion:

It is important to state when an agreement comes into effect to avoid unintended contractual obligations. The preceding provision makes clear that execution by a corporate officer is necessary to make the agreement effective. To avoid any unnecessary expense for the franchisee, it also clearly directs the franchisee to refrain from any expenditure until the agreement is in effect.

This provision also accounts for the fact that a long time can pass between when a prospective franchisee first applies for a franchise and when the parties' franchise agreement is executed. As a result,

> a disappointed prospect may claim that the negotiations, preliminary agreements, and actions undertaken in preparation for the franchise, viewed in the aggregate, created an enforceable right to a franchise, giving rise to breach of contract and related claims against a franchisor that no longer wishes to proceed with the transaction.[560]

The above provision seeks to extinguish any ambiguity as to when the franchisee/franchisor relationship arises. For example, in *Herald Hotel Associates v. Ramada Franchise Sys., Inc.*, a prospective Ramada franchisee started the process by submitting a license application and a $100,000 license application fee.[561] After Ramada notified the prospective franchisee of the approved application, the parties negotiated terms of a proposed license agreement. However, more than a year passed in which the prospective franchisee failed to sign the license agreement and failed to renovate the hotel. After a nearby hotel submitted an application to become a Ramada franchisee, the prospective franchisee objected based on the exclusive territory in the proposed license agreement. The prospective franchisee ultimately filed suit, alleging that Ramada breached the license application by failing to grant

559. For a discussion of transfer or assignment rights, see generally Chapter 7.

560. Kevin M. Shelley & Jonathan J. Toronto, *Preliminary Agreements: How to Avoid Unintended Contractual Obligations*, 25 FRANCHISE L.J. 47, 48 (Fall 2005).

561. BUS FRANCHISE GUIDE (CCH) ¶ 10,078 (N.Y. Sup. Ct. 1992).

the franchise. Because the license application provided that "Ramada and Applicant agree to enter into a Ramada license agreement in the form attached hereto," the court denied Ramada's motion for summary judgment.[562] The court concluded that there was a binding and enforceable obligation to enter into the license agreement. The unintended contractual obligations in *Herald Hotel* arose from an ambiguous preliminary agreement (created by the language in the application), but prior to a final franchise agreement.[563]

Unlike *Herald Hotel Associates*, in *L&E Corp. v. Days Inns of Am., Inc.*, the franchisor avoided an unintended contractual obligation by clearly stating when the franchise agreement became binding.[564] While the potential franchisee, L&E Corporation, had submitted a license application, there was no executed license agreement. Instead, Days Inns sent L&E Corporation a letter stating that the application had been approved, but Days Inns would not be bound absent *the execution and delivery of a license agreement* to L&E Corporation.[565] Ultimately, the parties did not execute the license agreement.[566] The franchisee brought an action against Days Inns seeking an injunction requiring Days Inns to issue the franchise. The district court granted L&E Corporation's injunction and Days Inns was compelled to issue L&E Corporation a ten-year license agreement.[567] The Fourth Circuit Court of Appeals reversed and held that the unambiguous language of the license application clearly required execution and delivery of the license agreement.[568] In other words, Days Inns' disclaimers in the license application and subsequent acceptance letter were unequivocal. The court also held that "the district court's decision to treat [the preconditions] as mere formalities, avoidable on the grounds of fairness and public policy, was error."[569]

As the preceding cases demonstrate, an executed franchise agreement is not always required to bind parties. Accordingly, a provision stating when the agreement comes into effect helps prevent an unintended franchise relationship. Both the franchisee and the franchisor benefit from unequivocally knowing when the franchise relationship begins.

---

562. *Id.*

563. *Id. See also* Stetzer v. Dunkin' Donuts, Inc., 87 F. Supp. 2d 104 (D. Conn. 2000) (refusing to grant summary judgment where letter agreement may have granted plaintiff right to open new franchise location even though franchise agreement was never executed for that location).

564. 992 F.2d 55 (4th Cir. 1993).

565. *Id.* at 57.

566. *Id.*

567. *Id.*

568. *Id.* at 58 ("The district court's fundamental error lay in its refusal to give effect to Days Inns' unequivocal disclaimers in the license application and the March 31 letter.").

569. *Id.* at 59. For an additional example, *see* Ross v. Culver Franchising System, Inc., No. 01 C 3830, 2004 WL 1898235 (N.D. Ill. Aug. 13, 2004) (dismissing plaintiffs' contract claim because undisputed evidence showed that the plaintiffs knew they were required to sign a franchise agreement and pay a $42,000 franchise fee in order to establish a franchise relationship).

N. Severability

Except as otherwise provided in this Agreement, if for any reason whatsoever, any term or condition of this Agreement or the application thereof to any party or circumstance shall, to any extent be invalid, unenforceable, contrary to or in conflict with any applicable present or future law or regulation, all other terms and conditions of this Agreement and/or the application of such terms and conditions to the Parties or circumstance shall not be affected thereby and each term and condition of this Agreement shall be separately valid and enforceable to the fullest extent permitted by law.

Discussion:

Most contracts include a severability clause stating that the unenforceability of one clause has no effect on the enforceability of the remaining clauses.[570] This is a typical contract term, and it is important for it to appear in a franchise agreement.[571] It should be noted that an agreement may not be capable of severance depending on the object of the law that is being infringed.[572]

Although the clause is typically boilerplate, if there is a particular area of concern with respect to an aspect of an agreement,[573] drafters may review relevant case law in drafting the clause for severability. In some instances, and unlike the sample clause, the franchisor will reserve to itself the right to terminate the agreement if the unenforceable provision is viewed as of such importance that its unenforceability would fundamentally alter the relationship. For example, a franchisor of a business offering medical services may want to reserve the right to terminate an agreement if a state enacts a law that prohibits a franchisor from collecting royalties based on revenues derived from the practice of medicine. In such event, the franchisor would not want any court to sever the payment provision from the rest of the agreement.

O. Notices

All written notices, consents, approvals, authorizations and reports, permitted or required to be delivered by this Agreement or the Operations Manual will be deemed to be delivered:

---

570. *See* Peter C. Lagarias, *Uniformity in California Franchise Agreements*, 21 FRANCHISE L.J. 136, 139 (Winter 2002).

571. *See* Kevin M. Kennedy, *Drafting an Enforceable Franchise Agreement Arbitration Clause*, 22 FRANCHISE L.J. 112, 113, 115 (Fall 2002) ("[T]o make it less likely that a decision invalidating the venue provision of an arbitration clause would invalidate the clause in its entirety, the franchisor should consider adding an arbitration-specific severability clause" and "a franchisor that wants to limit its risk should [also] . . . make clear that any limitations on damages are severable from the arbitration agreement itself. That way, if a court concludes that the damage limitation is unenforceable under an applicable state or federal statute, the arbitration clause will not be affected.").

572. *See, e.g.*, Unlimited Opportunity, Inc. v. Waadah, 861 N.W.2d 437, 442–44 (Neb. 2015) (the court reasoned "public policy considerations dictate our conclusion that such [non-compete] agreements should not be severable" and held that the entire non-compete clause was invalid and unenforceable); *see generally* Sanchez v. CleanNet USA, Inc., 78 F. Supp. 3d 747, 757 (N.D. Ill. 2015) ("'In determining whether it is appropriate to sever an unconscionable provision from an agreement and enforce the remainder of the agreement, Illinois courts are to consider whether the provisions operate independently of each other or whether the valid provisions are so closely connected with unenforceable provisions that to do so would be tantamount to rewriting the Agreement.'").

573. Enforceability of jury trial waivers, for example, is often an area of concern. *See infra* Section S.

1. at the time delivered by hand;
2. at the time delivered electronically;
3. one (1) business day after being placed in the hands of a nationally recognized commercial courier service for next business day delivery; or
4. three (3) business days after placement in the U.S. Mail.

Any notice must be sent to the party to be notified at its most current principal business address (or email address) of which the notifying party has notice; except that, it will always be deemed acceptable to send notice to you at the address of the Franchised Business.

Discussion:

Notice provisions are important, and often an afterthought in most franchise agreements. They can sometimes "trip up" a franchisor who fails to adhere strictly to the agreement's requirements regarding written notice. Strict compliance with the notice provision will be particularly important when a franchisor seeks to default or terminate a franchisee. If a franchisor fails to provide notice in accordance with the terms of the agreement, it creates risk that a court may find that the termination was unlawful.[574] Franchisors also should remember that some state franchise statutes include specific requirements with respect to how particular notices must be provided.[575] From the franchisor's drafting standpoint, it wants to be able to provide effective notice to the franchisee in the fastest and least cumbersome way possible. Many franchise agreements still do not permit the delivery of official notice by e-mail, but as a majority of all communication is now done by e-mail, it seems to be the least cumbersome way for a franchisor to deliver notice.

Many agreements provide that notice is not deemed delivered until received, and often not unless you have a signed receipt. However, given that during the term of the agreement, most notices are delivered by the franchisor, the franchisor may not want to require the franchisee to have to sign upon receipt in order for the notice to be effective. The signature requirement is particularly troublesome when a franchisor is trying to deliver a notice of default or termination and the franchisee refuses to accept the notice.

---

574. For example, in Tim Hortons USA, Inc. v. Singh, the court held that notice by e-mail was adequate even though the franchise agreement did not specifically authorize notice in that form. Case No. 16-civ-23041, 2017 WL 1326285 (S.D. Fla. Apr. 5, 2017) (also noting that while "[d]oughnuts usually make people happy," "the doughnut business at issue here has generated disputes and bad feelings, not to mention litigation"). The court relied on Florida law that found strict compliance with a notice provision unnecessary if a party has actual notice. *Id.* at *8. A similar challenge applying a different state's law or without actual notice could result in a court finding e-mail notice was inadequate.

575. *See, e.g.*, CAL. BUS. & PROF. CODE § 20030(b) (requiring that all notices of termination or nonrenewal must be "posted by registered, certified or other receipted mail, delivered by telegram or personally delivered to the franchisee"); *see, e.g.*, KAN. STAT. § 8-2414(a) (requiring notices for the cancellation, termination, or nonrenewal of franchise agreements between dealers and manufacturers or distributors to "be given by certified mail and the period of time given in the notice prior to cancellation, termination or nonrenewal [to] be computed from the date of mailing thereof"); *see, e.g.*, ME. REV. STAT. § 1366(1) (requiring notices of termination or nonrenewal for franchise agreements between a manufacturer and a distributor or dealer of power equipment, machinery, and/or appliances to "[b]e sent by registered, certified or other receipted mail, delivered by telegram or personally delivered to the distributor or dealer").

In addition, the franchisor should consider how to handle situations of abandonment if it utilizes a signed receipt system or even just an e-mail notice system. If the franchisee abandons its business operations, a typical franchise agreement will allow the franchisor to terminate, as discussed in Chapter 8. However, if the franchisor lacks a home address or personal e-mail address for the franchisee, it may be difficult for the franchisor to prove that it provided adequate notice of termination, since the franchisee may never pick up mail sent to the old business address, and the franchisor will want to cut off the terminated franchisee's access to brand-based e-mail and other systems immediately upon termination. In anticipation of this situation, many franchisors require a home mailing address for a franchisee as a backup notice address.

Franchisors should consider whether the phrase "most current . . . email address . . . of which the notifying party has notice" is reasonable within the structure of their system. In a large system, the number of franchisor e-mail addresses of which the franchisee is aware may be extremely broad and include a variety of personnel whom the franchisor does not wish to have involved in legal matters. In some instances, it is better to draft this clause to provide a specific franchisor e-mail address for service of notices so that requests are reviewed promptly and never overlooked.

P. Headings and Article Numbers

The headings, article numbers and table of contents appearing in this Agreement or any schedule hereto are inserted for convenience of reference only and shall not in any way affect the construction or interpretation of this Agreement.

Discussion:
The clause regarding headings and article numbers speaks to the general interpretation of the agreement. This clause is drafted so that the user is absolutely clear on the intention behind headings and article numbers. As the headings are often meant as a short form term describing the contents of the section, it is fair to disclaim that they have any contractual weight or authority. The failure to include this type of clause invites a court to interpret the short title as part of its contractual construction and perhaps make a finding that the short title somehow limits rights or obligations under the agreement.

Q. Time of the Essence

Time shall be of the essence of this Agreement and of each and every part hereof.

Discussion:
It is very common for contracts to stipulate that time is of the essence. This sample clause is bilateral and requires both parties to fulfill their respective obligations in as timely a manner as possible. Some franchise agreements instead may be worded

unilaterally, so that time is of the essence with respect to the franchisee's obligations. Typically, the parties can waive the "time is of the essence" provision under certain circumstances.[576] Oftentimes, such an ability to waive the "time is of the essence" provision will be drafted into the agreement. The failure to include a provision stating that time is of the essence may bring into question whether a party can rely on the strict time periods specified by the contract.[577]

R. Force Majeure

> Franchisor shall not be liable to Franchisee for any failure or delay in performing any obligation, in whole or in part, under this Agreement if such failure or delay results directly or indirectly from wars (declared or not), insurrections, riots, fires, floods, explosions, earthquakes, accidents, epidemic or quarantine restrictions, acts of God, any act of government or governmental priorities, transportation failures or delays, embargoes, material or parts shortages, strikes, labor trouble causing a cessation or slow down or interruption of work (including labor troubles or other delays at a supplier's facility), events where an export license is refused or withdrawn, or any other cause beyond Franchisor's reasonable control.

Discussion:

Force majeure provisions are included in contracts to suspend or excuse performance in the face of certain events—usually events beyond either party's control. The goal of these provisions is to allocate and manage unforeseeable risk. Depending on how the provision is tailored, a party's obligation to perform may be suspended during the "force majeure event." The unforeseeable event may also lead to the termination of the agreement if performance becomes impossible.

Although it is common for distributor contracts in the product distribution context to include force majeure provisions that temporarily excuse the manufacturer or supplier's obligations during times of some sort of extenuating external circumstance, it is less common to include force majeure provisions in franchise agreements. The franchisors typically either choose not to include force majeure provisions at all (given that franchisors may have fewer contractual obligations than the franchisee) or limit the clause in favor of the franchisor, particularly if the franchisor supplies products to the franchisee (for example, gasoline or cars).[578]

---

576. *See* Stetzer v. Dunkin' Donuts, Inc., 87 F. Supp. 2d 104, 112 (D. Conn. 2000) ("Under Massachusetts law, a party can waive a time-is-of-the-essence provision through speech or conduct indicating that the provision is no longer of importance.").

577. *See id.* at 111 ("The fact that a contract states a date for performance does not necessarily make time of the essence."); *see also* Pack 2000, Inc. v. Cushman, 89 A.3d 869, 886 (Conn. 2014) (citation omitted) ("It is well settled that, '[when] a time for performance is stated in an agreement, a party's tender of performance within a reasonable time thereafter will be considered substantial performance unless the parties intended that time for performance be of the essence. [When] the agreement does not specifically state that time is of the essence, it is presumed not to be unless the parties have expressed a contrary intent.'").

578. *See, e.g.*, Wootton Enterprises, Inc. v. Subaru of America, Inc., 134 F. Supp. 2d 698 (D. Ma. 2001) (examining a force majeure provision and finding that franchisee failed to establish that franchisor late vehicle delivery breached the franchise agreement).

From the franchisor's perspective, it is typically not helpful to include a force majeure clause that applies to the franchisee's obligations, as that opens the door for a nonperforming franchisee to cite external circumstances as the reason for its nonperformance in a host of areas, including quality assurance. On the other hand, if such a provision is included, the franchisor could consider requiring the franchisee to pay liquidated damages up to the amount of business continuation insurance proceeds in the event that the franchisee's business is destroyed. Such a provision would require the franchisor to account for individual state laws that place limits on the availability of liquidated damages, whether through a state addendum or otherwise, but could allow both parties to the agreement to mitigate their respective risks.

Still, the inclusion or exclusion of a force majeure provision will not prevent a party from asserting a force majeure defense in a breach of contract case. Functionally, a claim of force majeure is equivalent to an affirmative defense.[579]

In the litigation context, a force majeure defense ultimately may not carry the day, but it very well may raise factual issues that would be subject to discovery and could survive dispositive motion practice. Still, if a franchisor does wish to include bilateral clauses, the agreement should expressly require the franchisee to make all payments notwithstanding any claim of force majeure, and make plain that the franchisee's economic hardship, whatever its cause or seriousness, is not force majeure.

Particularly in the wake of the economic downturn during 2007 through 2009, franchisees and franchisors used force majeure to argue that the unforeseeable economic meltdown excused nonperformance. For example, in *Route 6 Outparcels, LLC v. Ruby Tuesdays*,[580] the lessee claimed that the "global economic downturn"—events entirely outside its control and through no fault of its own—prevented it from constructing a restaurant and caused it to breach a commercial lease agreement. Under the terms of the lease agreement, a change in financial circumstances was not among the enumerated list of force majeure triggering events. Even assuming that the severe economic downturn fell within the catchall language of the lease agreement's force majeure clause, the lessee failed to demonstrate that it was prevented from complying with its obligations under the lease due to events entirely outside of its control. "While [the restaurant], of course, had no control over the world economy, the decisions it made with respect to how to cope with the financial downturn—notwithstanding that its options may have been limited—remained within [the lessee's] power and control."[581]

Impossibility, impracticability, and frustration are closely related to the force majeure defense and often asserted in franchise litigation. For instance in *Days Inn of Am., Inc. v. Patel*, a franchisee did not deny that he breached the franchise

579. 30 Williston on Contracts § 77:31 (4th ed.).

580. 88 A.D.3d 1224 (N.Y. App. Div. 2011).

581. *Id.* at 1226 (noting that "financial hardship is not grounds for avoiding performance under a contract"). *See also* Great Lakes Gas Transmission Ltd. P'ship v. Essar Steel Minnesota, LLC, 871 F. Supp. 2d 843 (D. Minn. 2012) (holding that the "worldwide financial crisis" in conjunction with the force majeure clause in a contract for the transportation of natural gas to buyer's steel plant did not excuse buyer's duty to pay for transportation of gas).

agreement when he failed to pay royalty fees and his facility fell below minimum acceptable standards.[582] Instead, the franchisee argued that a road closure prevented easy access to his facility for more than a year and it became commercially impossible to perform his duties under the franchise agreement. Applying New Jersey law, the court held that "simple inability to pay does not create an impossibility or impracticability which excuses a party's performance of his contractual obligations."[583] Moreover, while the road closure might have affected the franchise's patronage, it had no effect on the franchisee's ability or obligation to comply with the franchisor's quality assurance standards. A force majeure provision can help clarify which of these unforeseen events will suspend an agreement's obligations.

S. Waiver of Jury Trial

WITH RESPECT TO ANY PROCEEDING NOT SUBJECT TO ARBITRATION, THE PARTIES HEREBY AGREE TO WAIVE TRIAL BY JURY IN ANY ACTION, PROCEEDING OR COUNTERCLAIM, WHETHER AT LAW OR EQUITY, REGARDLESS OF WHICH PARTY BRINGS SUIT.

THIS WAIVER WILL APPLY TO ANY MATTER WHATSOEVER BETWEEN THE PARTIES HERETO WHICH ARISES OUT OF OR IS RELATED IN ANY WAY TO THIS AGREEMENT, THE PERFORMANCE OF EITHER PARTY, AND/OR FRANCHISEE'S PURCHASE FROM FRANCHISOR OF THE FRANCHISE AND/OR ANY GOODS OR SERVICES.

Discussion:

A party's right to a jury trial, guaranteed by the Seventh Amendment to the U.S. Constitution, may be contractually waived in franchise agreements in some jurisdictions. Franchisors often wish to include in franchise agreements a contractual jury waiver to eliminate the uncertainty that jury trials inject into what otherwise may be, from a franchisor's perspective, a desirable judicial forum. On the other hand, franchisees often seek to preserve the right to a jury trial, so that they have the full range of tools available if they find themselves in a dispute with a franchisor, who will likely have more resources to bring to the lawsuit.

In the majority of U.S. jurisdictions that allow contractual jury trial waivers, a party's waiver of the right to a jury must be "knowing, willing and intelligent," and courts have developed various factors to determine if, in particular circumstances, that standard has been met.[584] The contractual jury waiver must be conspicuous and

582. 88 F. Supp. 2d 928, 933 (C.D. Ill. 2000).

583. *Id.*

584. *See, e.g.*, Aetna Ins. Co. v. Kennedy, 301 U.S. 389, 393 (1937) (noting "as the right of jury trial is fundamental, courts indulge every reasonable presumption against waiver," and holding parties had not waived right to jury trial); Tracinda Corp v. DaimlerChrysler AG, 502 F.3d 212 (3d Cir. 2007) (affirming that "[t]o be valid, a jury waiver must be made knowingly and voluntarily based on the facts of the case" and holding that "when a valid

prominent, leading drafters to consider where to place the provision in the contract and to emphasize them through bold-faced type, capital letters, larger font, underscoring, or some combination, in the fashion of the preceding sample provision.[585]

For example, in *Century 21 Real Estate LLC v. All Professional Realty, Inc.*,[586] the waiver was not in the original franchise agreement. Instead, it was written in bold and capital letters directly above the signature line on the renewal contract. The court found that the waiver was enforceable because its placement was sufficiently conspicuous and prominent.[587] Alternatively, the jury waiver provision in *G&R Moojestic Treats, Inc. v. Maggiemoo's Int'l, LLC*, appeared on page 49 of a single-spaced agreement prepared by the franchisor and the terms were not open to negotiation.[588] The court held that the waiver's placement was not sufficiently conspicuous.[589]

In some jurisdictions, however, all jury waivers in franchise agreements are prohibited as a matter of state statutory franchise law.[590] Other jurisdictions may not uphold jury waivers based on their courts' views of franchise public policy, even without a specific statutory prohibition on such waivers.[591]

Depending on the facts, courts may not uphold jury waivers if, in applying their jurisdiction's particular waiver test, they determine that the agreement was not negotiated and/or that the parties' bargaining power was significantly unequal—circumstances that often exist in franchising. That was the case in *Ohio Learning Centers, LLC, v. Sylvan Learning, Inc.*,[592] where the court commented that Sylvan had a far superior bargaining power during negotiations and the jury waiver provisions were not at all conspicuous.[593] In view of the differences in state law and individual facts, enforceability is not certain and one should counsel clients accordingly.

---

contractual jury trial waiver provision applies to a signatory corporation, the waiver also applies to nonsignatory directors and officers seeking to invoke the waiver as agents of the corporation").

585. *See, e.g.*, Dunkin' Donuts Franchising, LLC v. SAI Food & Hospitality, LLC, No. 11-CV-01484, 2013 U.S. Dist. LEXIS 35942 (E.D. Mo. Mar. 15, 2013); Cousins Subs Sys., Inc. v. Better Subs Dev. Inc., No. RDB-10-1932, 2011 WL 4585541 (E.D. Wis. Sept. 30, 2011).

586. No. Civ. 2:10–2751 WBS GGH, 2012 WL 2682761 (E.D. Cal. July 6, 2012).

587. *Id.* at *5.

588. Case No. 1:04-cv-01694-WMN, Doc. 79, at 14–15 (D. Md. Mar. 10, 2005).

589. *Id.*

590. *See, e.g.*, MINN. R. 2860.4400(J) ("It shall be unfair and inequitable for any person to . . . require a Franchisee to waive his or her rights to a jury trial . . ."); Carrel v. George Weston Bakeries Distribution, Inc., No. 1:05-CV-1769-SEB-JPG, 2006 WL 2524124, at *2 (S.D. Ind. Aug. 29, 2006) (contractual jury waivers violate Indiana Deceptive Practices Act § 23-2-2.7-1(10), which prohibits franchise agreements from including terms that limit "litigation brought for breach of the agreement in any manner whatsoever"). Moreover, California and Georgia prohibit all pre-litigation jury waiver clauses. Grafton Partners LP v. Superior Court, 116 P.3d 479 (Cal. 2005); Bank South, N.A. v. Howard, 264 Ga. 339, 444 S.E.2d 799 (1994).

591. *See e.g.*, Goodyear Tire & Rubber Co. v. Tualation Tire & Auto, Inc., 908 P.2d 300, BUS FRANCHISE GUIDE (CCH) 10,838 (Or. 1995) (public policy underlying franchise act rendered jury waiver unenforceable even in absence of statutory provision concerning jury right or waiver).

592. No. RDB-10-1932, 2012 WL 3025106 (D.M. July 24, 2012).

593. *Id.* at *8 (denying Sylvan's motion to strike Ohio Learning Centers' demand for a jury trial). *But see* AAMCO Transmissions, Inc. v. Baker, No. 06-CV-05252, 2008 WL 5272781 (E.D. Pa. Dec. 18, 2008) (enforcing a jury waiver where there was no significant disparity in bargaining power between the franchisee and franchisor).

Courts are also split as to which party carries the burden of proving a waiver of jury rights. The majority of courts place the burden on the party seeking to enforce the waiver.[594] This approach is rooted in the Supreme Court's holding that, "as the right of jury trial is fundamental, courts [should] indulge every reasonable presumption against waiver."[595] Still, a number of courts impose the burden on the party objecting to the jury trial waiver.[596]

As a result, those who draft franchise agreements, as well as those who counsel franchisors and franchisees about them, should review and understand the applicable law and trends with respect to jury waivers in all relevant jurisdictions, both with respect to drafting requirements and other elements of enforceability. Given that most franchisors use the same form of franchise agreement in all states, franchisors may choose to include a general jury waiver in their standard franchise agreement and then handle jurisdictional and situational differences through state-specific addenda or negotiated changes.[597]

T. Damages Waiver

> Franchisee hereby waives to the fullest extent permitted by law, any right to or claim for any punitive, exemplary, incidental, indirect, special or consequential damages (including, without limitation, lost profits) against Franchisor arising out of any cause whatsoever (whether such cause be based in contract, negligence, strict liability, other tort or otherwise) and agrees that in the event of a dispute, Franchisee's recovery is limited to actual damages. If any other term of this Agreement is found or determined to be unconscionable or unenforceable for any reason, the foregoing provisions will continue in full force and effect, including, without limitation, the waiver of any right to claim any consequential damages.

Discussion:

Franchisors often include some variety of a damages waiver or "damages cap" provision in an attempt to manage risk, whether in a judicial or arbitral forum. The preceding sample clause is an example of a franchisor's attempt to limit damages exposure at the outset of the franchise relationship.[598] Damages caps, however, are

594. *See, e.g.*, Phoenix Leasing Inc. v. Sure Broadcasting, Inc., 843 F. Supp. 1379 (D. Nev. 1994) (noting that an "informal survey indicated that the majority of courts place the burden on the party seeking enforcement of a prelitigation contractual waiver" and therefore following that approach); Bevill Co. v. Sprint/United Management Co., No. 01–2524–CM, 2006 WL 2921006 (D. Kan. Oct. 11, 2006) ("the majority of courts have decided that the burden lies with the party seeking to enforce the contractual waiver").

595. *Aetna Ins. Co.*, 301 U.S. at 393.

596. KMC Co. v. Irving Trust Co., 757 F.2d 752, 758 (6th Cir. 1985) ("[I]n the context of an express contractual waiver the objecting party should have the burden of demonstrating that its consent to the provision was not knowing and voluntary.").

597. While a franchisor may elect to insert a choice-of-law provision in their franchise agreement so that the contract will be construed under the laws of a jurisdiction that enforces jury waivers, courts may invalidate the choice-of-law provision if neither the parties nor the transaction has any relationship with the selected state. For a full discussion of the enforceability of choice-of-law provisions, *see supra* Chapter 8, Section I(C).

598. Joseph J. Fittante, Jr. & Dennis E. Wieczorek, *Advanced Drafting*, ABA 27th Forum on Franchising 24 (2004).

not consistently enforceable and may be void under statutory or common law, either in their entirety or in part, depending on the jurisdiction.

In at least 11 states, judges have statutory support for refusing to enforce a damages waiver provision.[599] For example, a court in Illinois held that because the Illinois franchise disclosure act makes the franchisors liable to franchisees for damages and attorneys' fees, the remedial limitations provision in the franchise agreement—which included a waiver of punitive damages and recovery of attorneys' fees and costs—was unenforceable.[600]

Even where there is no statutory bar to damages caps, courts are sometimes unwilling to enforce the provisions on a case-by-case basis. As with jury trial waivers, courts are concerned with the franchisees' unequal bargaining power. These courts turn to the doctrine of unconscionability to strike down damages caps. As one California court held, the punitive damages waiver was substantively unconscionable as it lacked mutuality; "a franchisor is more likely to be defending against punitive damages than seeking them."[601]

Still, in a number of jurisdictions damages waivers remain enforceable.[602] Courts cite a number of factors to support enforcement of damages caps, including:

1. a perception that the provision reflected an allocation risk between parties;
2. the presence of sophisticated parties;
3. the commercial context of the transaction;
4. the prominent and unambiguous language of the provision;
5. that the limitation would not be unconscionable under the Uniform Commercial Code (UCC); and
6. that there was a renewal of the agreement, without objection by the party later challenging the provision.[603]

Notably, a damages waiver provision might only apply to certain causes of action and certain types of damages. If the claim against the franchisor is for fraud

599. *See* Cal. Bus. & Prof. Code §§ 20010, 20040; Conn. Gen. Stat. §§ 42-133f, 42-133g; 1987 Ill. Laws Ch. 815 §§ 704/41, 705/26; Ind. Code Ann. §§ 23-4-4.7-1, 23-4-4.5-28; Iowa Code §§ 523H.4, 523H.14; MD. Ann. Bus. Occ. & Prof. §§ 14-226, 14-227; Mich. Comp. Laws §§ 445.1527(b), 445.1531; Minn. R. §§ 80C.21, 80C.17; R.I. Gen. Law §§ 19-28.1-15, 19-28.1-21; S.D. Codified Laws §§ 37-5A-86, 37-5A-83, 37-5A-83, 37-5A-85; Wis. Stat. Ann. §§ 135.025, 135.06.

600. Sanchez v. CleanNet USA, Inc., 78 F. Supp. 3d 747, 757 (N.D. Ill. 2015).

601. IJL Dominicana S.A. v. It's Just Lunch Int'l, LLC, No. CV08-5417-VAP, 2009 WL 305187, at *4 (C.D. Cal. Feb. 6, 2009).

602. *See, e.g.*, Dunkin' Donuts Franchised Restaurants LLC v. Manassas Donut Inc., No. 1:07CV446(JCC), 2008 WL 110474, at *6 (E.D. Va. Jan. 8, 2008) (granting franchisor's motion to strike franchisee's jury demand and claim for punitive damages); Silver v. JTH Tax, Inc., 2005 WL 1668060, at *2 (E.D. Va. June 21, 2005) (concluding that under the law of either New York or Virginia the provision of the franchise agreement waiving any claim for punitive damages was enforceable); Keating v. Baskin-Robbins USA Co., 2001 WL 407017, at *15 (E.D.N.C. Mar. 27, 2001) (finding that punitive damages were inappropriate in light of explicit waiver in franchise agreement).

603. Edward Wood Dunham, *Enforcing Contract Terms Designed to Manage Franchisor Risk*, 19 Franchise L.J. 91, 97 (Winter 2000); *see also* Omni Corp. v. Sonitrol Corp., 303 Fed. Appx. 908, 909–10 (2d Cir. 2008) (limitation of damages clause enforceable, including because "the premises at issue were maintained and controlled by Omni, a commercial entity" and "Omni was better able to discern and ensure that the premises were reasonably maintained to minimize the risk of flooding than was [its counterparty]").

or fraudulent inducement, for example, the damages waiver may be unenforceable—as would the rest of the franchise agreement.[604] A court might also be willing to acknowledge waiver of some category of damages but not all, as a party must be left with an appropriate remedy for breach.[605]

U. Reasonable Business Judgment

> Whenever Franchisor reserves discretion in a particular area or where Franchisor agrees to exercise its rights reasonably or in good faith, Franchisor will satisfy its obligations whenever it exercises reasonable business judgment in making a decision or exercising a right. Franchisor's decisions or actions will be deemed to be the result of reasonable business judgment, even if other reasonable or even arguably preferable alternatives are available, if Franchisor's decisions or actions are intended, in whole or significant part, to promote or benefit the System generally even if the decision or action also promotes Franchisor's financial or other individual interests. Examples of items that will promote or benefit the System include, without limitation, enhancing the value of the trademarks, improving customer service and satisfaction, improving product quality, improving uniformity, enhancing or encouraging modernization and improving the competitive position of the System.

Discussion:
As discussed in Chapter 3, Section, VII(v) some drafters have begun to avoid the word "discretion" in franchise agreements. This is mostly because that term at times has become a red flag for courts that may expose the franchisor to claims under the common law covenant of good faith and fair dealing over the franchisor's exercise of discretion.[606]

The covenant of good faith and fair dealing generally requires that when a contract grants discretion to one party, that party is required to exercise discretion in a fair and reasonable manner, consistent with the reasonable expectations of parties.[607] To establish a breach of the implied covenant of good faith and fair dealing claim, a plaintiff must show a failure or refusal to discharge contractual responsibil-

---

604. 28 Williston on Contracts § 70:220 (4th ed.).

605. *See e.g.*, Select Pork, Inc. v. Babcock Swine, Inc., 640 F.2d 147 (8th Cir. 1981) (holding limitation on damages unconscionable and unenforceable where seller knew at the time of contracting that it did not have enough product to meet the buyer's request, and where seller instead tendered a nonconforming product, because "[h]ad [seller] delivered the promised [product], then the clause limiting damages would have been reasonable . . . and the Uniform Commercial Code do[es] not require plaintiffs to be held to a remedial limitation which they thought would be applicable to the [product] which they agreed to buy"); Tokyo Ohka Kogyo Am., Inc. v. Huntsman Propylene Oxide LLC, 35 F. Supp. 3d 1316, 1334–35 (D. Or. 2014) (holding damages limitation was procedurally and substantively unconscionable because it was "fundamentally unfair" to enforce a limitation clause that left plaintiff without the appropriate remedy); Frank's Maint. & Eng'g, Inc. v. C. A. Roberts Co., 86 Ill. App. 3d 980, 989 (1st Dist. 1980) (limitation on damages cannot be enforced if it deprives "contracting party of reasonable protection against a breach").

606. For a thorough discussion of the rise of reasonable business judgment provisions in franchise agreements, *see generally* Brian B. Schnell & Ronald K. Gardner, Jr., *Battle Over the Franchisor Business Judgment Rule and the Path to Peace*, 35 Franchise L.J. 167 (Fall 2015).

607. Restatement (Second) of Contracts § 205.

ities. As one jurisdiction puts it, this failure is "prompted not by an honest mistake, bad judgment, or negligence," but by a deliberate act, "which frustrates the agreed common purpose and disappoints the reasonable expectations of the other party, thereby depriving that party of the benefits of the agreement."[608]

The good faith and fair dealing standard may yield unpredictable results. For example, in *Burger King Corp. v. E-Z Eating, 41 Corp.*,[609] applying the good faith standard, the Eleventh Circuit upheld Burger King Corporation's right to impose the Value Menu on the franchisees. The court analyzed the franchise agreement and concluded that the franchisees agreed to changes in "standards, specifications, and procedures" that became necessary.[610] A year later, a Florida District Court—reviewing a similar franchise agreement—nonetheless denied Burger King Corporation's motion to dismiss its franchisees' claim that adding a certain product to the Value Menu breached the implied covenant of good faith and fair dealing, noting that the plaintiffs had alleged that Burger King Corporation had admitted that the sale of the new Value Meal product could lead to bankruptcy of its franchisees.[611] But six months later, the same Florida District Court ultimately dismissed the plaintiffs' good faith and fair dealing claim, noting that an inference of bad faith does not arise "simply because an exercise of contractual discretion has some marginal economic impact on the plaintiff."[612]

To address this problem, some drafters have begun using the phrase "reasonable business judgment."[613] The purpose of that phrase is to give the franchisor some flexibility in its decision-making abilities under the agreement without facing judicial scrutiny of that decision making. More specifically, the franchisor reserves the right to use reasonable business judgment in making decisions that affect the franchisees. Provisions often explicitly state that the standard is met even if "other reasonable or arguably preferable alternatives are available, if the decision or action is intended to promote or benefit the system generally"—even if it also promotes the franchisor's individual interests.[614] Some drafters go even further to disclaim any harm that franchisor's reasonable business judgment might cause.

There is limited case law discussing reasonable business judgment in the franchise context. For example, in *In re Sizzler Restaurants International, Inc.*,[615] a restaurant franchisee asserted claims for breach of the licensing agreement and the implied covenant of good faith and fair dealing. The court held:

608. 27 Fla. Jur. 2d *Franchise Contracts* § 14.

609. 572 F.3d 1306 (11th Cir. 2009).

610. *Id.* at 1314.

611. Nat'l Franchisee Ass'n v. Burger King Corp., 715 F. Supp. 2d 1232, 1245 (S.D. Fla. May 20, 2010).

612. Nat'l Franchisee Ass'n v. Burger King Corp., No. 09-23435-CIV, 2010 WL 4811912, at *4–6 (S.D. Fla. Nov. 19, 2010).

613. *See* Schnell & Gardner, *supra* note 606, at 168.

614. *Id.* at 169.

615. 225 B.R. 466 (Bankr. C.D. Cal. 1998).

> The inquiry into [the franchisor's] decision-making process is not an inquiry that looks to results, but more appropriately should examine the actual decision-making process to determine whether it was legitimate, i.e. honest or within accepted commercial practices. This court declines to second-guess the result reached, as long as the decision making process was honest or was within accepted commercial practices.[616]

The court concluded that as long as it was undisputed that the franchisor had a legitimate business reason for their discretionary decision, the franchisee could not maintain a claim for breach of implied covenant of good faith and fair dealing.[617]

It is worth emphasizing that the business judgment rule is not the standard for *every* decision a franchisor makes that might have an effect on the franchisee. Rather, it is the standard a court might use to determine if the franchisor complied with the implied covenant of good faith and fair dealing when the franchisor does not have an absolute right to make a decision. In other words, it is the standard required by the terms of the franchise agreement when the franchisor has the discretion to make a decision.[618]

V. Entire Agreement, Modifications, and No Reliance

> This Agreement contains the entire agreement between the Parties hereto as it relates to the franchising of the Franchised Business at the Premises, and there are no representations, inducements, promises, agreements, arrangements or undertakings, oral or written, between the Parties relating to the franchising of the Franchised Business at the Premises other than those set forth herein, and no party has relied on any representation, inducement, promise, agreement, arrangement, undertaking, of any type or form, that is not set forth in this Agreement. No agreement of any kind relating to the matters covered by this Agreement shall be binding upon either party unless and until the same has been made in writing and executed by all interested parties. This provision is not intended to disclaim the representations Franchisor made solely in the franchise disclosure document that Franchisor furnished to Franchisee.
>
> This Agreement may not be amended, modified or rescinded, or any performance requirement waived, except by a written document signed by Franchisee and an authorized representative of Franchisor. This provision does not apply to changes in the Manual, which Franchisor may modify unilaterally. The Parties expressly agree that this Agreement may not be amended or modified, or any performance standard changed, by course of dealing, by special indulgences or benefits Franchisor bestows on Franchisee, or by inference from a party's conduct.

---

616. *Id.* at 474.

617. *Id.* at 475.

618. However, not all courts make this distinction so clearly. *See* Ernie Haire Ford, Inc. v. Ford Motor Co., 260 F.3d 1285, 1290–92 (11th Cir. 2001) (holding that, though car manufacturer's decision was not in the best interest of its dealer, "it was neither capricious nor in contravention of the parties' reasonable expectations" and therefore manufacturer was entitled to summary judgment on breach of good faith and fair dealing provision).

Discussion:

Integration, no-reliance, and no oral modifications clauses are among the most important of the general provisions in any commercial contract, and are of utmost importance in franchise agreements, where disputes over what the parties promised each other are common. The purpose of the integration clause is to capture the parties' contractual acknowledgment that the only understanding and promises between them are those appearing within the "four corners" of the written franchise agreement, and that the rights and obligations as written in the franchise agreement supersede any prior agreements, discussions, or representations of any kind. The requirement that all amendments and modifications be in an authorized, signed writing serves a similar purpose. These provisions are important not only so that the parties each understand the bounds of their contractual responsibilities and rights during the regular course, but also as a matter of contract interpretation and construction if a dispute ends up in litigation or arbitration.

In very simple terms, the integration clause and modifications language affect whether extrinsic evidence—or "parol evidence"—may be introduced in a dispute. Particularly from the franchisor's perspective, the clause's aim is to demonstrate to a court (and, before that, to counsel contemplating a claim) that the parties plainly intended that anything outside the written document (like a pre-signing conversation) does not and cannot form the basis for any contractual duty or right and, therefore, cannot support any claim of breach. As a broad generalization, the franchisors typically seek to rely on integration clauses in franchise contract disputes while the franchisees very often seek to convince a court that the parties' contract encompassed more than what appears in the written agreement's provisions, based on alleged oral statements, correspondence, marketing materials, or other evidence. Courts' receptiveness to integration clauses in general, and those in franchise agreements in particular, varies by jurisdiction and depends largely on the law, facts, conduct, and equities in an particular case.

A court's receptiveness to the franchise agreement's integration clause is also closely intertwined with the court's treatment of the parol evidence rule. At common law, the parol evidence rule is as follows:

1. A binding integrated agreement discharges prior agreements to the extent that it is inconsistent with them.
2. A binding completely integrated agreement discharges prior agreements to the extent that they are within its scope.
3. An integrated agreement that is not binding or that is voidable or avoided does not discharge a prior agreement. But an integrated agreement, even though not binding, may be effective to render inoperative a term which would have been part of the agreement if it had not been integrated.[619]

619. Restatement (Second) Contracts § 213 (1981).

In some jurisdictions, even in the absence of an integration clause, the parol evidence rule creates a presumption that a writing is a total integration. Other jurisdictions have elected to modify the parol evidence rule.[620] Accordingly, an integration clause seeks to give the parol evidence rule full effect. In *G.I.M. Sec. & Sound, Inc. v. LoJack Corp.*,[621] the court held under both Massachusetts and New York law, integration clauses bar reference to pre-agreement representations. Alternatively, the Fifth Circuit Court of Appeals in *Water Craft Mgmt., L.L.C. v. Mercury Marine*,[622] did not end its analysis based on the franchise agreement's integration clause: "A contract's integration clause does not automatically bar consideration of parol evidence, but if an agreement contains an integration clause, we must examine the facts and the contract's substance to determine whether the agreement properly reflected the parties' intentions."[623]

Drafters often intend that an integration clause also bar fraud claims based on representations outside the written agreement, but in some jurisdictions an integration clause alone is not sufficient for that purpose.[624] Accordingly, franchise agreements should contain separate no-reliance language that makes plain that the parties have not relied on matters outside the four corners of the agreement. Many franchise agreements call out no-reliance provisions separately from the integration clause, sometimes in bolded or otherwise emphasized form. The purpose of no-reliance language is to derail plaintiff's ability to prove an essential element of a fraud claim—reasonable reliance on an alleged representation. A party cannot reasonably rely on a representation, the argument goes, if he or she has disclaimed reliance in the contract. Again, however, courts take different views of no-reliance clauses in fraud cases depending on the applicable state law and the facts with which they are presented. Thus, drafters must use much care in crafting integration, modification, and no-reliance clauses, and should counsel their clients that these clauses do not inoculate against all claims or improper conduct.

620. *See, e.g.*, Borah v. McCandless, 205 P.3d 1209, 1217 (Idaho 2009) (IDAHO CODE § 28-2-202 "was 'intended to liberalize the parol evidence rule and to abolish the presumption that a writing is a total integration' and 'require that the court make a definite finding that the parties intended a total integration before consistent additional terms are to be excluded'").

621. No. 10–CV–4701 (PKC)(ARL), 2014 WL 4675854, at *1 (E.D.N.Y. Sept. 19, 2014).

622. 426 F. App'x 232, 236 (5th Cir. 2011).

623. *Id.*

624. *See, e.g.*, Cousins Subs Sys. Inc. v. Better Subs Dev. Inc., No. 09-C-0336, 2011 WL 4585541, at *9 (E.D. Wis. Sept. 30, 2011) (granting summary judgment on negligent misrepresentation claim because the integration clause barred such claims, but finding that integration clauses are not enforceable for intentional fraud); Hockey Enterprises, Inc. v. Talafous, No. Civ. 10-2943 DWF/JSM, 2012 WL 72979, at *9 (D. Minn. Jan. 10, 2012) (holding that franchisee's negligent misrepresentation claim was not barred by an integration clause in a franchise agreement); Next Generation Grp., LLC v. Sylvan Learning Centers, LLC, No. CIV. CBB-11-0986, 2012 WL 37397, at *4 (D. Md. Jan. 5, 2012) ("[T]he law in Maryland . . . is that a plaintiff can successfully bring a tort action for fraud that is based on false pre-contract promises by the defendant even if (1) the written contract contains an integration clause and if (2) the pre-contractual promises that constitute the fraud are not mentioned in the written contract.").

TABLE OF CASES

A

B

C

D

E

F

G

H

I

J

K

L

M

N

O

P

Q

R

S

T

U

V

W

X

Y

Z

INDEX

Note: Information found in footnotes is indicated by an n and footnote number following the page number.

A

B

C

G

H

I

J

K

L

M

N

O

P

S

T

U

V

W